Guts

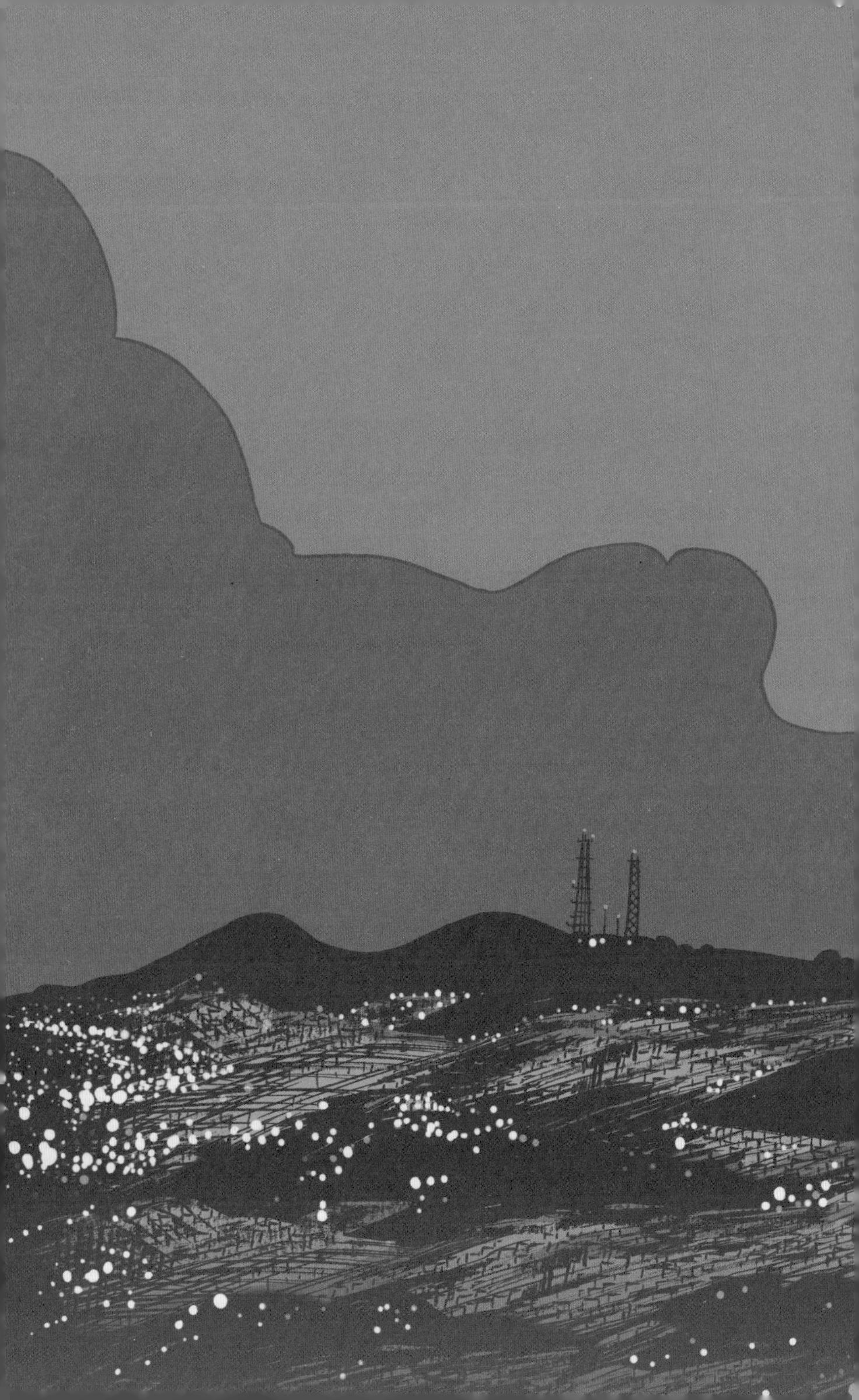

Guts

Raina Telgemeier
with color by Braden Lamb

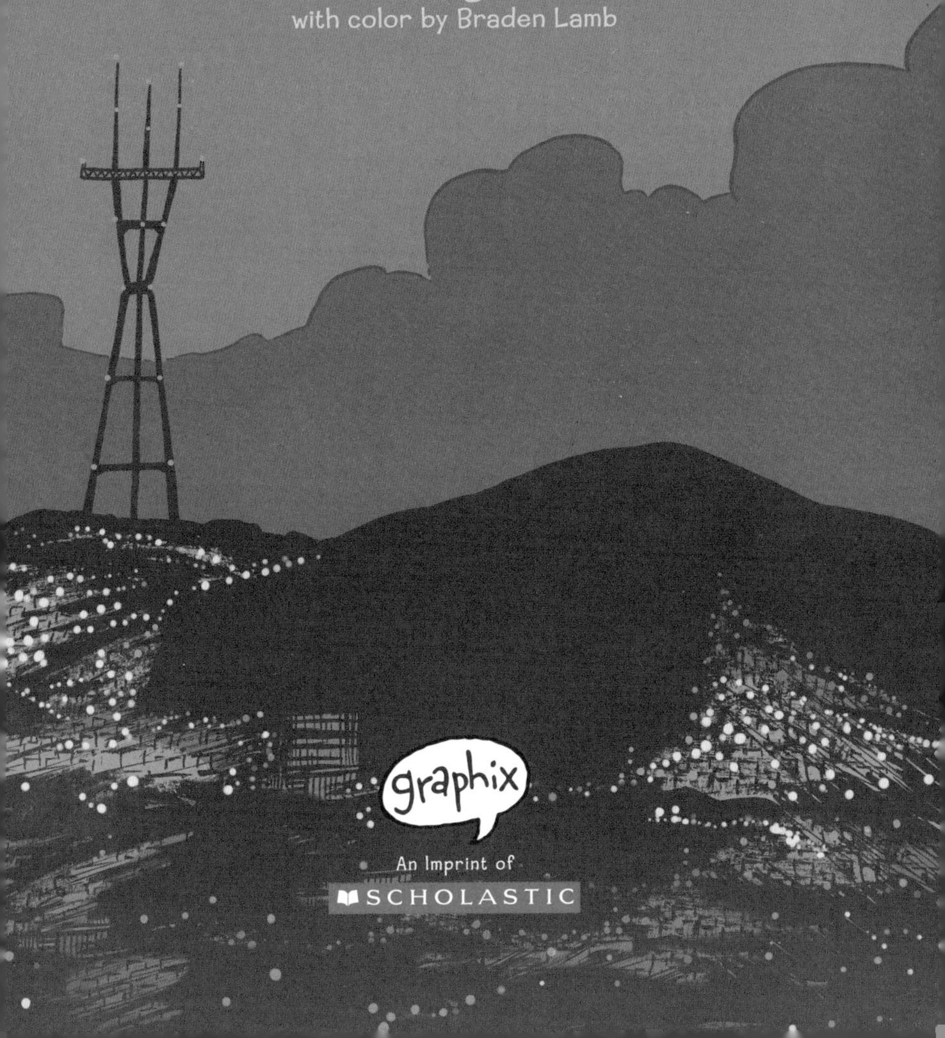

graphix
An Imprint of
SCHOLASTIC

All rights reserved. Published by Graphix, an imprint of Scholastic Inc.,
Publishers since 1920. SCHOLASTIC, GRAPHIX, and associated logos are trademarks
and/or registered trademarks of Scholastic Inc. All other trademarks are the
property of their respective owners and are used without permission.

The publisher does not have any control over and does not assume any
responsibility for author or third-party websites or their content.

This graphic novel is based on personal experiences, though certain
characters, places, and incidents have been modified in service
of the story.

Library of Congress Cataloging-in-Publication Data

Names: Telgemeier, Raina, author, illustrator.
Title: Guts / Raina Telgemeier ; with color by Braden Lamb.
Description: First edition. | New York, NY : Graphix logo, an imprint of Scholastic, 2019.
Identifiers: LCCN 2018050676 (print) | LCCN 2018060290 (ebook)
ISBN 978-0-545-85253-1 (ebook)
ISBN 978-0-545-85251-7 (hardcover : alk. paper)
ISBN 978-0-545-85250-0 (pbk. : alk. paper)
Subjects: LCSH: Stress in children. | Children–Physiology. | Stomach–Diseases.
Classification: LCC BF723.S75 (ebook) | LCC BF723.S75 T45 2019 (print) | DDC 155.4/189042–dc23
LC record available at https://lccn.loc.gov/2018050676

10 9 8 7 6 5 4 3 2 1   19 20 21 22 23
Printed in China   62
First edition, September 2019
Edited by Cassandra Pelham Fulton
Lettering by Jesse Post
Book design by Phil Falco
Author photo by Joseph Fanvu
Publisher: David Saylor

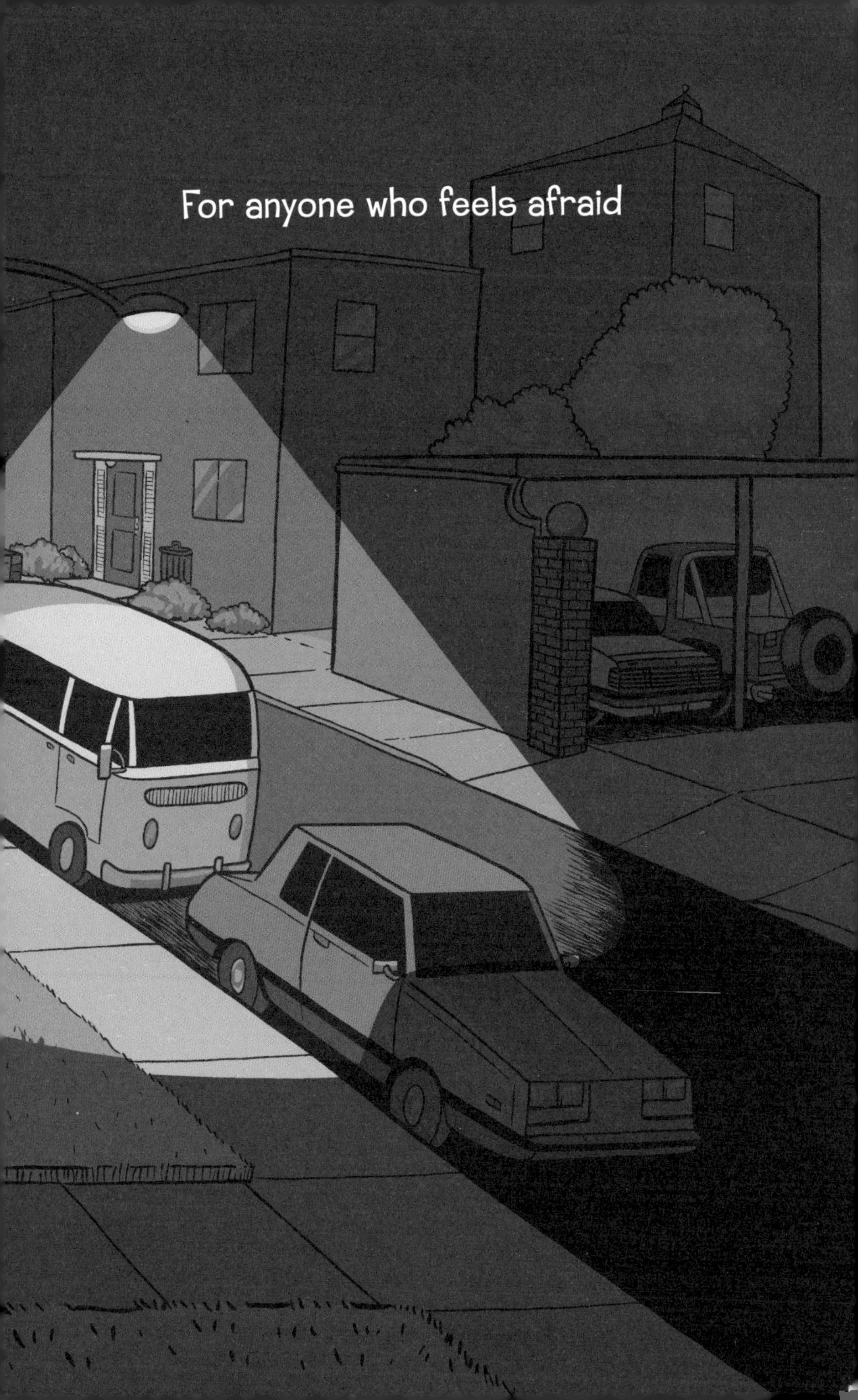
For anyone who feels afraid

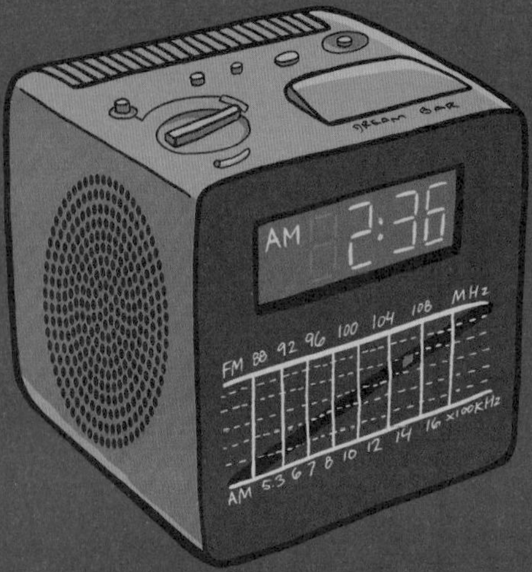

DREAM BAR
AM 2:36
FM 88 92 96 100 104 108 MHz
AM 5.3 6 7 8 10 12 14 16 x100KHz

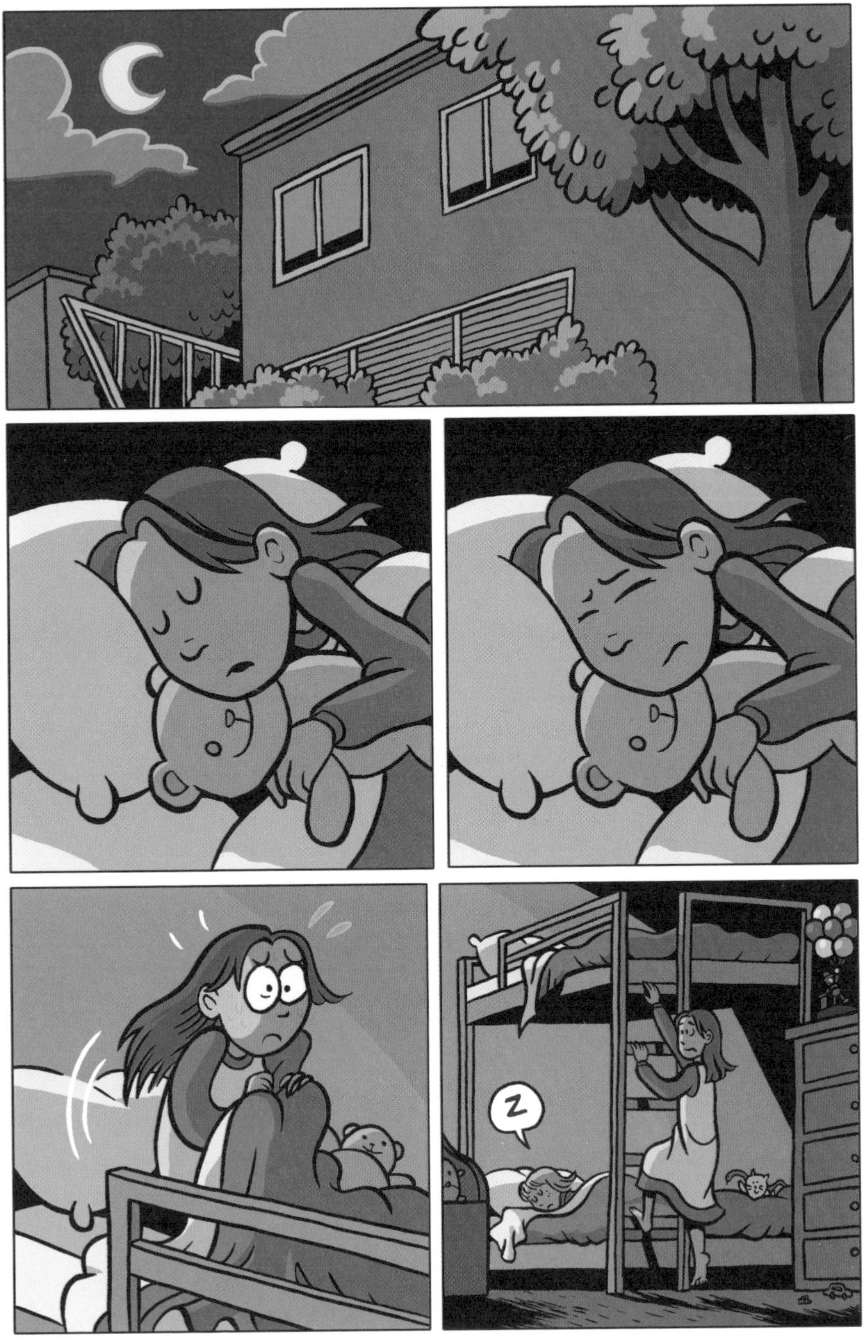
Z

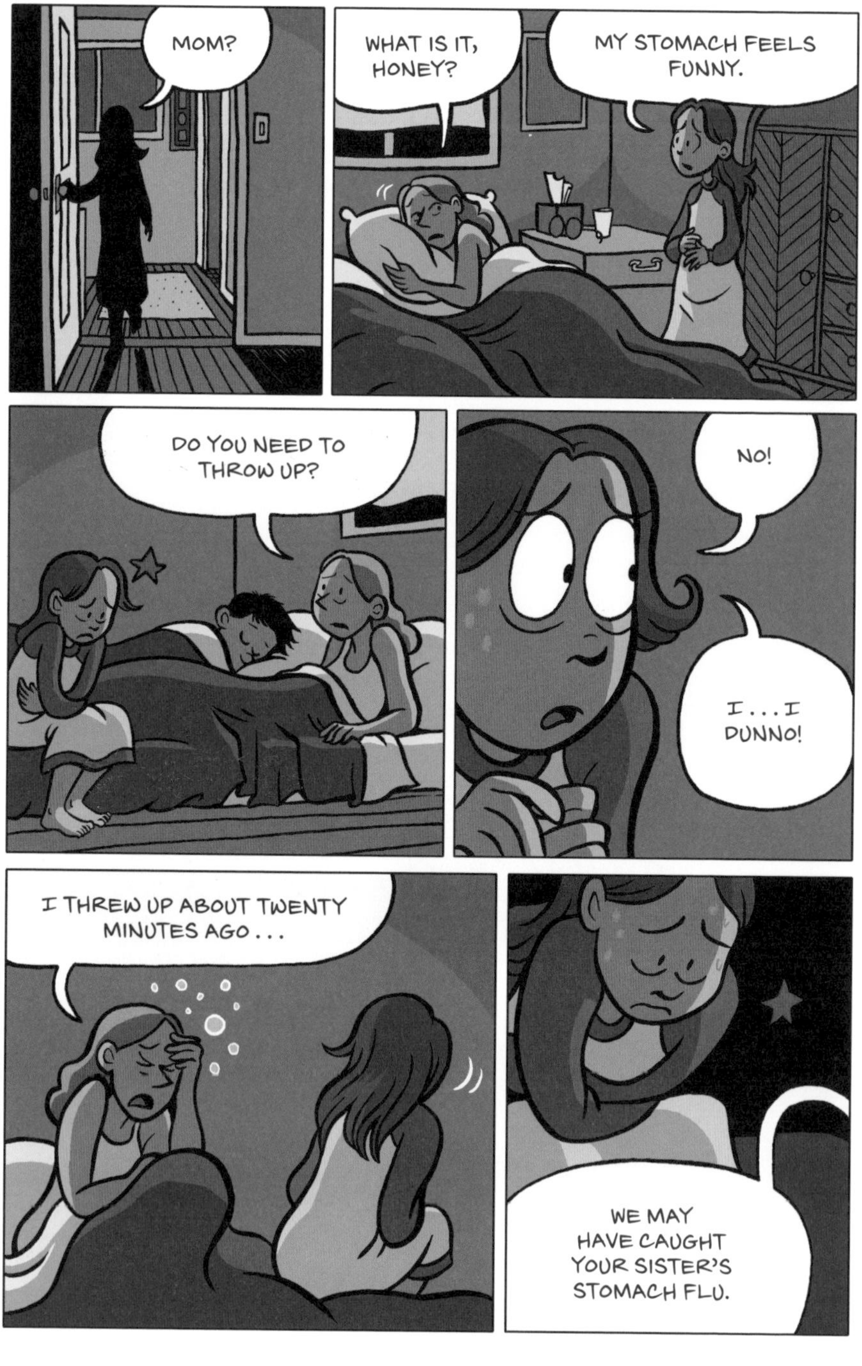
MOM?
WHAT IS IT, HONEY?
MY STOMACH FEELS FUNNY.
DO YOU NEED TO THROW UP?
NO!
I . . . I DUNNO!
I THREW UP ABOUT TWENTY MINUTES AGO . . .
WE MAY HAVE CAUGHT YOUR SISTER'S STOMACH FLU.

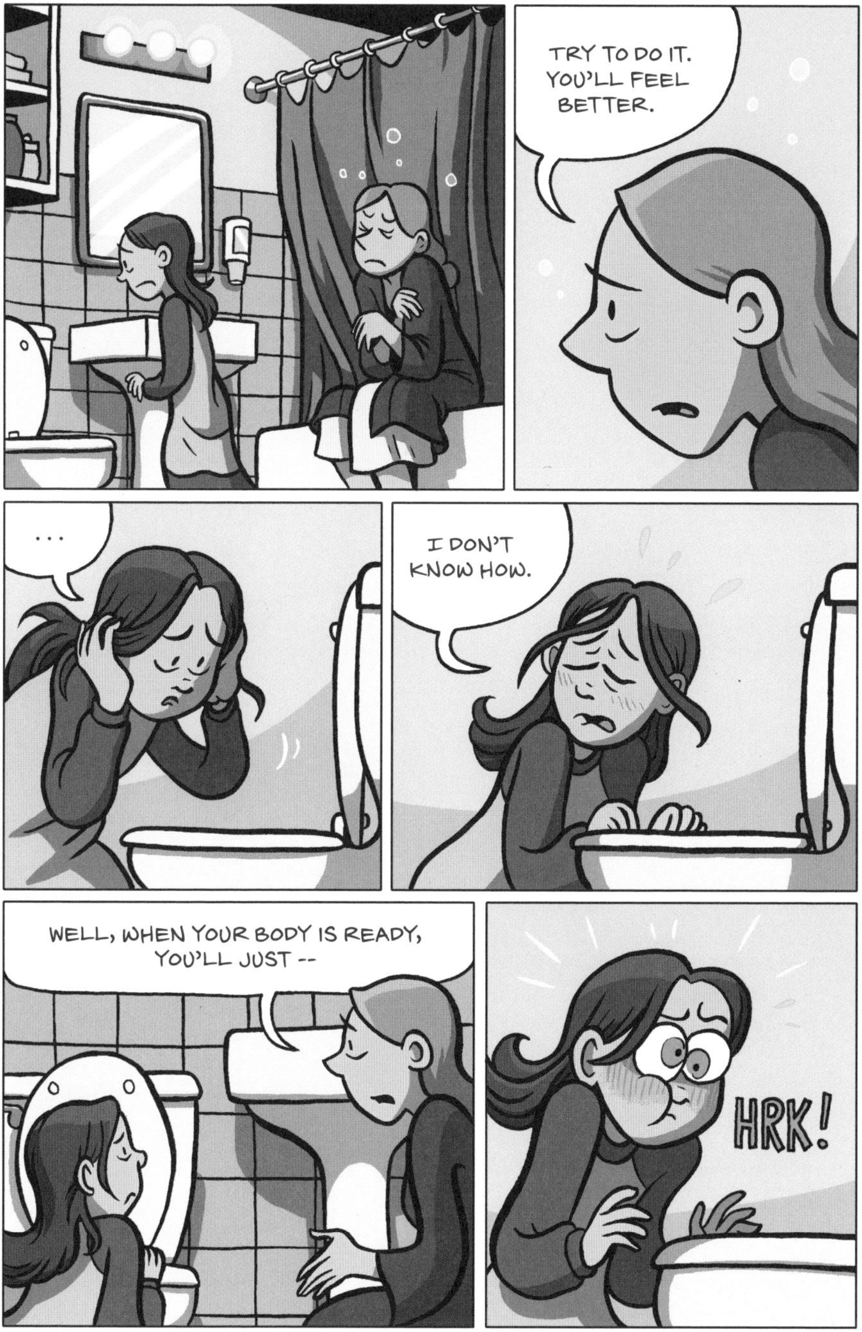
TRY TO DO IT. YOU'LL FEEL BETTER.
...
I DON'T KNOW HOW.
WELL, WHEN YOUR BODY IS READY, YOU'LL JUST --
HRK!

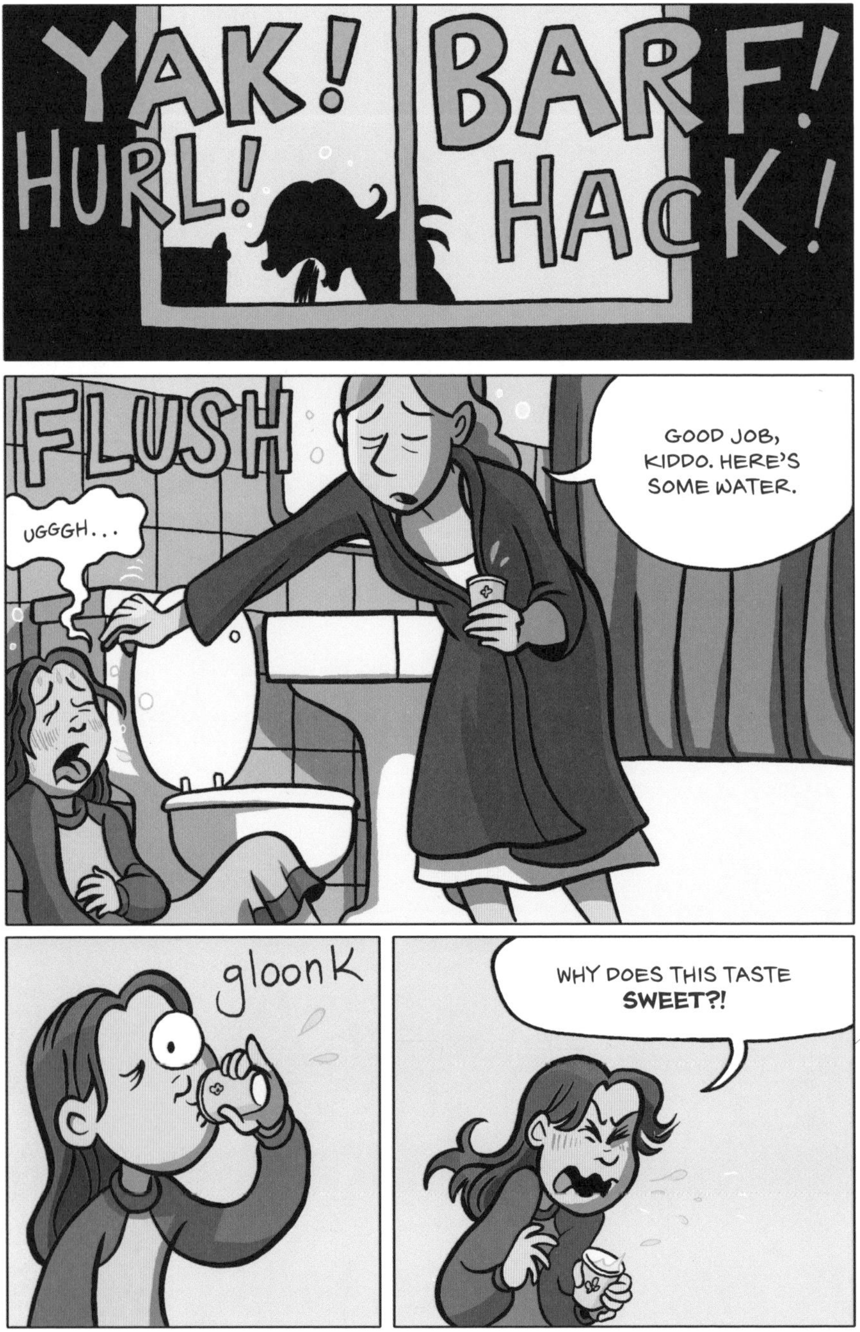
YAK!
BARF!
HURL!
HACK!
FLUSH
UGGGH...
GOOD JOB, KIDDO. HERE'S SOME WATER.
gloonk
WHY DOES THIS TASTE **SWEET?!**

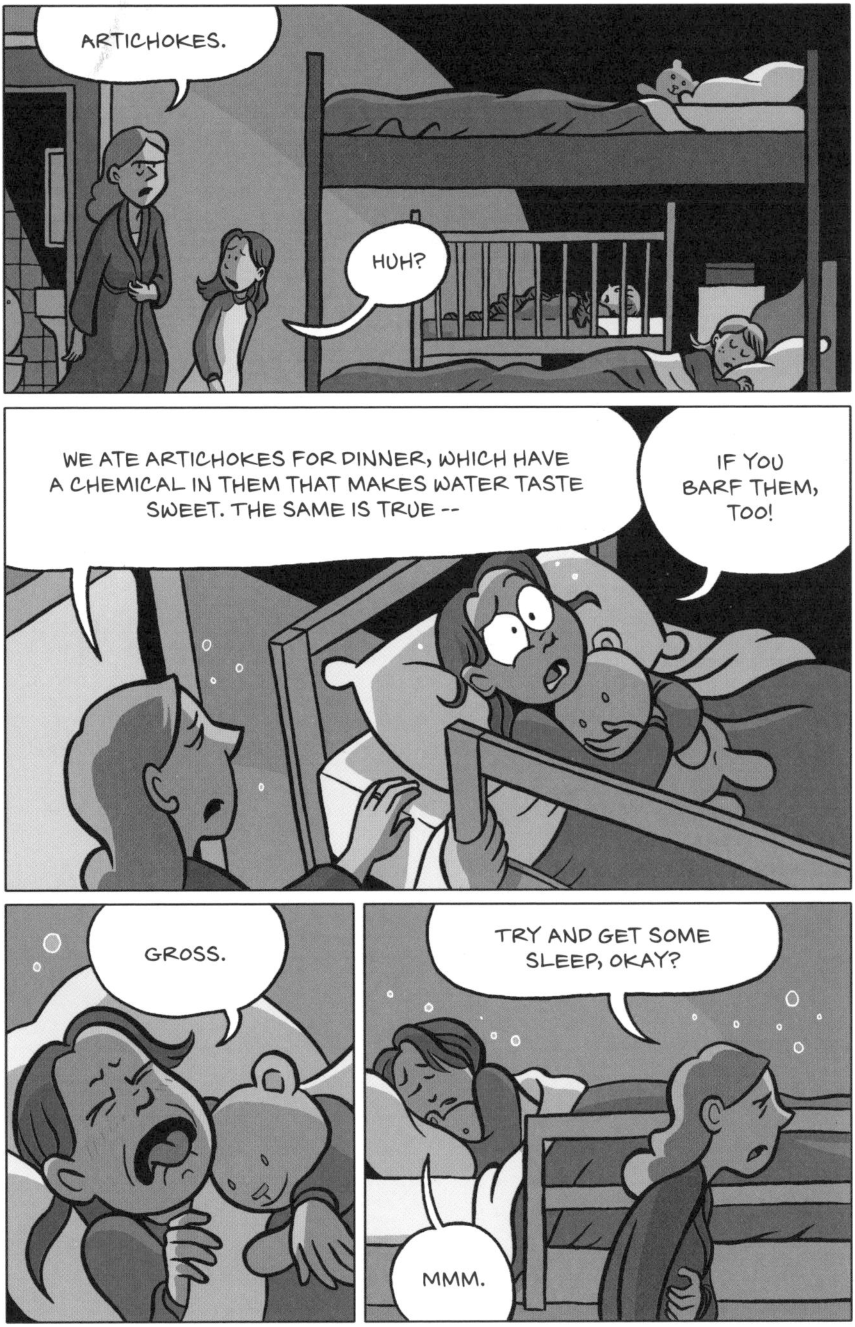
ARTICHOKES.
HUH?
WE ATE ARTICHOKES FOR DINNER, WHICH HAVE A CHEMICAL IN THEM THAT MAKES WATER TASTE SWEET. THE SAME IS TRUE --
IF YOU BARF THEM, TOO!
GROSS.
TRY AND GET SOME SLEEP, OKAY?
MMM.

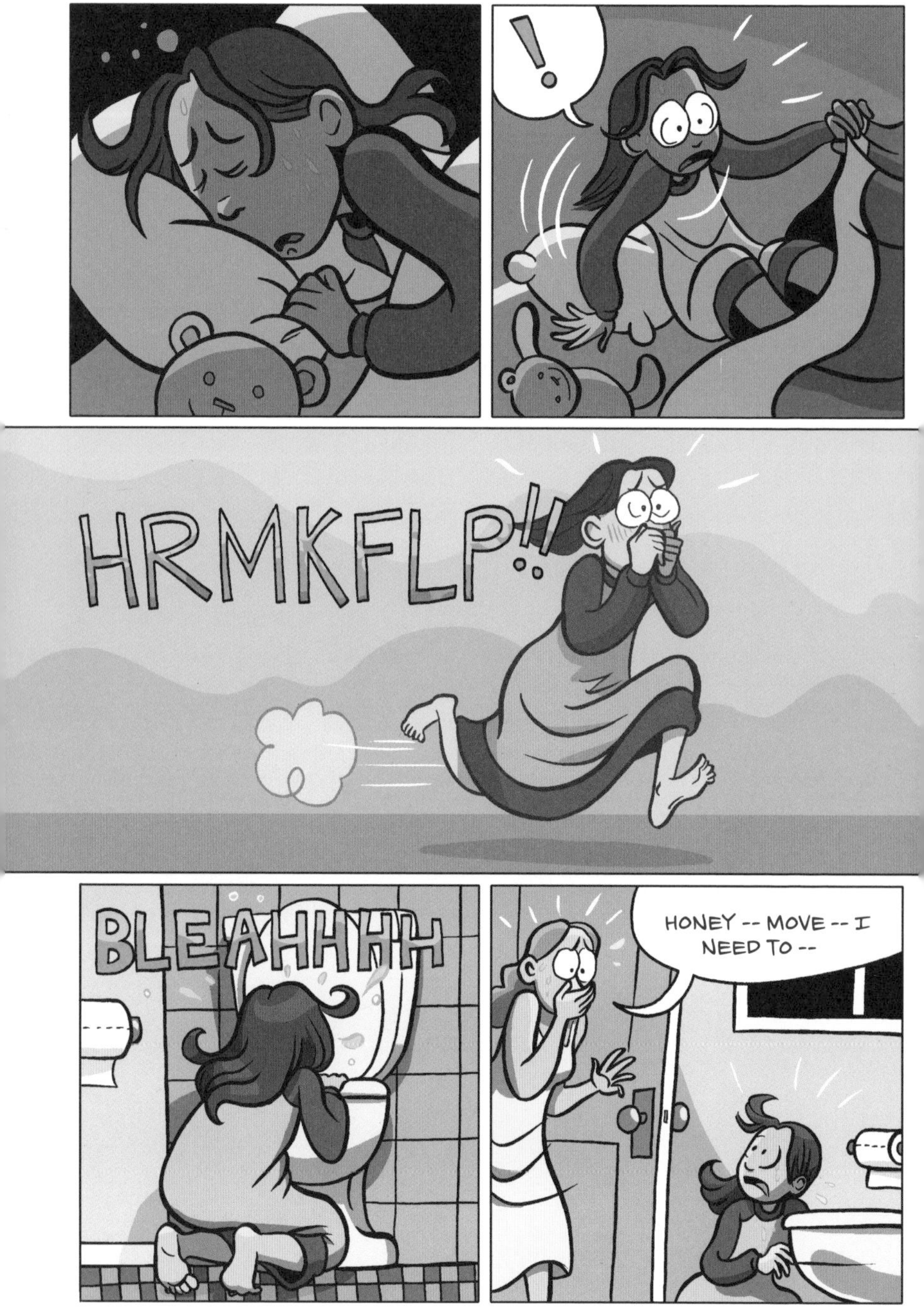
!
HRMKFLP!!
BLEAHHHH
HONEY -- MOVE -- I NEED TO --

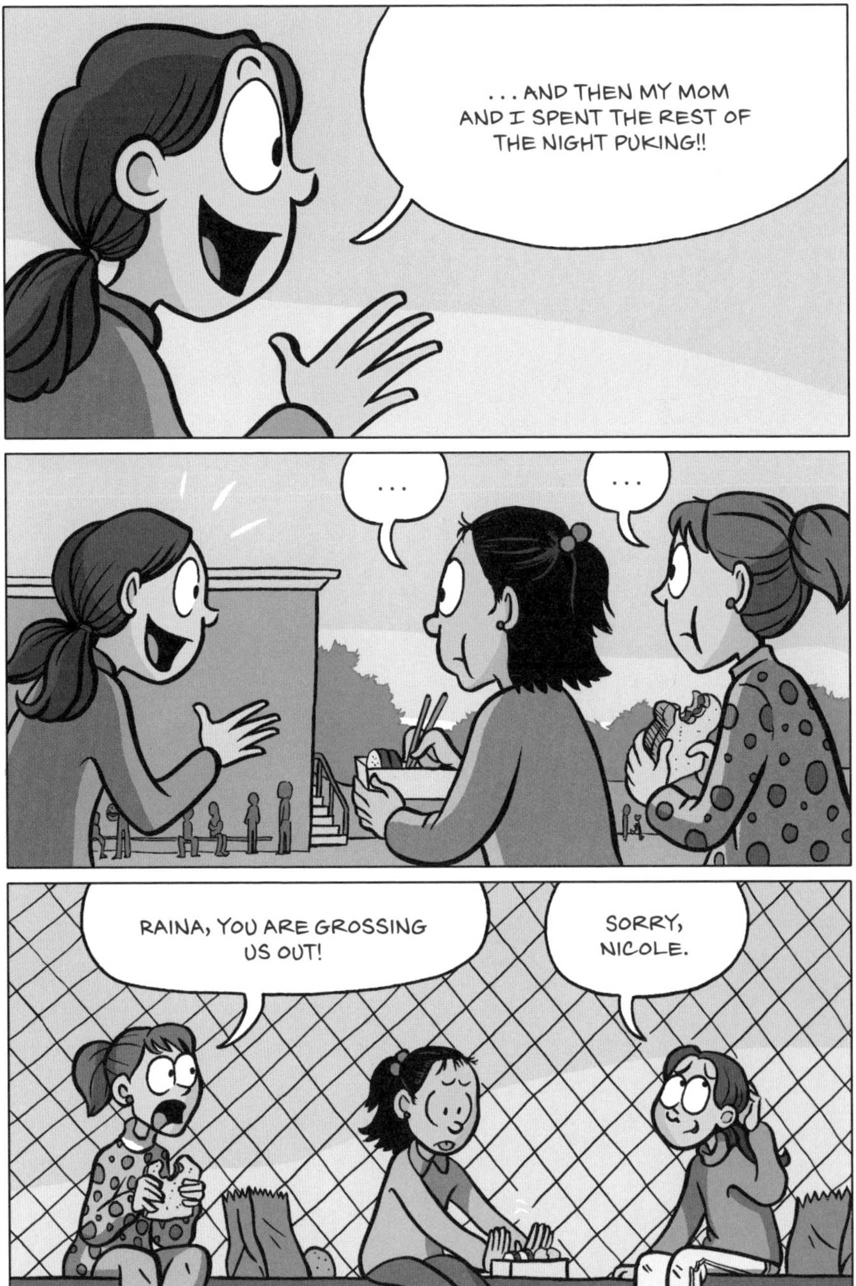
. . . AND THEN MY MOM AND I SPENT THE REST OF THE NIGHT PUKING!!
. . .
. . .
RAINA, YOU ARE GROSSING US OUT!
SORRY, NICOLE.

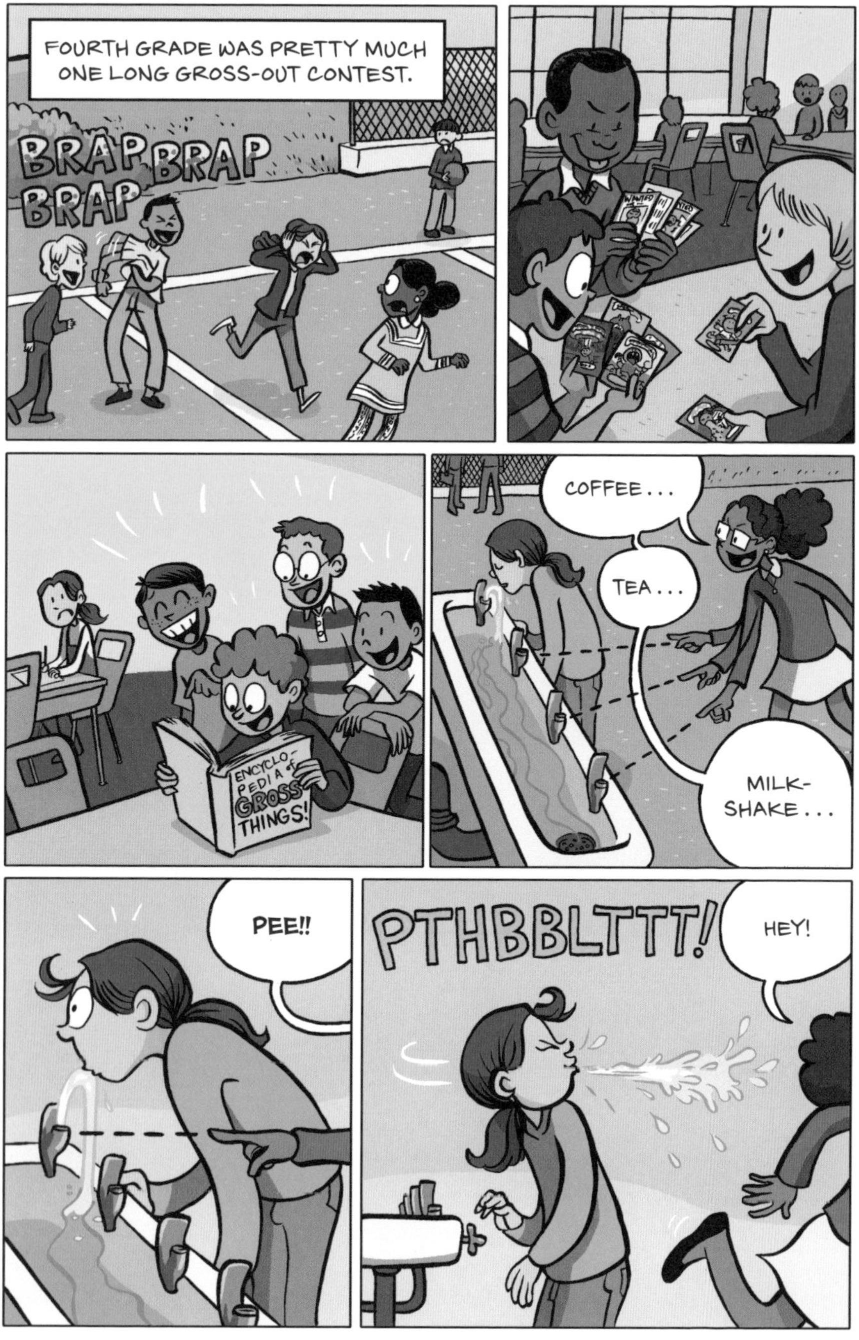
FOURTH GRADE WAS PRETTY MUCH ONE LONG GROSS-OUT CONTEST.
BRAP BRAP
BRAP
ENCYCLOPEDIA of GROSS THINGS!
COFFEE...
TEA...
MILK-SHAKE...
PEE!!
PTHBBLTTT!
HEY!

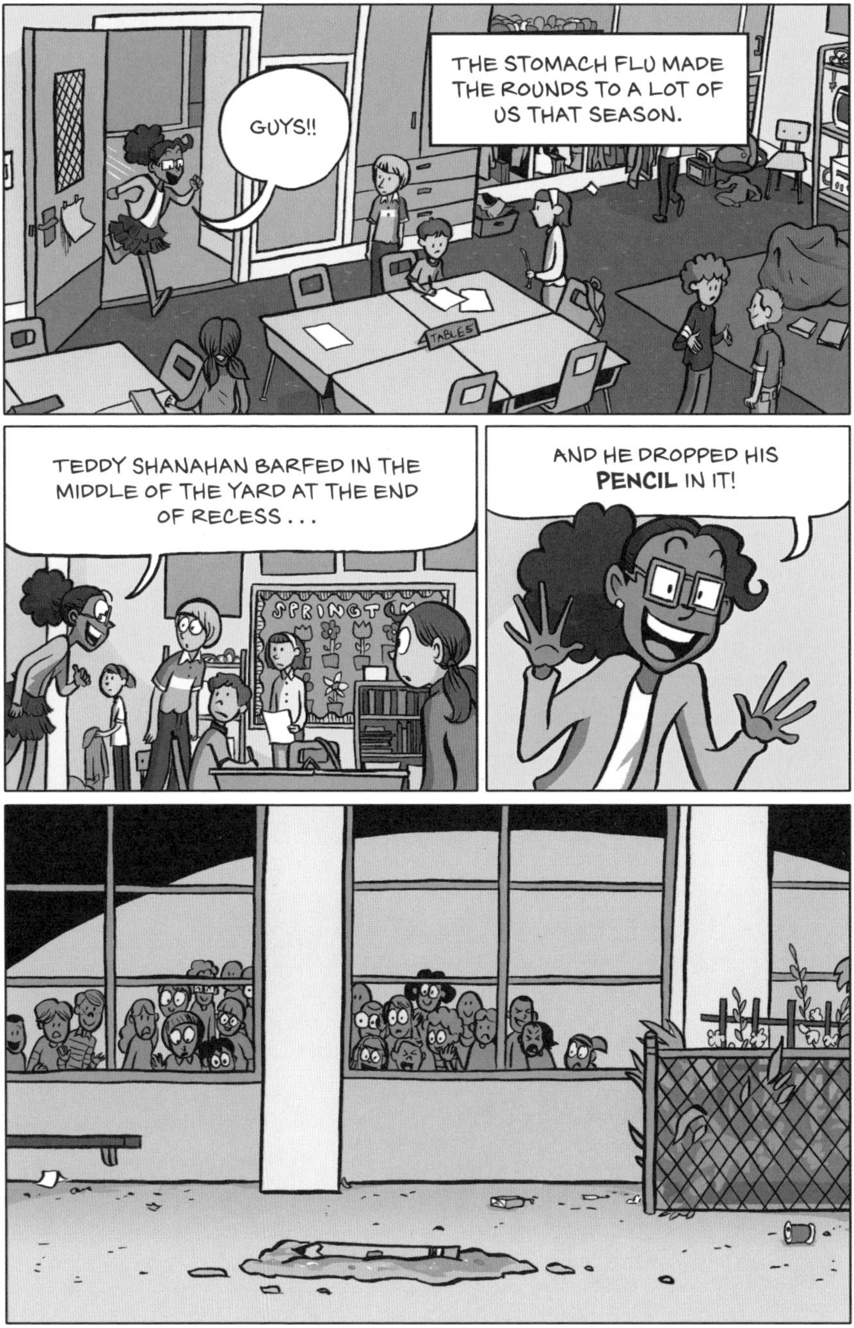
GUYS!!
THE STOMACH FLU MADE THE ROUNDS TO A LOT OF US THAT SEASON.
TEDDY SHANAHAN BARFED IN THE MIDDLE OF THE YARD AT THE END OF RECESS . . .
AND HE DROPPED HIS **PENCIL** IN IT!

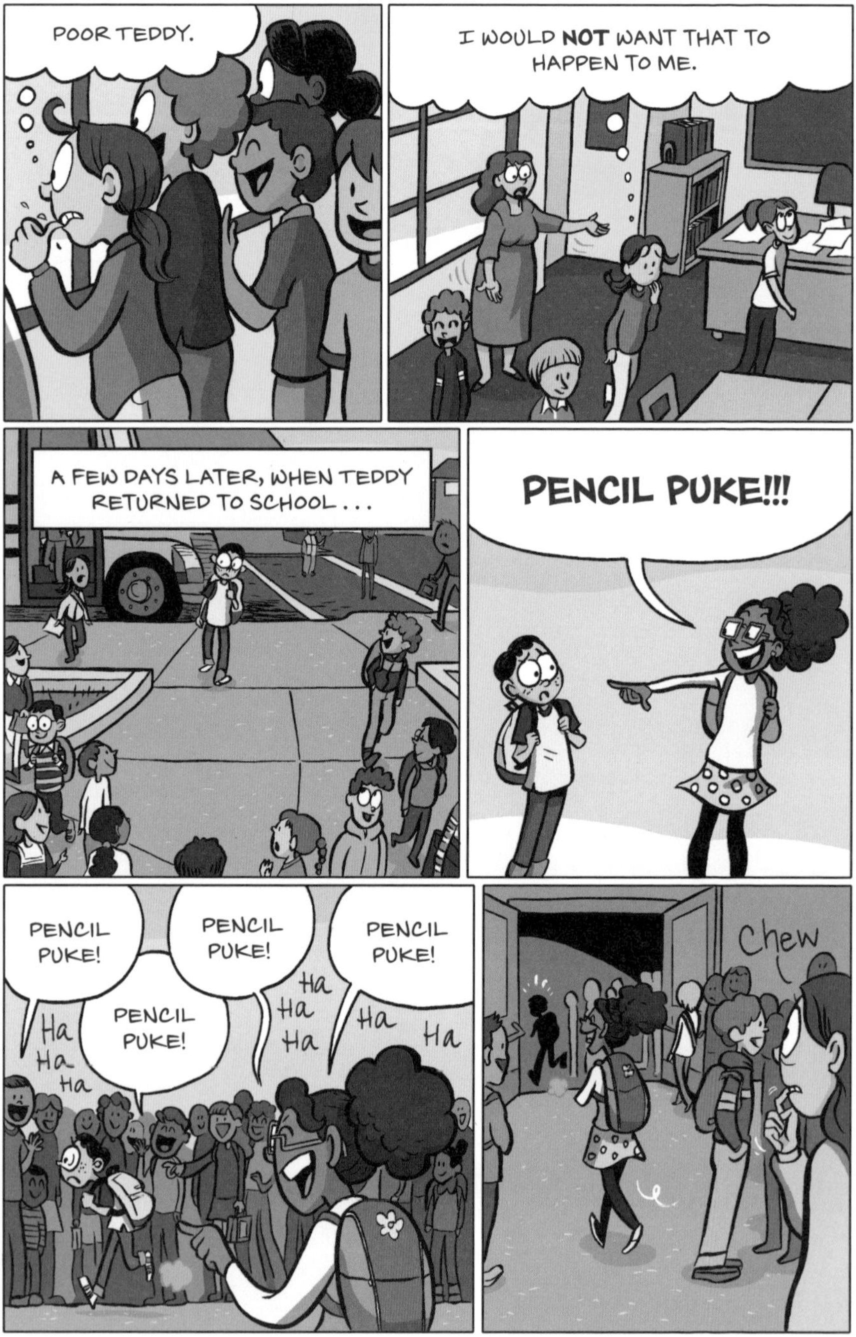

POOR TEDDY.
I WOULD **NOT** WANT THAT TO HAPPEN TO ME.
A FEW DAYS LATER, WHEN TEDDY RETURNED TO SCHOOL . . .
PENCIL PUKE!!!
PENCIL PUKE!
PENCIL PUKE!
PENCIL PUKE!
PENCIL PUKE!
Ha Ha Ha
Ha Ha Ha
Ha
Ha
Chew

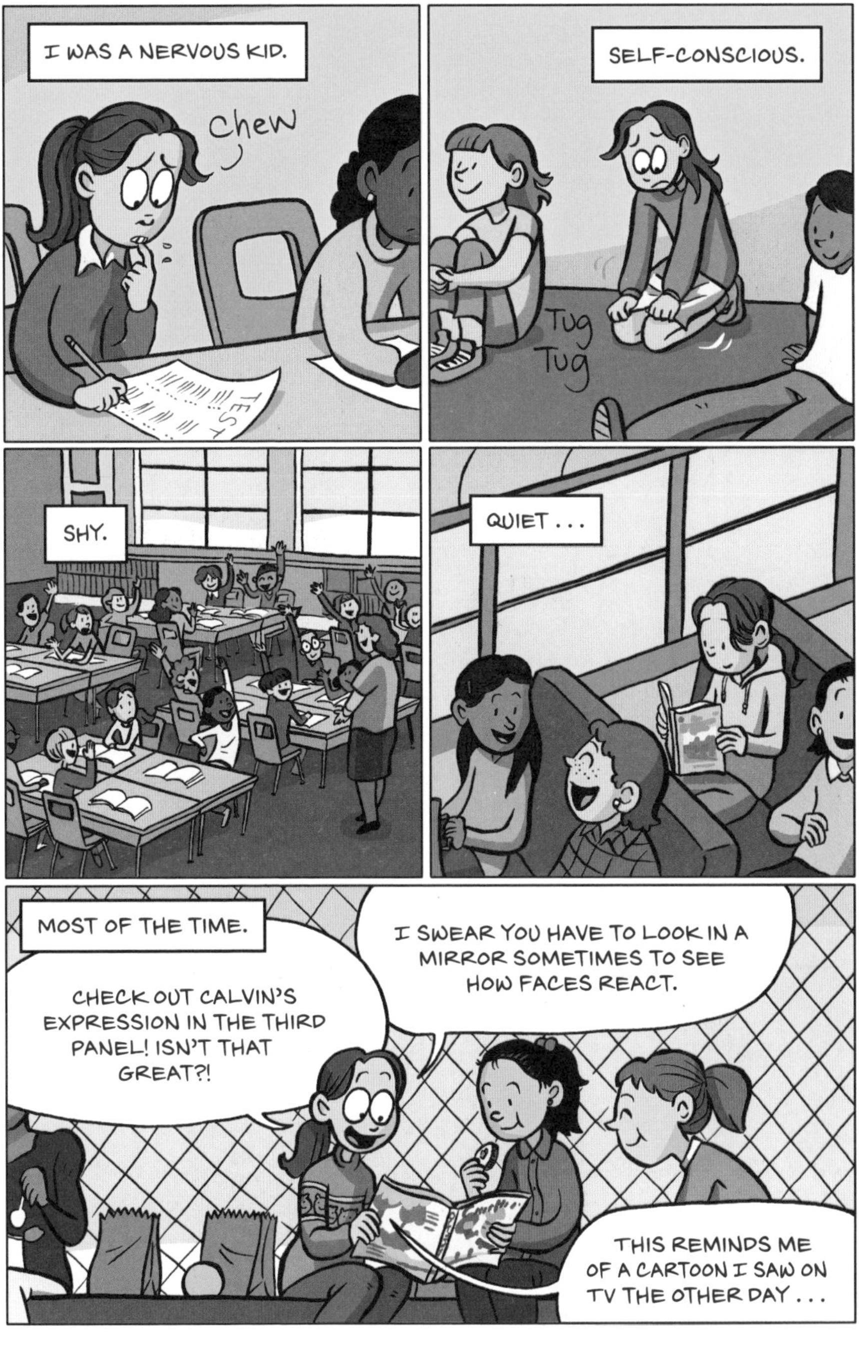
I WAS A NERVOUS KID.
Chew
TEST
SELF-CONSCIOUS.
Tug
Tug
SHY.
QUIET . . .
MOST OF THE TIME.
CHECK OUT CALVIN'S EXPRESSION IN THE THIRD PANEL! ISN'T THAT GREAT?!
I SWEAR YOU HAVE TO LOOK IN A MIRROR SOMETIMES TO SEE HOW FACES REACT.
THIS REMINDS ME OF A CARTOON I SAW ON TV THE OTHER DAY . . .

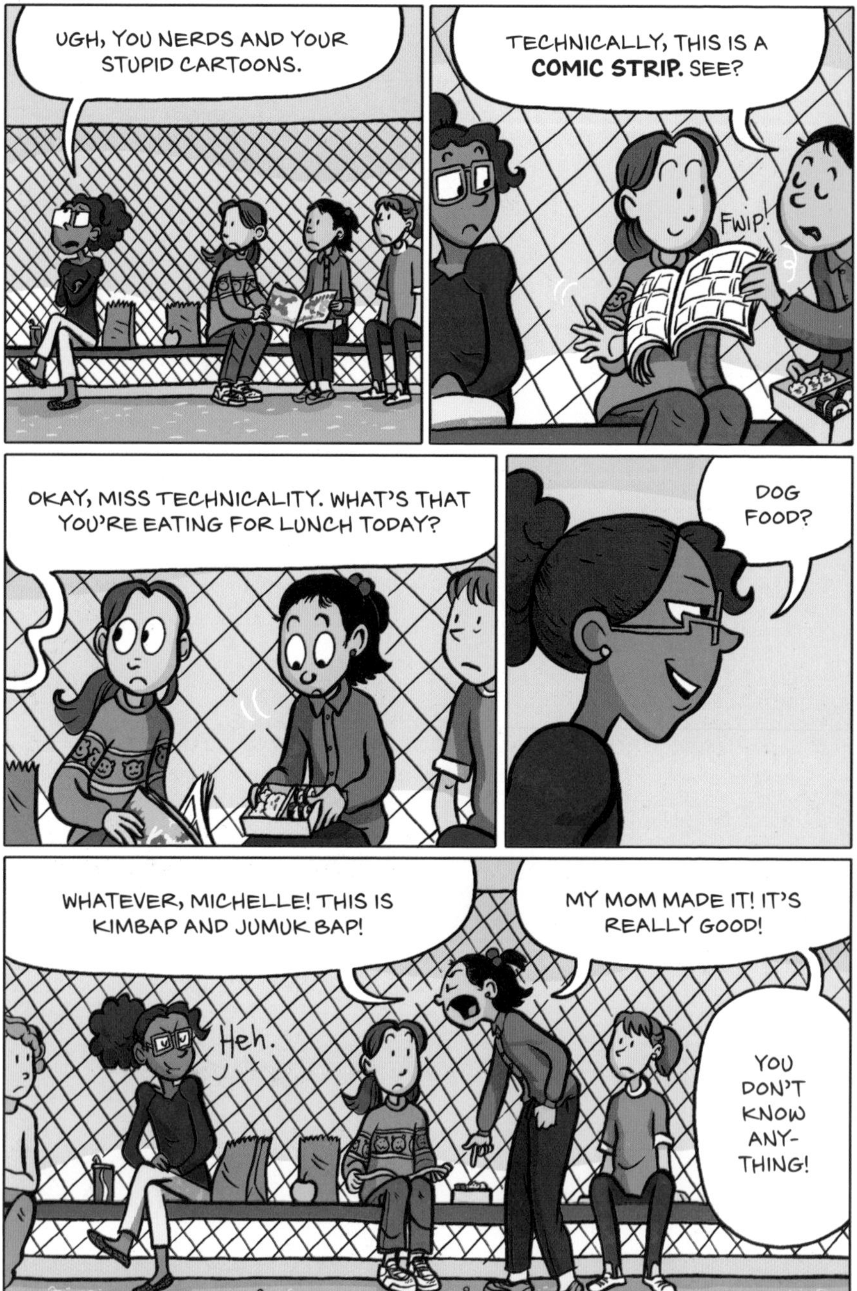
UGH, YOU NERDS AND YOUR STUPID CARTOONS.
TECHNICALLY, THIS IS A **COMIC STRIP.** SEE?
FWIP!
OKAY, MISS TECHNICALITY. WHAT'S THAT YOU'RE EATING FOR LUNCH TODAY?
DOG FOOD?
WHATEVER, MICHELLE! THIS IS KIMBAP AND JUMUK BAP!
MY MOM MADE IT! IT'S REALLY GOOD!
Heh.
YOU DON'T KNOW ANY-THING!

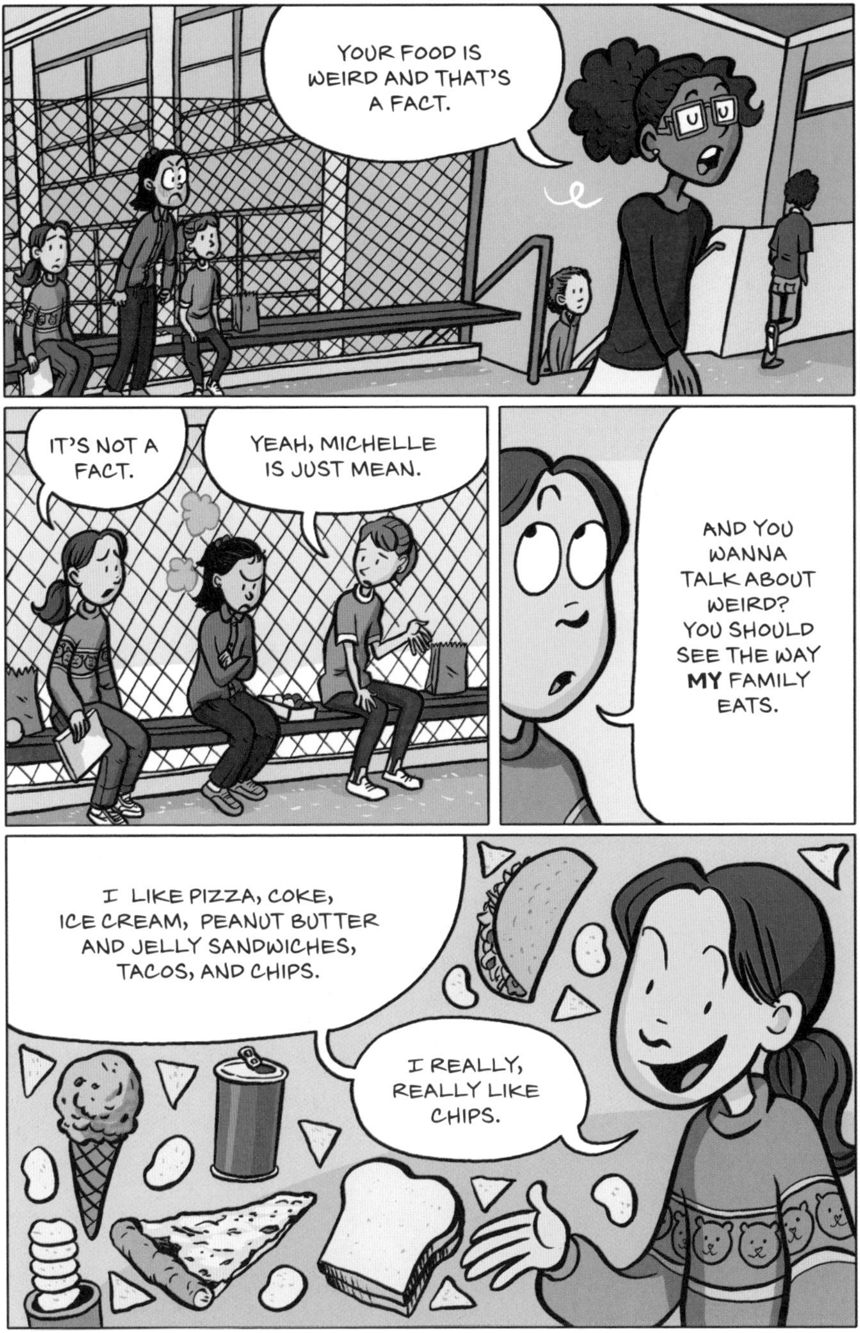
YOUR FOOD IS WEIRD AND THAT'S A FACT.
IT'S NOT A FACT.
YEAH, MICHELLE IS JUST MEAN.
AND YOU WANNA TALK ABOUT WEIRD? YOU SHOULD SEE THE WAY **MY** FAMILY EATS.
I LIKE PIZZA, COKE, ICE CREAM, PEANUT BUTTER AND JELLY SANDWICHES, TACOS, AND CHIPS.
I REALLY, REALLY LIKE CHIPS.

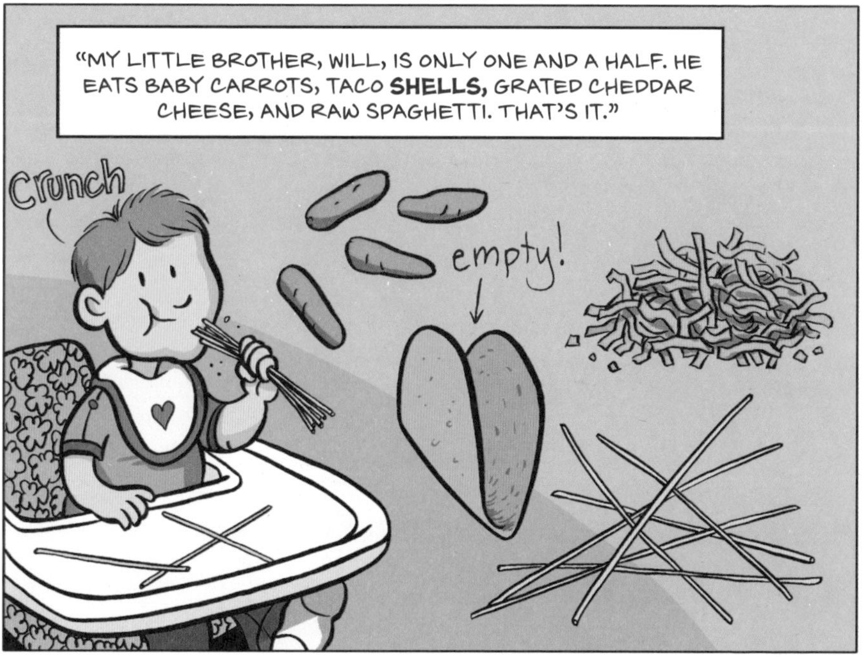
"MY LITTLE BROTHER, WILL, IS ONLY ONE AND A HALF. HE EATS BABY CARROTS, TACO **SHELLS,** GRATED CHEDDAR CHEESE, AND RAW SPAGHETTI. THAT'S IT."
Crunch
empty!

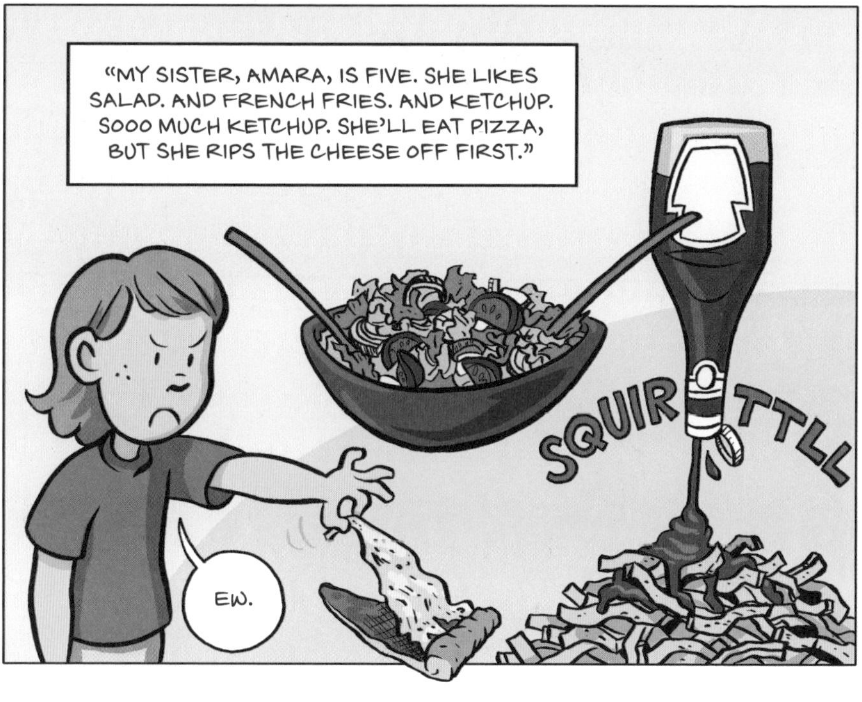
"MY SISTER, AMARA, IS FIVE. SHE LIKES SALAD. AND FRENCH FRIES. AND KETCHUP. SOOO MUCH KETCHUP. SHE'LL EAT PIZZA, BUT SHE RIPS THE CHEESE OFF FIRST."
SQUIRTTLL
EW.

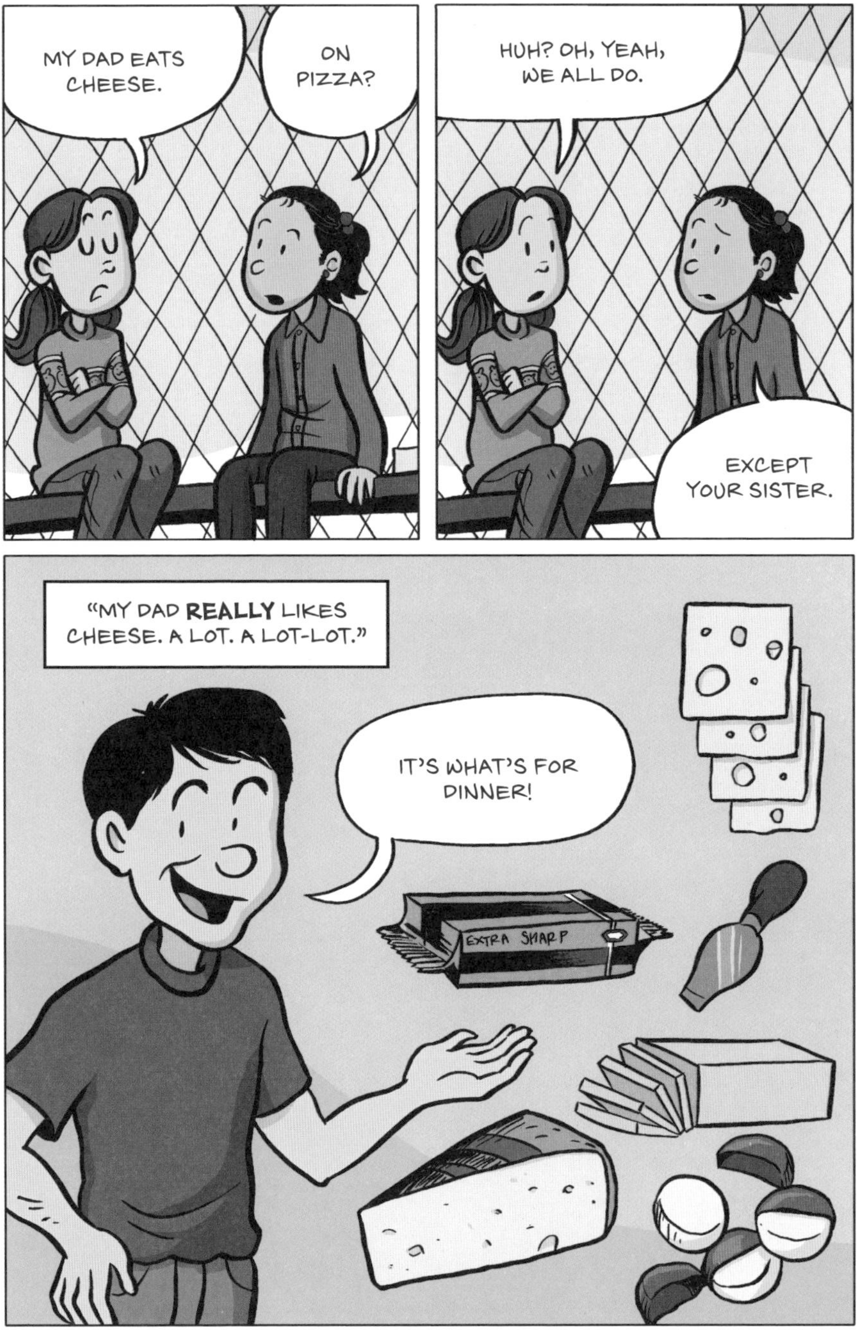
MY DAD EATS CHEESE.
ON PIZZA?
HUH? OH, YEAH, WE ALL DO.
EXCEPT YOUR SISTER.
"MY DAD **REALLY** LIKES CHEESE. A LOT. A LOT-LOT."
IT'S WHAT'S FOR DINNER!
EXTRA SHARP

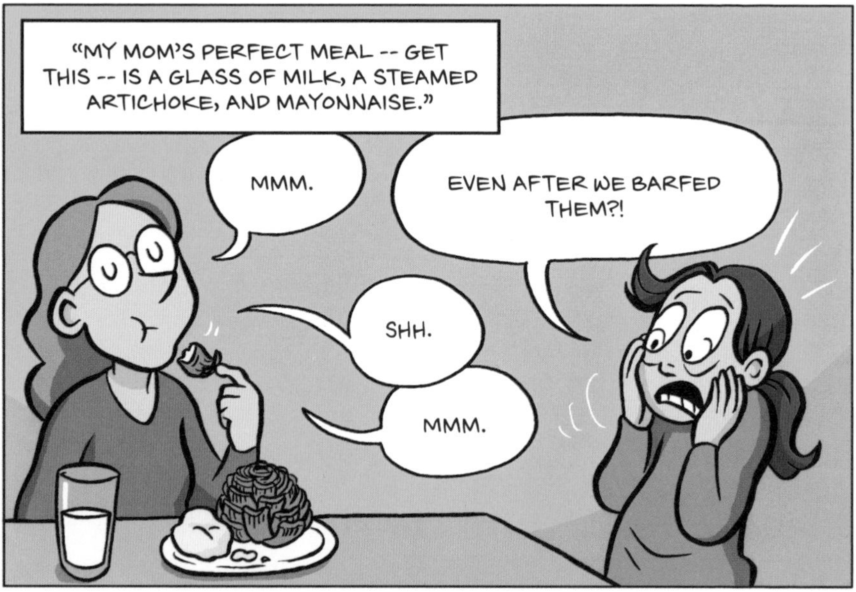
"MY MOM'S PERFECT MEAL -- GET THIS -- IS A GLASS OF MILK, A STEAMED ARTICHOKE, AND MAYONNAISE."
MMM.
EVEN AFTER WE BARFED THEM?!
SHH.
MMM.

ANATOMY

of a "normal dinner" at our house

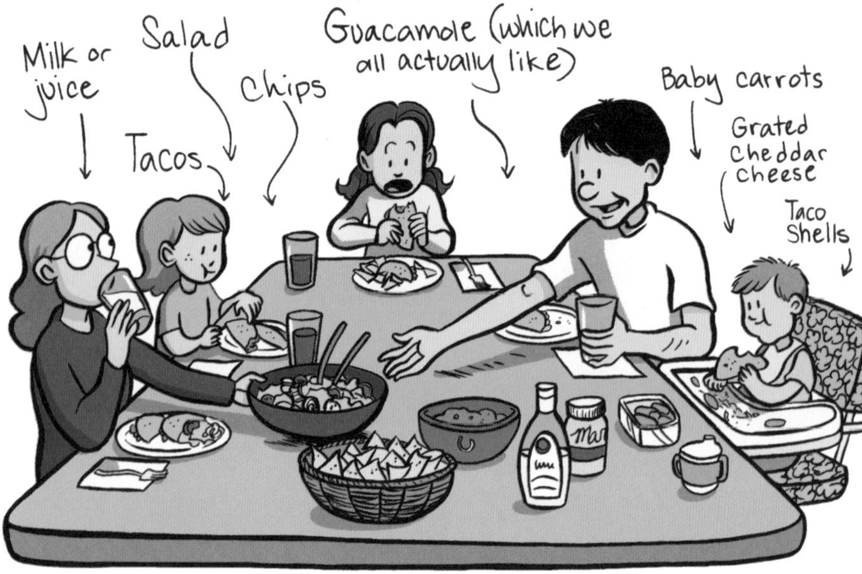
Milk or juice
Salad
Tacos
Chips
Guacamole (which we all actually like)
Baby carrots
Grated Cheddar cheese
Taco Shells

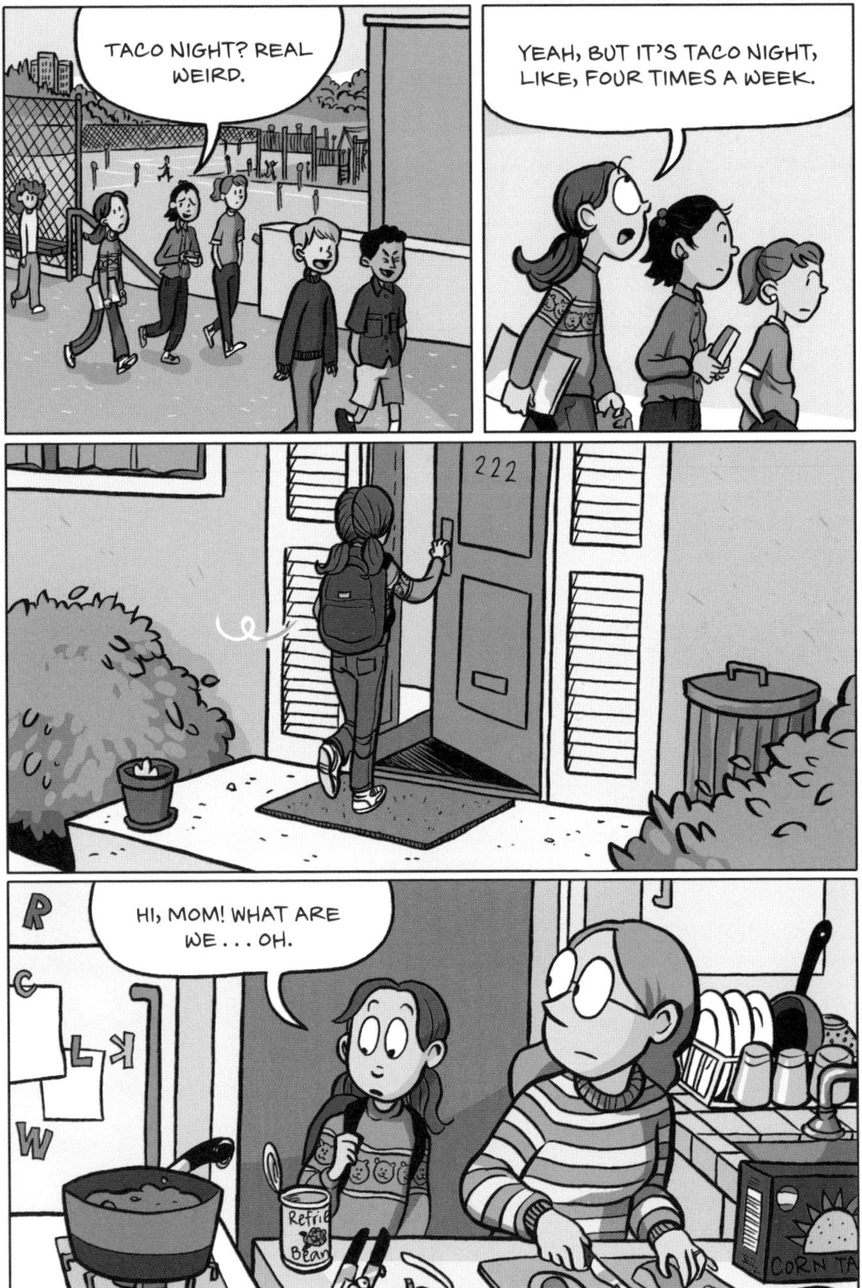
TACO NIGHT? REAL WEIRD.
YEAH, BUT IT'S TACO NIGHT, LIKE, FOUR TIMES A WEEK.
222
HI, MOM! WHAT ARE WE . . . OH.

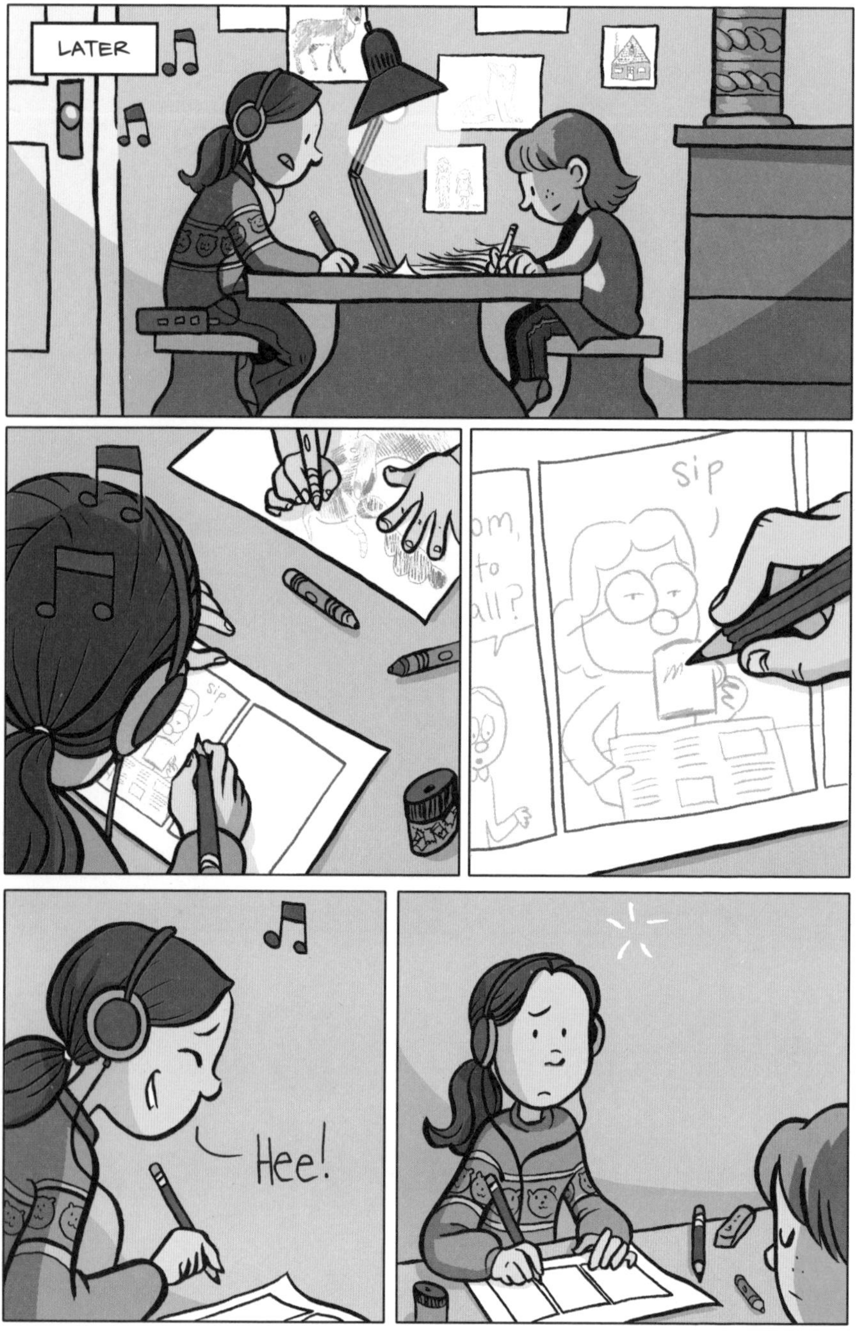
LATER
sip
sip
Hee!

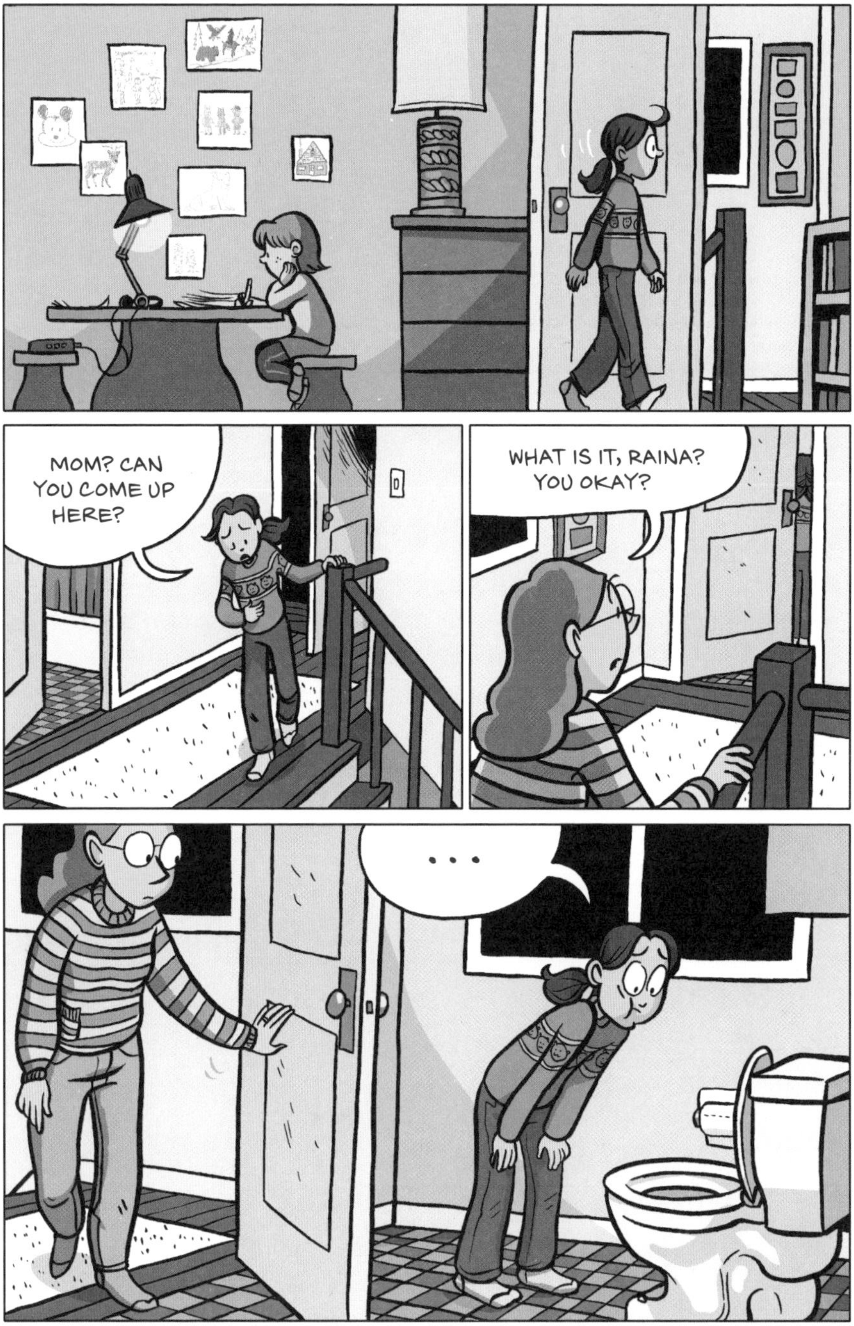
MOM? CAN YOU COME UP HERE?
WHAT IS IT, RAINA? YOU OKAY?
. . .

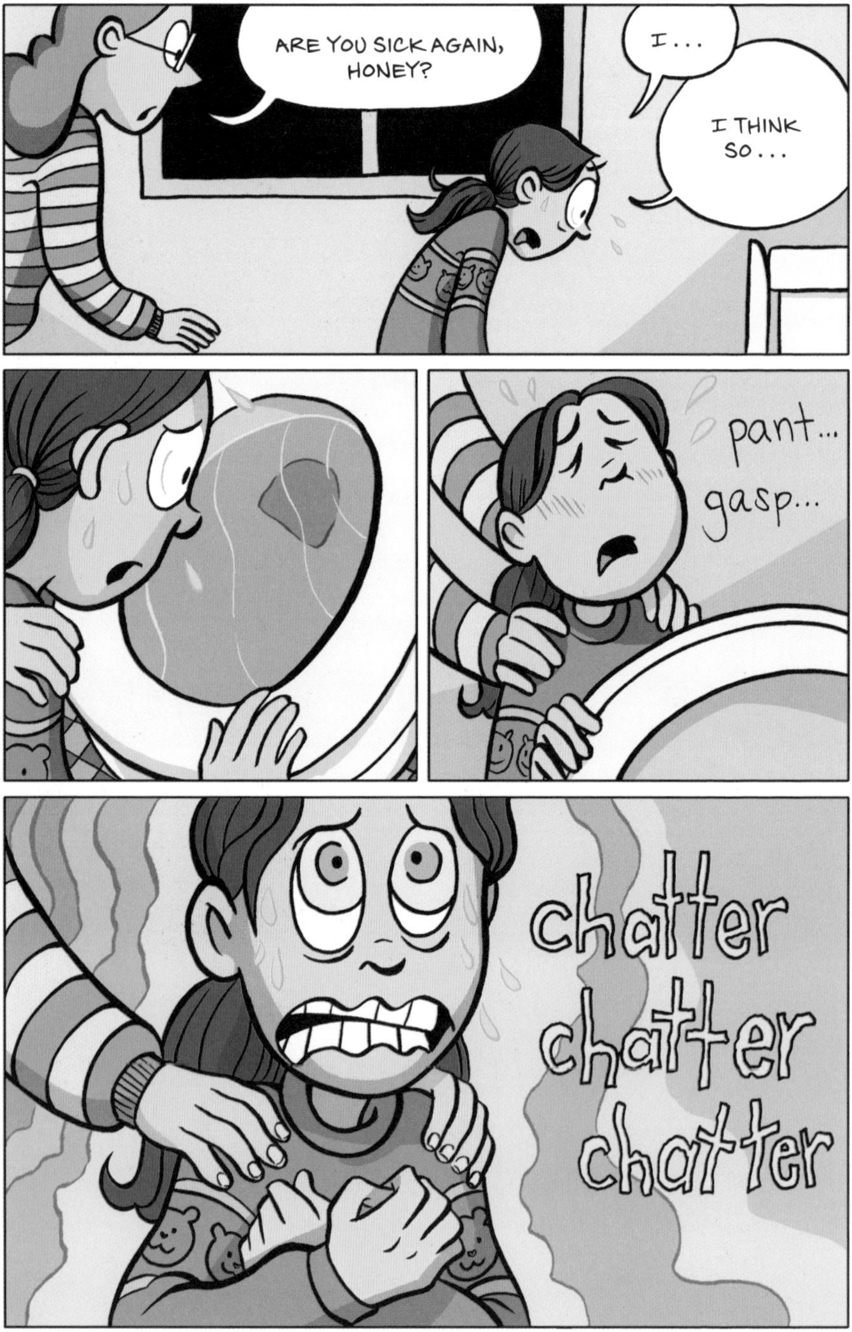
ARE YOU SICK AGAIN, HONEY?
I...
I THINK SO...
pant...
gasp...
chatter
chatter
chatter

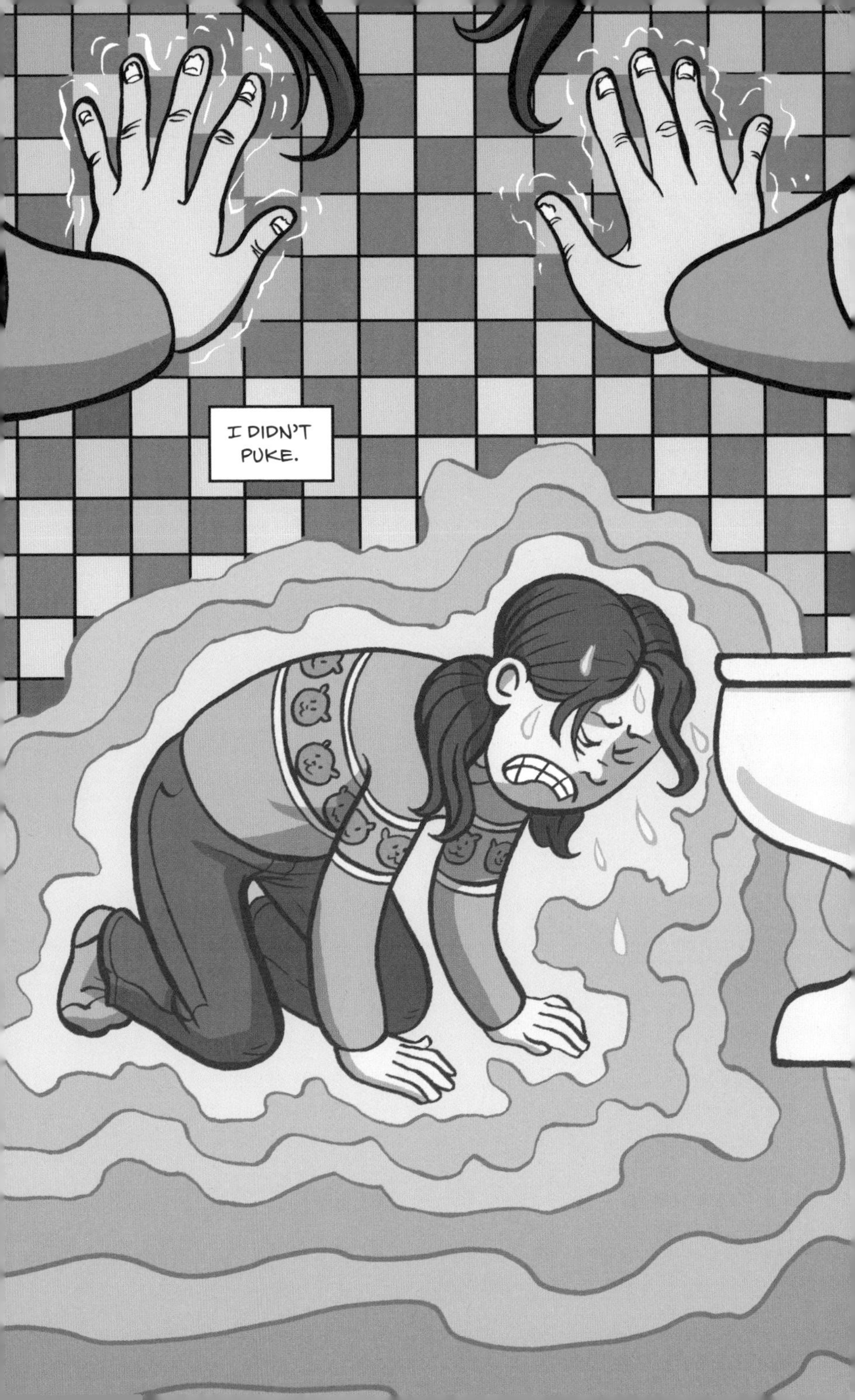
I DIDN'T PUKE.

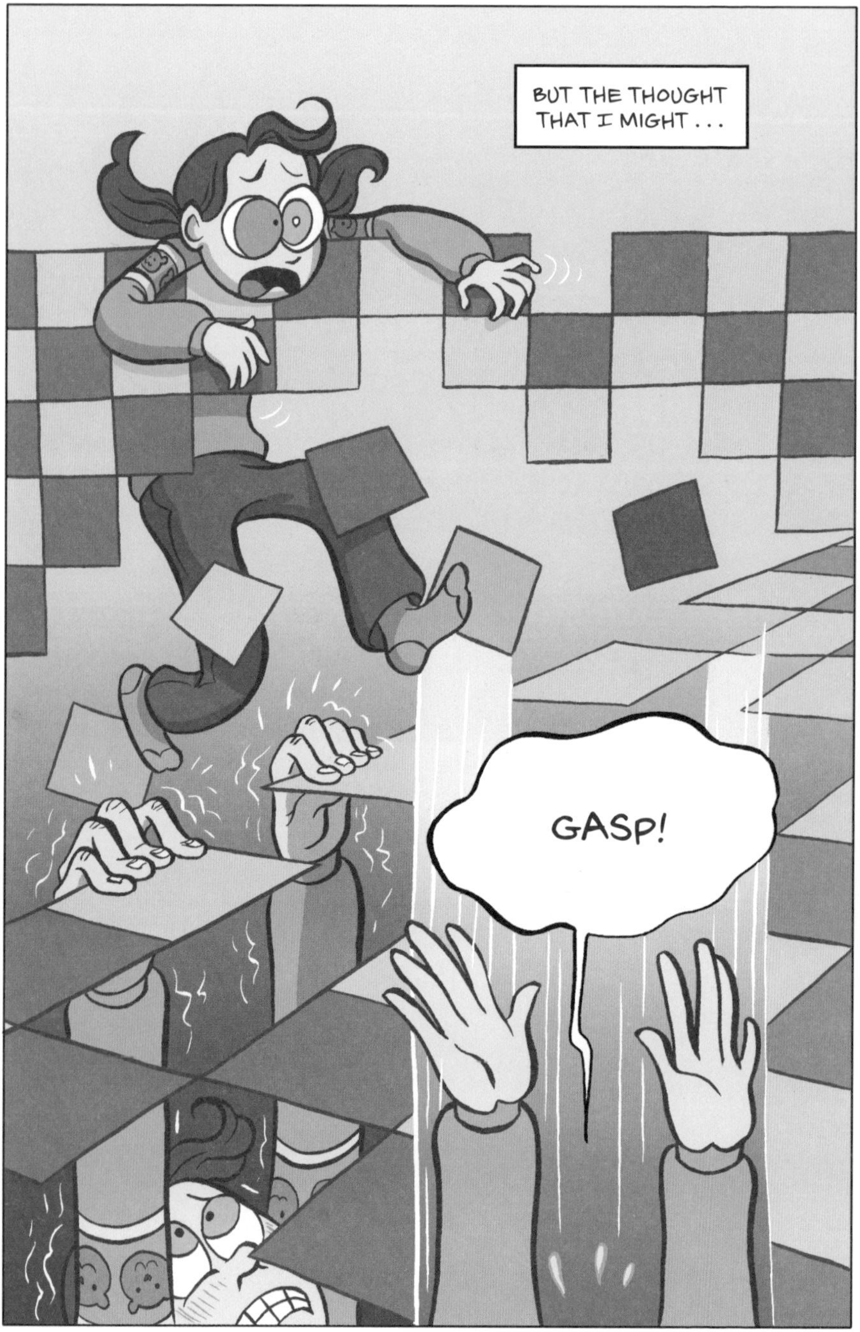
BUT THE THOUGHT THAT I MIGHT . . .
GASP!

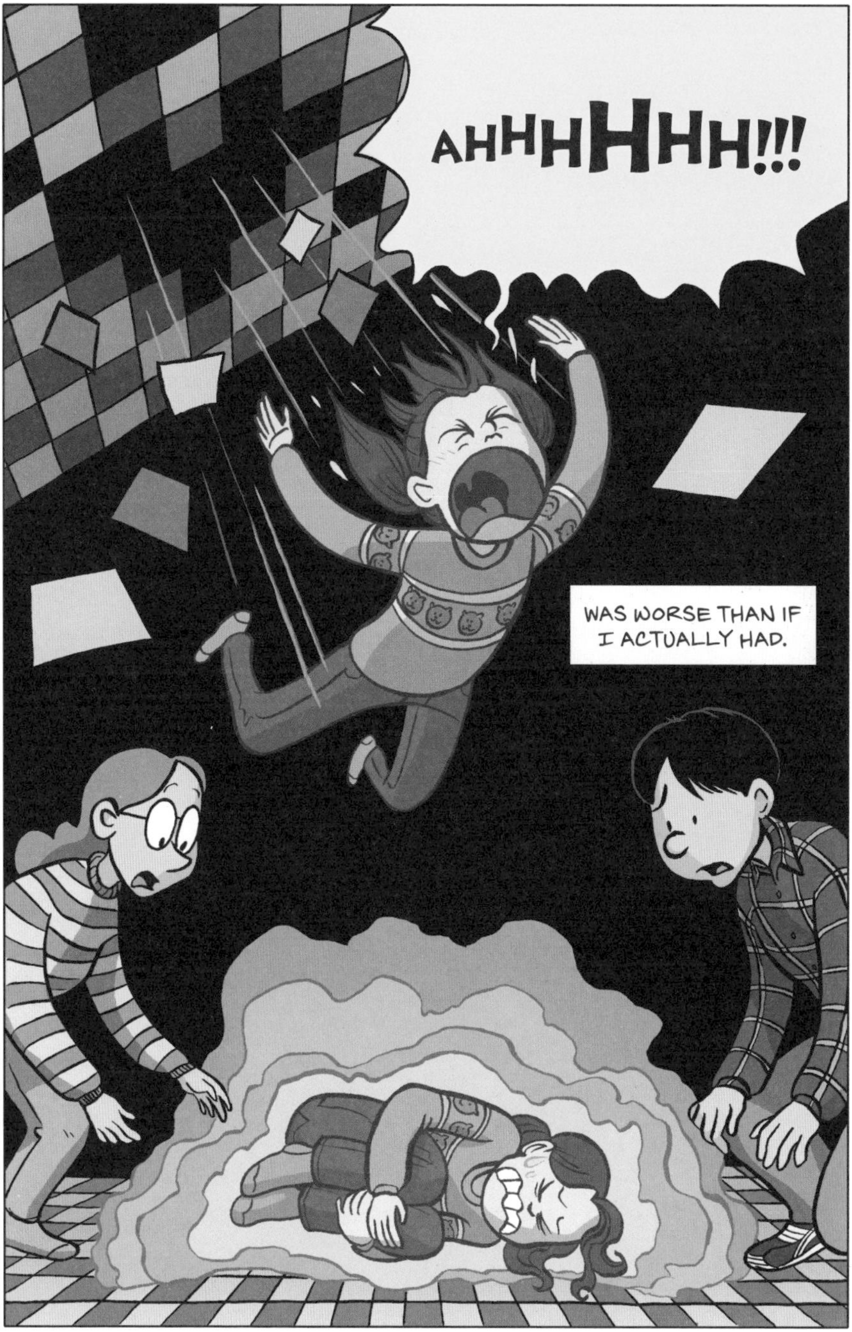
AHHHHHH!!!
WAS WORSE THAN IF I ACTUALLY HAD.

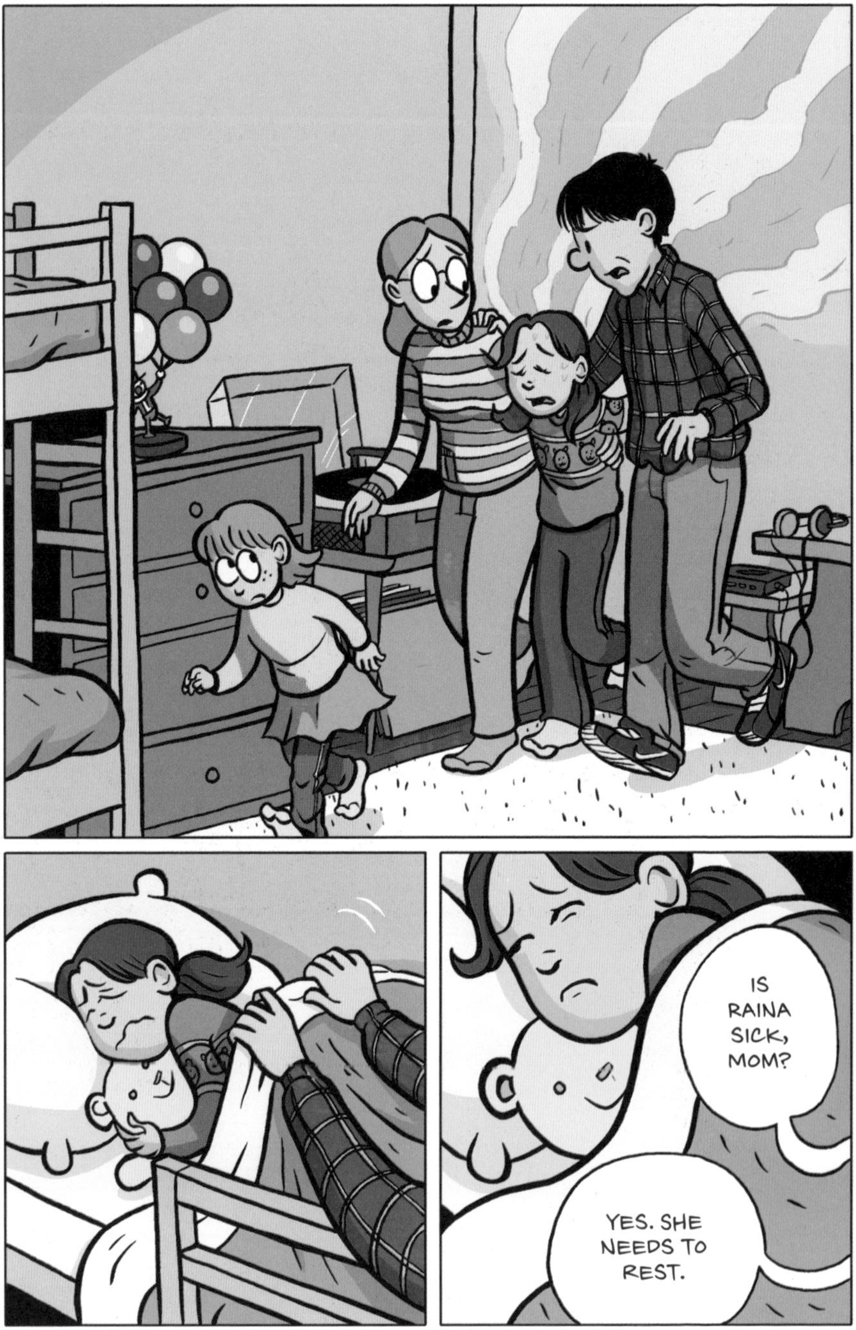
IS RAINA SICK, MOM?
YES. SHE NEEDS TO REST.

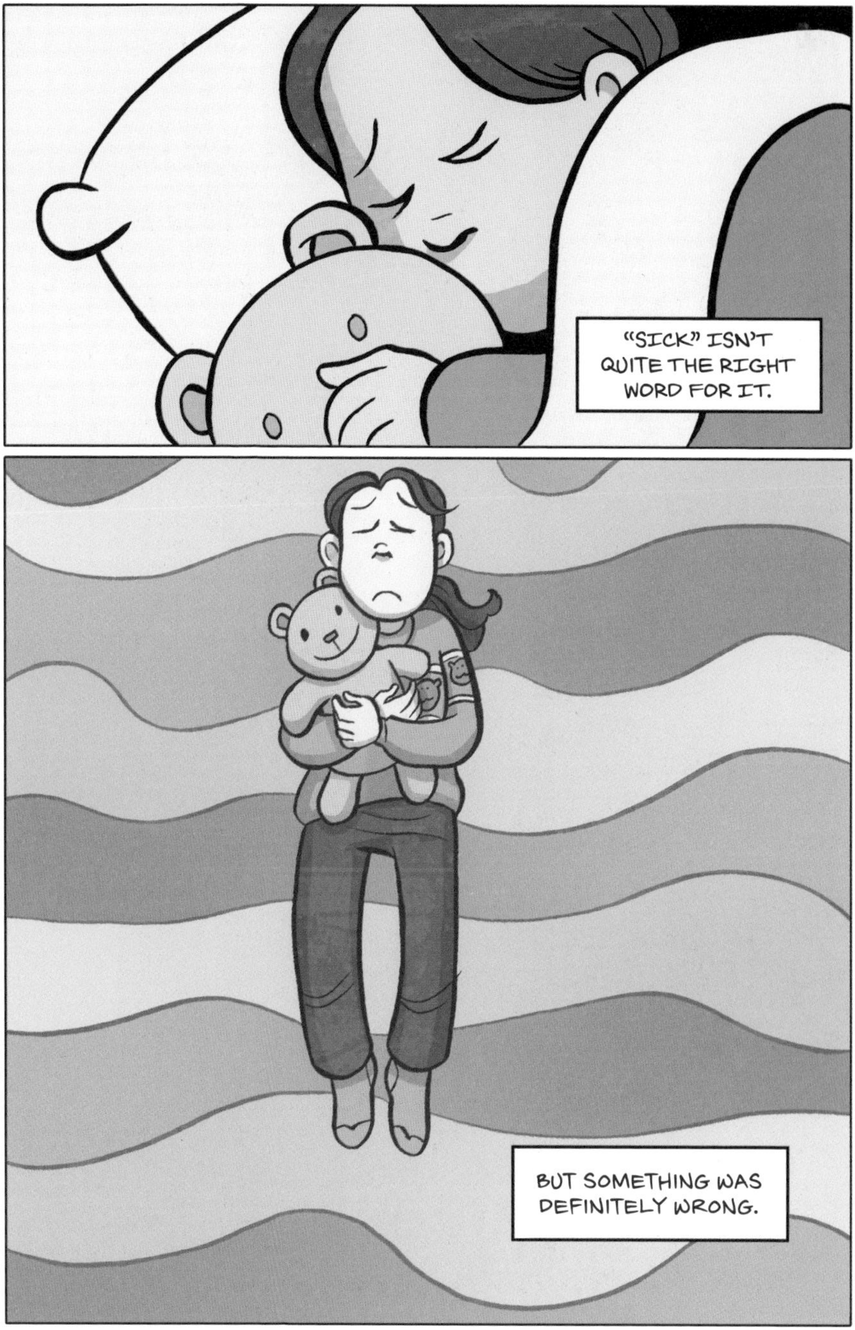
"SICK" ISN'T QUITE THE RIGHT WORD FOR IT.
BUT SOMETHING WAS DEFINITELY WRONG.

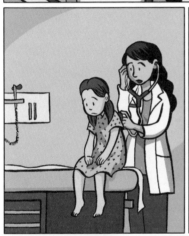

HEALTHY AS A HORSE!

COULD BE YOUR HORMONES KICKING IN . . . MIGHT HAVE BEEN A LITTLE FOOD POISONING.

COULD BE. BUT NONE OF THAT EXPLAINED WHY I HAD BEEN SO **SCARED.**

OKAY, CLASS, GETTING BACK TO THE QUIZ . . .

2. After dinner, 5/8 of the pizza is left over. That night, your sister eats 2/8 of the pizza. How much is left after that?

3. Henry spent 4/9 of his allowance on baseball cards. What fraction

IS THAT WITH OR WITHOUT THE CHEESE?

TABLE 3

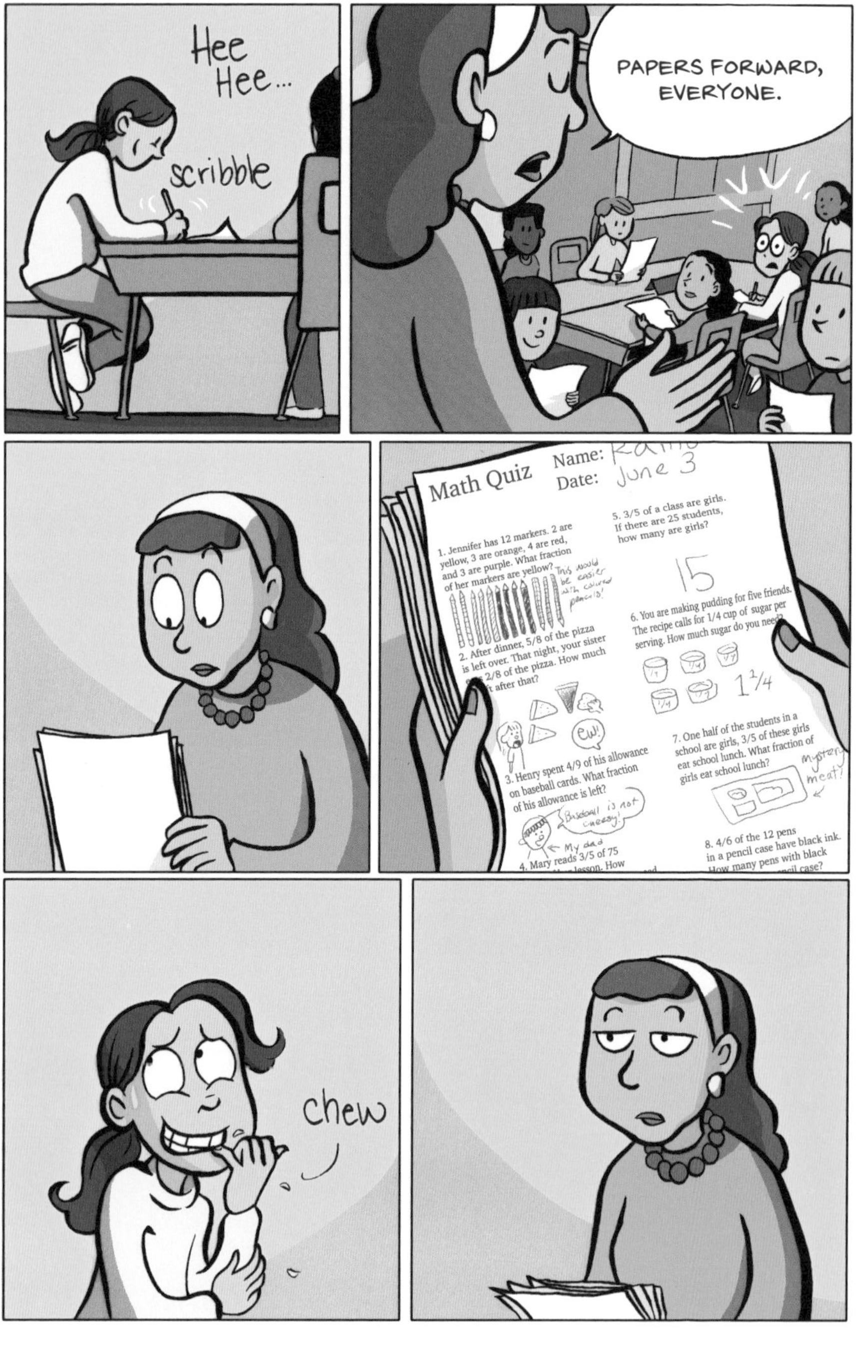
Hee
Hee...
scribble
PAPERS FORWARD, EVERYONE.
Math Quiz
Name:
Date: June 3
1. Jennifer has 12 markers. 2 are yellow, 3 are orange, 4 are red, and 3 are purple. What fraction of her markers are yellow?
This would be easier with colored pencils!
2. After dinner, 5/8 of the pizza is left over. That night, your sister
2/8 of the pizza. How much
after that?
Ew!
3. Henry spent 4/9 of his allowance on baseball cards. What fraction of his allowance is left?
Baseball is not cheesy!
My dad
4. Mary reads 3/5 of 75
5. 3/5 of a class are girls. If there are 25 students, how many are girls?
15
6. You are making pudding for five friends. The recipe calls for 1/4 cup of sugar per serving. How much sugar do you need?
1 1/4
7. One half of the students in a school are girls, 3/5 of these girls eat school lunch. What fraction of girls eat school lunch?
Mystery meat!
8. 4/6 of the 12 pens in a pencil case have black ink.
How many pens with black
chew

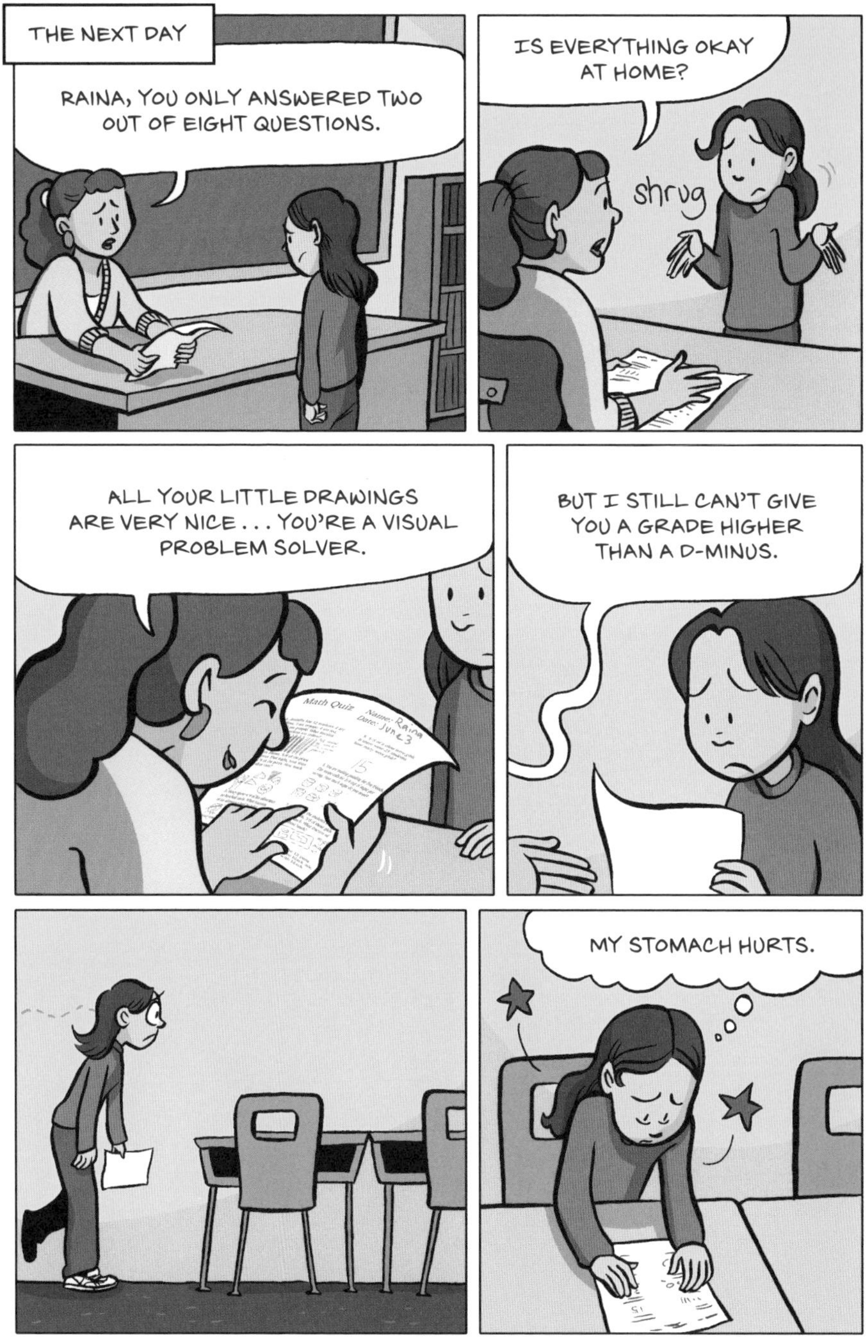
THE NEXT DAY
RAINA, YOU ONLY ANSWERED TWO OUT OF EIGHT QUESTIONS.
IS EVERYTHING OKAY AT HOME?
shrug
ALL YOUR LITTLE DRAWINGS ARE VERY NICE . . . YOU'RE A VISUAL PROBLEM SOLVER.
Math Quiz
Name: Raina
Date: June 3
BUT I STILL CAN'T GIVE YOU A GRADE HIGHER THAN A D-MINUS.
MY STOMACH HURTS.

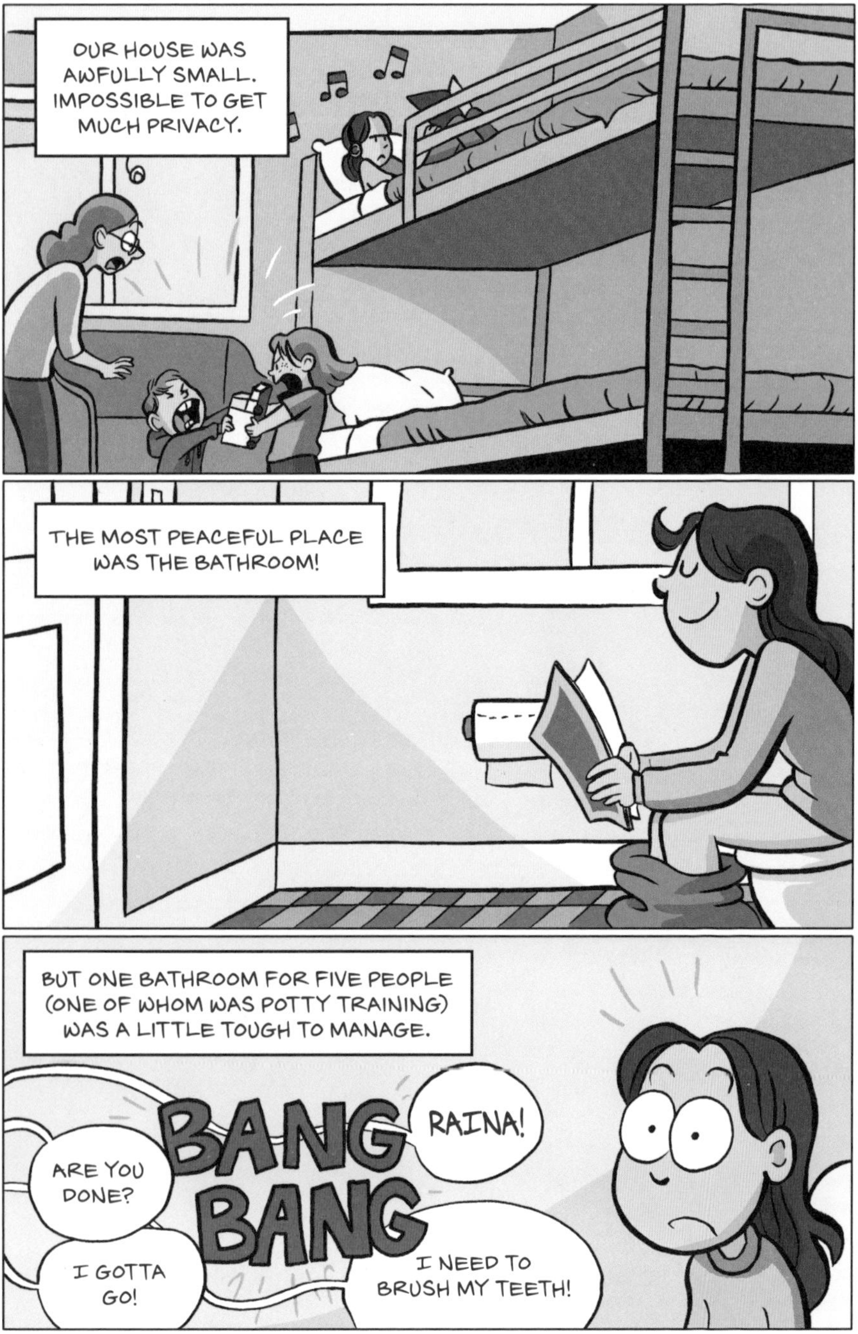
OUR HOUSE WAS AWFULLY SMALL. IMPOSSIBLE TO GET MUCH PRIVACY.
THE MOST PEACEFUL PLACE WAS THE BATHROOM!
BUT ONE BATHROOM FOR FIVE PEOPLE (ONE OF WHOM WAS POTTY TRAINING) WAS A LITTLE TOUGH TO MANAGE.
BANG
RAINA!
ARE YOU DONE?
BANG
I GOTTA GO!
I NEED TO BRUSH MY TEETH!

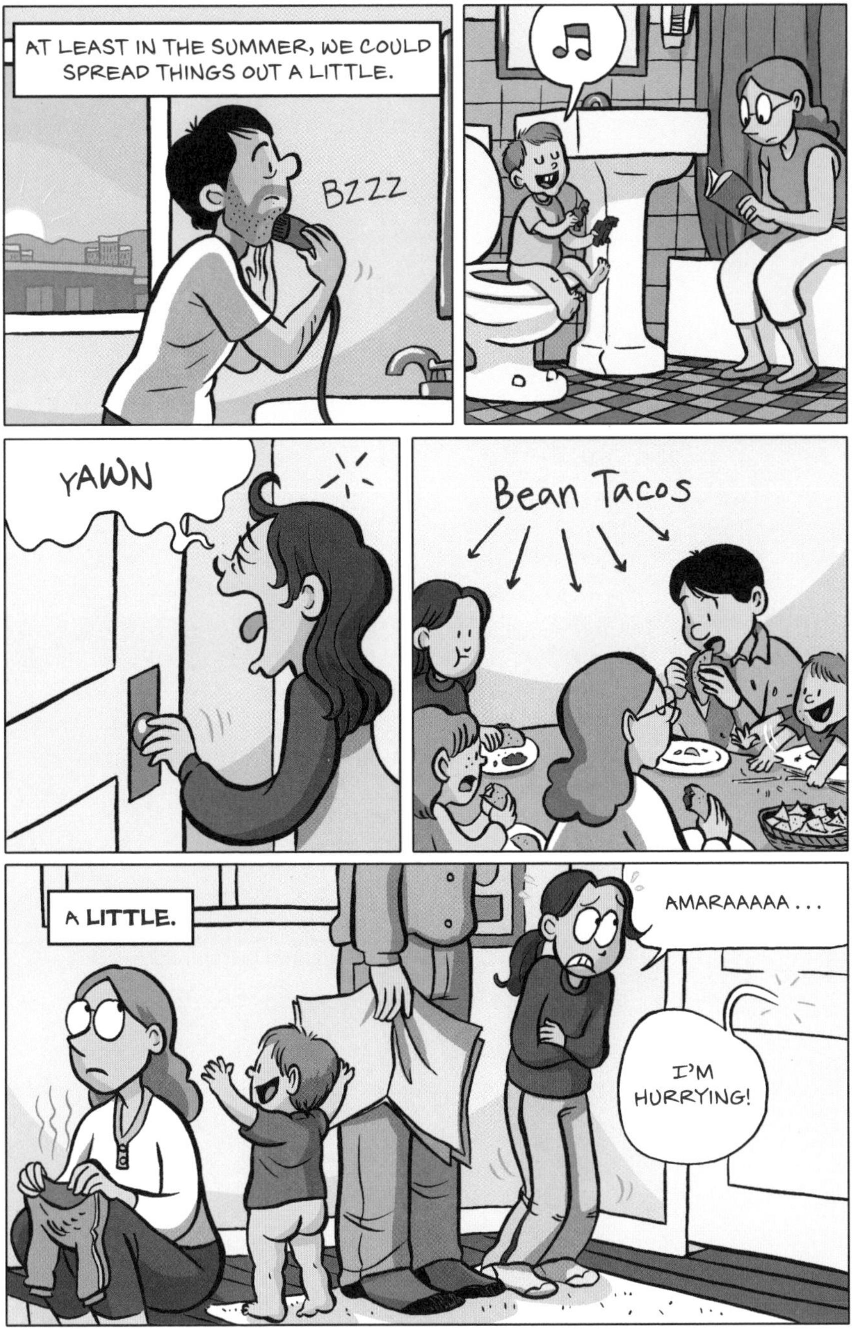
AT LEAST IN THE SUMMER, WE COULD SPREAD THINGS OUT A LITTLE.
BZZZ
YAWN
Bean Tacos
A LITTLE.
AMARAAAAA . . .
I'M HURRYING!

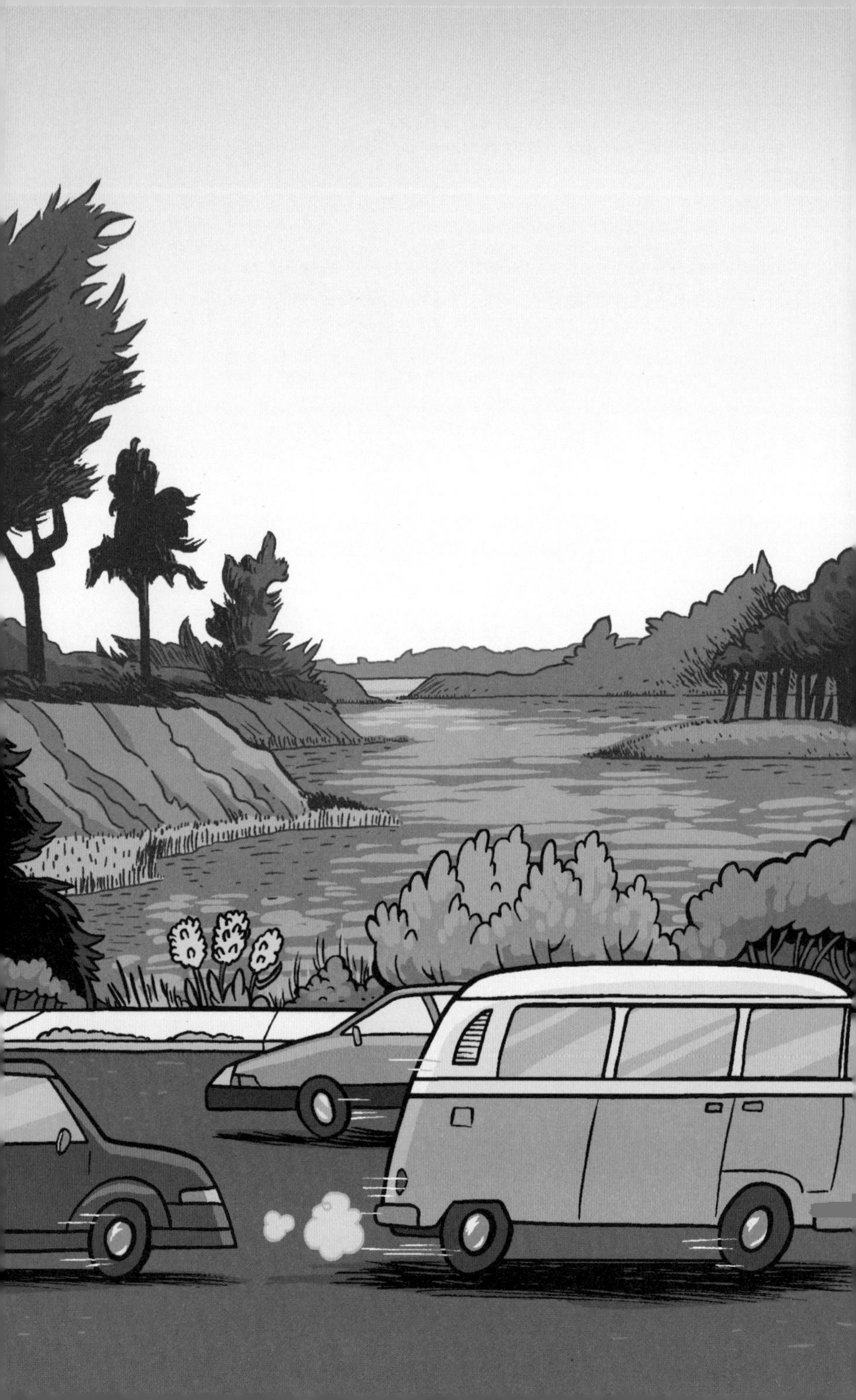

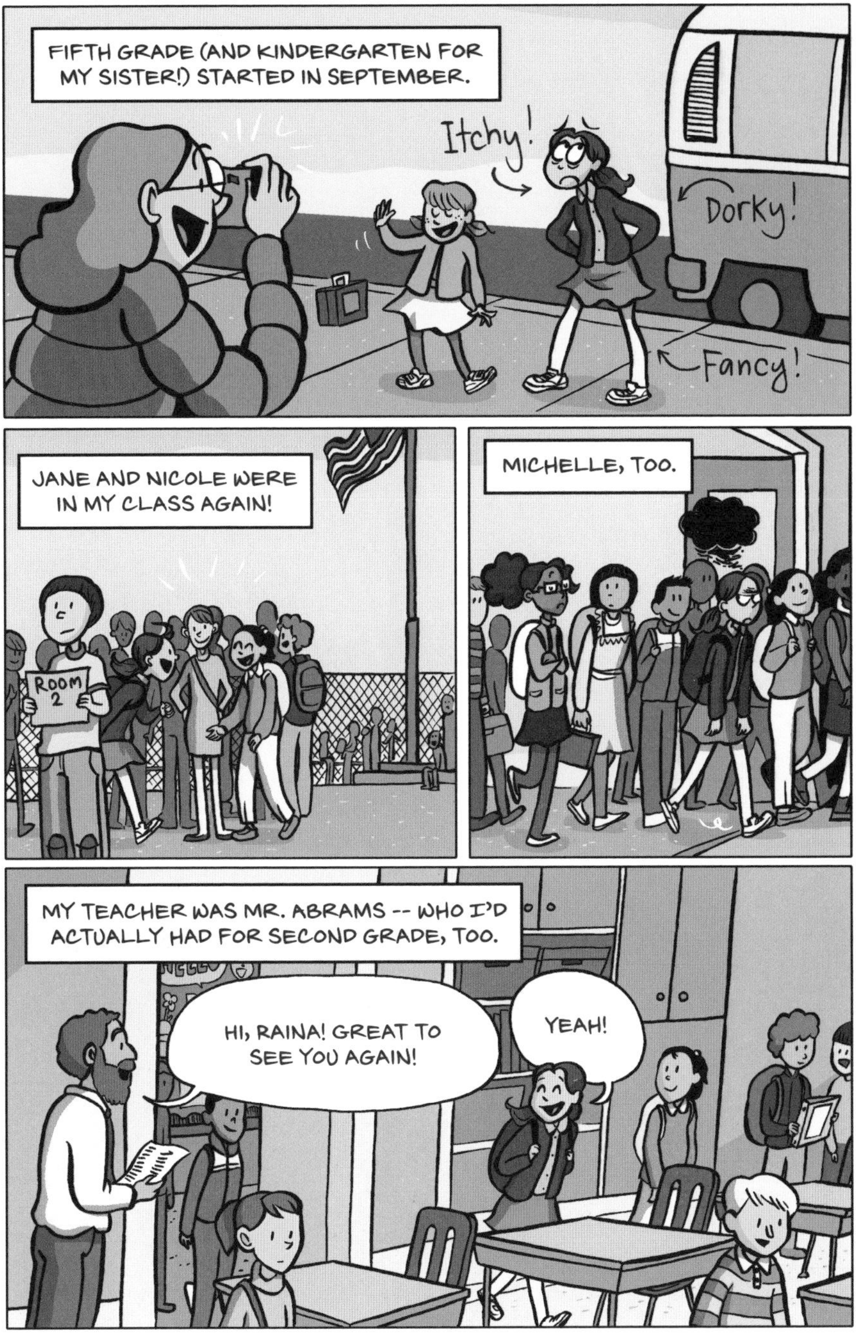
FIFTH GRADE (AND KINDERGARTEN FOR MY SISTER!) STARTED IN SEPTEMBER.
Itchy!
Dorky!
Fancy!
JANE AND NICOLE WERE IN MY CLASS AGAIN!
ROOM 2
MICHELLE, TOO.
MY TEACHER WAS MR. ABRAMS -- WHO I'D ACTUALLY HAD FOR SECOND GRADE, TOO.
HI, RAINA! GREAT TO SEE YOU AGAIN!
YEAH!

ONE OF THE THINGS OUR CLASS WOULD BE DOING THIS YEAR WAS THE

LDI!

THAT STANDS FOR **L**ECTURE, **D**EMONSTRATION, OR **I**NSTRUCTION!

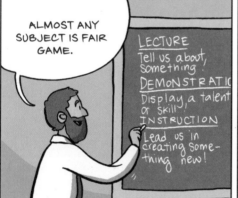

ALMOST ANY SUBJECT IS FAIR GAME.

LECTURE
Tell us about something!
DEMONSTRATIO
Display a talent or skill
INSTRUCTION
Lead us in creating something new!

LDIs WILL BE GIVEN ORALLY EVERY TUESDAY. YOU CAN SUBMIT PROPOSALS TO ME ANYTIME!

YES, TAI?

CAN I DEMONSTRATE HOW TO BURP THE ALPHABET?

Ha Ha Ha Ha Ha

34

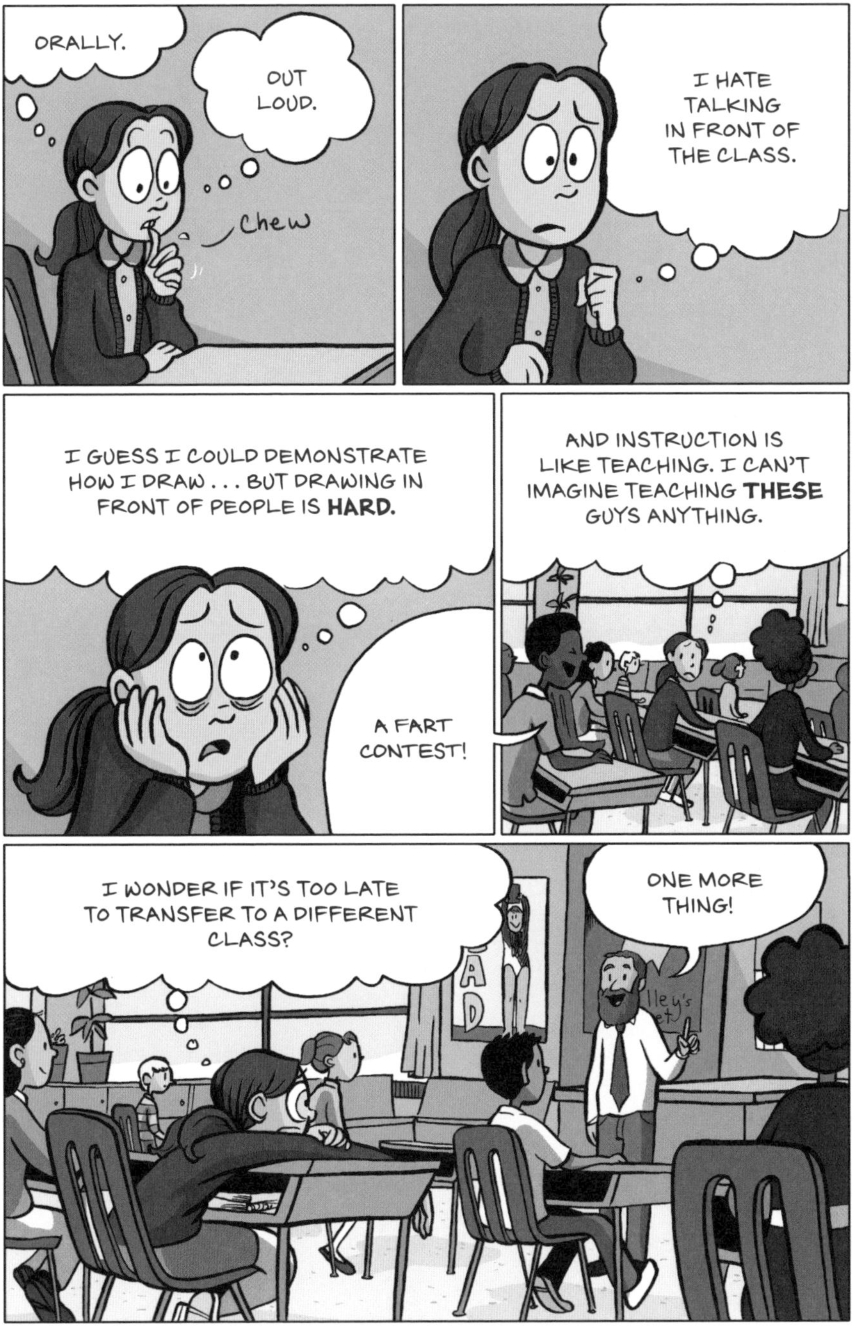
ORALLY.
OUT LOUD.
Chew
I HATE TALKING IN FRONT OF THE CLASS.
I GUESS I COULD DEMONSTRATE HOW I DRAW . . . BUT DRAWING IN FRONT OF PEOPLE IS **HARD.**
A FART CONTEST!
AND INSTRUCTION IS LIKE TEACHING. I CAN'T IMAGINE TEACHING **THESE** GUYS ANYTHING.
I WONDER IF IT'S TOO LATE TO TRANSFER TO A DIFFERENT CLASS?
ONE MORE THING!

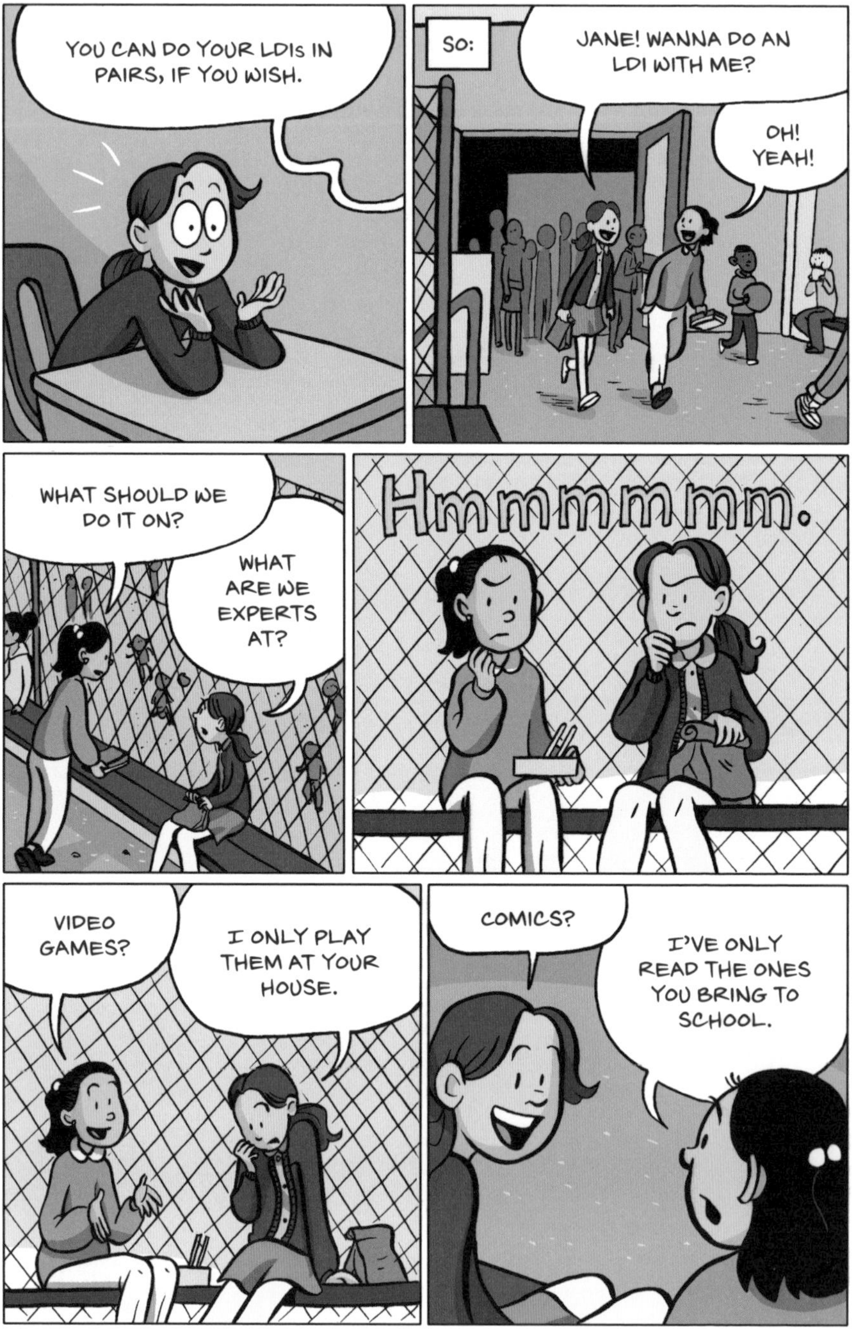
YOU CAN DO YOUR LDIs IN PAIRS, IF YOU WISH.
SO:
JANE! WANNA DO AN LDI WITH ME?
OH! YEAH!
WHAT SHOULD WE DO IT ON?
WHAT ARE WE EXPERTS AT?
Hmmmmmm.
VIDEO GAMES?
I ONLY PLAY THEM AT YOUR HOUSE.
COMICS?
I'VE ONLY READ THE ONES YOU BRING TO SCHOOL.

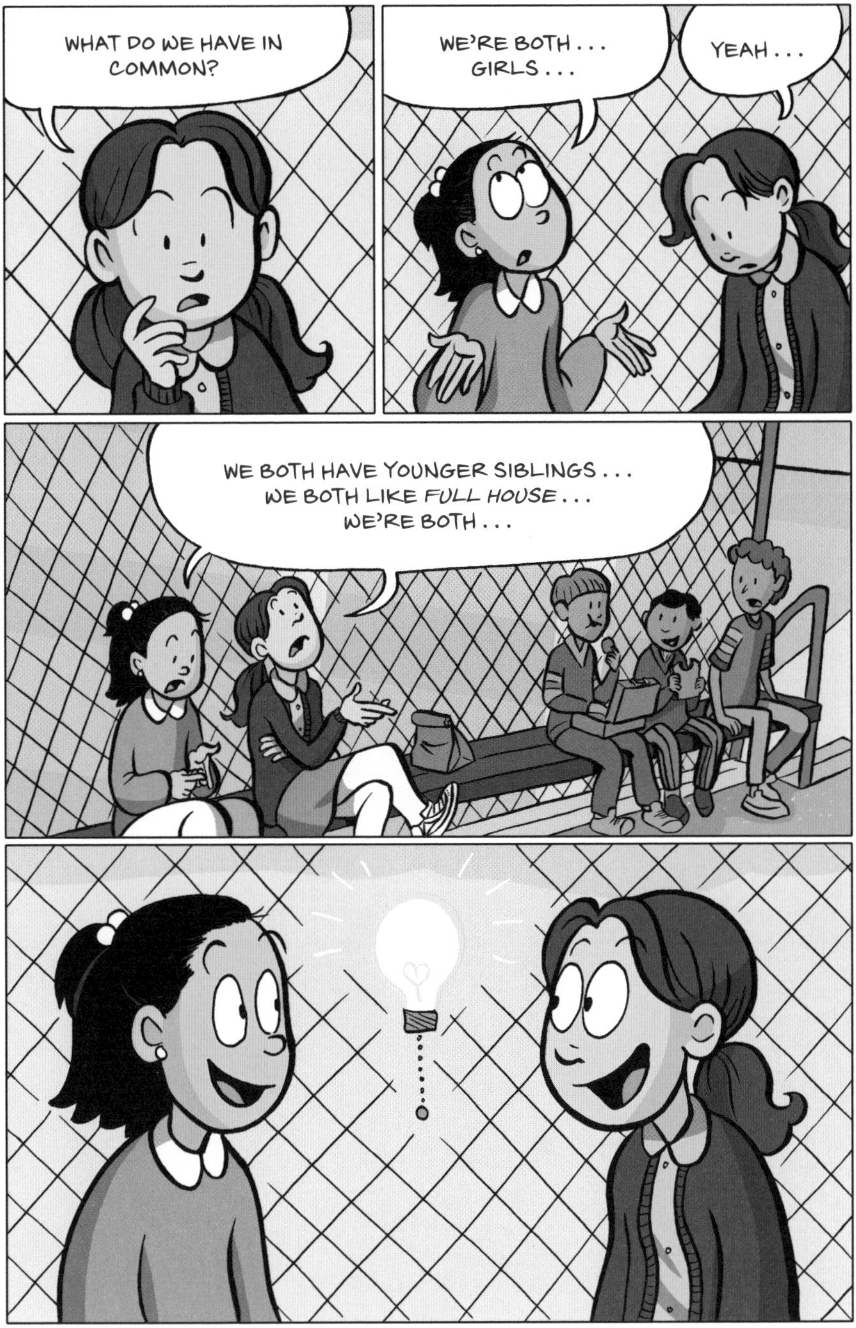
WHAT DO WE HAVE IN COMMON?
WE'RE BOTH . . . GIRLS . . .
YEAH . . .
WE BOTH HAVE YOUNGER SIBLINGS . . . WE BOTH LIKE *FULL HOUSE* . . . WE'RE BOTH . . .

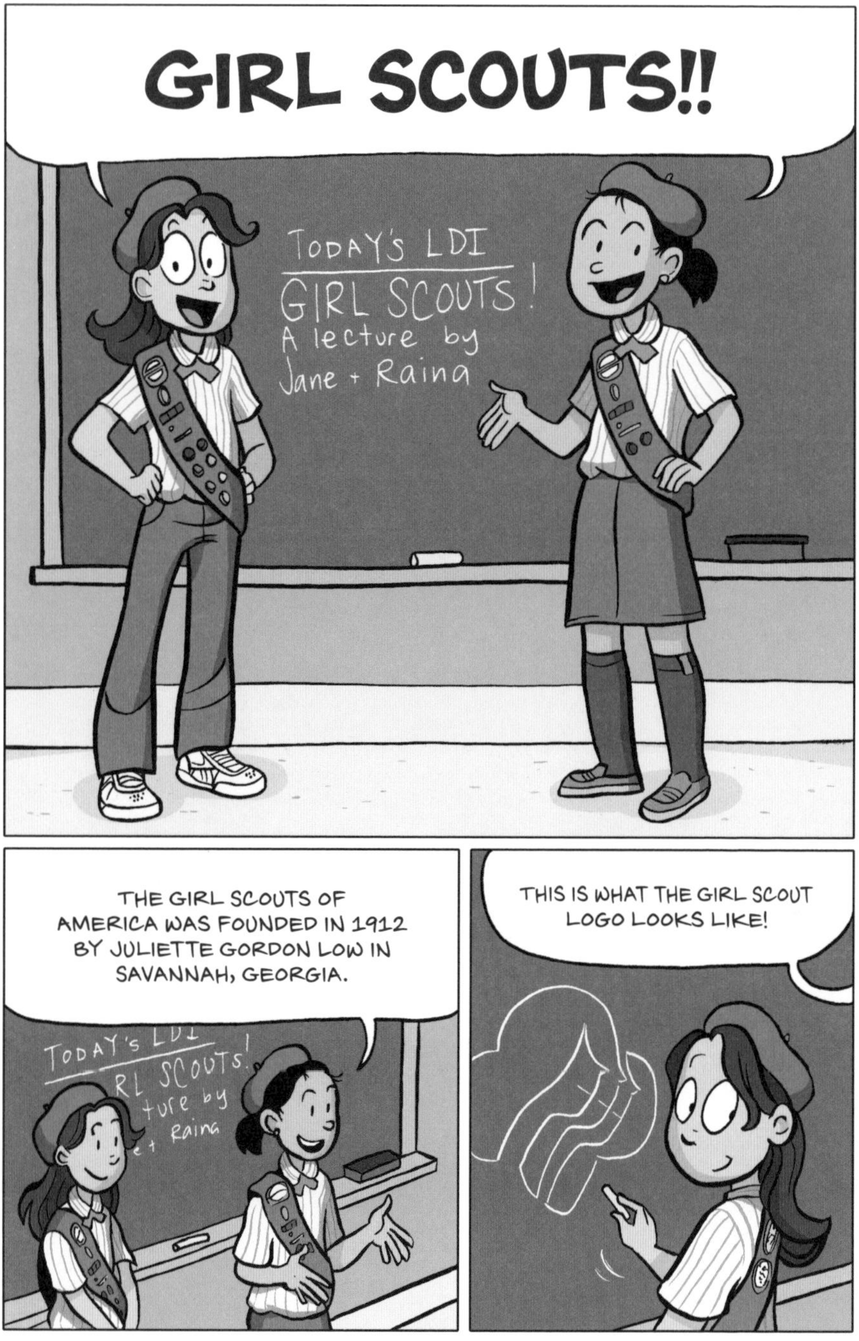
GIRL SCOUTS!!
TODAY'S LDI
GIRL SCOUTS!
A lecture by
Jane + Raina
THE GIRL SCOUTS OF AMERICA WAS FOUNDED IN 1912 BY JULIETTE GORDON LOW IN SAVANNAH, GEORGIA.
THIS IS WHAT THE GIRL SCOUT LOGO LOOKS LIKE!

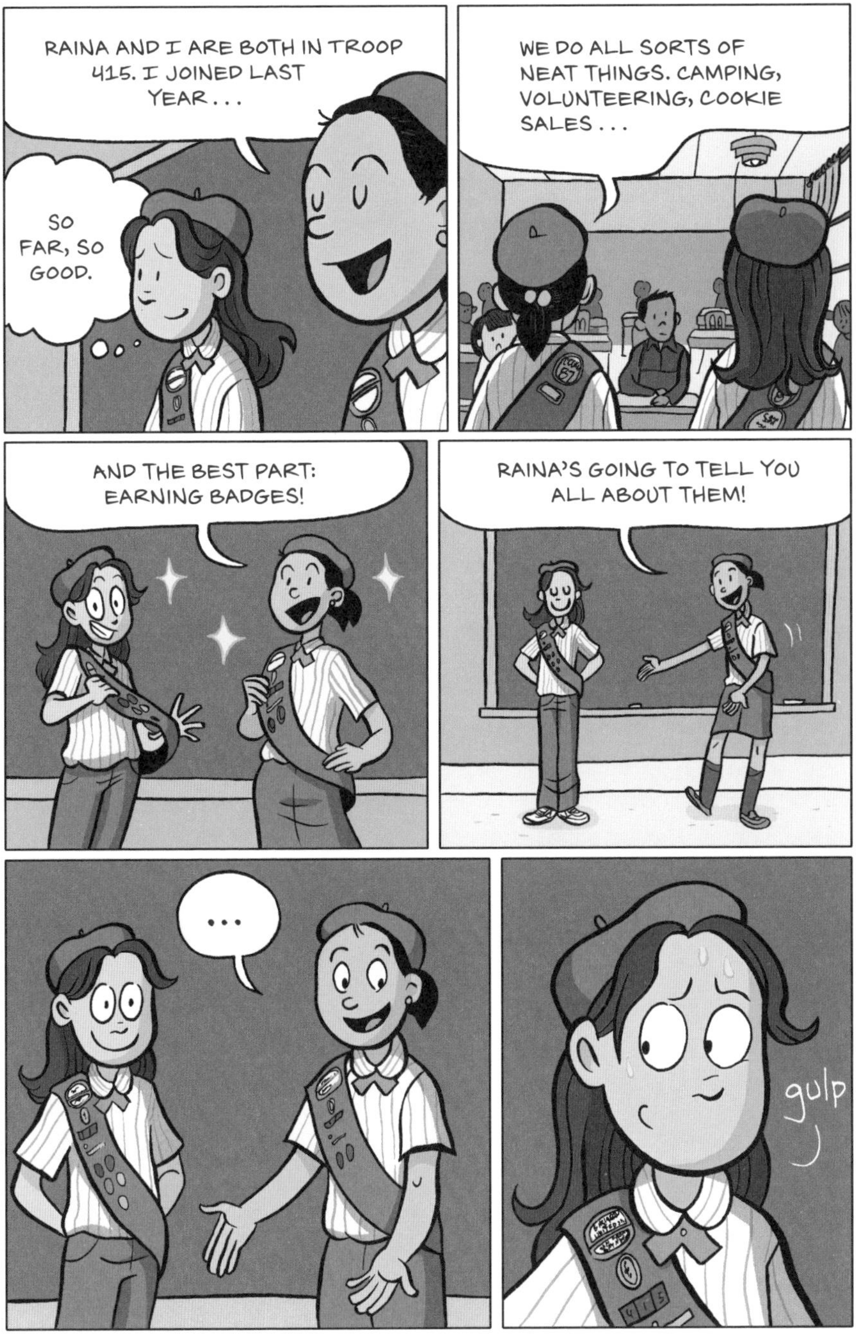
RAINA AND I ARE BOTH IN TROOP 415. I JOINED LAST YEAR...
SO FAR, SO GOOD.
WE DO ALL SORTS OF NEAT THINGS. CAMPING, VOLUNTEERING, COOKIE SALES...
AND THE BEST PART: EARNING BADGES!
RAINA'S GOING TO TELL YOU ALL ABOUT THEM!
...
gulp

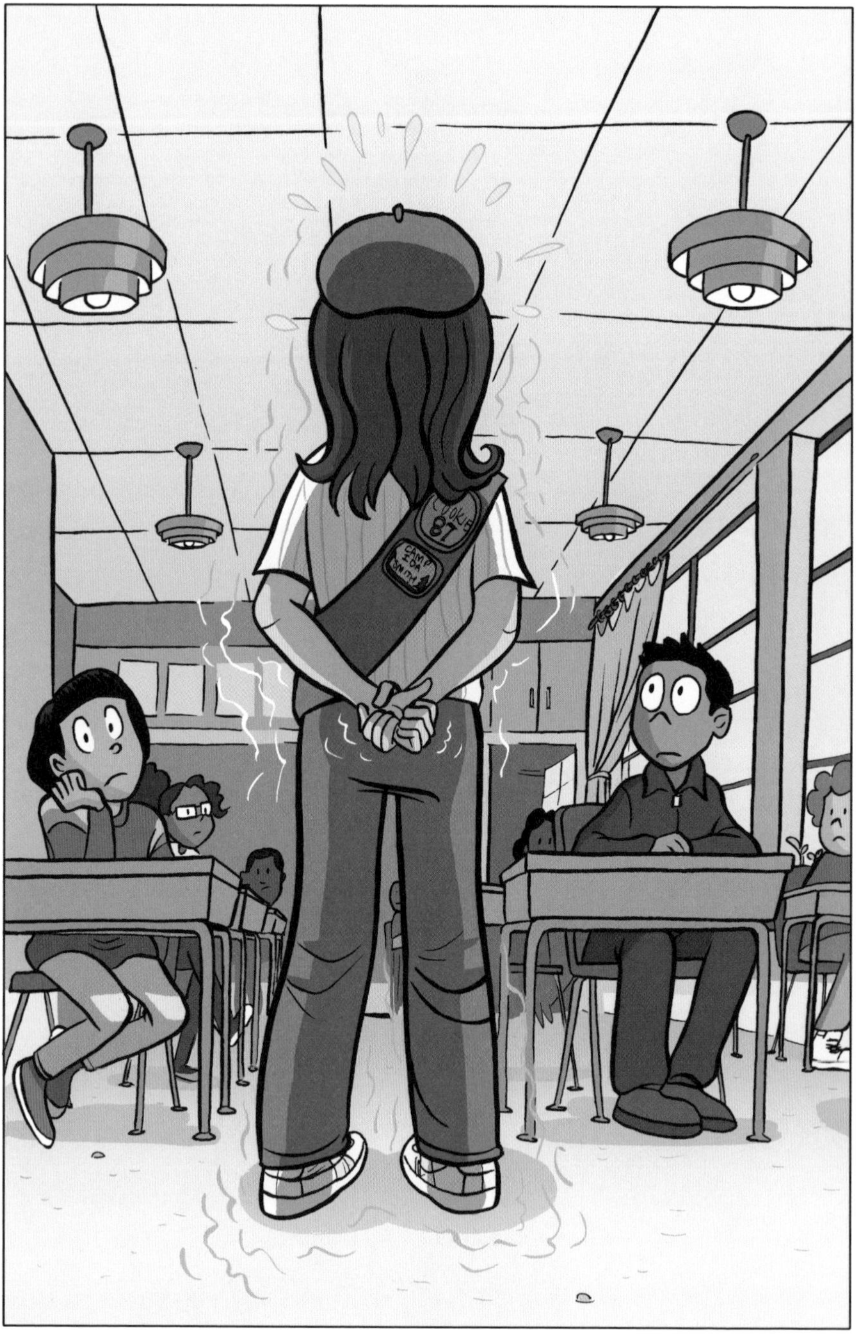
COOKIE 87
CAMP IDA SMITH

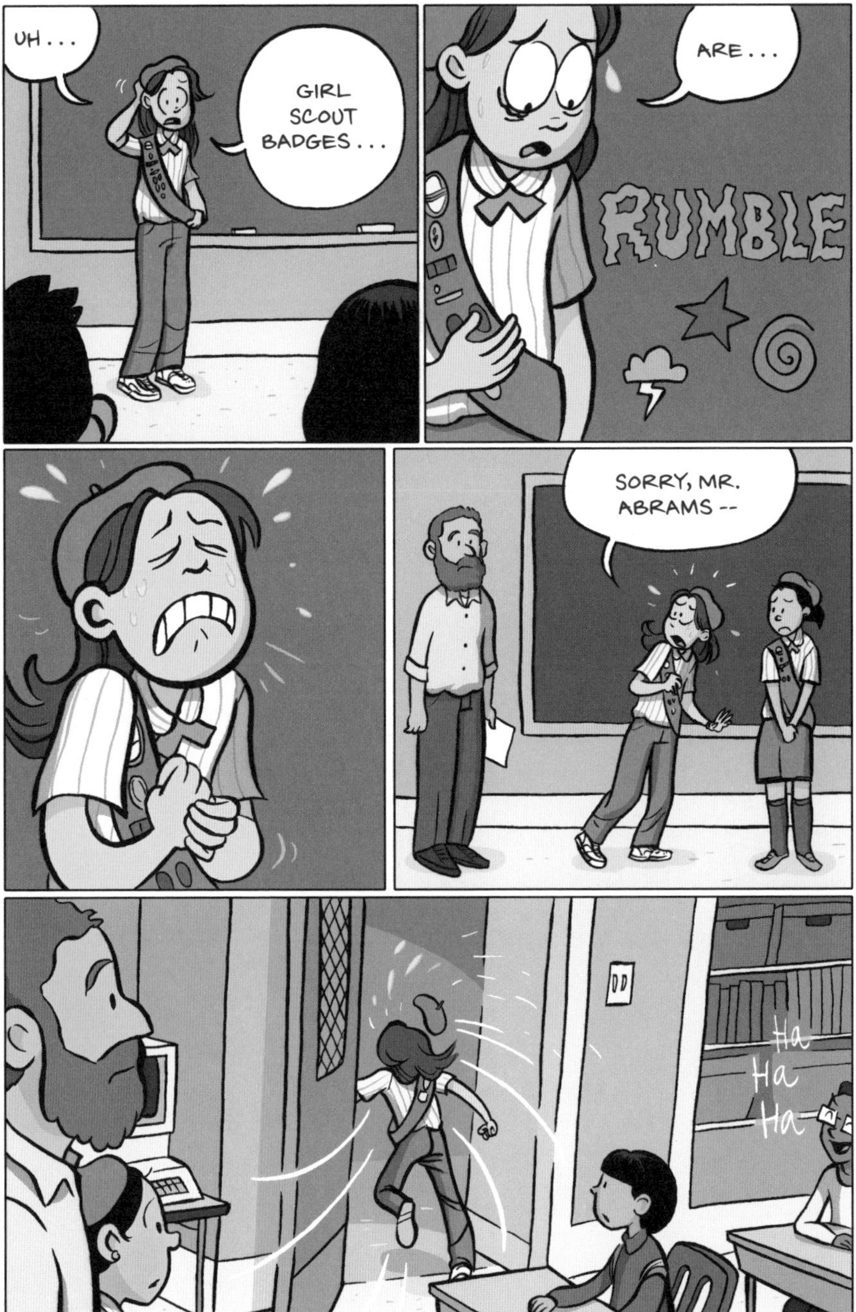

UH . . .
GIRL SCOUT BADGES . . .
ARE . . .
RUMBLE
SORRY, MR. ABRAMS --
Ha Ha Ha

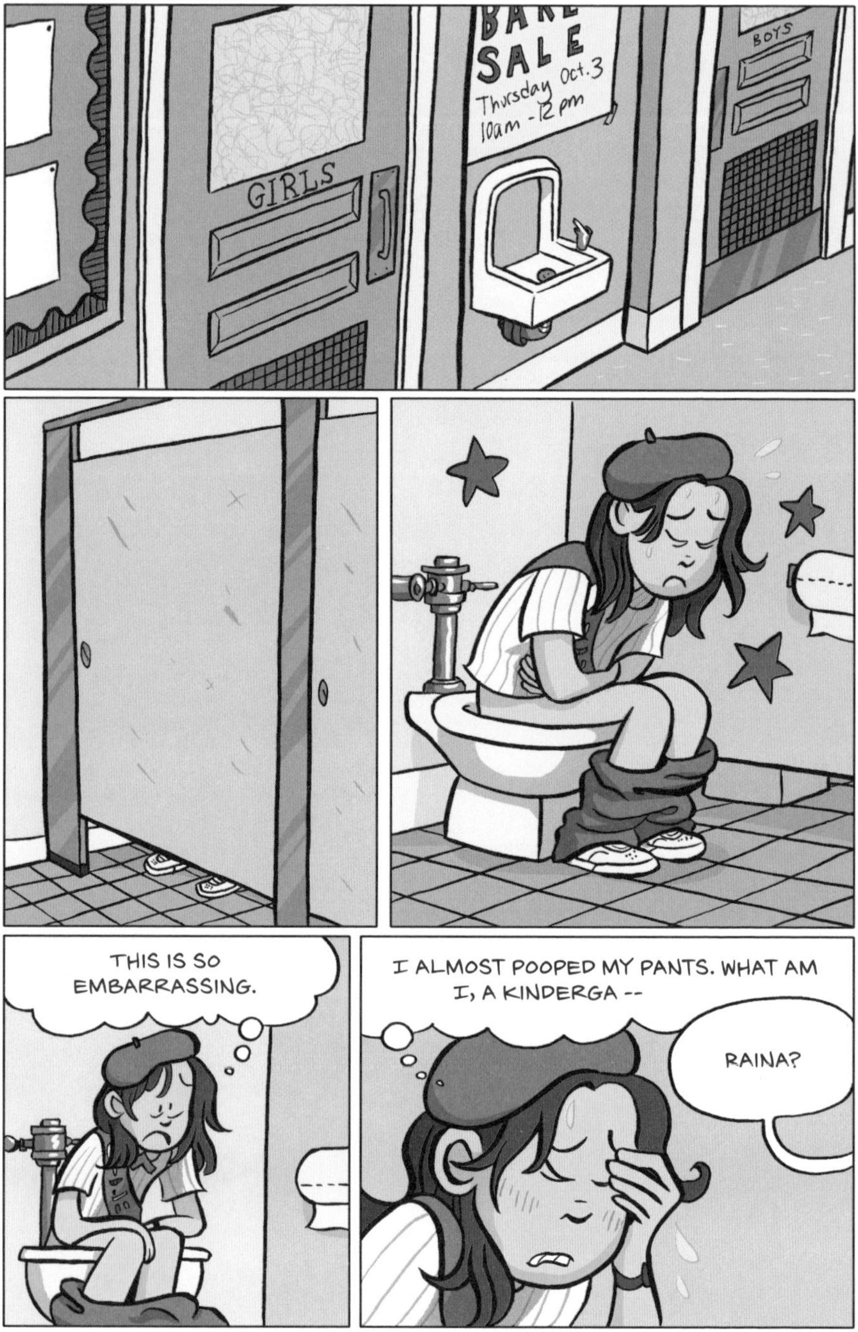
BAKE SALE
Thursday Oct. 3
10am - 12pm
GIRLS
BOYS
THIS IS SO EMBARRASSING.
I ALMOST POOPED MY PANTS. WHAT AM I, A KINDERGA --
RAINA?

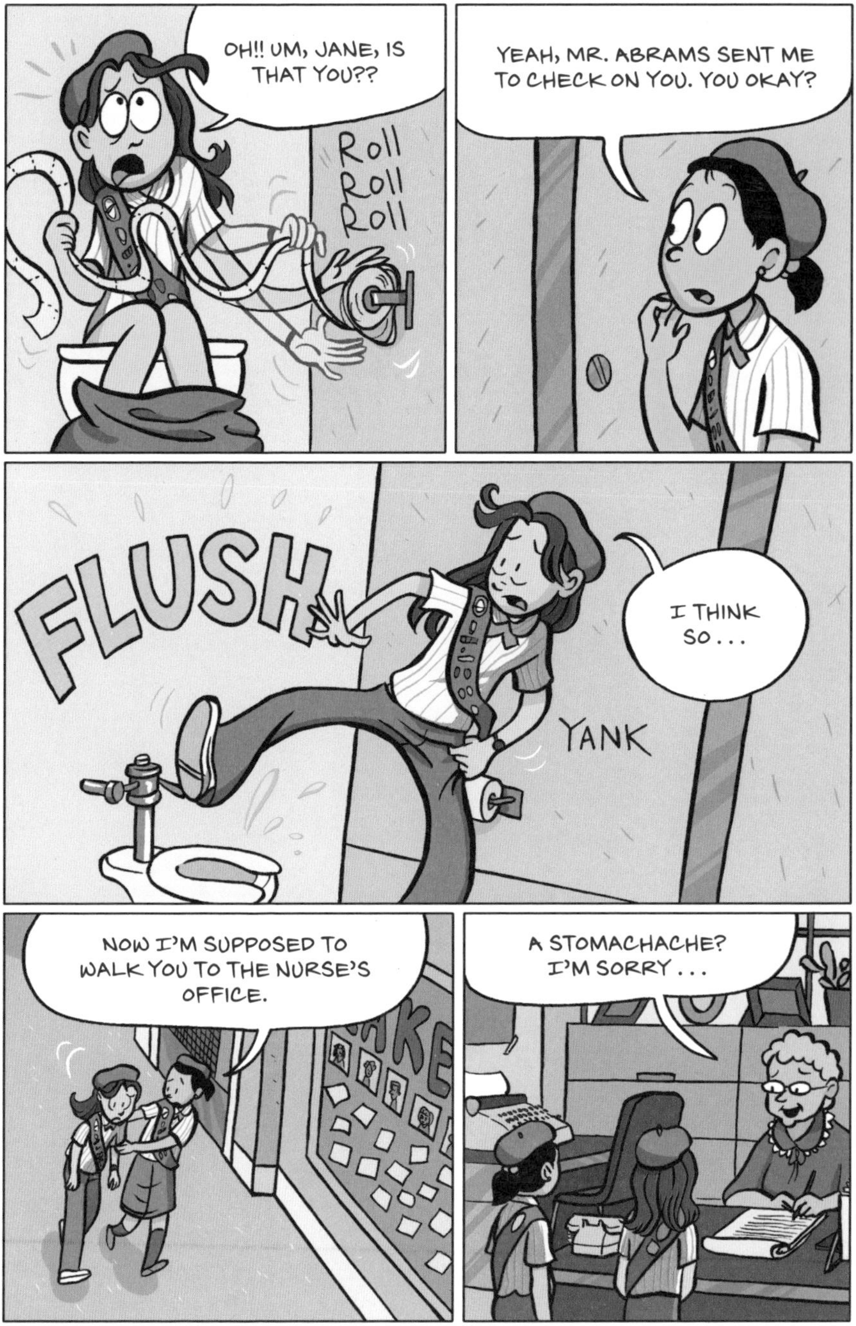
OH!! UM, JANE, IS THAT YOU??
Roll Roll Roll
YEAH, MR. ABRAMS SENT ME TO CHECK ON YOU. YOU OKAY?
FLUSH
I THINK SO . . .
YANK
NOW I'M SUPPOSED TO WALK YOU TO THE NURSE'S OFFICE.
A STOMACHACHE? I'M SORRY . . .

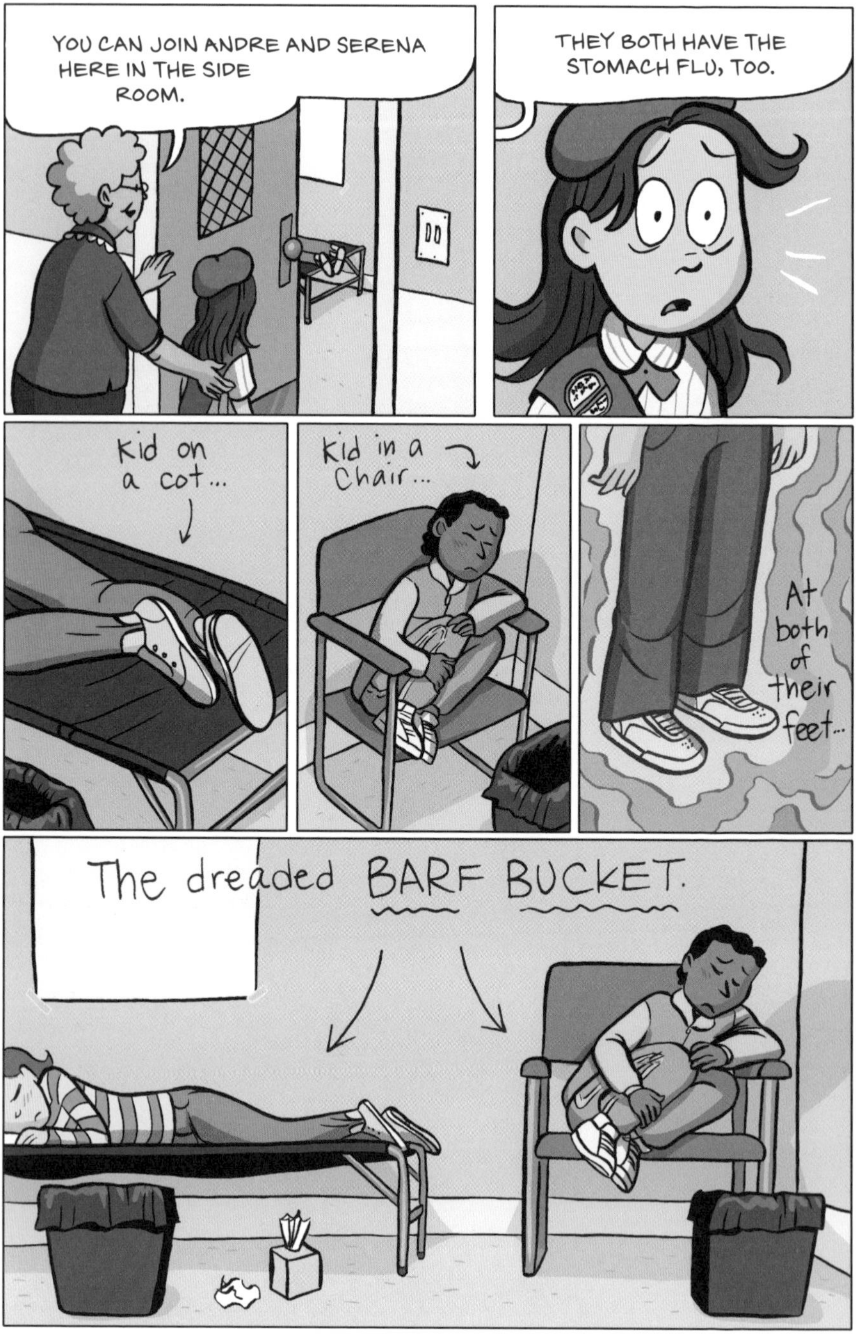
YOU CAN JOIN ANDRE AND SERENA HERE IN THE SIDE ROOM.
THEY BOTH HAVE THE STOMACH FLU, TOO.
Kid on a cot...
Kid in a Chair...
At both of their feet...
The dreaded BARF BUCKET.

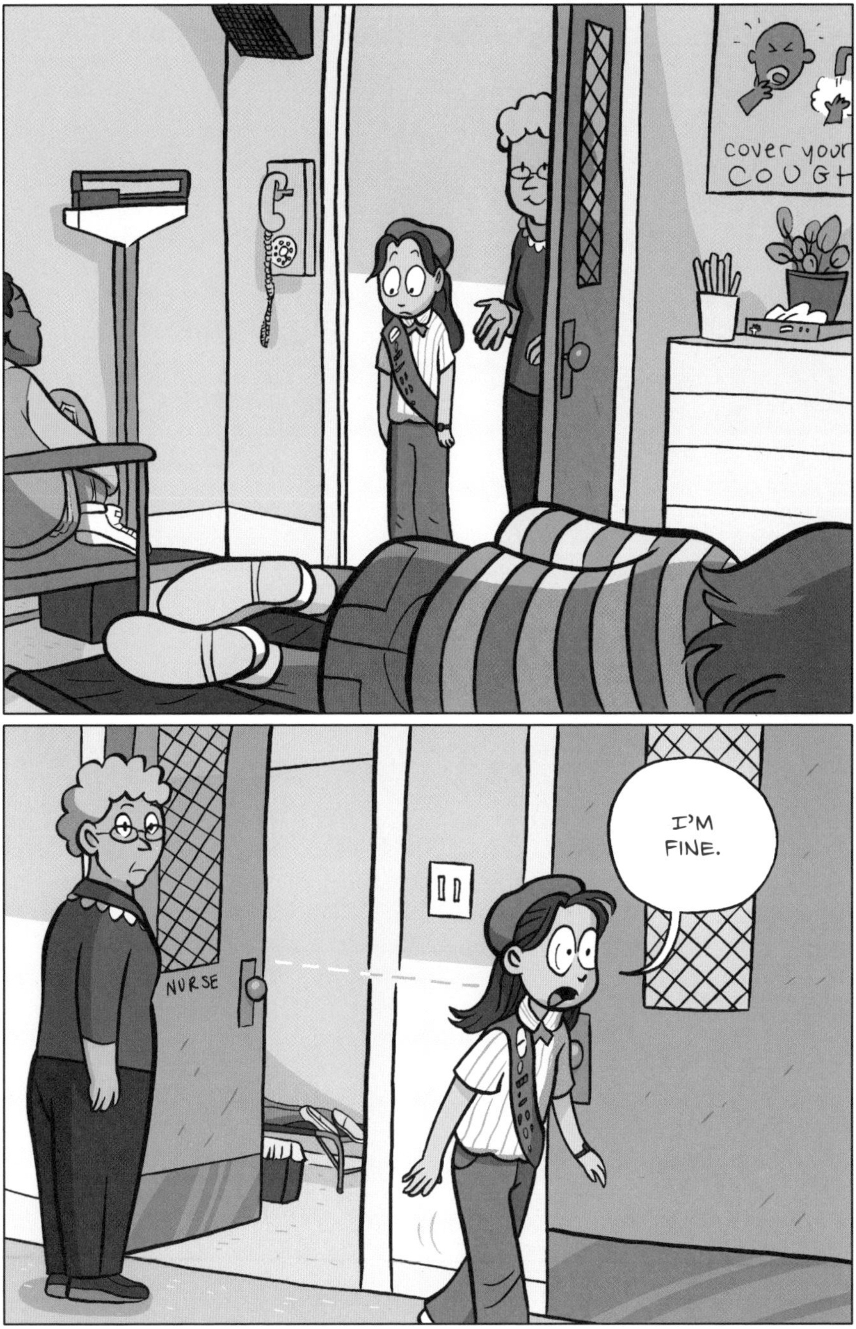
cover your
COUGH
NURSE
I'M FINE.

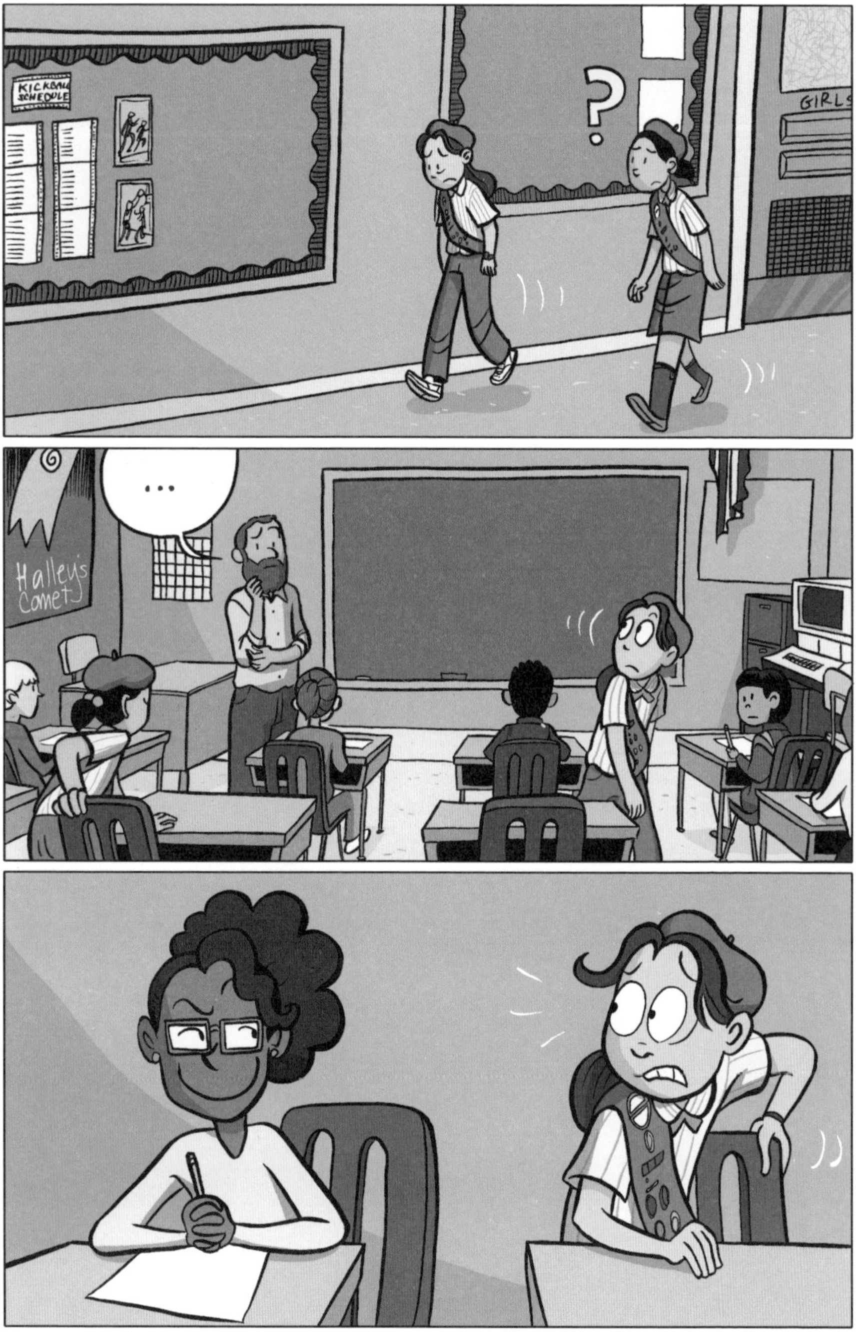
KICKBALL SCHEDULE
?
GIRLS
...
Halley's Comet

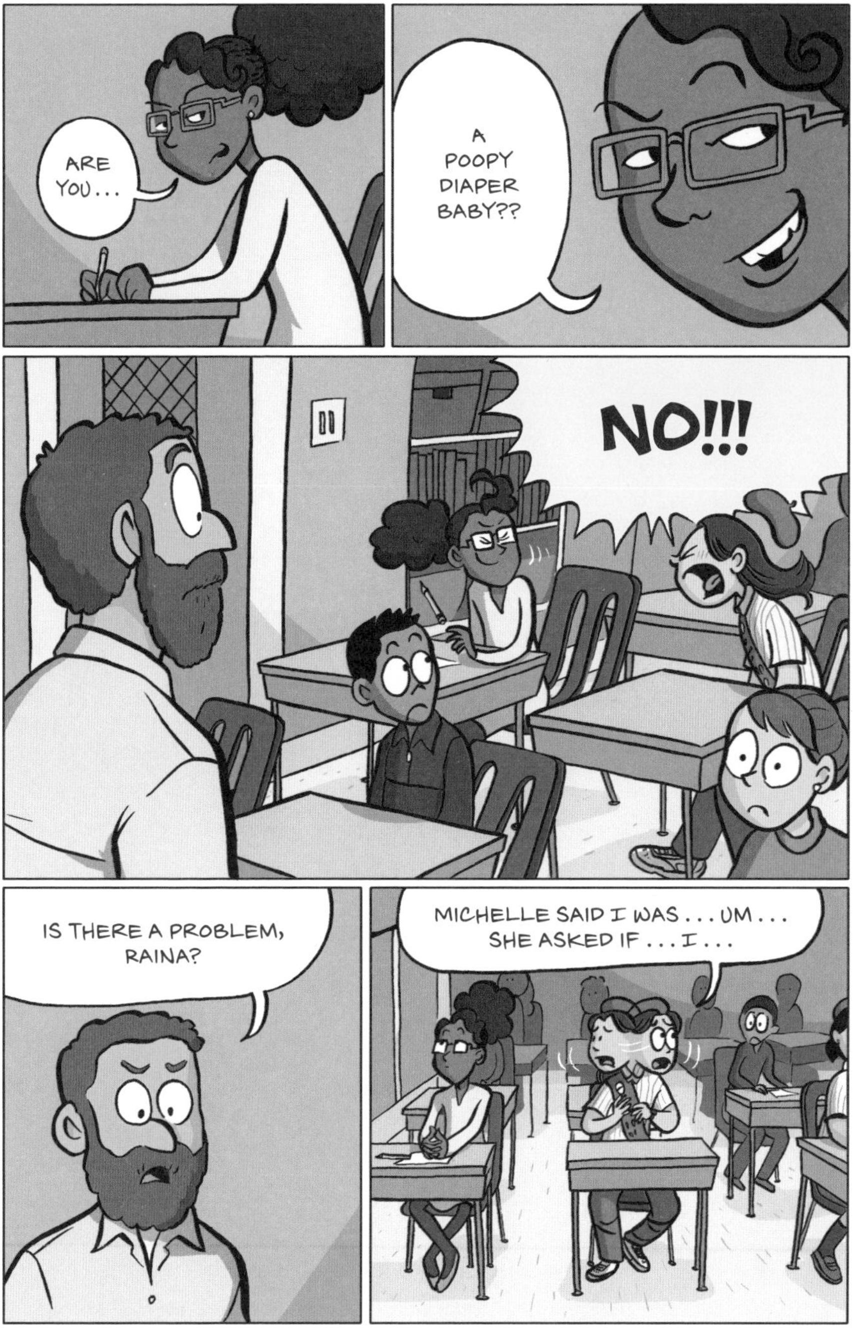
ARE YOU...
A POOPY DIAPER BABY??
NO!!!
IS THERE A PROBLEM, RAINA?
MICHELLE SAID I WAS... UM... SHE ASKED IF... I...

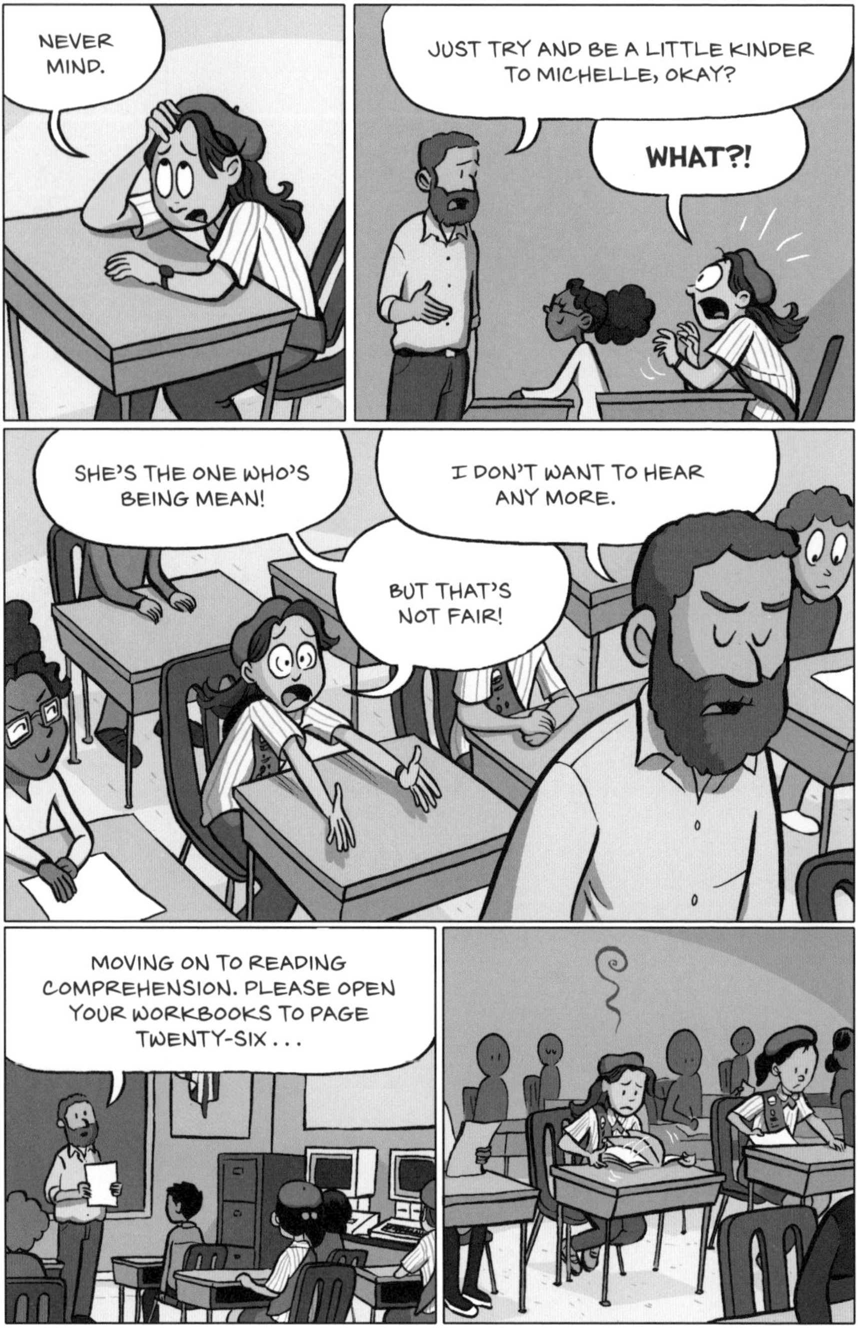
NEVER MIND.
JUST TRY AND BE A LITTLE KINDER TO MICHELLE, OKAY?
WHAT?!
SHE'S THE ONE WHO'S BEING MEAN!
I DON'T WANT TO HEAR ANY MORE.
BUT THAT'S NOT FAIR!
MOVING ON TO READING COMPREHENSION. PLEASE OPEN YOUR WORKBOOKS TO PAGE TWENTY-SIX . . .

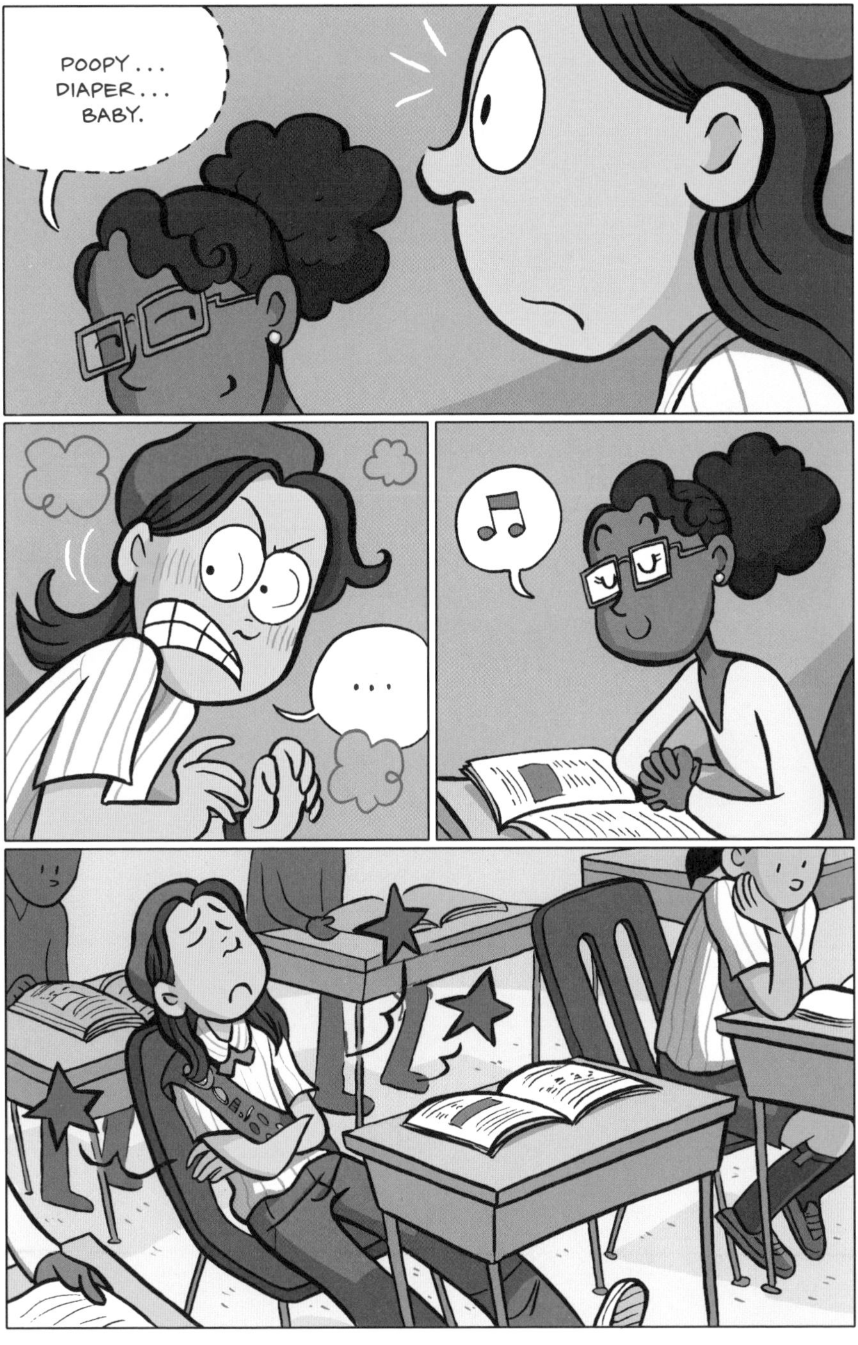
POOPY...
DIAPER...
BABY.
...

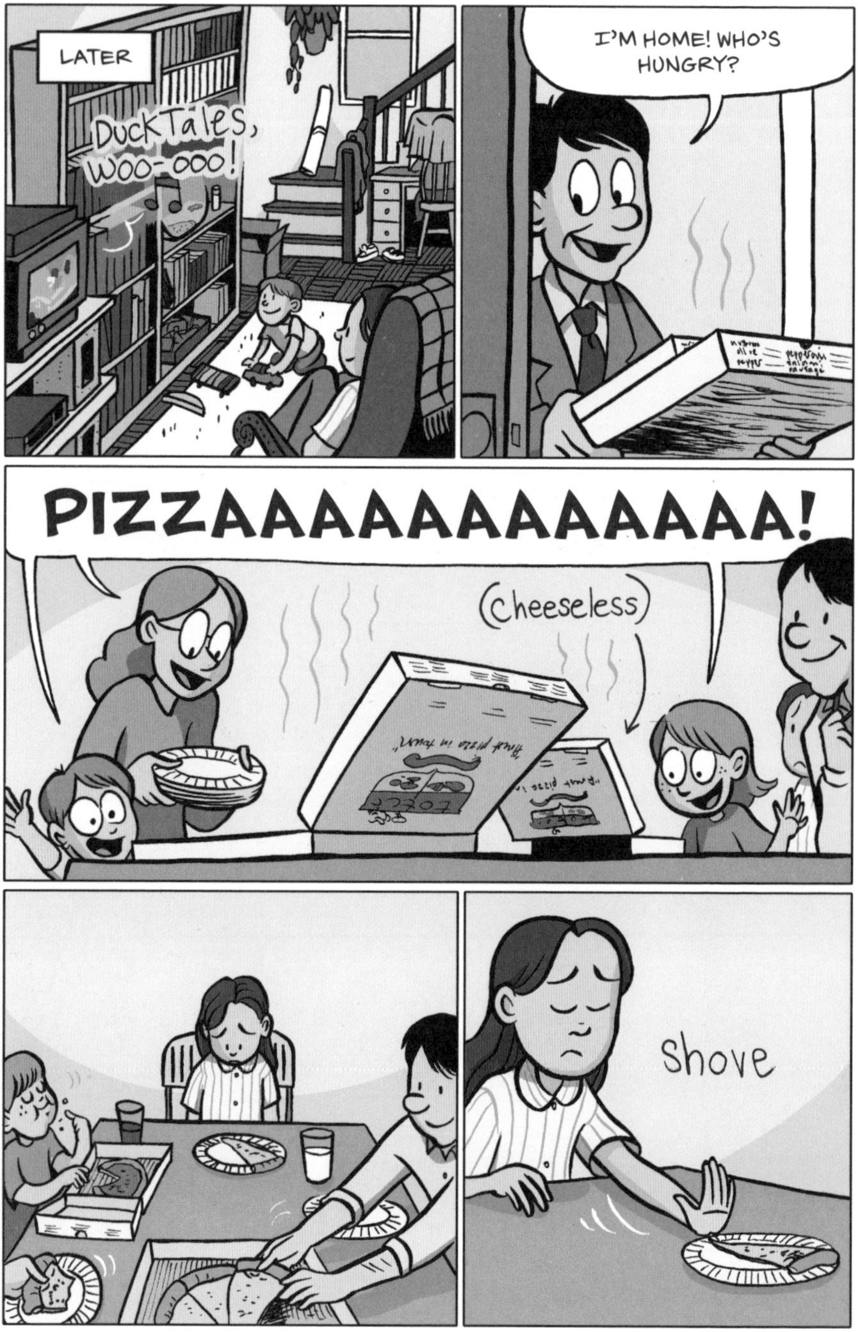
LATER
DuckTales, Woo-ooo!
I'M HOME! WHO'S HUNGRY?
PIZZAAAAAAAAAAAA!
(cheeseless)
Shove

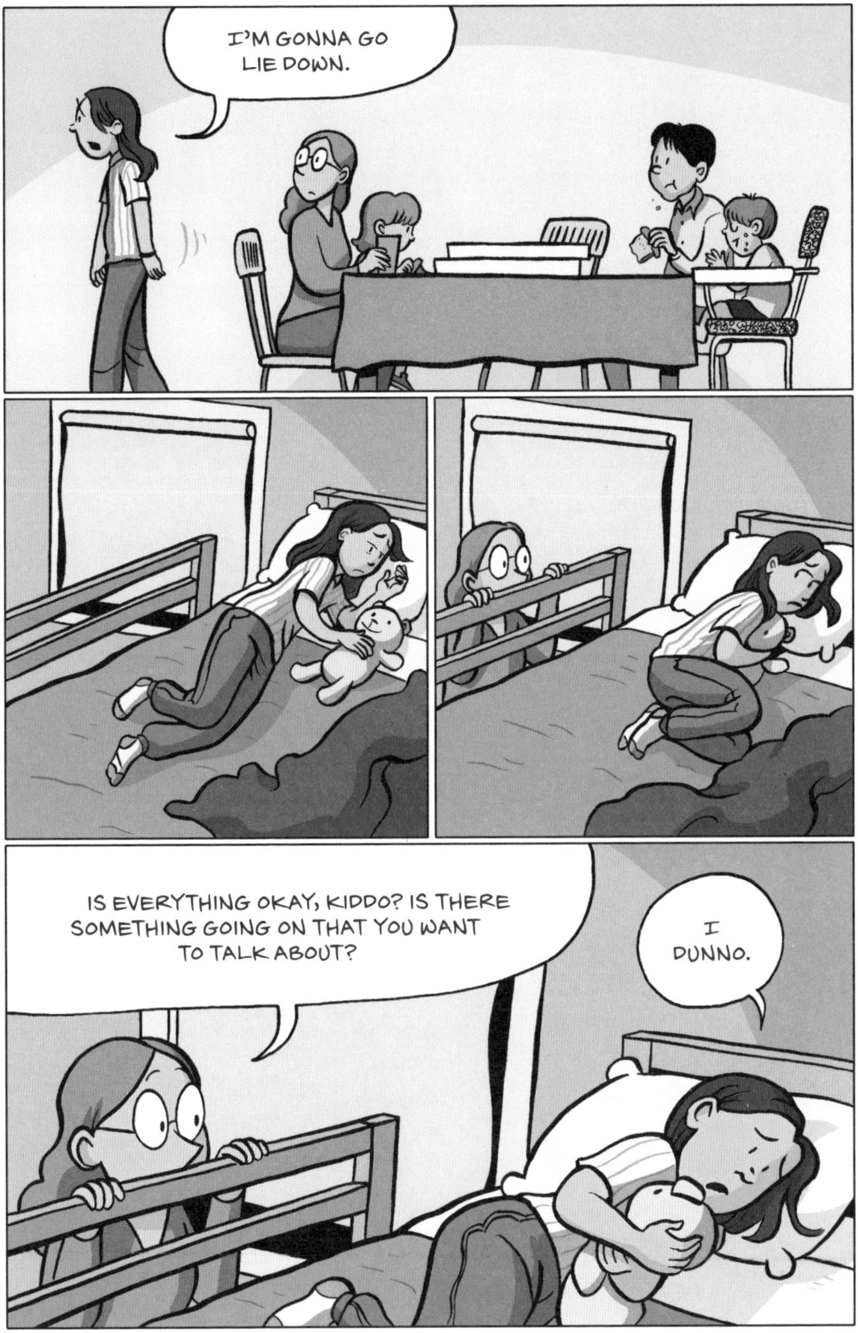

I'M GONNA GO LIE DOWN.
IS EVERYTHING OKAY, KIDDO? IS THERE SOMETHING GOING ON THAT YOU WANT TO TALK ABOUT?
I DUNNO.

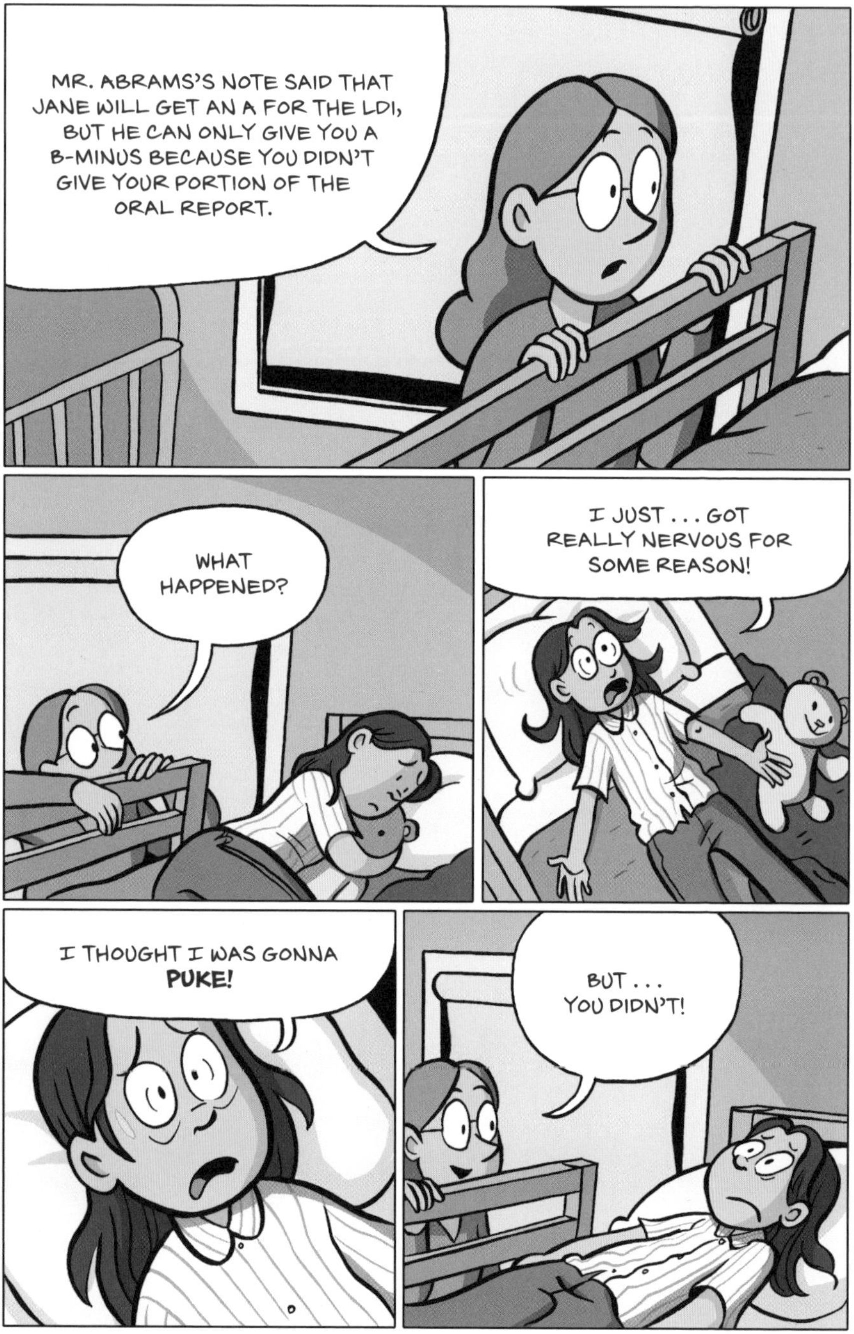
MR. ABRAMS'S NOTE SAID THAT JANE WILL GET AN A FOR THE LDI, BUT HE CAN ONLY GIVE YOU A B-MINUS BECAUSE YOU DIDN'T GIVE YOUR PORTION OF THE ORAL REPORT.
WHAT HAPPENED?
I JUST . . . GOT REALLY NERVOUS FOR SOME REASON!
I THOUGHT I WAS GONNA **PUKE!**
BUT . . . YOU DIDN'T!

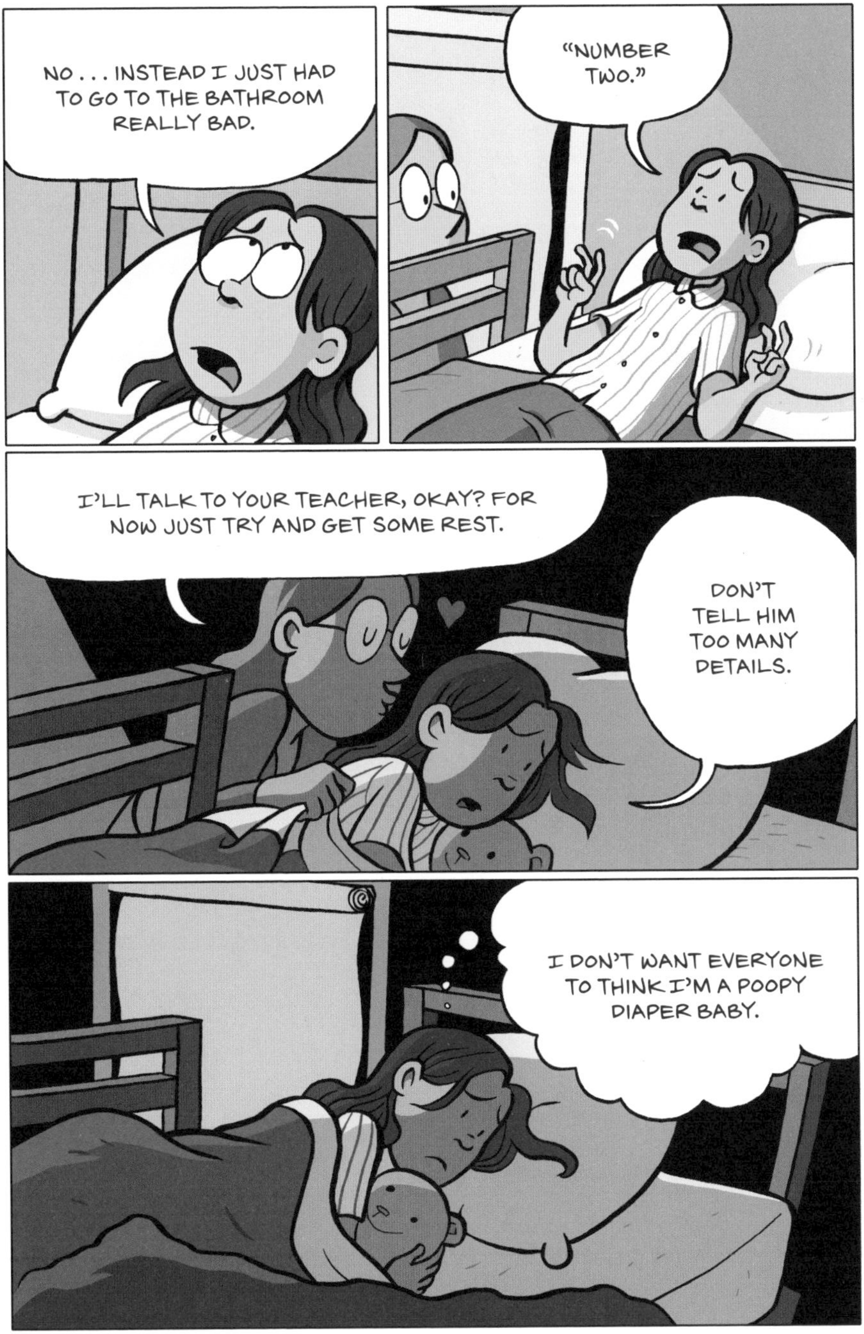
NO . . . INSTEAD I JUST HAD TO GO TO THE BATHROOM REALLY BAD.
"NUMBER TWO."
I'LL TALK TO YOUR TEACHER, OKAY? FOR NOW JUST TRY AND GET SOME REST.
DON'T TELL HIM TOO MANY DETAILS.
I DON'T WANT EVERYONE TO THINK I'M A POOPY DIAPER BABY.

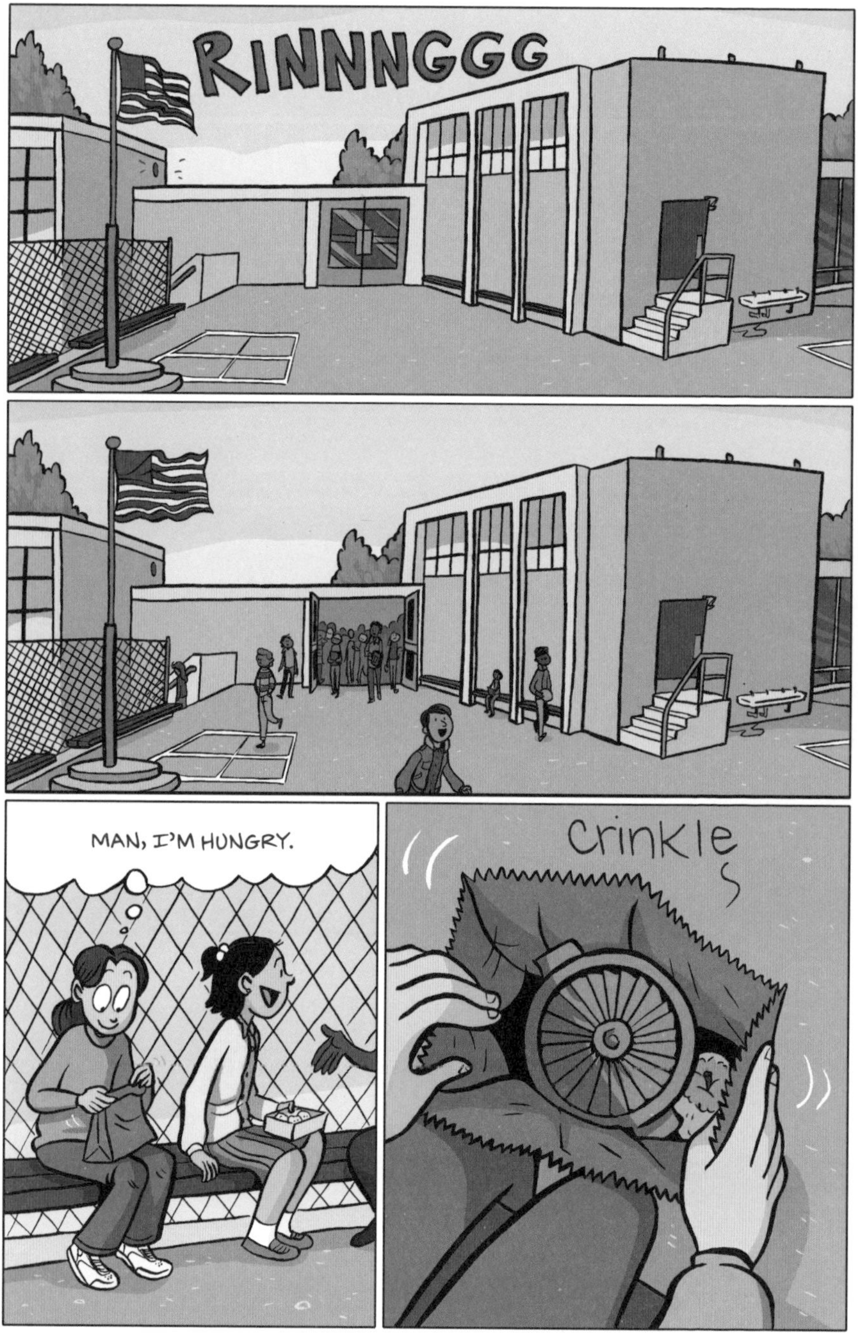
RINNNGGG
MAN, I'M HUNGRY.
Crinkle

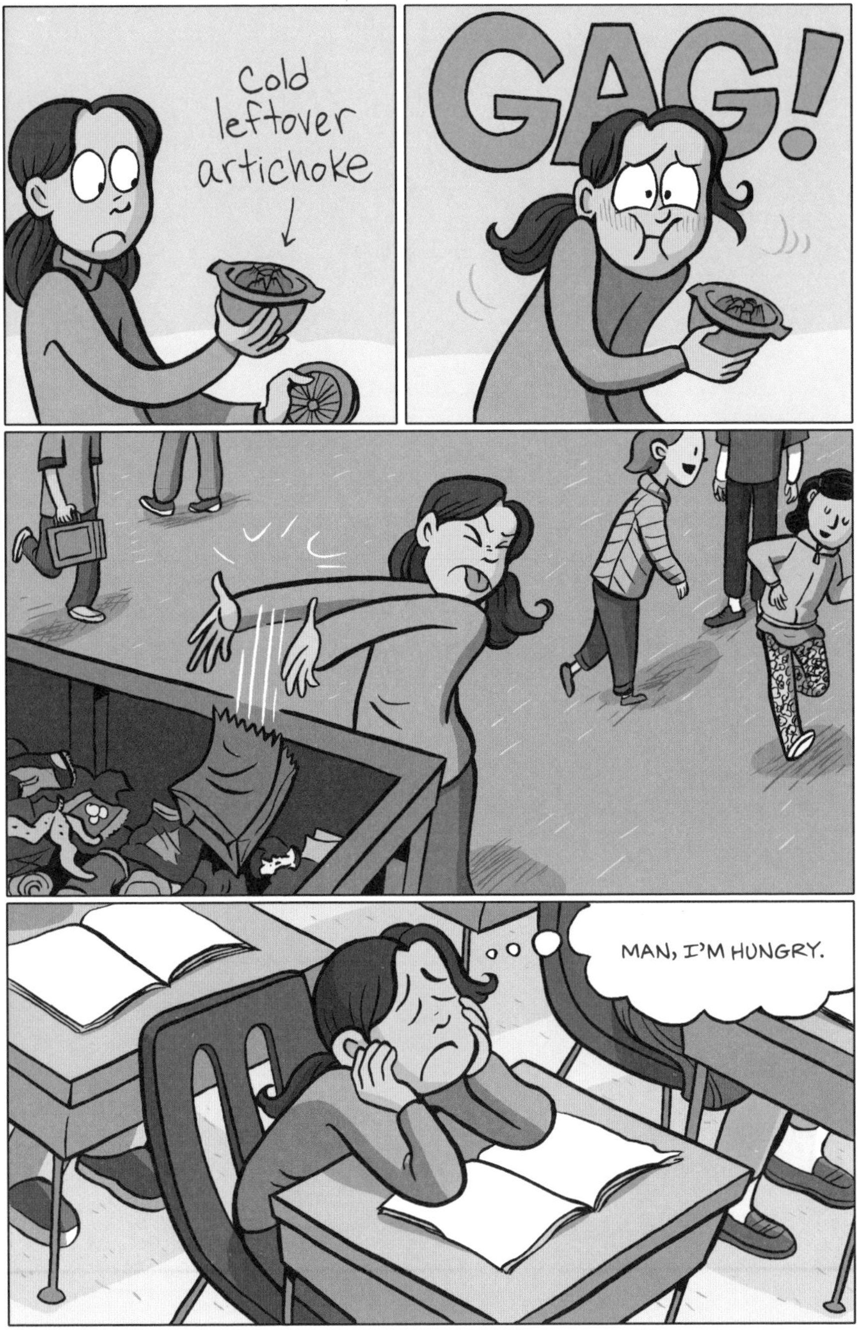
Cold leftover artichoke
GAG!
MAN, I'M HUNGRY.

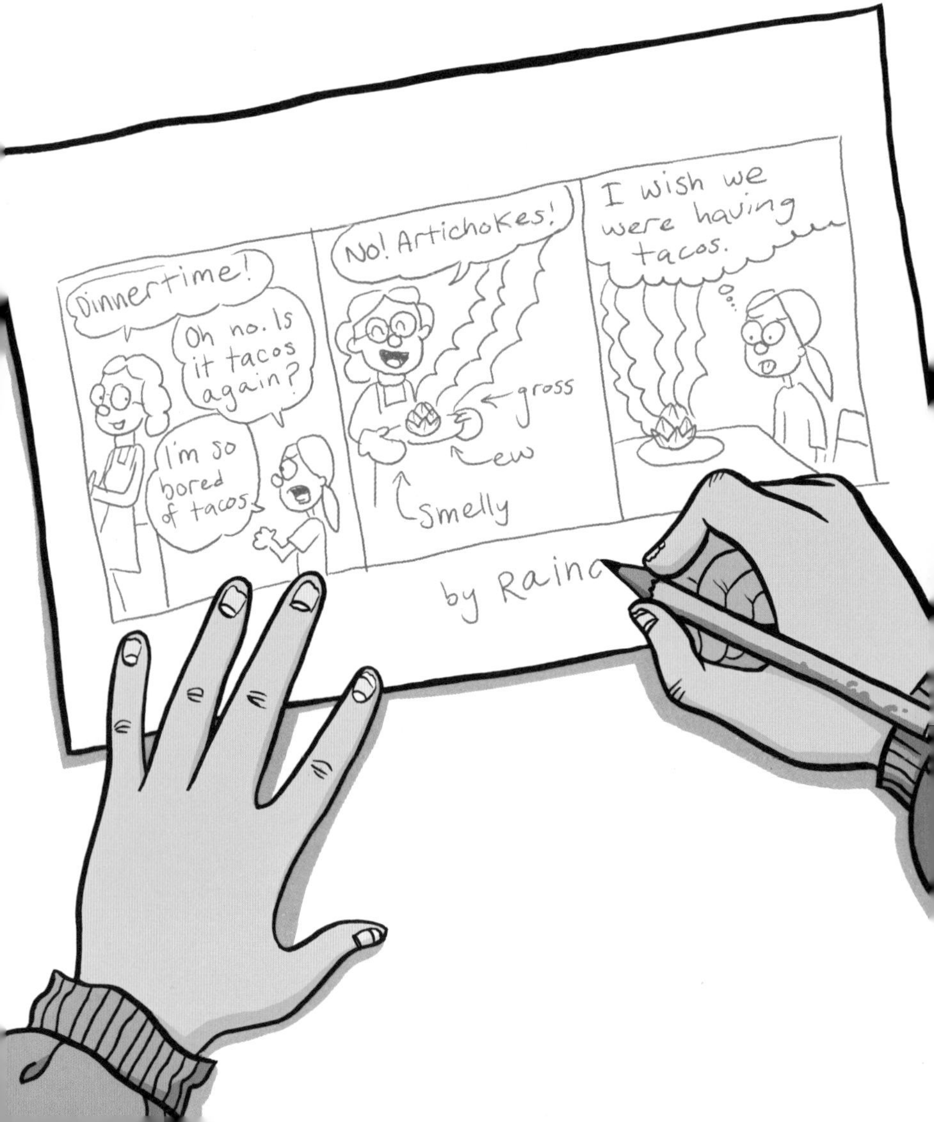
Dinnertime!
Oh no. Is it tacos again?
I'm so bored of tacos.
No! Artichokes!
gross
ew
smelly
I wish we were having tacos.
...
by Raina

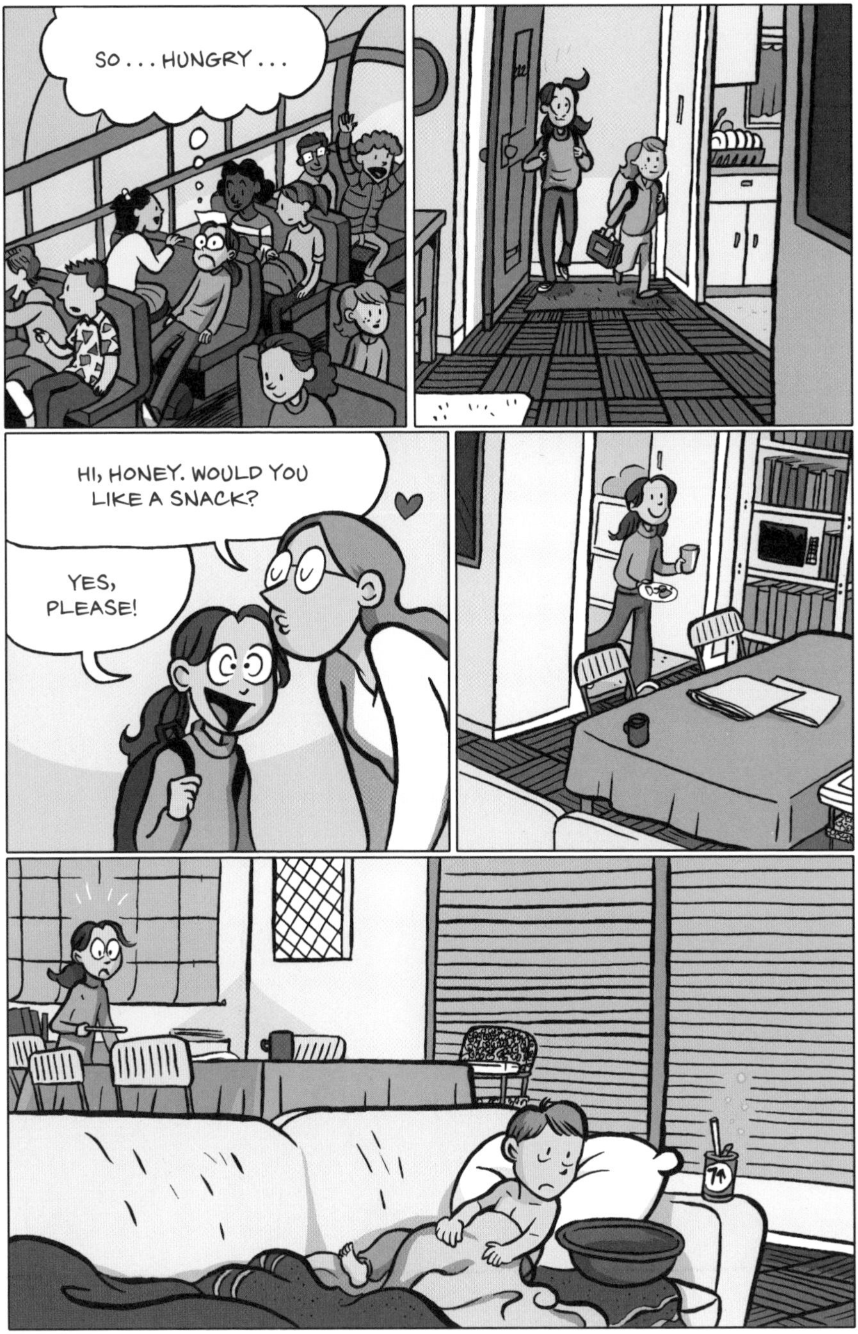
SO . . . HUNGRY . . .
HI, HONEY. WOULD YOU LIKE A SNACK?
YES, PLEASE!

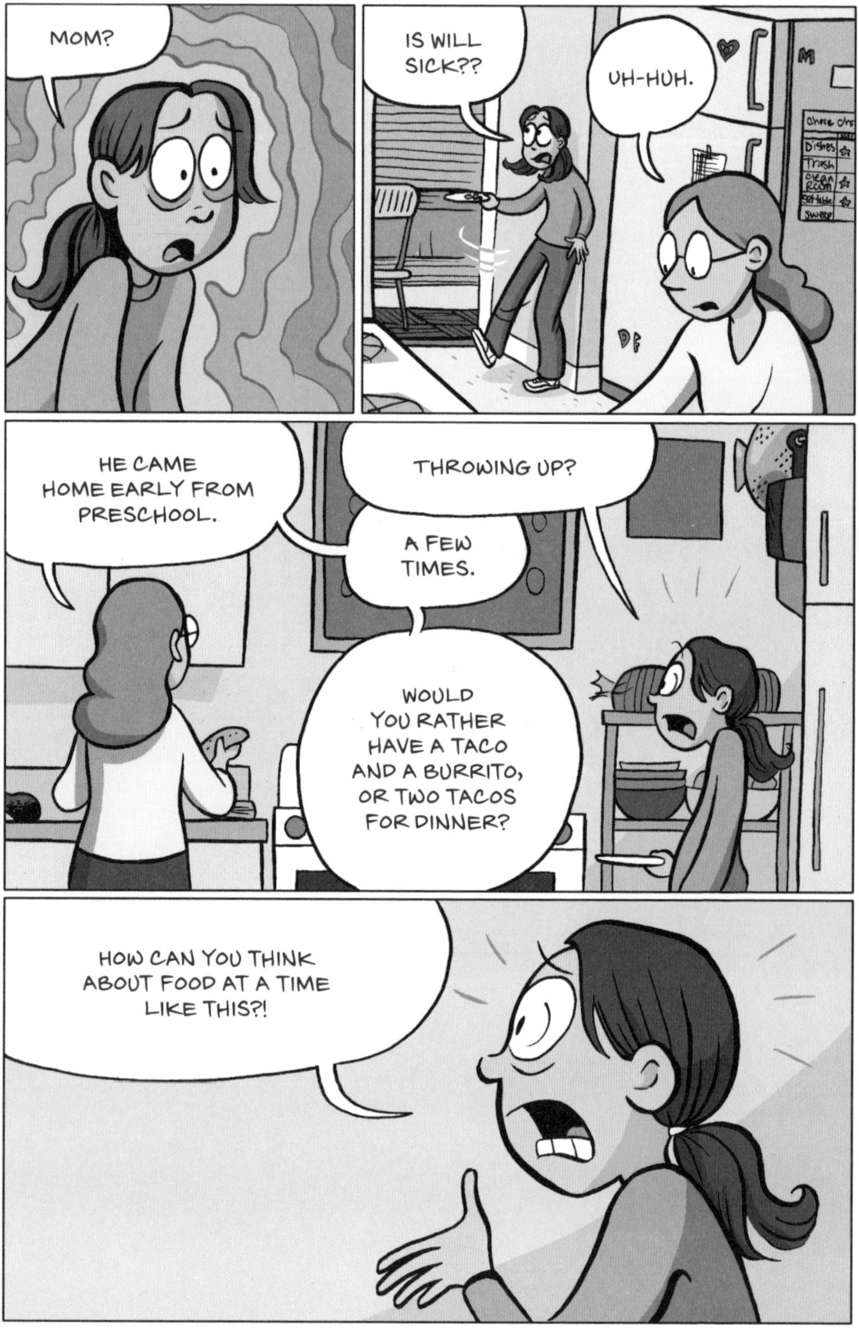
MOM?
IS WILL SICK??
UH-HUH.
Chore Chart
Dishes
Trash
Clean Room
Set table
Sweep
HE CAME HOME EARLY FROM PRESCHOOL.
THROWING UP?
A FEW TIMES.
WOULD YOU RATHER HAVE A TACO AND A BURRITO, OR TWO TACOS FOR DINNER?
HOW CAN YOU THINK ABOUT FOOD AT A TIME LIKE THIS?!

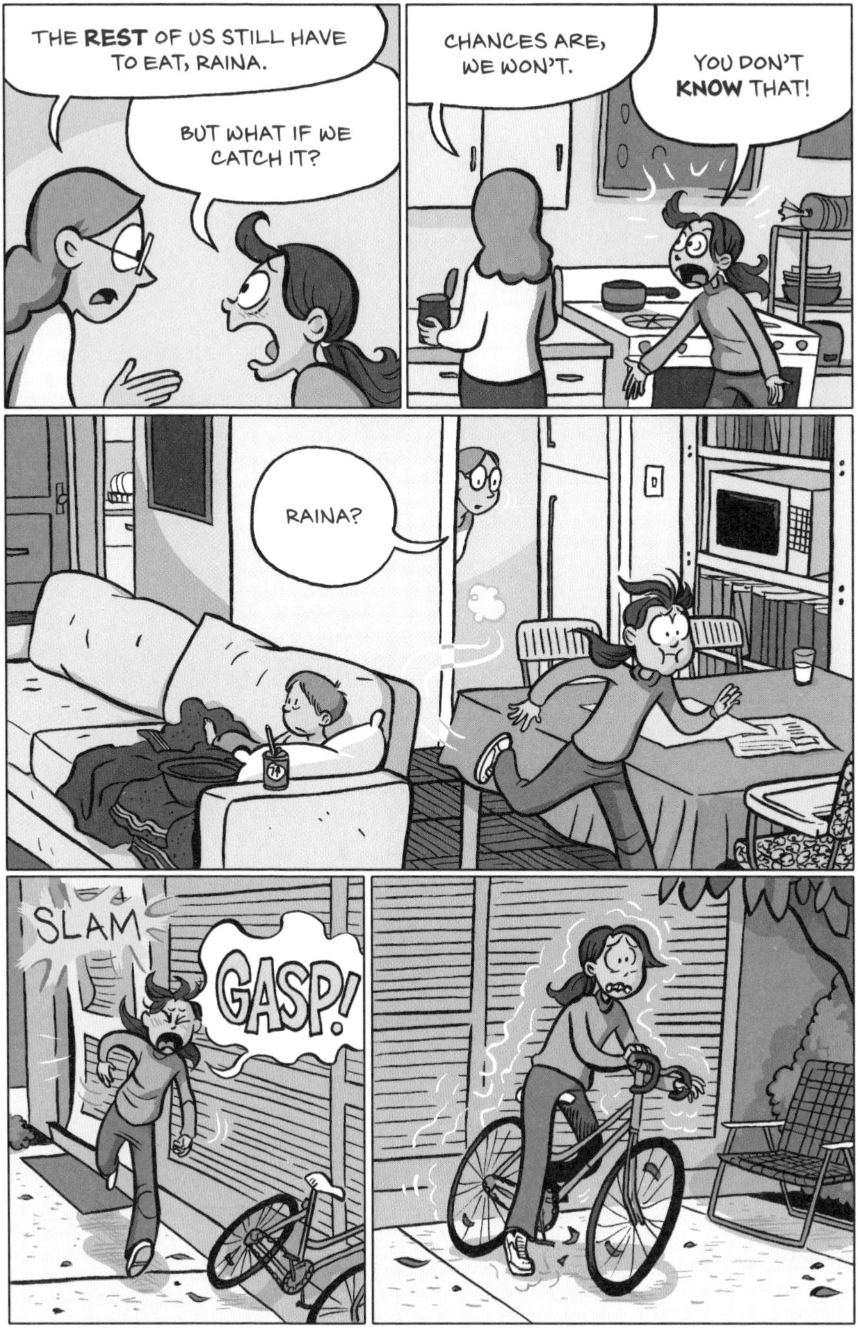
THE **REST** OF US STILL HAVE TO EAT, RAINA.
BUT WHAT IF WE CATCH IT?
CHANCES ARE, WE WON'T.
YOU DON'T **KNOW** THAT!
RAINA?
SLAM
GASP!

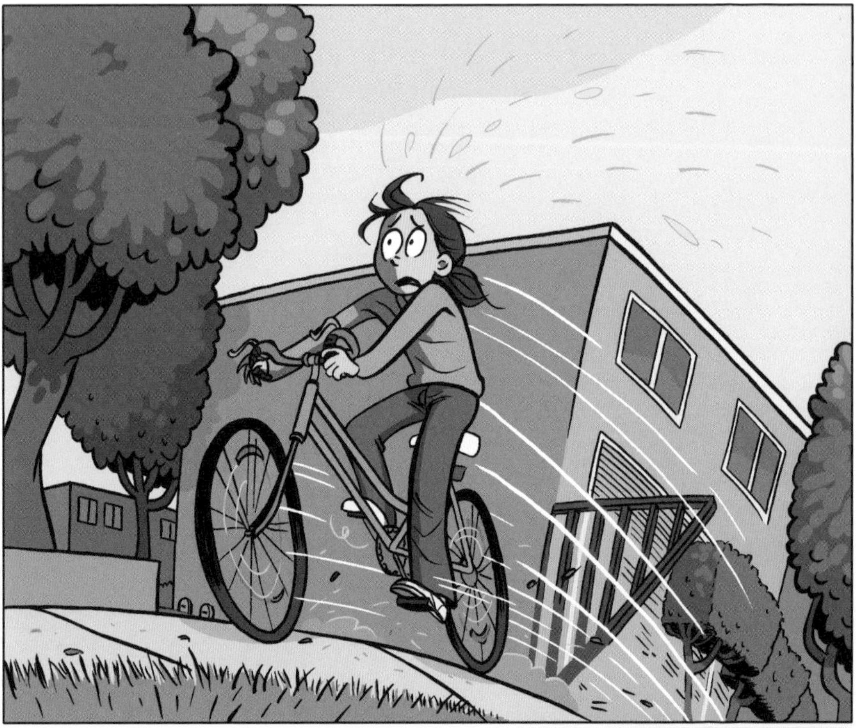

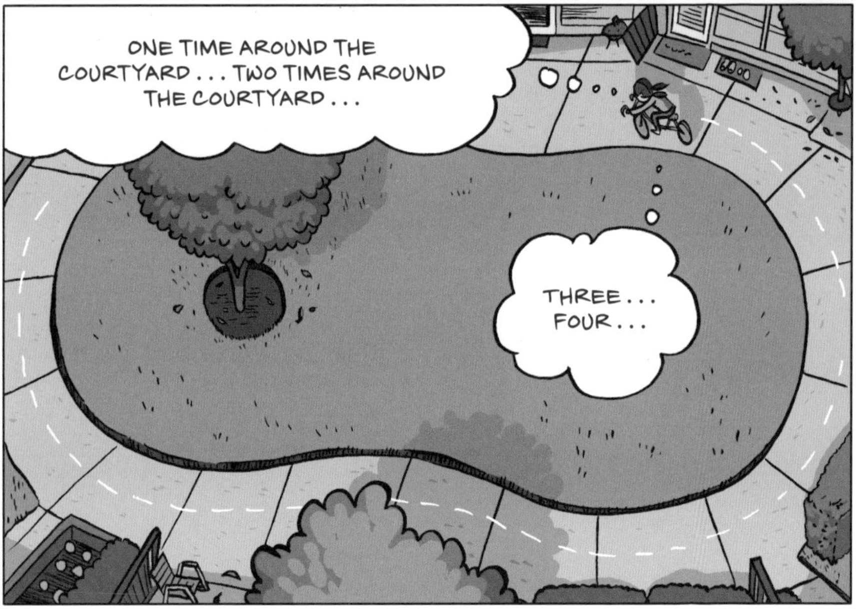
ONE TIME AROUND THE COURTYARD . . . TWO TIMES AROUND THE COURTYARD . . .
THREE . . . FOUR . . .

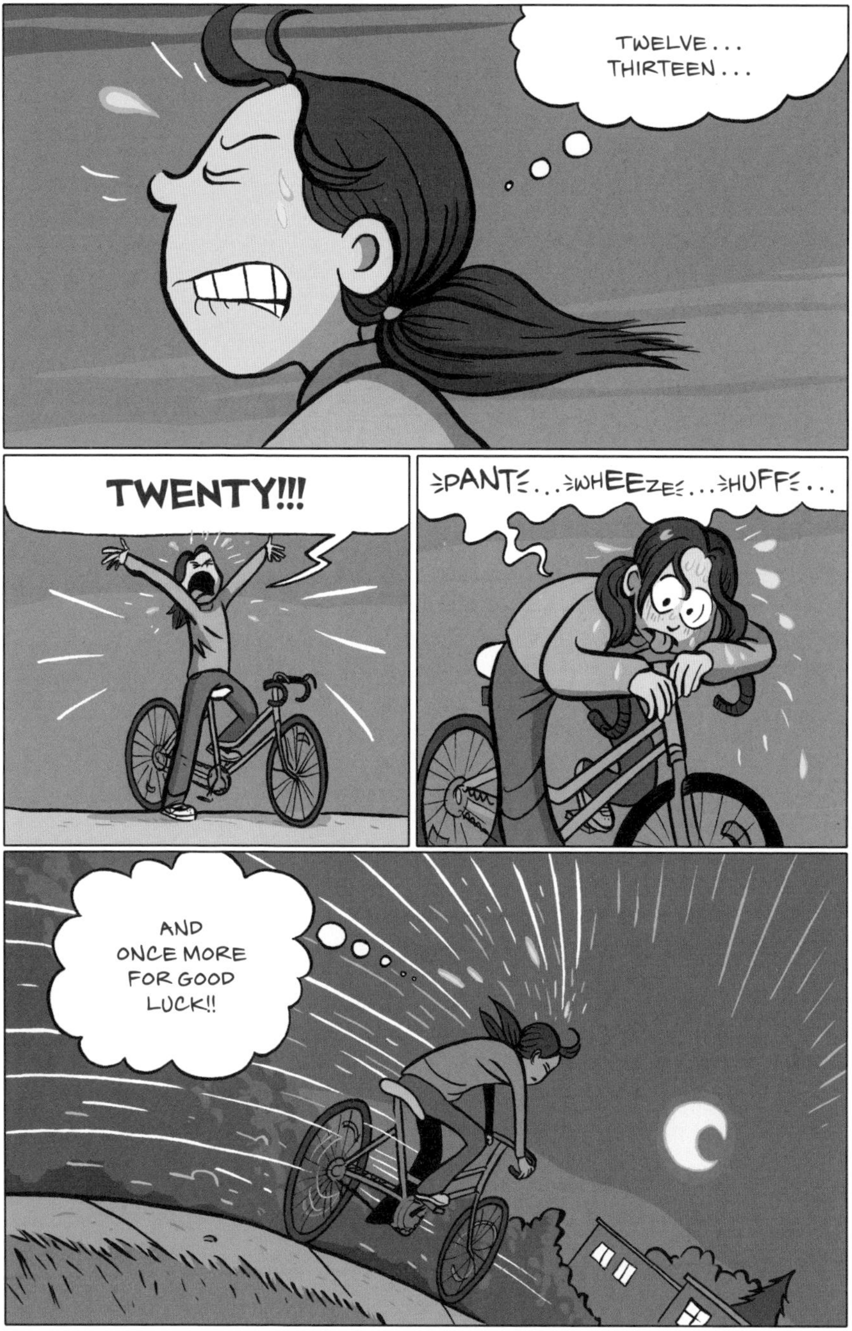
TWELVE...
THIRTEEN...
TWENTY!!!
PANT...WHEEZE...HUFF...
AND ONCE MORE FOR GOOD LUCK!!

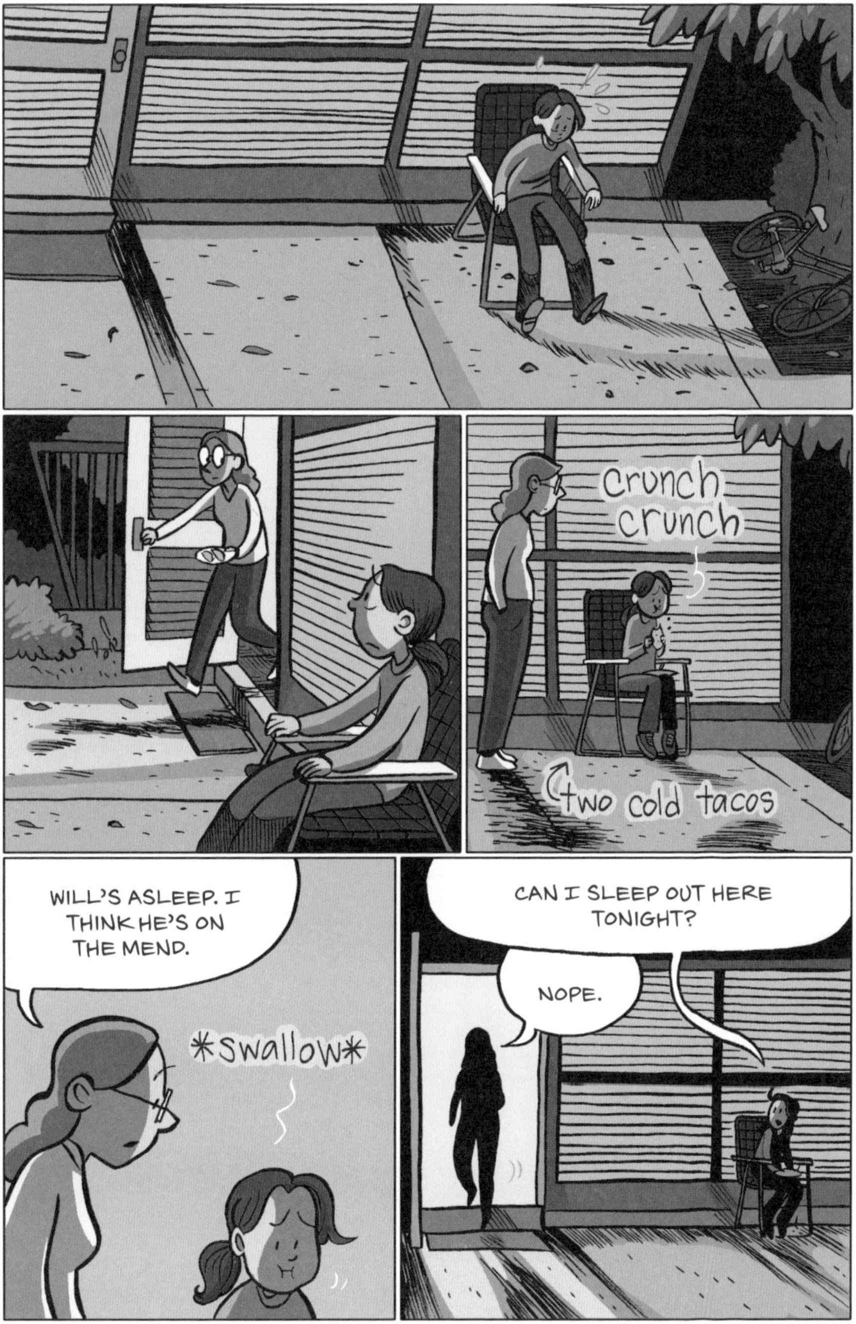
crunch
crunch
two cold tacos
WILL'S ASLEEP. I THINK HE'S ON THE MEND.
swallow
CAN I SLEEP OUT HERE TONIGHT?
NOPE.

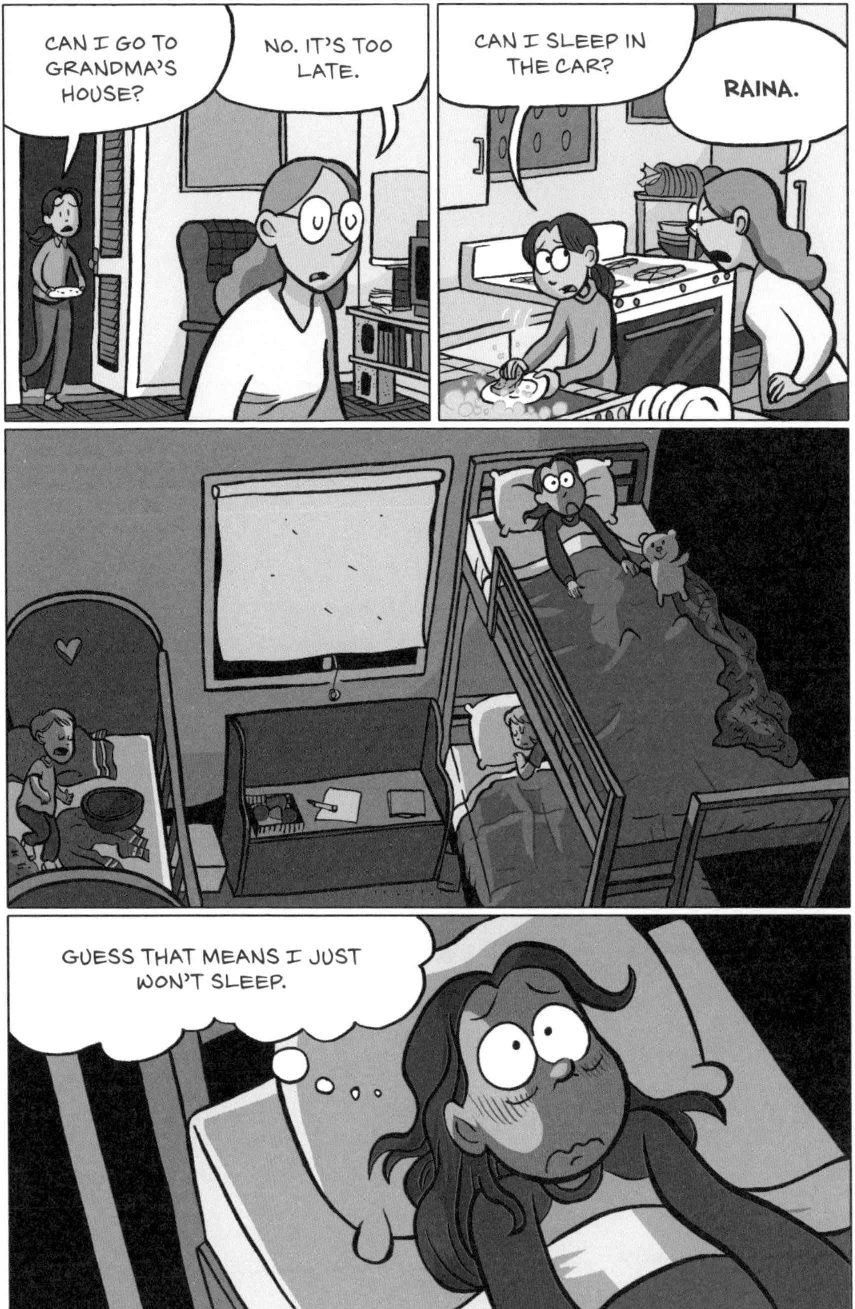
CAN I GO TO GRANDMA'S HOUSE?
NO. IT'S TOO LATE.
CAN I SLEEP IN THE CAR?
RAINA.
GUESS THAT MEANS I JUST WON'T SLEEP.

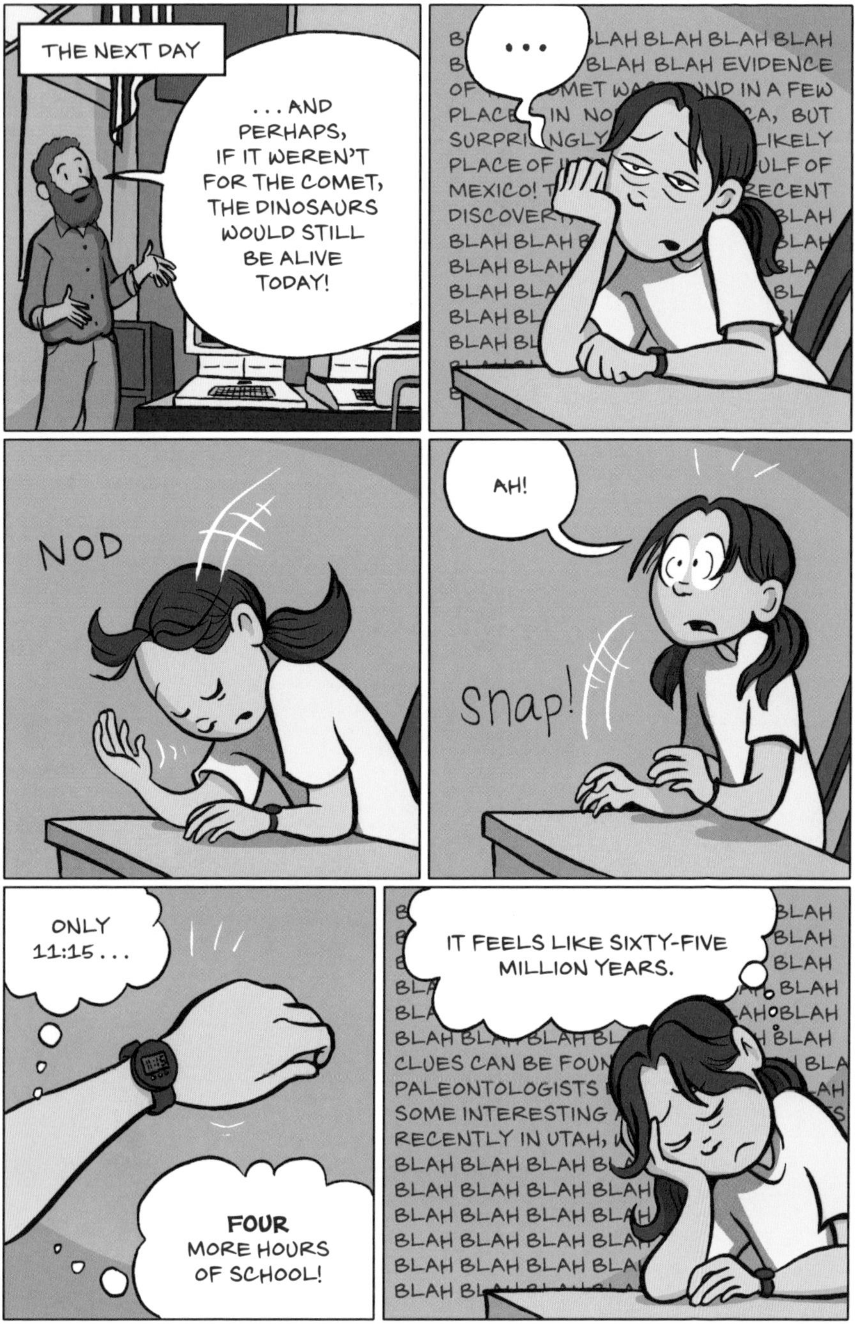
THE NEXT DAY
. . . AND PERHAPS, IF IT WEREN'T FOR THE COMET, THE DINOSAURS WOULD STILL BE ALIVE TODAY!
. . .
NOD
AH!
SNAP!
ONLY 11:15 . . .
FOUR MORE HOURS OF SCHOOL!
IT FEELS LIKE SIXTY-FIVE MILLION YEARS.

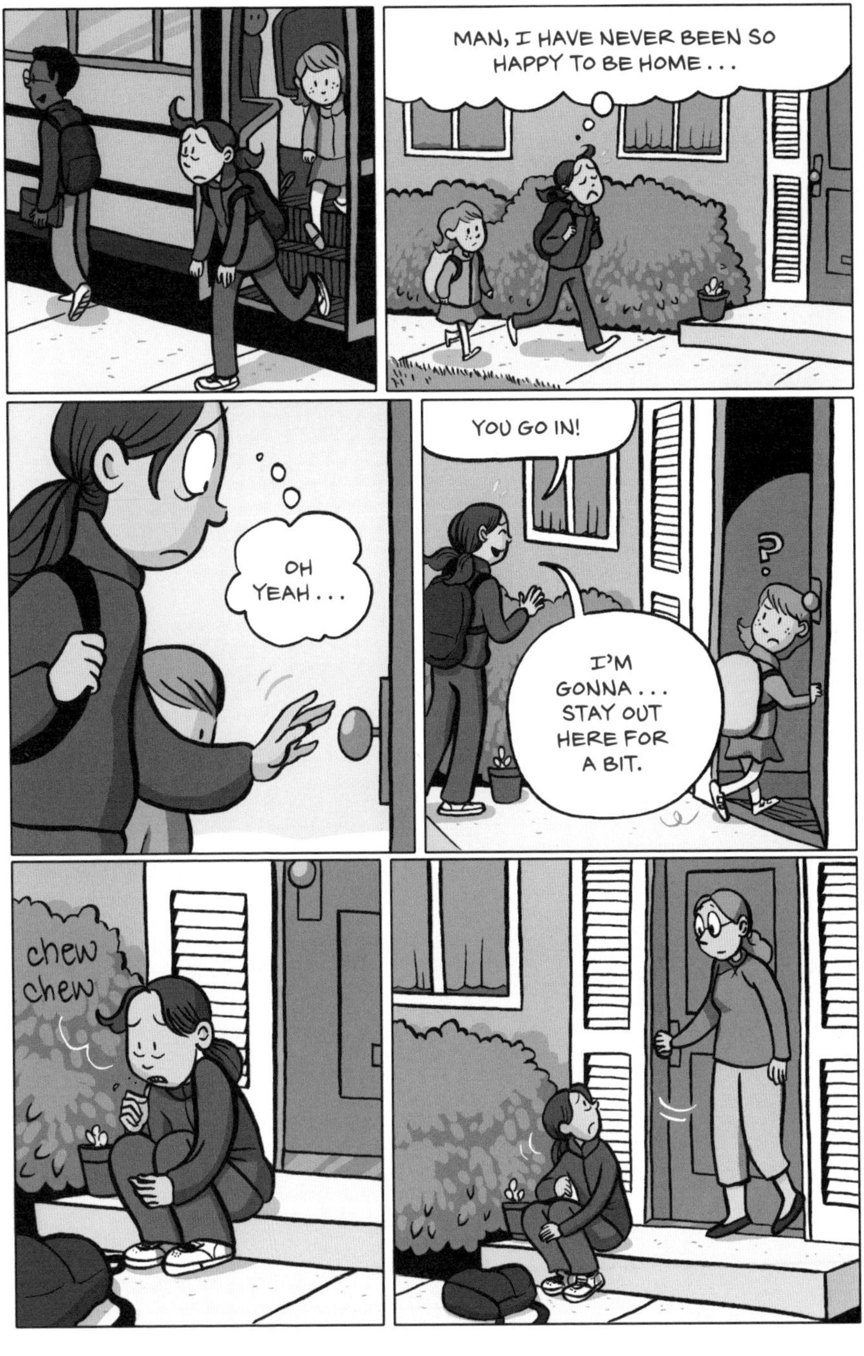
MAN, I HAVE NEVER BEEN SO HAPPY TO BE HOME . . .
OH YEAH . . .
YOU GO IN!
?
I'M GONNA . . . STAY OUT HERE FOR A BIT.
chew chew

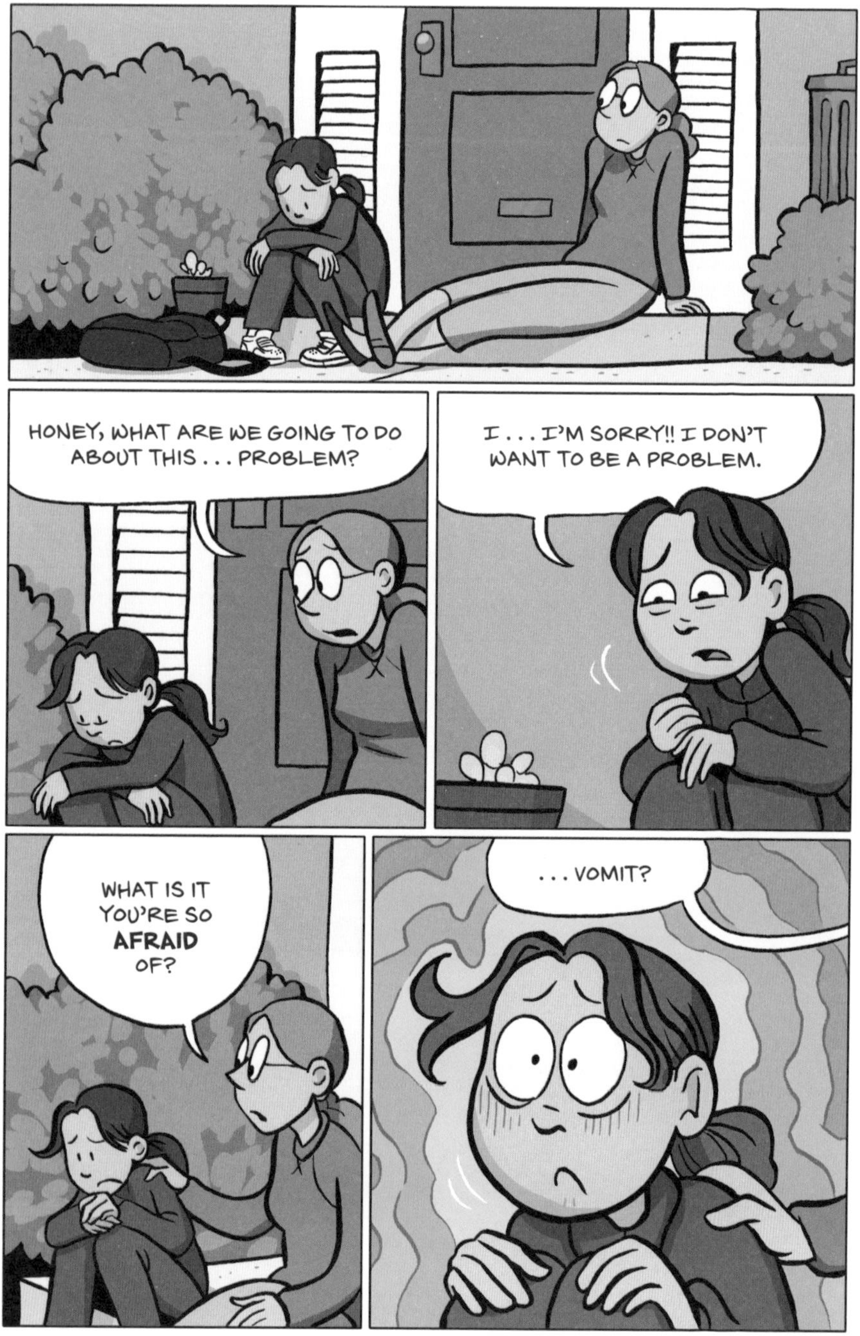
HONEY, WHAT ARE WE GOING TO DO ABOUT THIS . . . PROBLEM?
I . . . I'M SORRY!! I DON'T WANT TO BE A PROBLEM.
WHAT IS IT YOU'RE SO **AFRAID** OF?
. . . VOMIT?

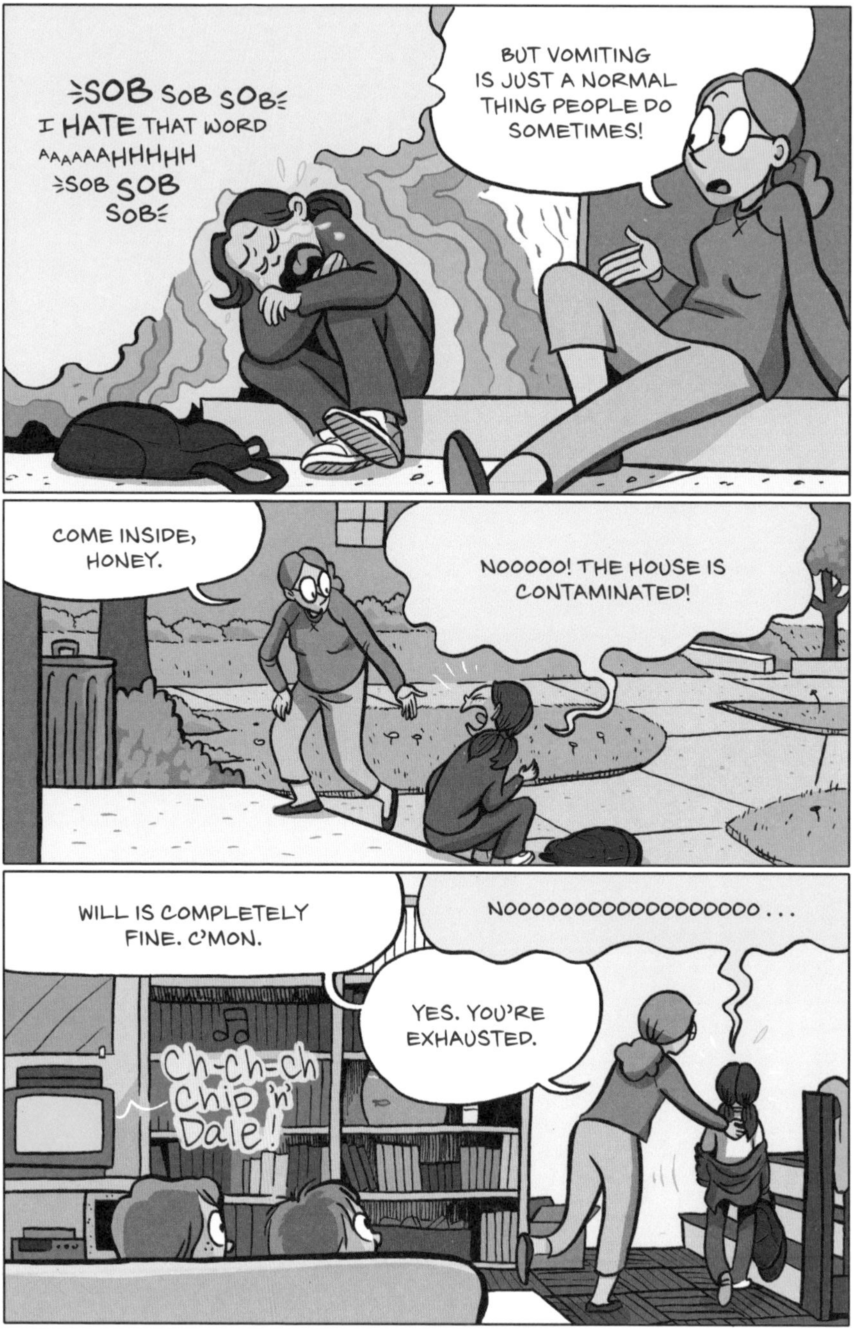

SOB SOB SOB
I HATE THAT WORD
AAAAAAHHHHH
SOB SOB SOB
BUT VOMITING IS JUST A NORMAL THING PEOPLE DO SOMETIMES!
COME INSIDE, HONEY.
NOOOOO! THE HOUSE IS CONTAMINATED!
WILL IS COMPLETELY FINE. C'MON.
NOOOOOOOOOOOOOOOOOO . . .
YES. YOU'RE EXHAUSTED.
Ch-ch-ch Chip 'n' Dale!

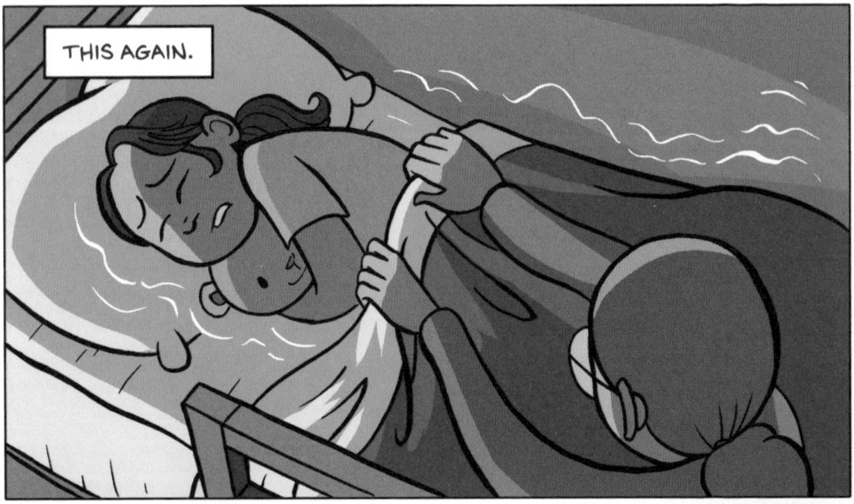
THIS AGAIN.

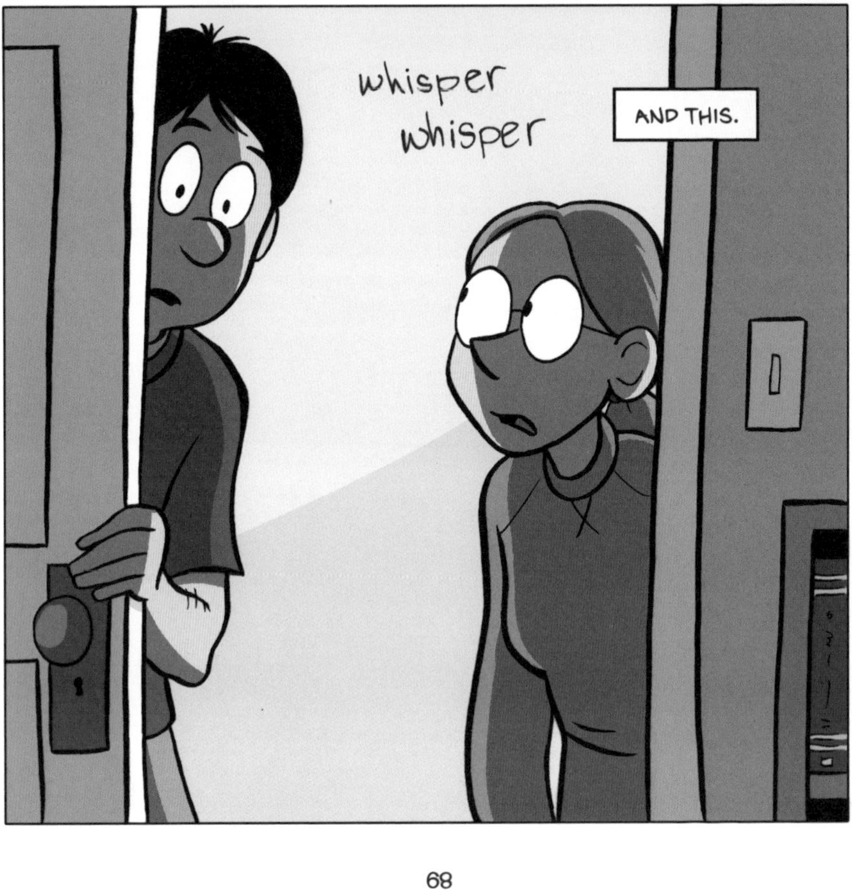
whisper
whisper
AND THIS.

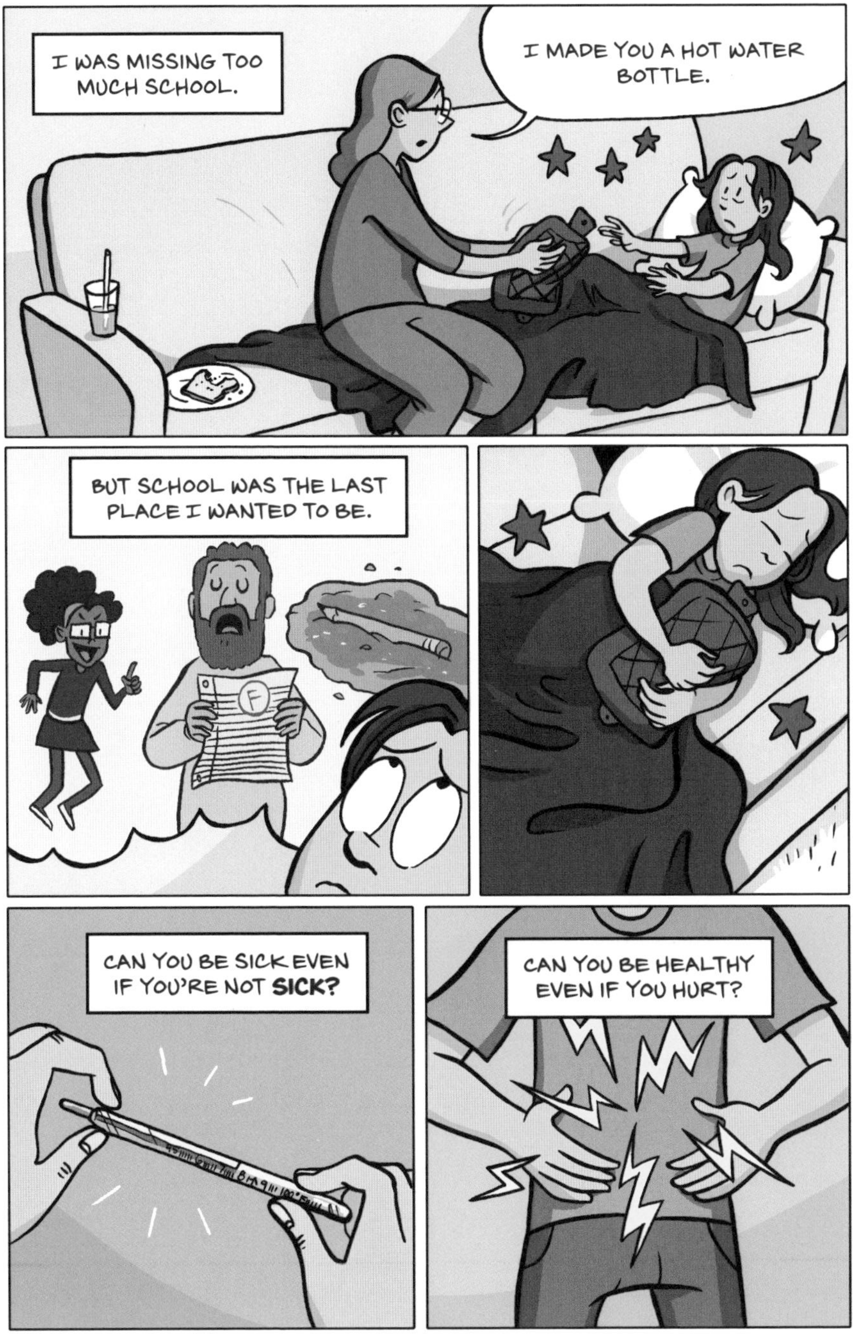
I WAS MISSING TOO MUCH SCHOOL.
I MADE YOU A HOT WATER BOTTLE.
BUT SCHOOL WAS THE LAST PLACE I WANTED TO BE.
F
CAN YOU BE SICK EVEN IF YOU'RE NOT **SICK?**
CAN YOU BE HEALTHY EVEN IF YOU HURT?

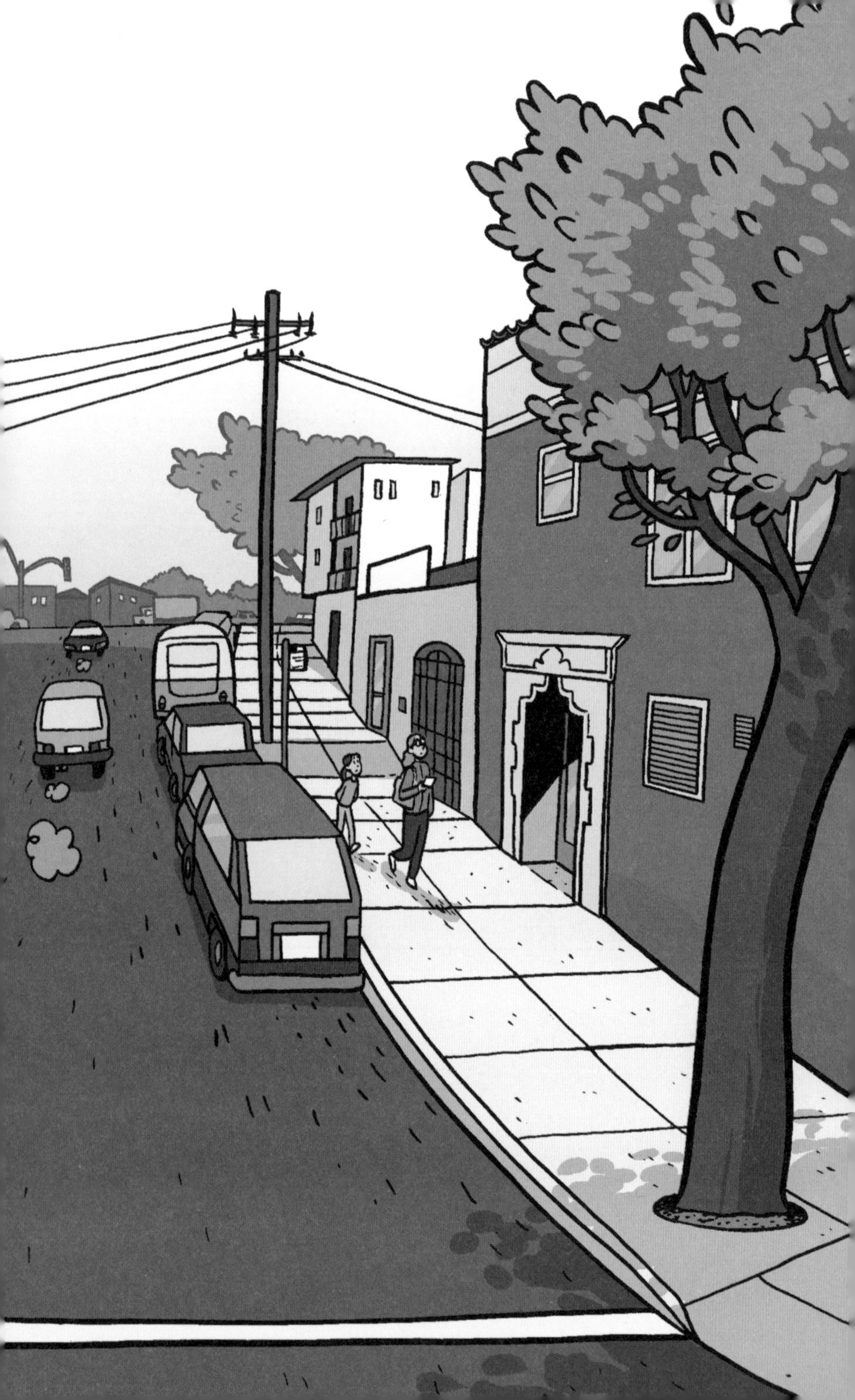

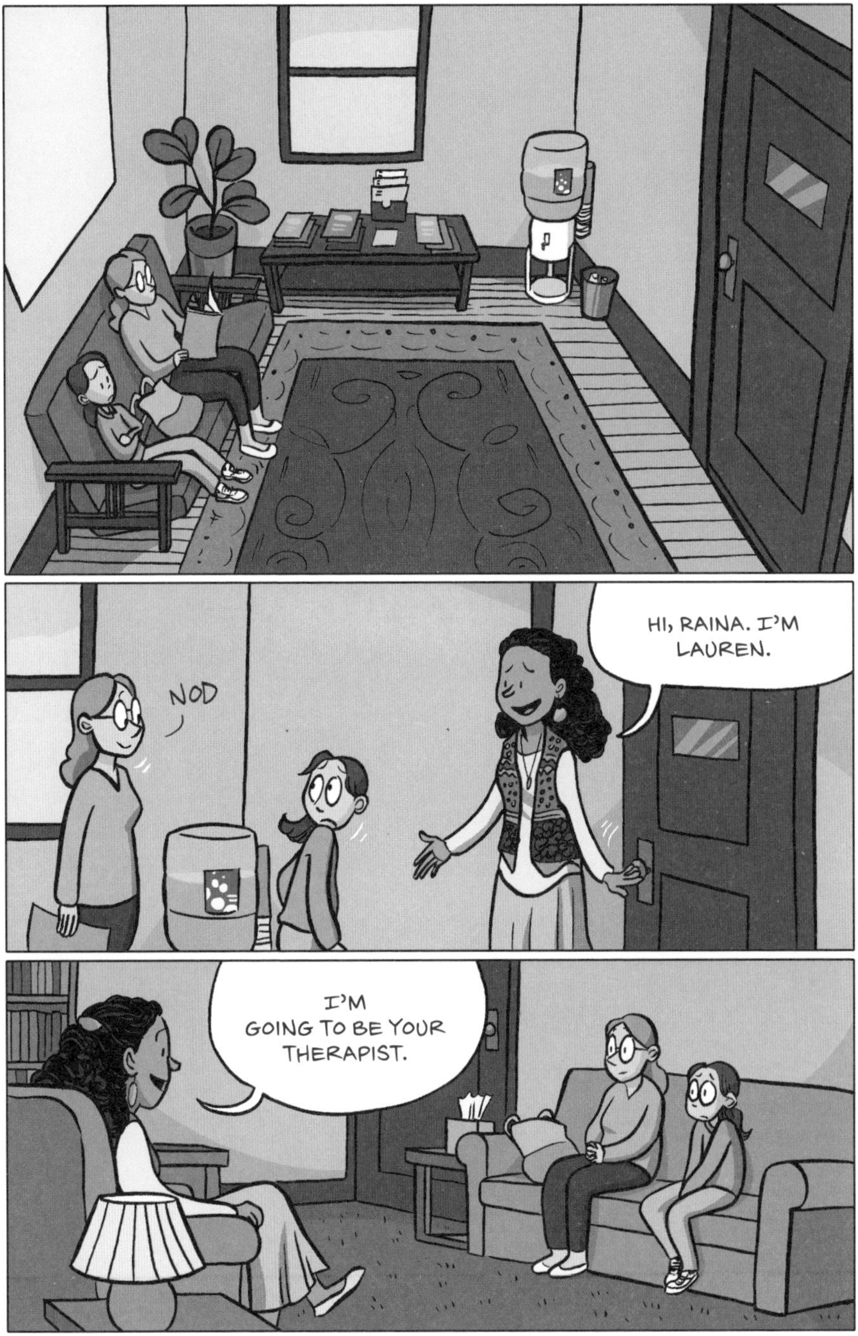
NOD
HI, RAINA. I'M LAUREN.
I'M GOING TO BE YOUR THERAPIST.

YOUR MOM AND DAD HAVE SPOKEN TO ME ABOUT WHAT'S BEEN GOING ON.

I'LL MEET WITH THEM OCCASIONALLY TO CHECK IN. BUT!

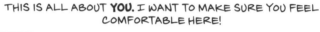

THIS IS ALL ABOUT **YOU.** I WANT TO MAKE SURE YOU FEEL COMFORTABLE HERE!

chew

THANK YOU, MRS. TELGEMEIER! SEE YOU IN A BIT.

GOOD LUCK!

CLICK!

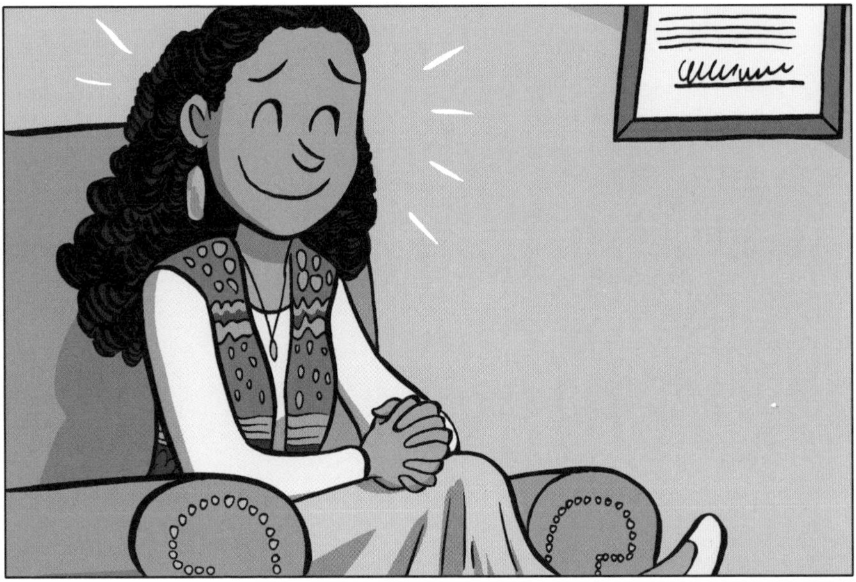

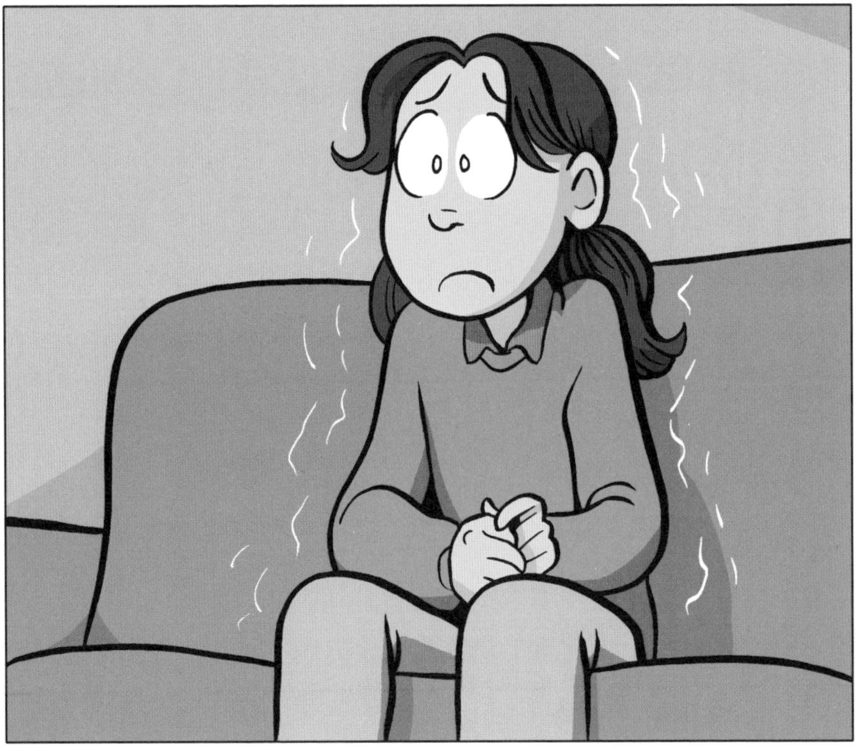

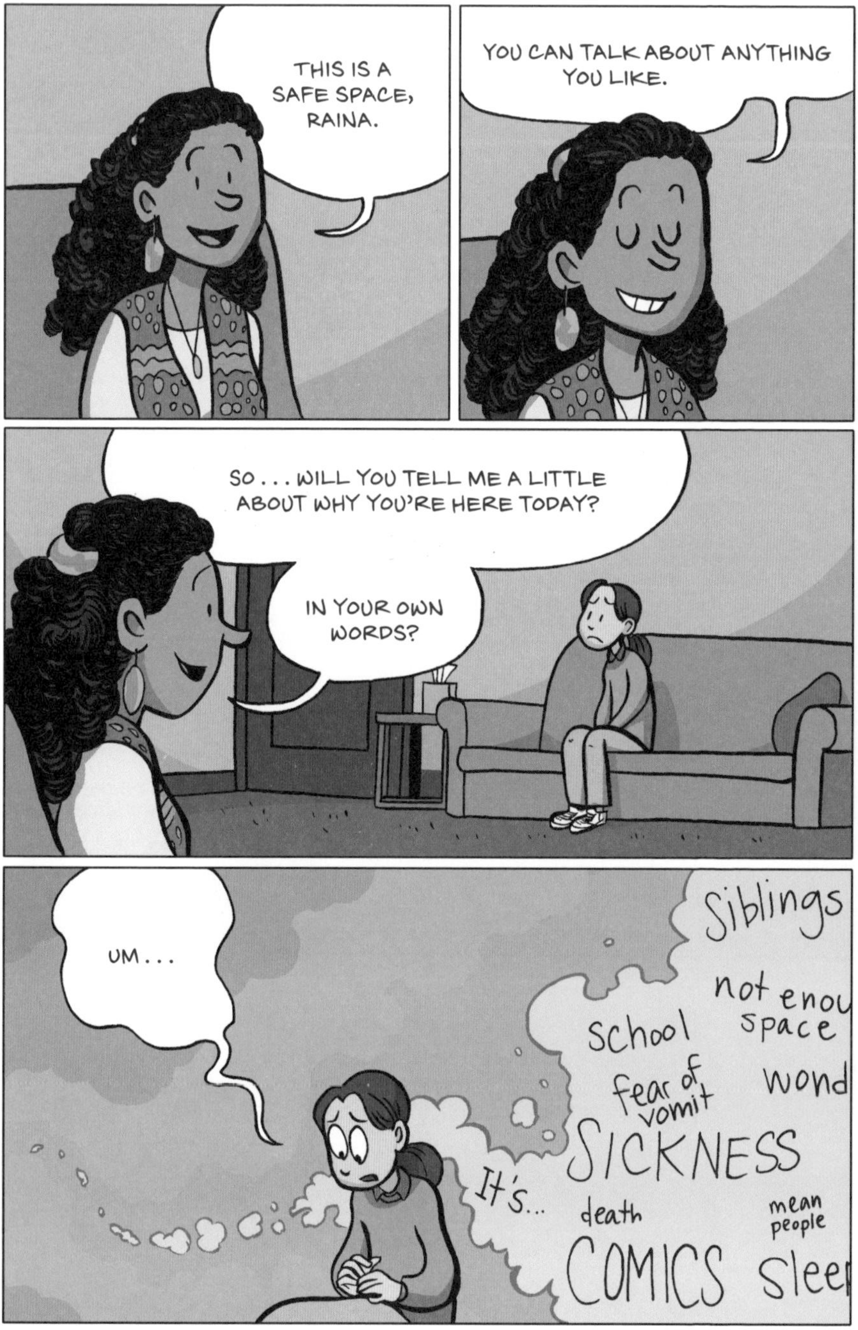
THIS IS A SAFE SPACE, RAINA.
YOU CAN TALK ABOUT ANYTHING YOU LIKE.
SO . . . WILL YOU TELL ME A LITTLE ABOUT WHY YOU'RE HERE TODAY?
IN YOUR OWN WORDS?
UM . . .
It's...
Siblings
not enou
space
School
fear of vomit
wond
SICKNESS
death
mean people
COMICS
slee

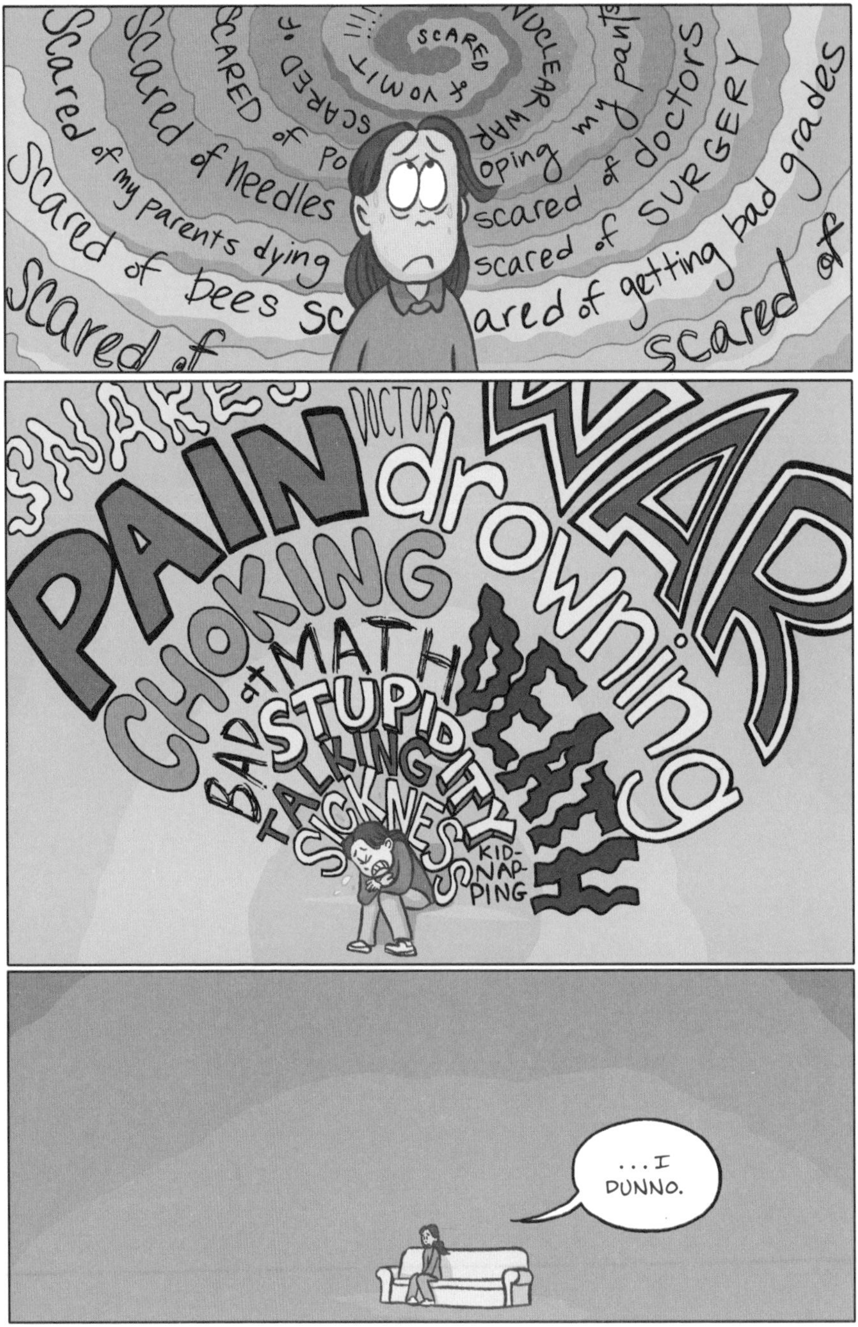
SCARED
of VOMIT
SCARED of
NUCLEAR WAR
my pants
SCARED of
Scared of Needles
scared of doctors
Scared of my parents dying
scared of SURGERY
Scared of bees
scared of
ared of getting bad grades
Scared of
Scared of
DOCTORS
WAR
PAIN
drowning
CHOKING
MATH
DEATH
BAD at
STUPIDITY
TALKING
SICKNESS
KID-NAP-PING
...I DUNNO.

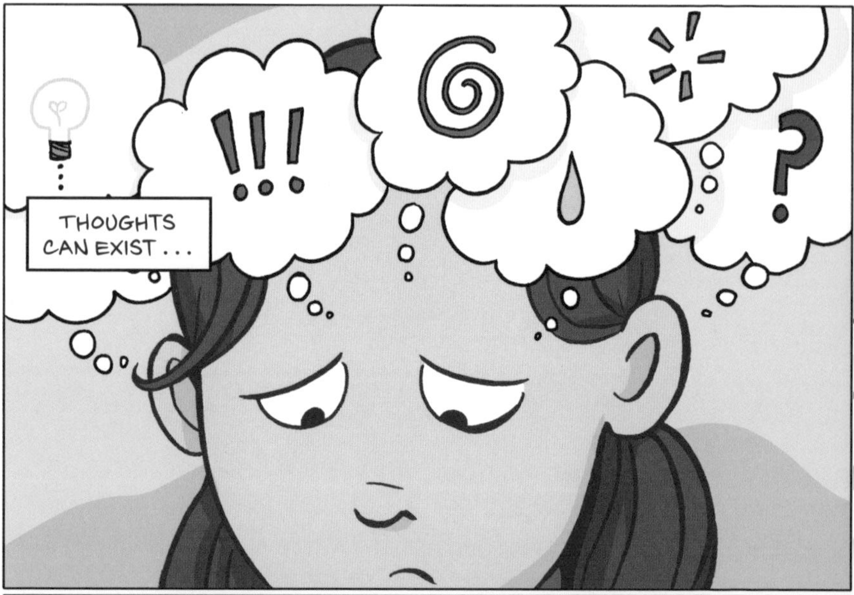
THOUGHTS CAN EXIST . . .
!!!
?

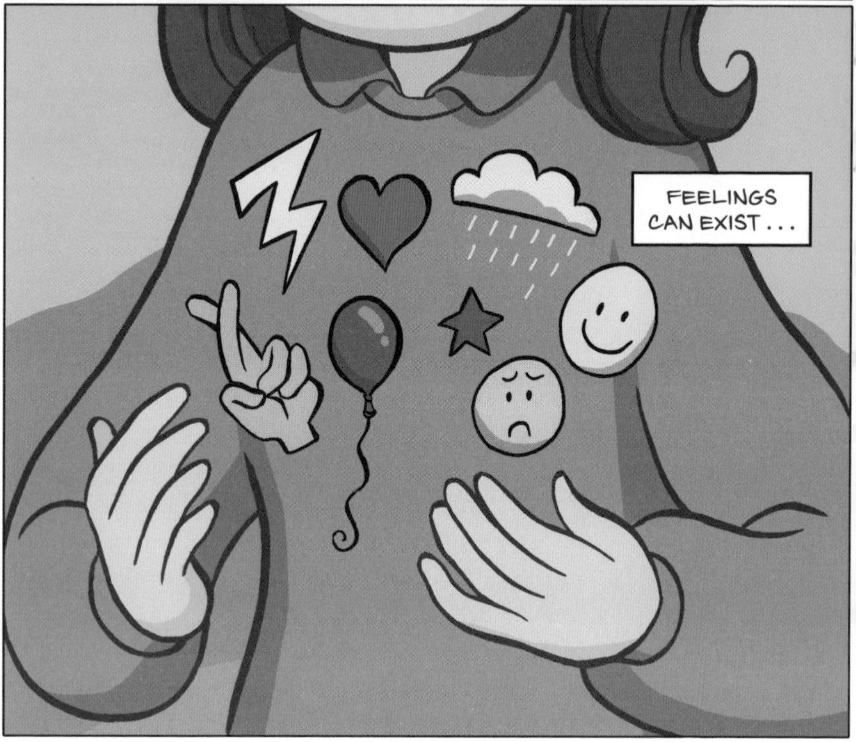
FEELINGS CAN EXIST . . .

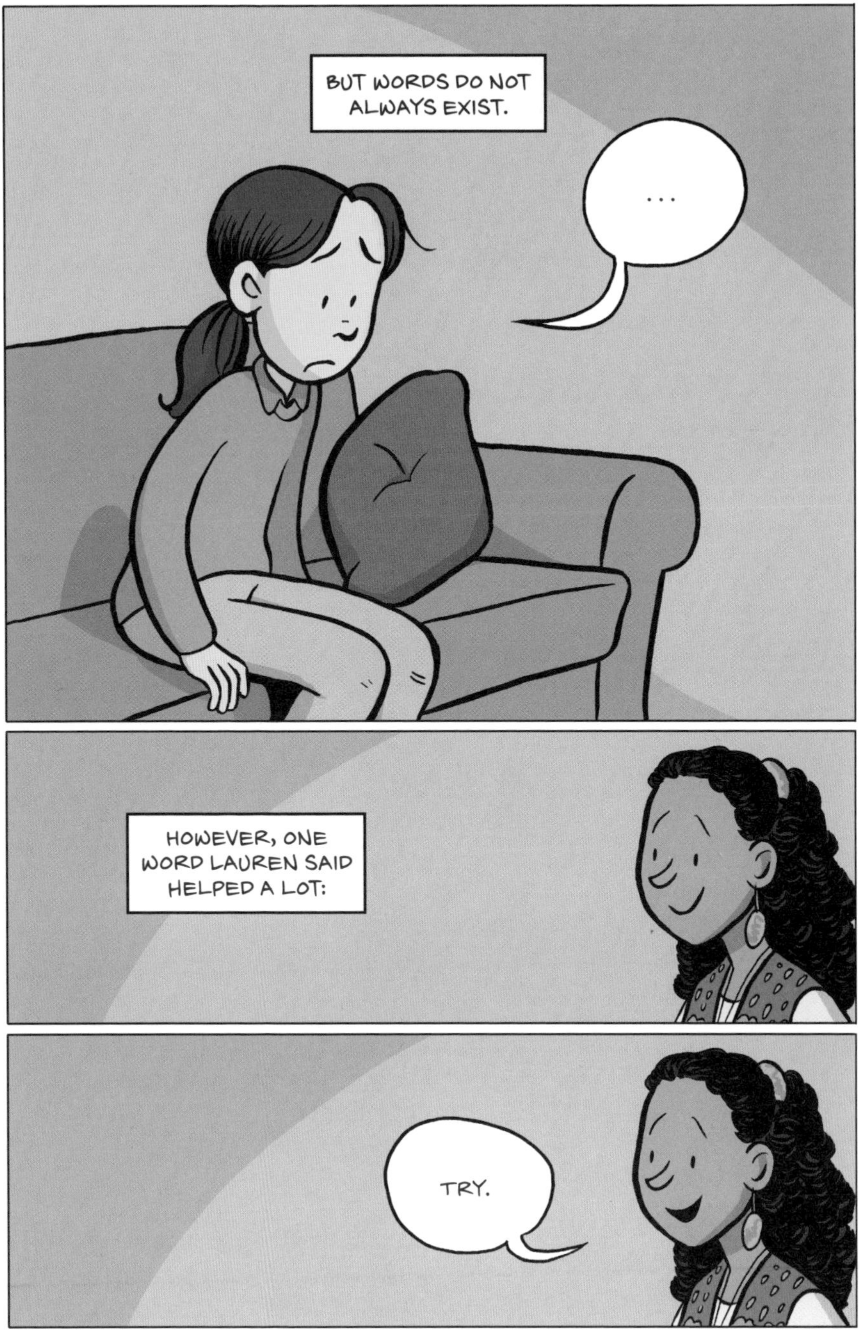
BUT WORDS DO NOT ALWAYS EXIST.
...
HOWEVER, ONE WORD LAUREN SAID HELPED A LOT:
TRY.

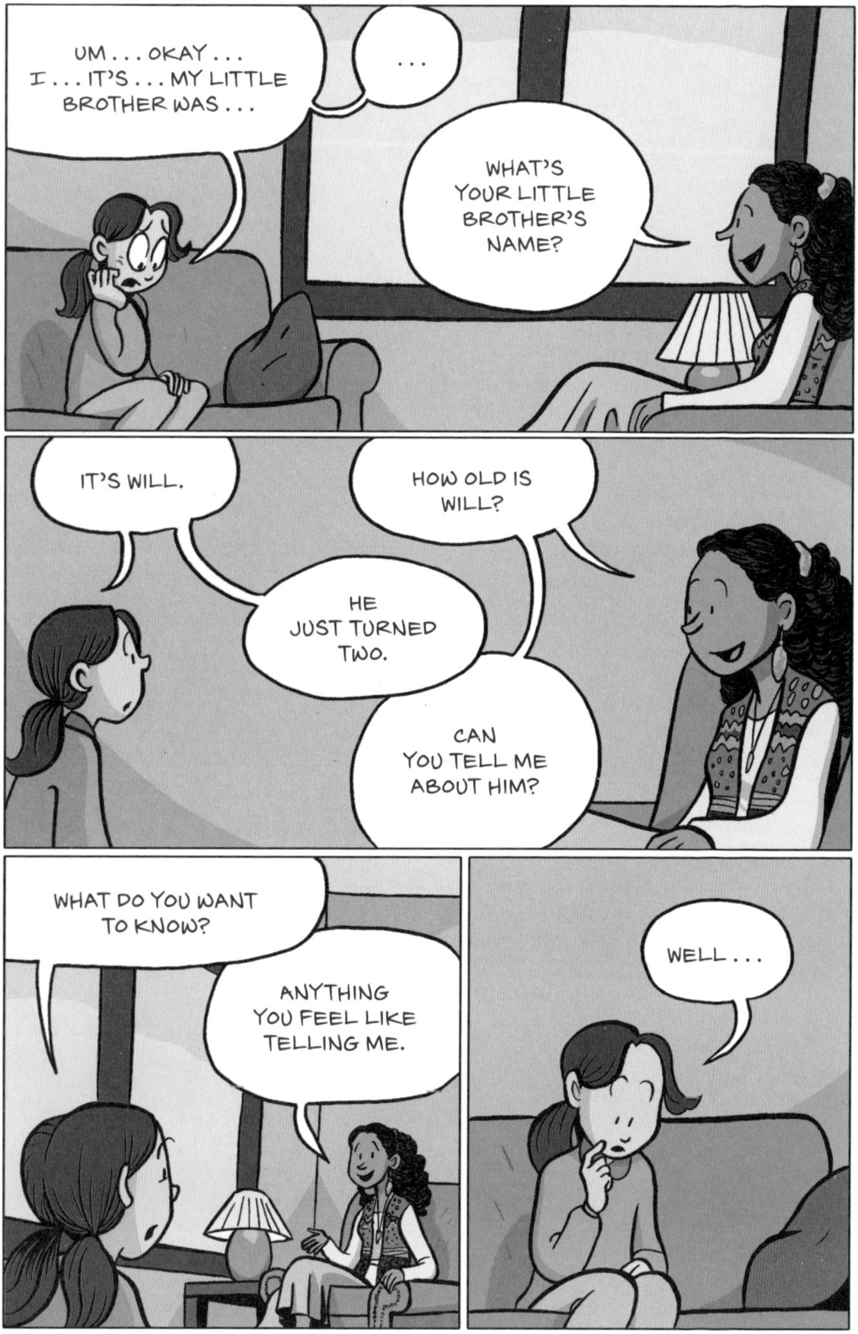
UM . . . OKAY . . . I . . . IT'S . . . MY LITTLE BROTHER WAS . . .
. . .
WHAT'S YOUR LITTLE BROTHER'S NAME?
IT'S WILL.
HOW OLD IS WILL?
HE JUST TURNED TWO.
CAN YOU TELL ME ABOUT HIM?
WHAT DO YOU WANT TO KNOW?
ANYTHING YOU FEEL LIKE TELLING ME.
WELL . . .

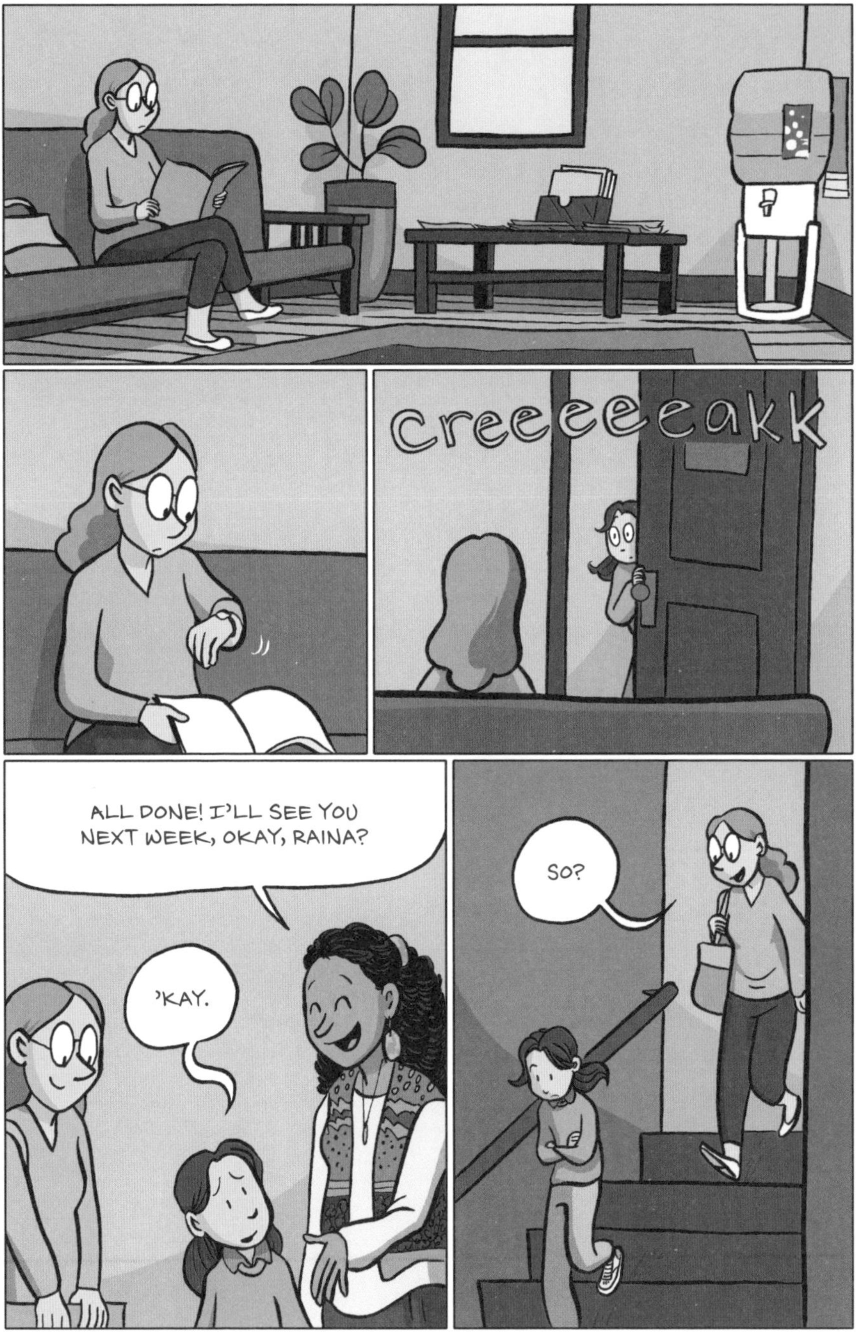
creeeeeakk
ALL DONE! I'LL SEE YOU NEXT WEEK, OKAY, RAINA?
'KAY.
SO?

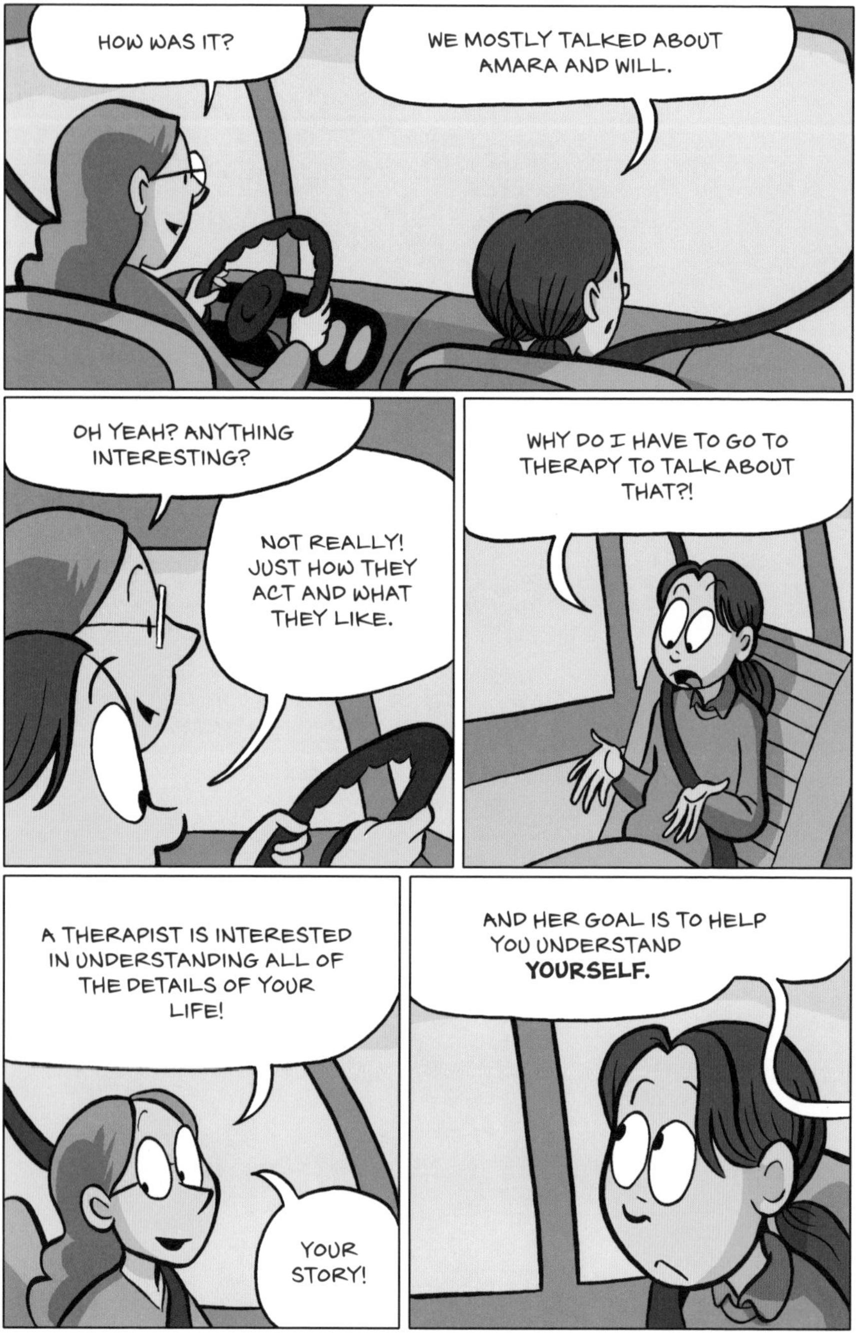
HOW WAS IT?
WE MOSTLY TALKED ABOUT AMARA AND WILL.
OH YEAH? ANYTHING INTERESTING?
NOT REALLY! JUST HOW THEY ACT AND WHAT THEY LIKE.
WHY DO I HAVE TO GO TO THERAPY TO TALK ABOUT THAT?!
A THERAPIST IS INTERESTED IN UNDERSTANDING ALL OF THE DETAILS OF YOUR LIFE!
YOUR STORY!
AND HER GOAL IS TO HELP YOU UNDERSTAND **YOURSELF.**

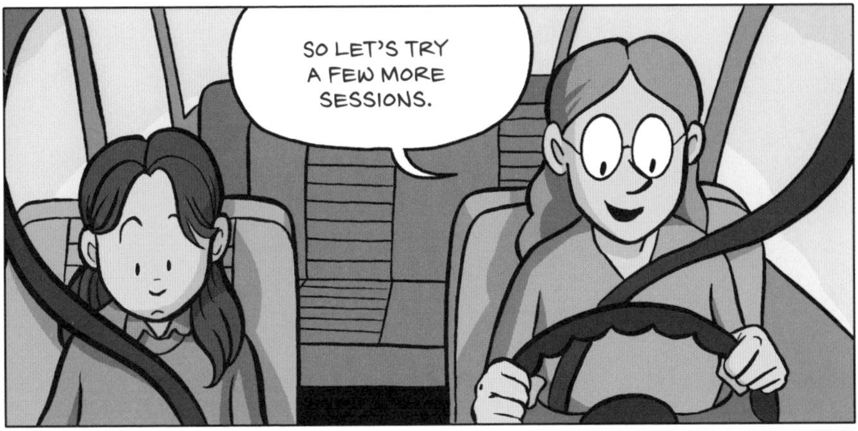
SO LET'S TRY A FEW MORE SESSIONS.
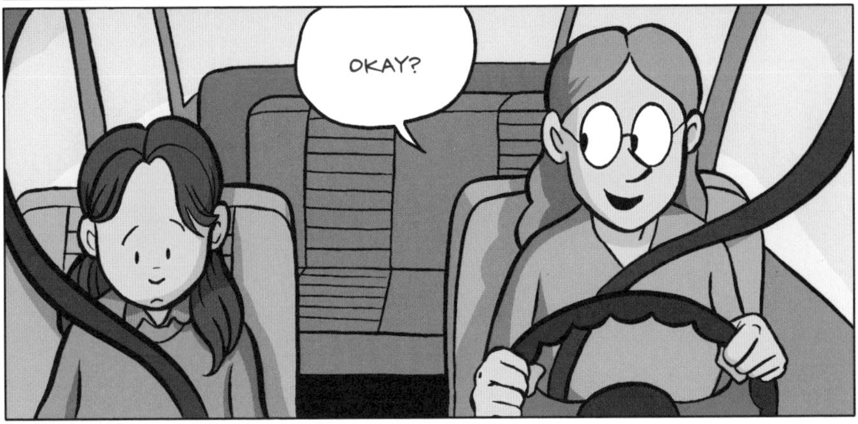
OKAY?
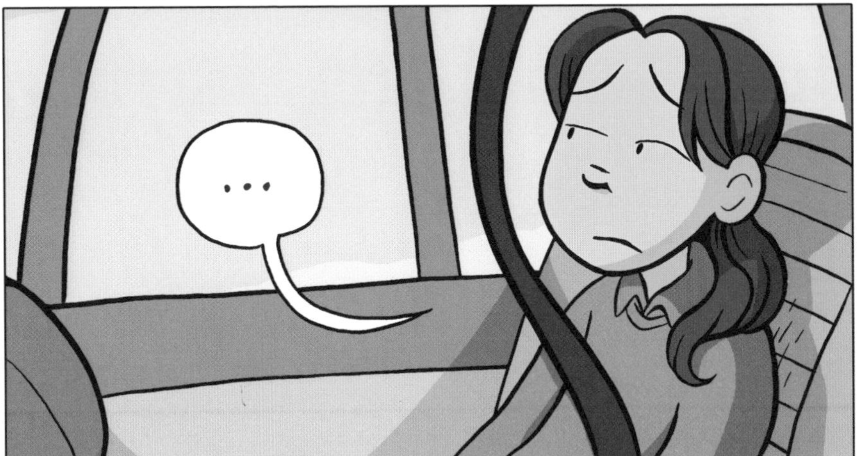
...

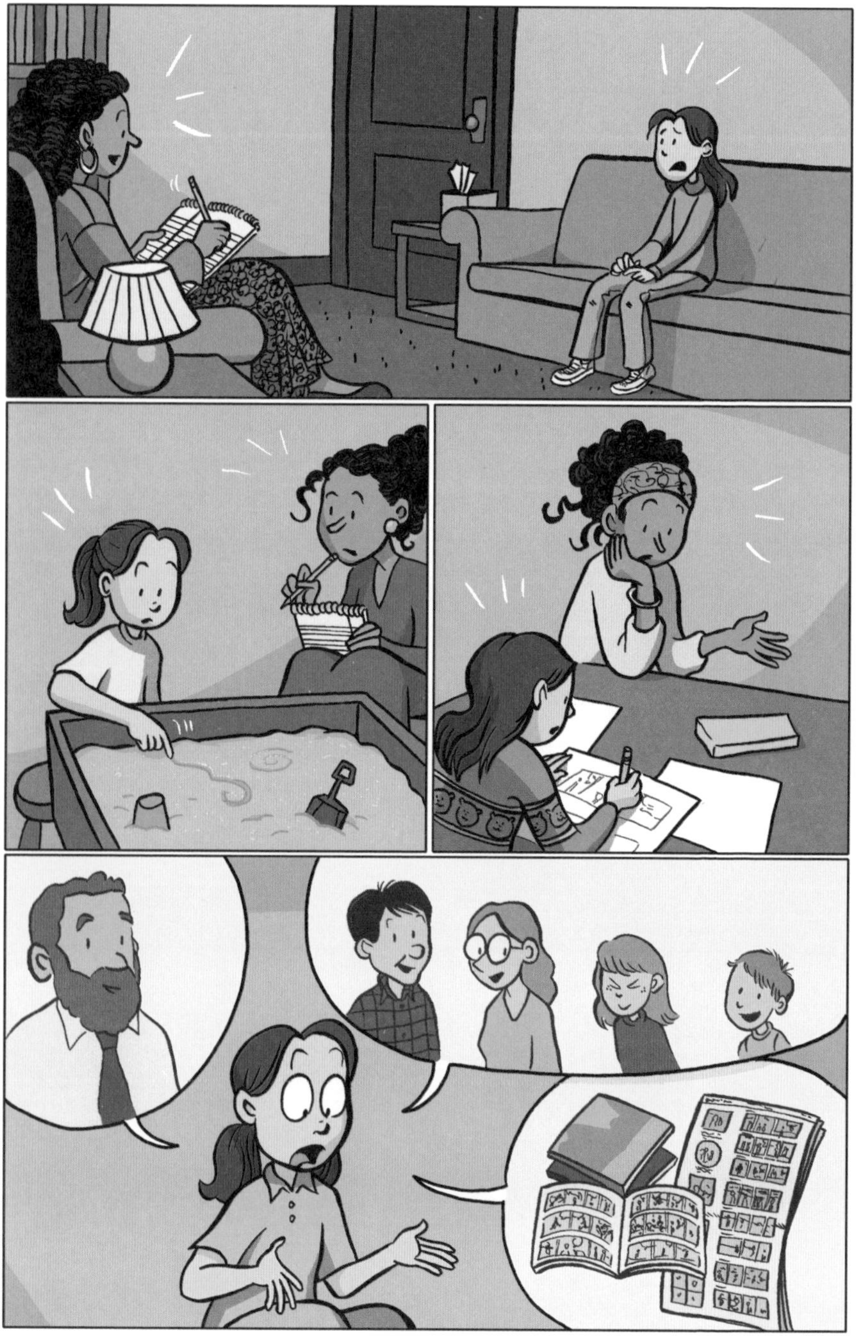

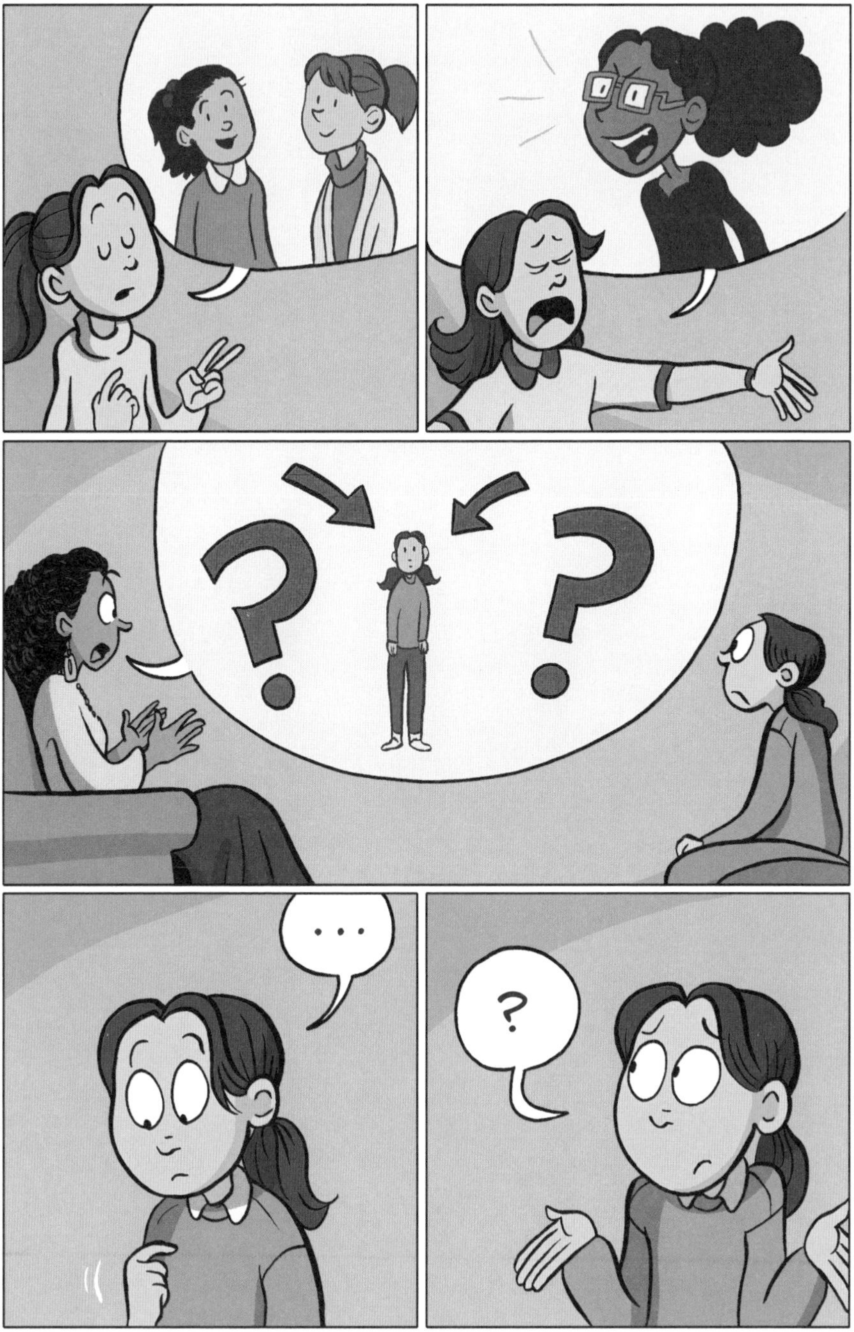
...
?

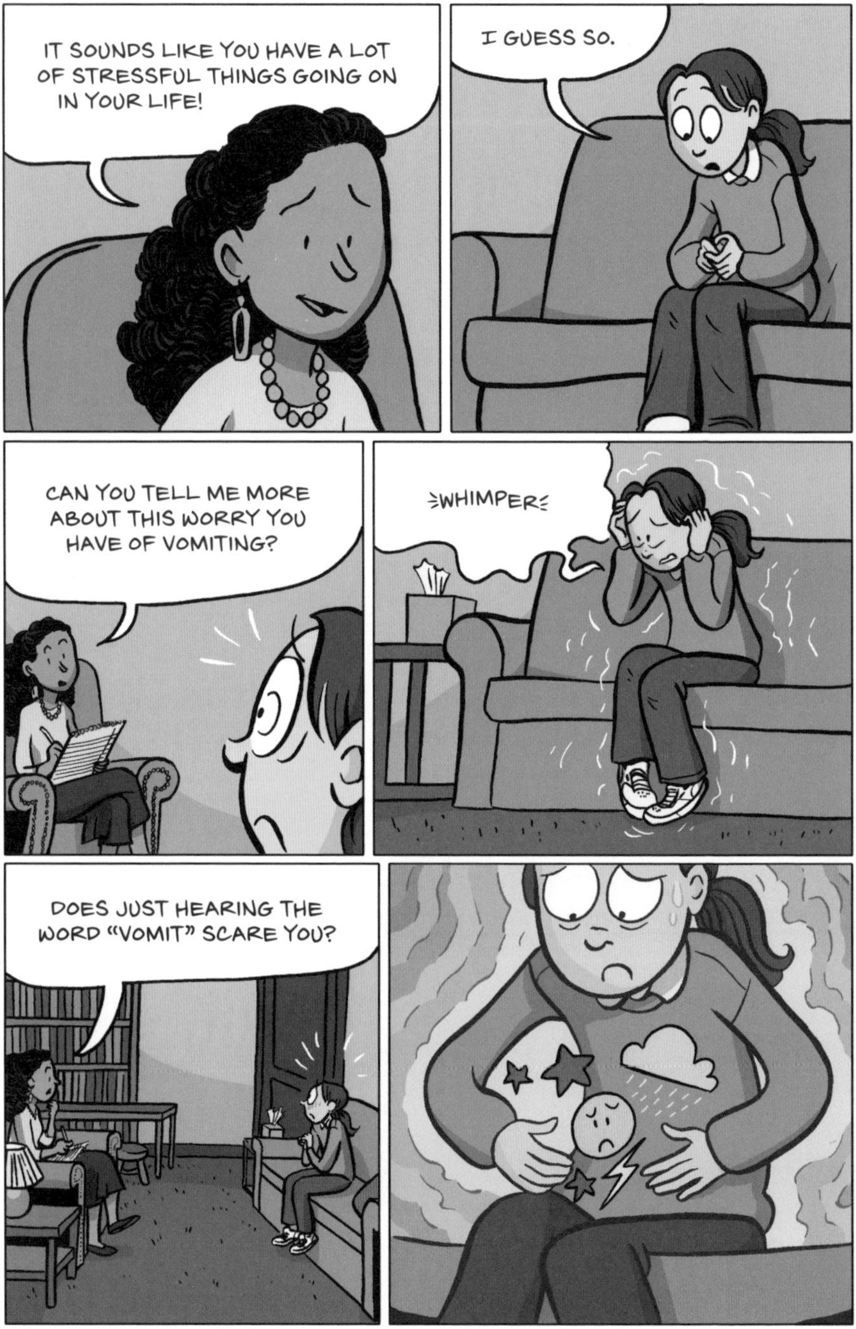
IT SOUNDS LIKE YOU HAVE A LOT OF STRESSFUL THINGS GOING ON IN YOUR LIFE!
I GUESS SO.
CAN YOU TELL ME MORE ABOUT THIS WORRY YOU HAVE OF VOMITING?
WHIMPER
DOES JUST HEARING THE WORD "VOMIT" SCARE YOU?

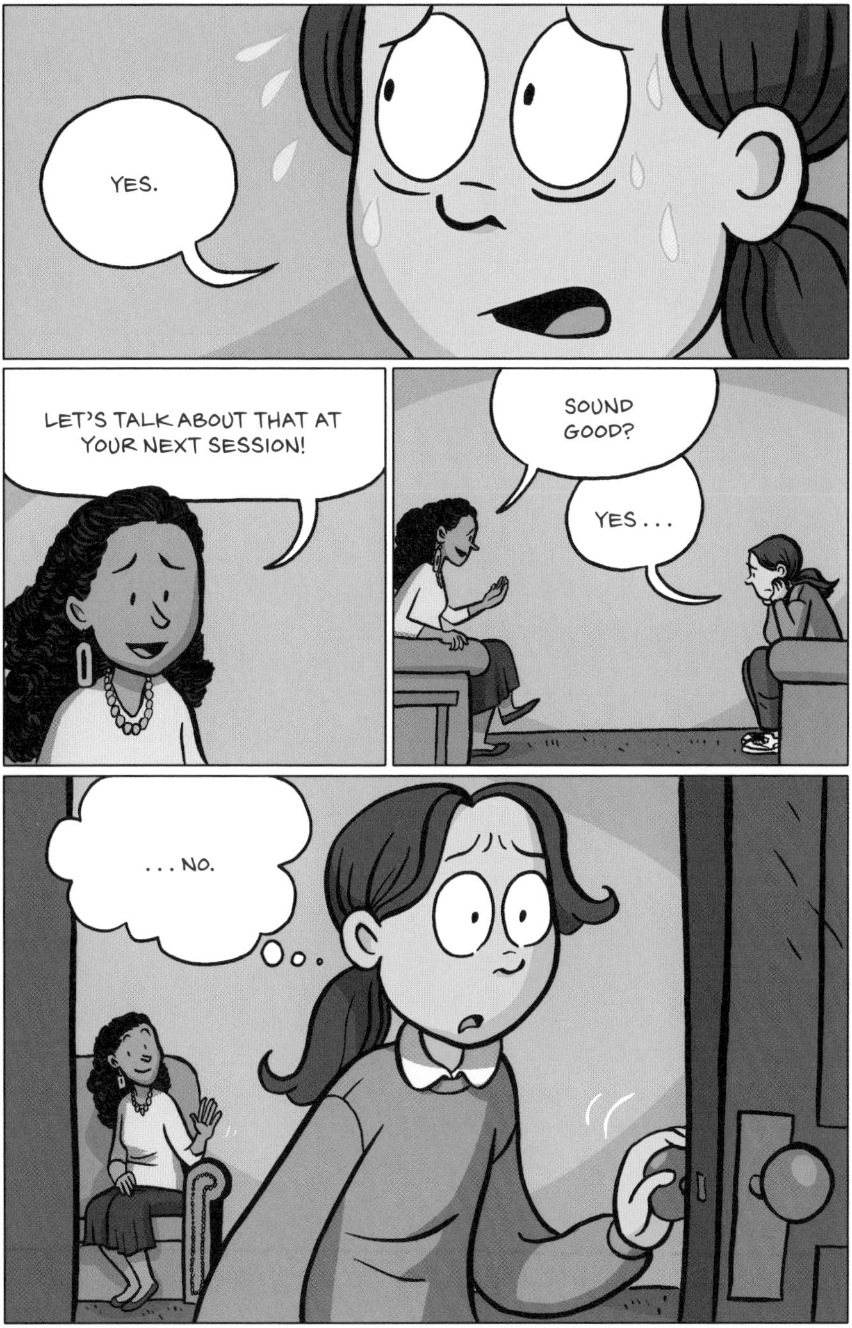
YES.
LET'S TALK ABOUT THAT AT YOUR NEXT SESSION!
SOUND GOOD?
YES . . .
. . . NO.

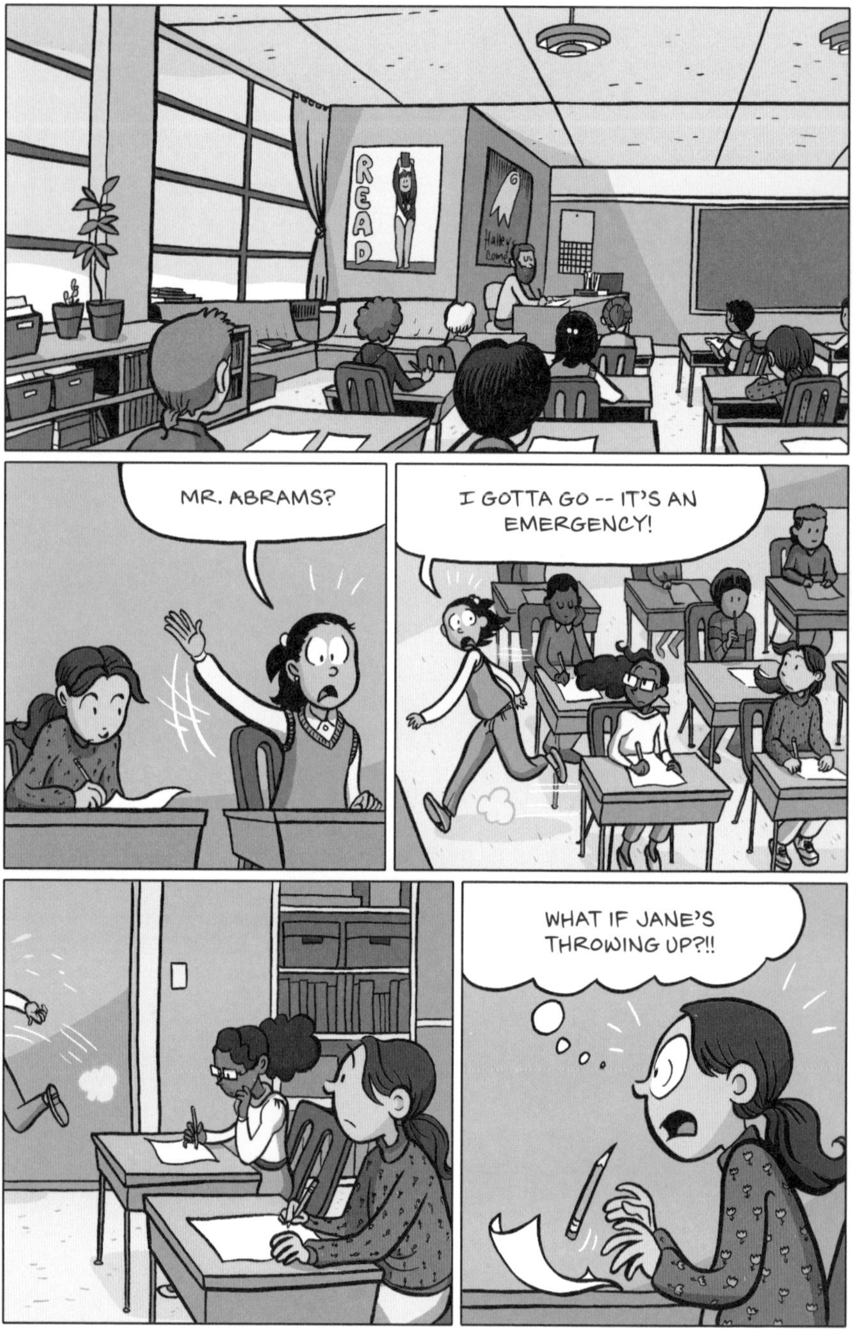
READ
MR. ABRAMS?
I GOTTA GO -- IT'S AN EMERGENCY!
WHAT IF JANE'S THROWING UP?!!

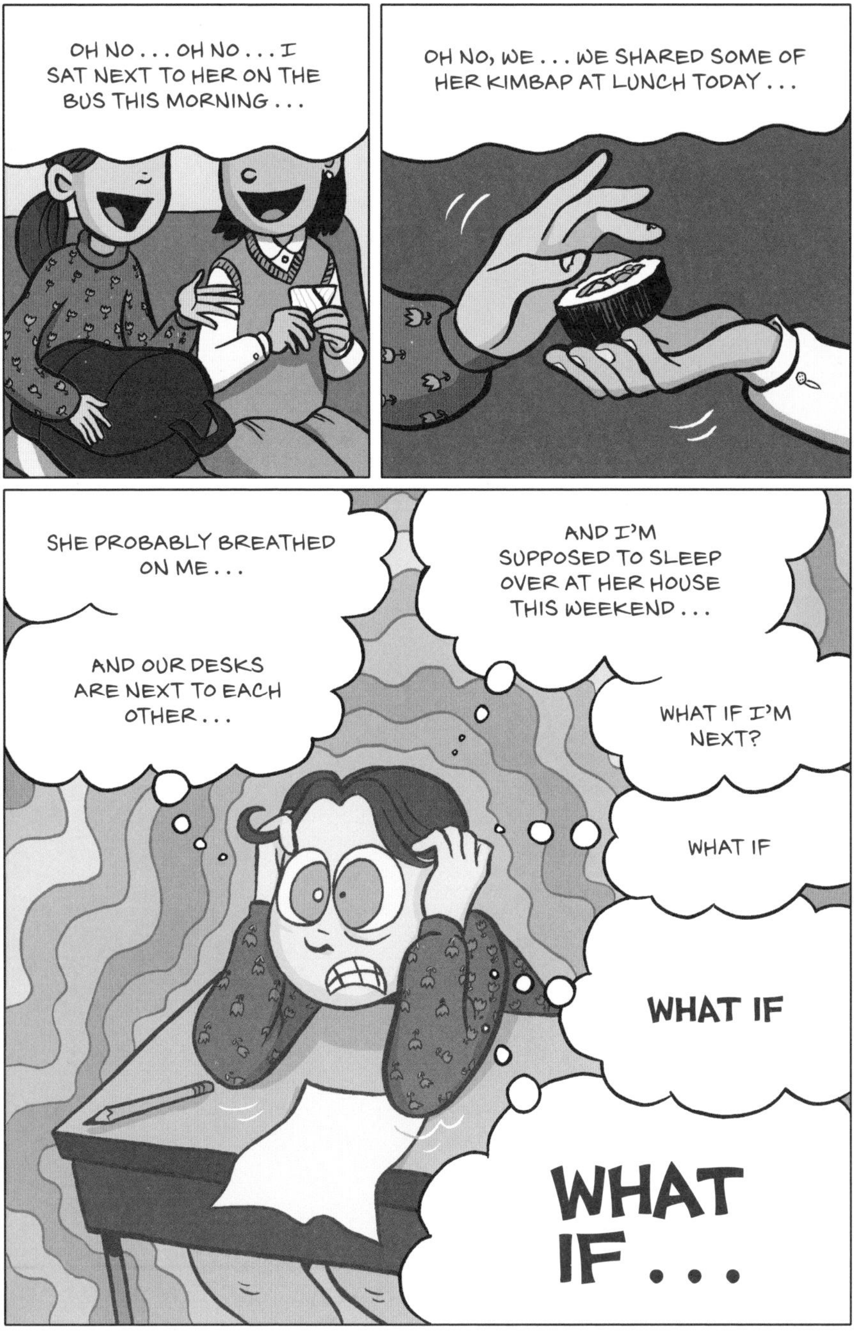
OH NO . . . OH NO . . . I SAT NEXT TO HER ON THE BUS THIS MORNING . . .
OH NO, WE . . . WE SHARED SOME OF HER KIMBAP AT LUNCH TODAY . . .
SHE PROBABLY BREATHED ON ME . . .
AND I'M SUPPOSED TO SLEEP OVER AT HER HOUSE THIS WEEKEND . . .
AND OUR DESKS ARE NEXT TO EACH OTHER . . .
WHAT IF I'M NEXT?
WHAT IF
WHAT IF
WHAT IF . . .

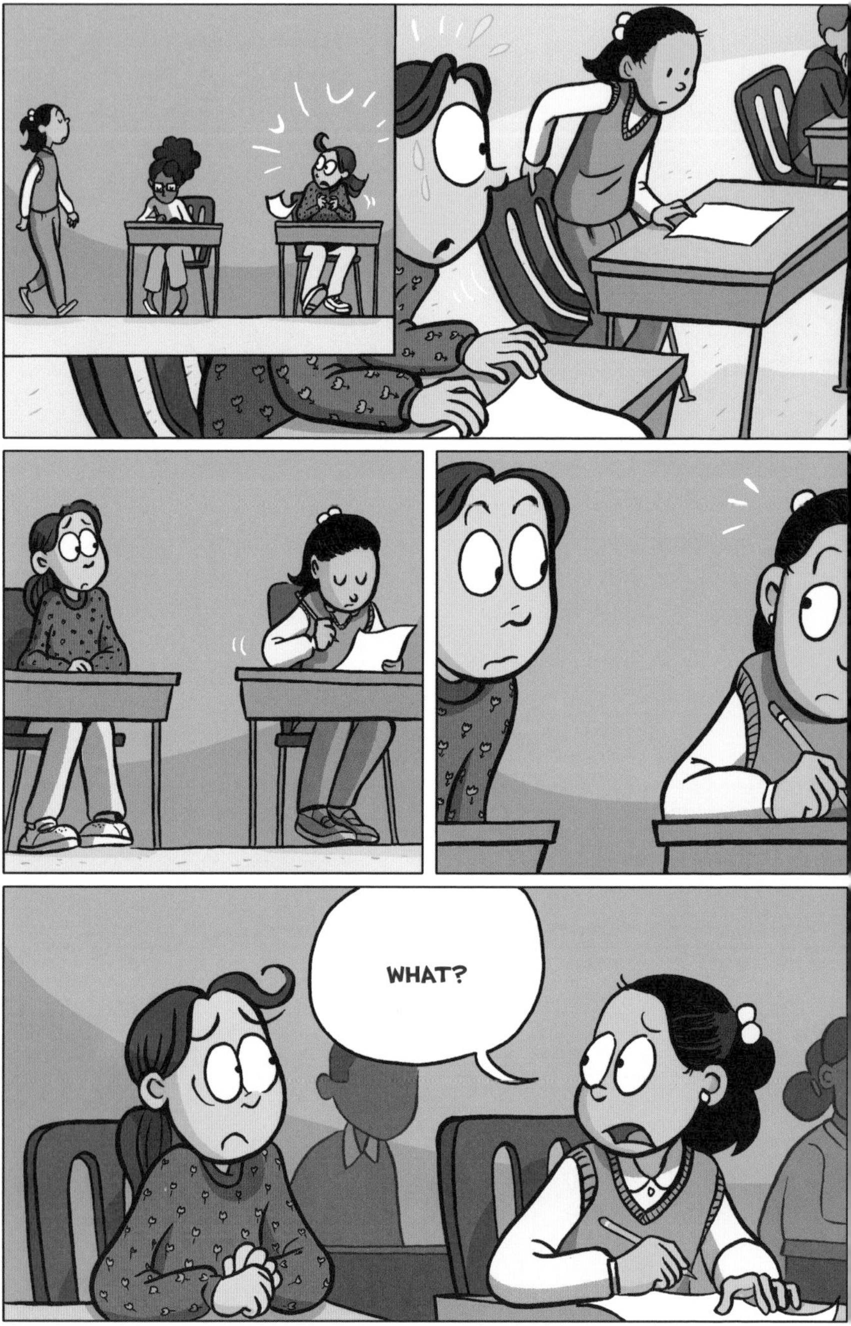
WHAT?

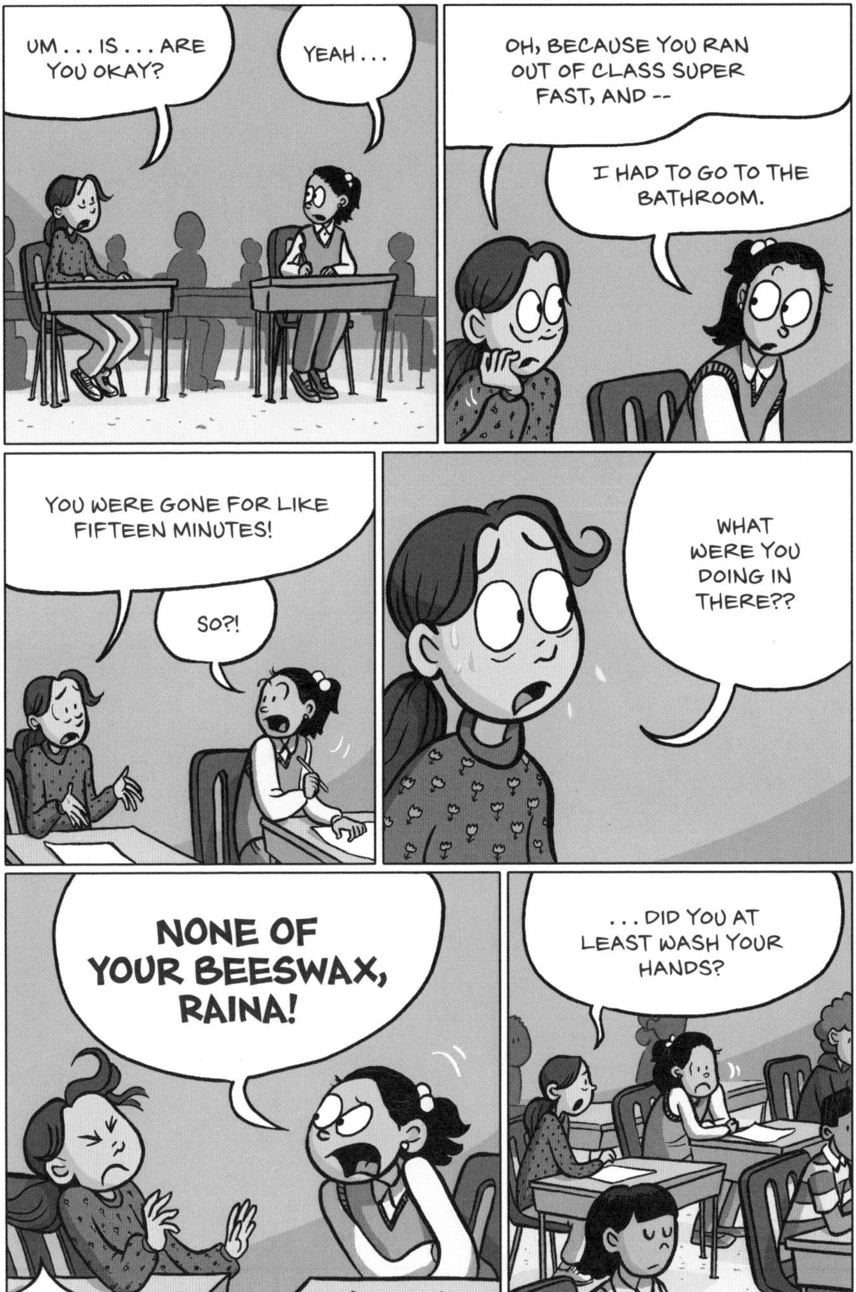
UM . . . IS . . . ARE YOU OKAY?
YEAH . . .
OH, BECAUSE YOU RAN OUT OF CLASS SUPER FAST, AND --
I HAD TO GO TO THE BATHROOM.
YOU WERE GONE FOR LIKE FIFTEEN MINUTES!
SO?!
WHAT WERE YOU DOING IN THERE??
NONE OF YOUR BEESWAX, RAINA!
. . . DID YOU AT LEAST WASH YOUR HANDS?

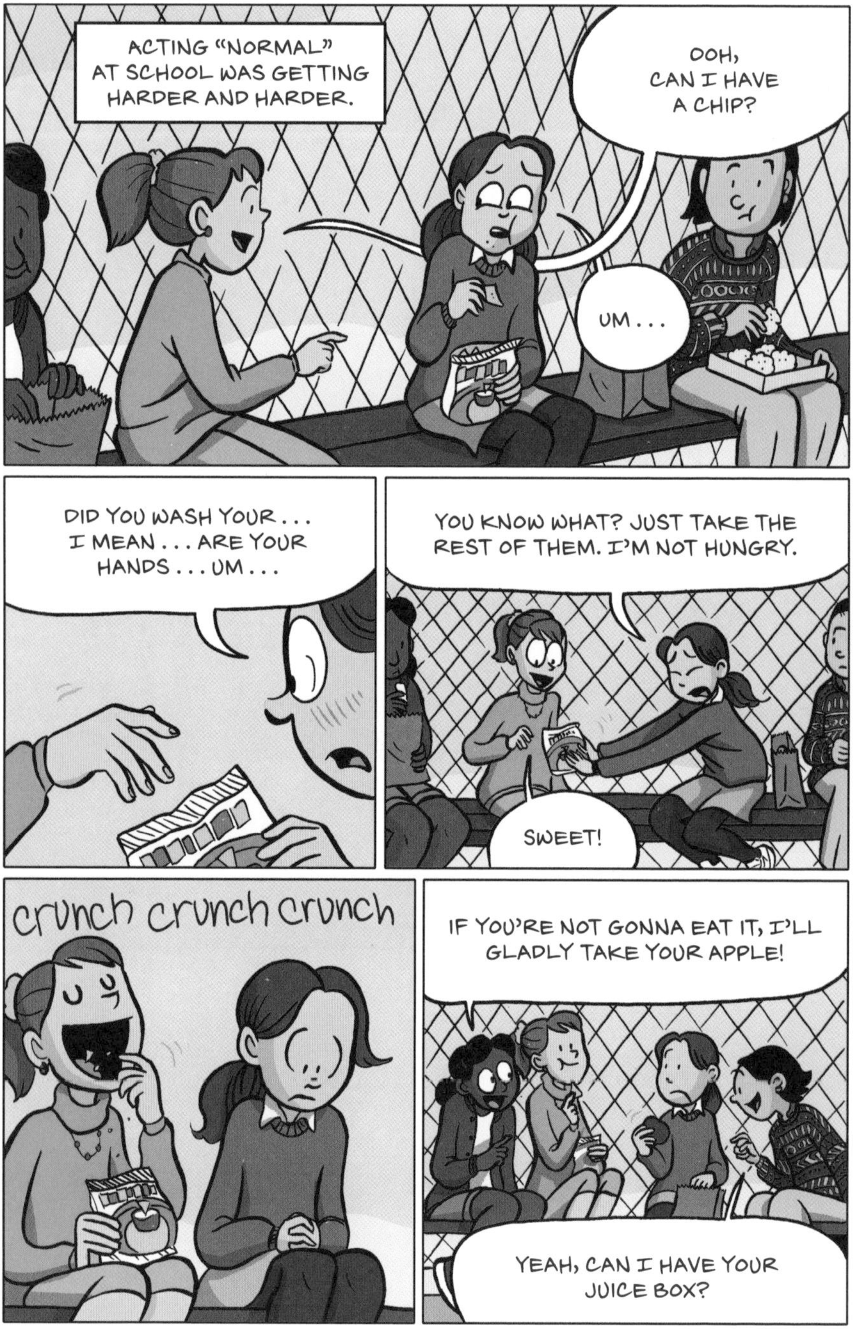
ACTING "NORMAL" AT SCHOOL WAS GETTING HARDER AND HARDER.
OOH, CAN I HAVE A CHIP?
UM . . .
DID YOU WASH YOUR . . . I MEAN . . . ARE YOUR HANDS . . . UM . . .
YOU KNOW WHAT? JUST TAKE THE REST OF THEM. I'M NOT HUNGRY.
SWEET!
crunch crunch crunch
IF YOU'RE NOT GONNA EAT IT, I'LL GLADLY TAKE YOUR APPLE!
YEAH, CAN I HAVE YOUR JUICE BOX?

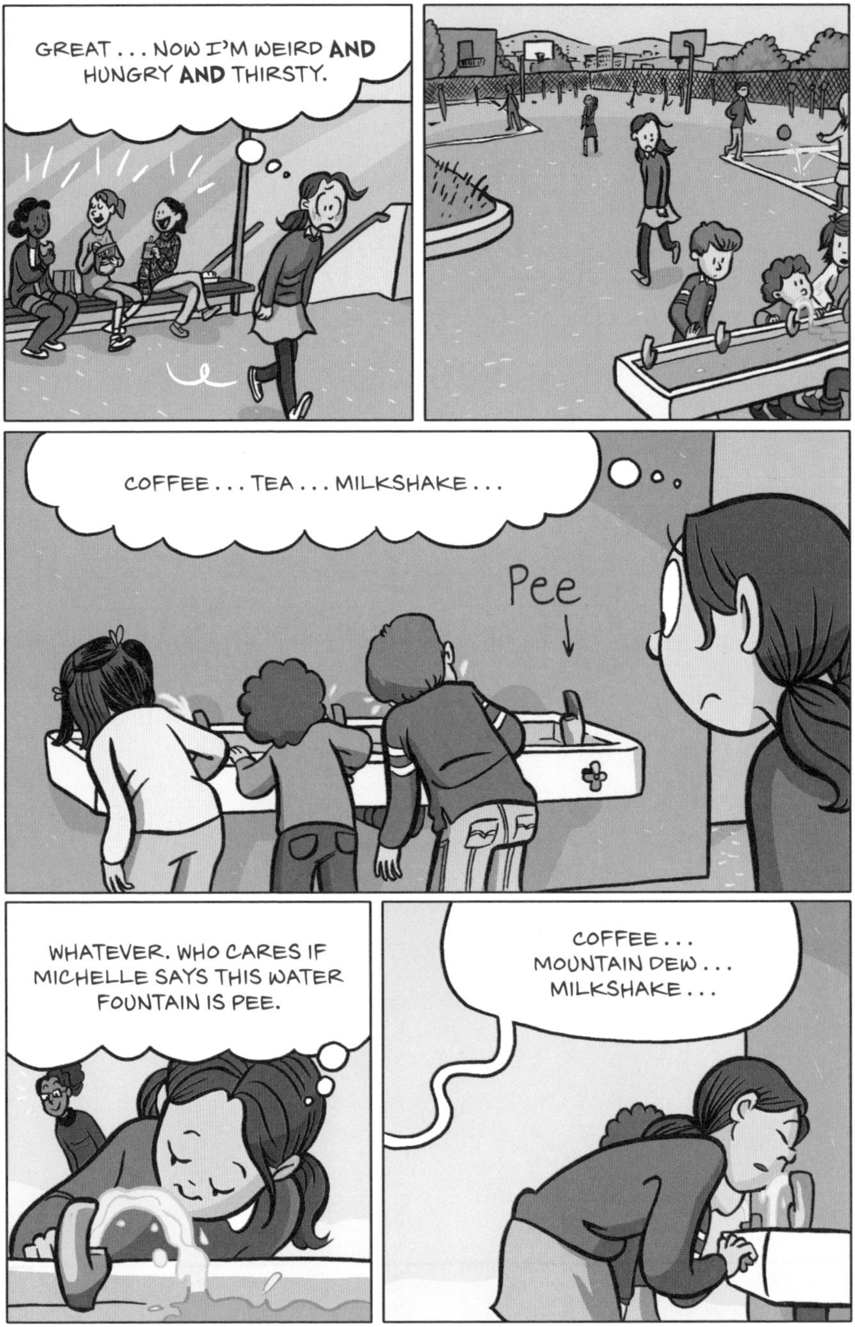
GREAT . . . NOW I'M WEIRD **AND** HUNGRY **AND** THIRSTY.
COFFEE . . . TEA . . . MILKSHAKE . . .
Pee
WHATEVER. WHO CARES IF MICHELLE SAYS THIS WATER FOUNTAIN IS PEE.
COFFEE . . . MOUNTAIN DEW . . . MILKSHAKE . . .

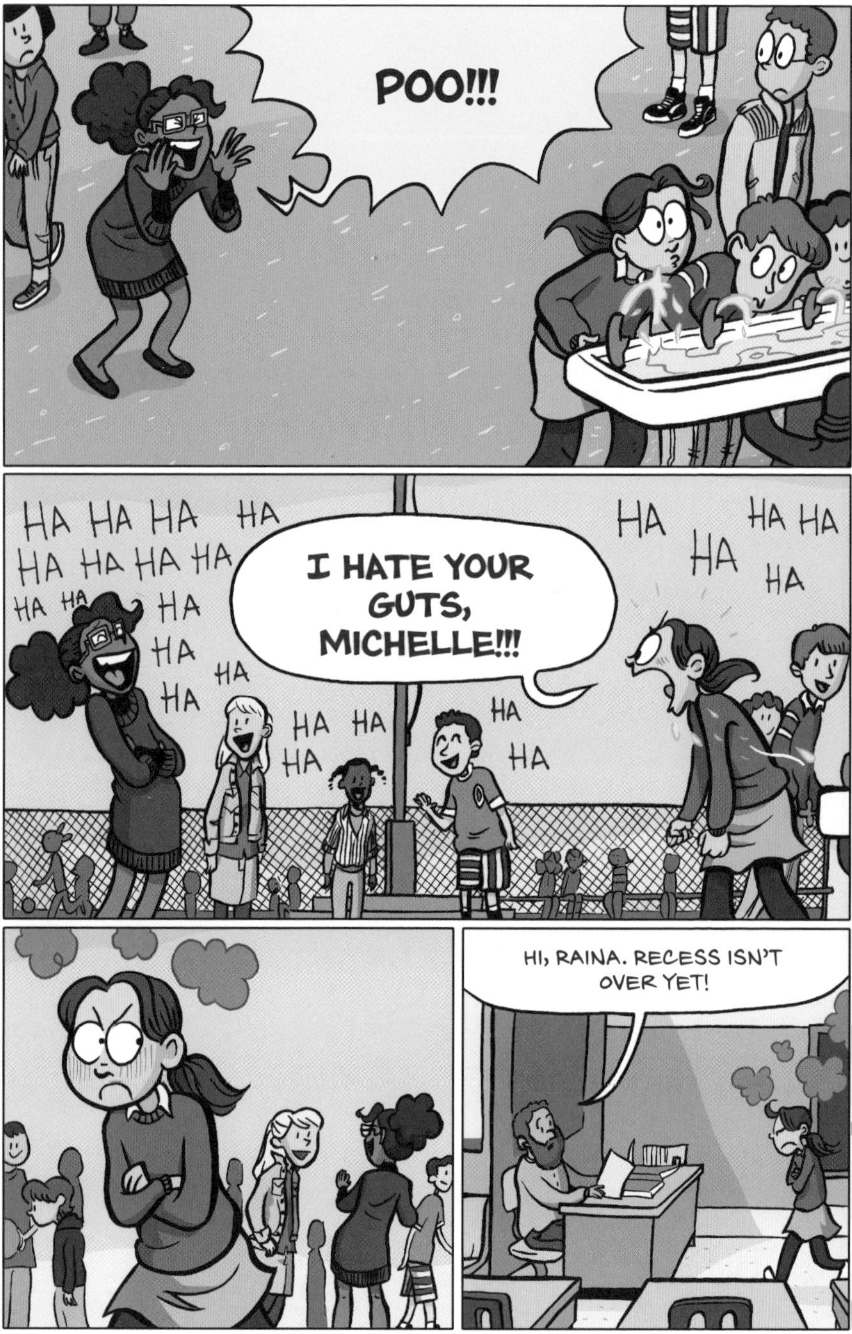
POO!!!
HA HA HA HA
HA HA HA HA
HA HA HA
HA
HA
HA
I HATE YOUR GUTS, MICHELLE!!!
HA HA
HA
HA
HA
HA HA HA
HA
HA
HA
HI, RAINA. RECESS ISN'T OVER YET!

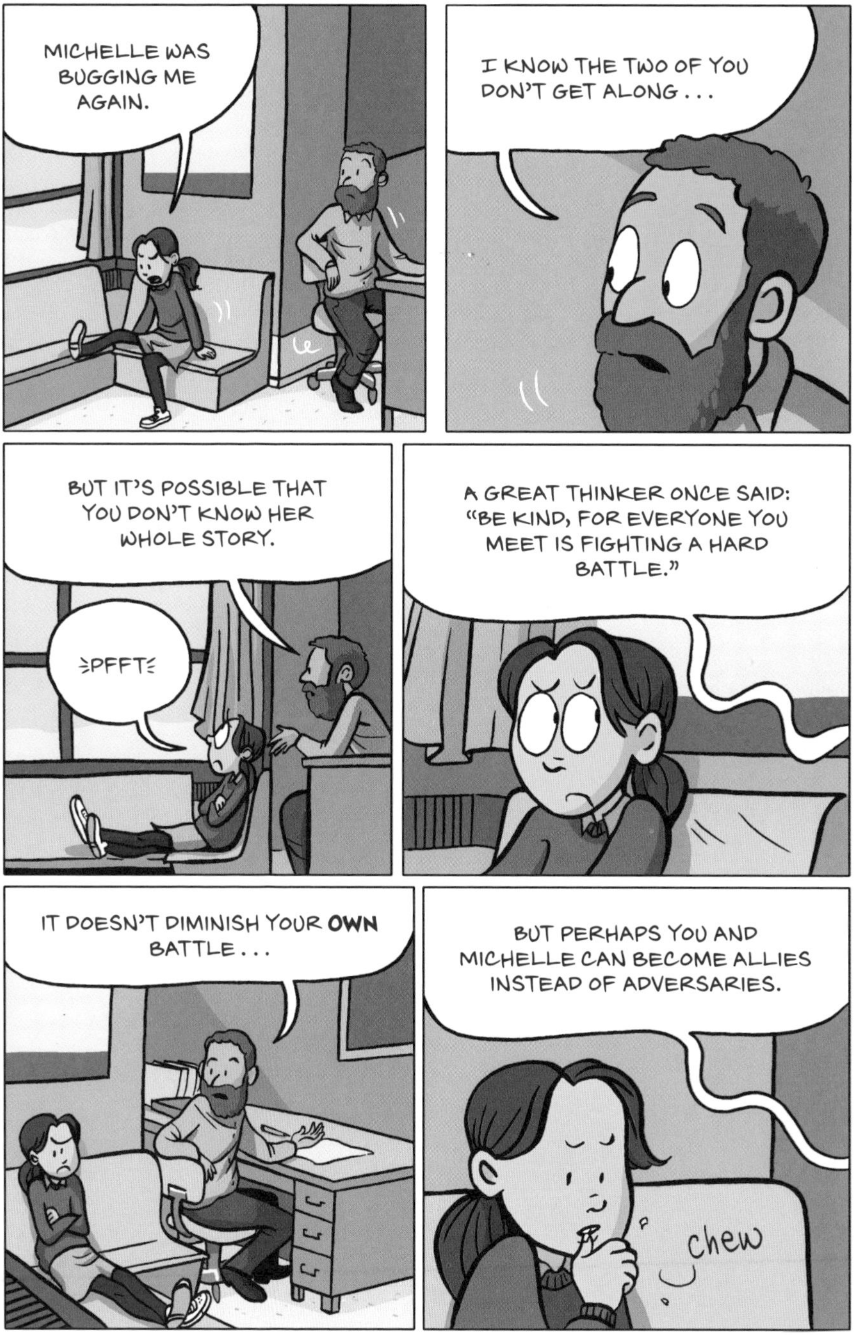

MICHELLE WAS BUGGING ME AGAIN.
I KNOW THE TWO OF YOU DON'T GET ALONG . . .
BUT IT'S POSSIBLE THAT YOU DON'T KNOW HER WHOLE STORY.
PFFT
A GREAT THINKER ONCE SAID: "BE KIND, FOR EVERYONE YOU MEET IS FIGHTING A HARD BATTLE."
IT DOESN'T DIMINISH YOUR **OWN** BATTLE . . .
BUT PERHAPS YOU AND MICHELLE CAN BECOME ALLIES INSTEAD OF ADVERSARIES.
chew

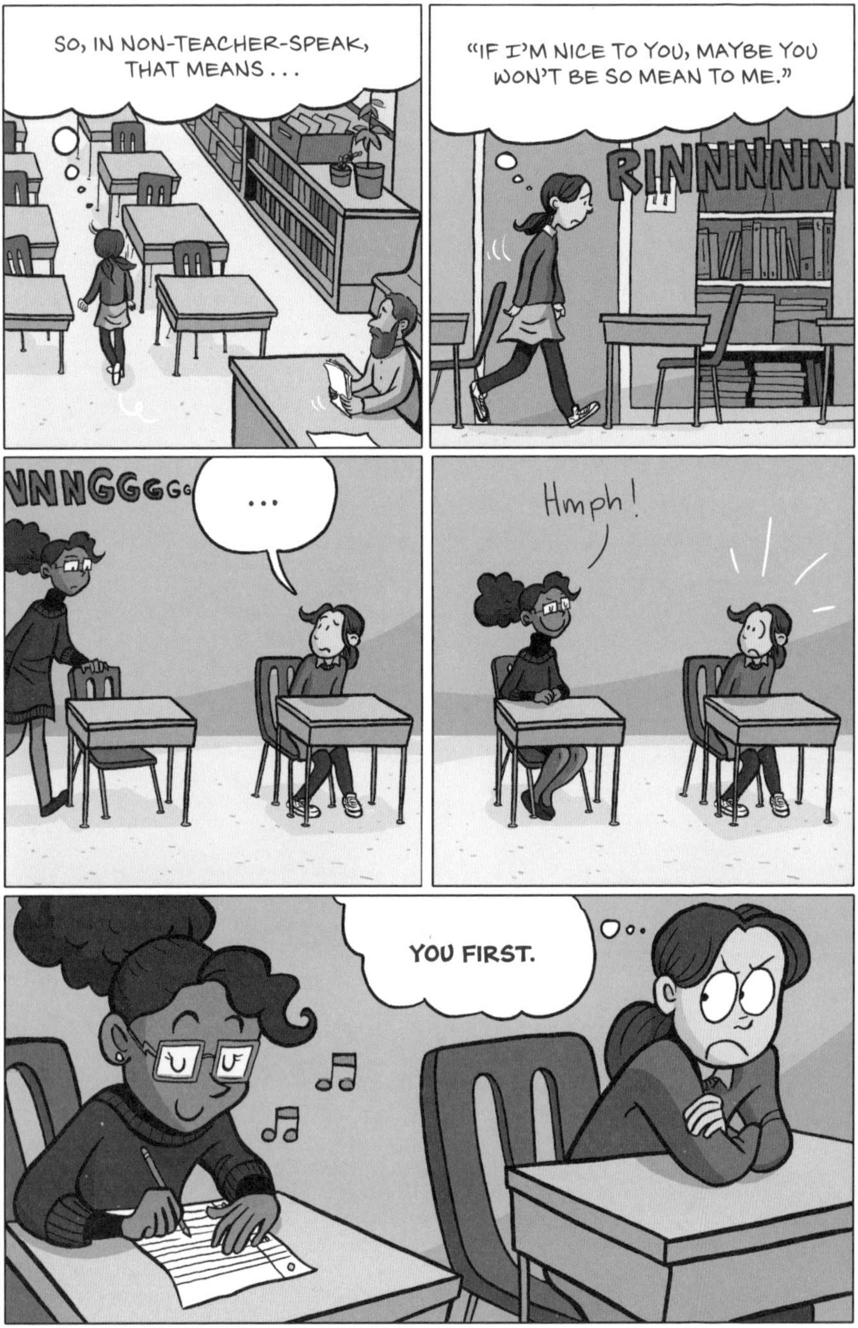
SO, IN NON-TEACHER-SPEAK, THAT MEANS . . .
"IF I'M NICE TO YOU, MAYBE YOU WON'T BE SO MEAN TO ME."
RINNNNNNNNGGGGG
...
Hmph!
YOU FIRST.

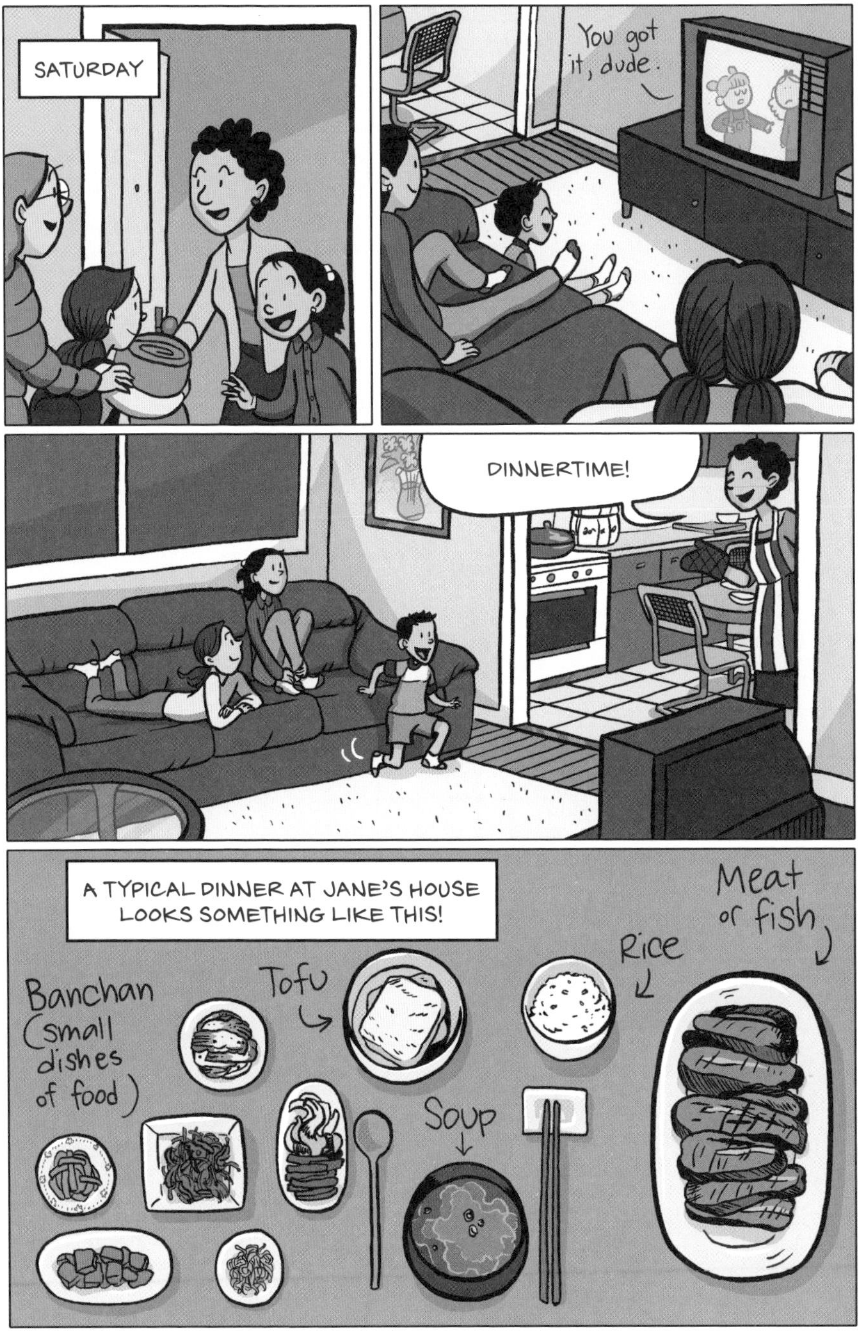
SATURDAY
You got it, dude.
DINNERTIME!
A TYPICAL DINNER AT JANE'S HOUSE LOOKS SOMETHING LIKE THIS!
Meat or fish
Rice
Tofu
Banchan (small dishes of food)
Soup

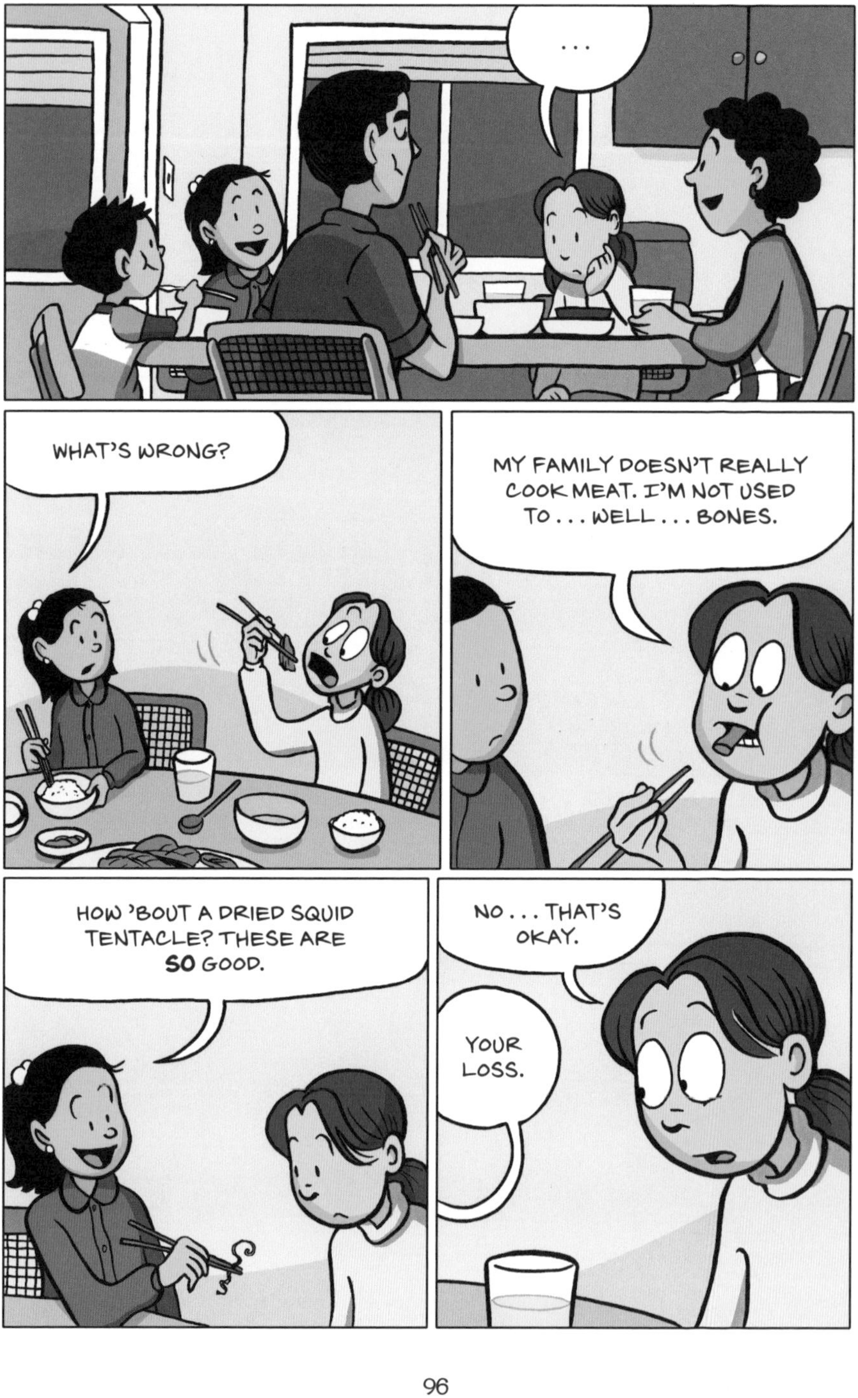
...
WHAT'S WRONG?
MY FAMILY DOESN'T REALLY COOK MEAT. I'M NOT USED TO . . . WELL . . . BONES.
HOW 'BOUT A DRIED SQUID TENTACLE? THESE ARE **SO** GOOD.
NO . . . THAT'S OKAY.
YOUR LOSS.

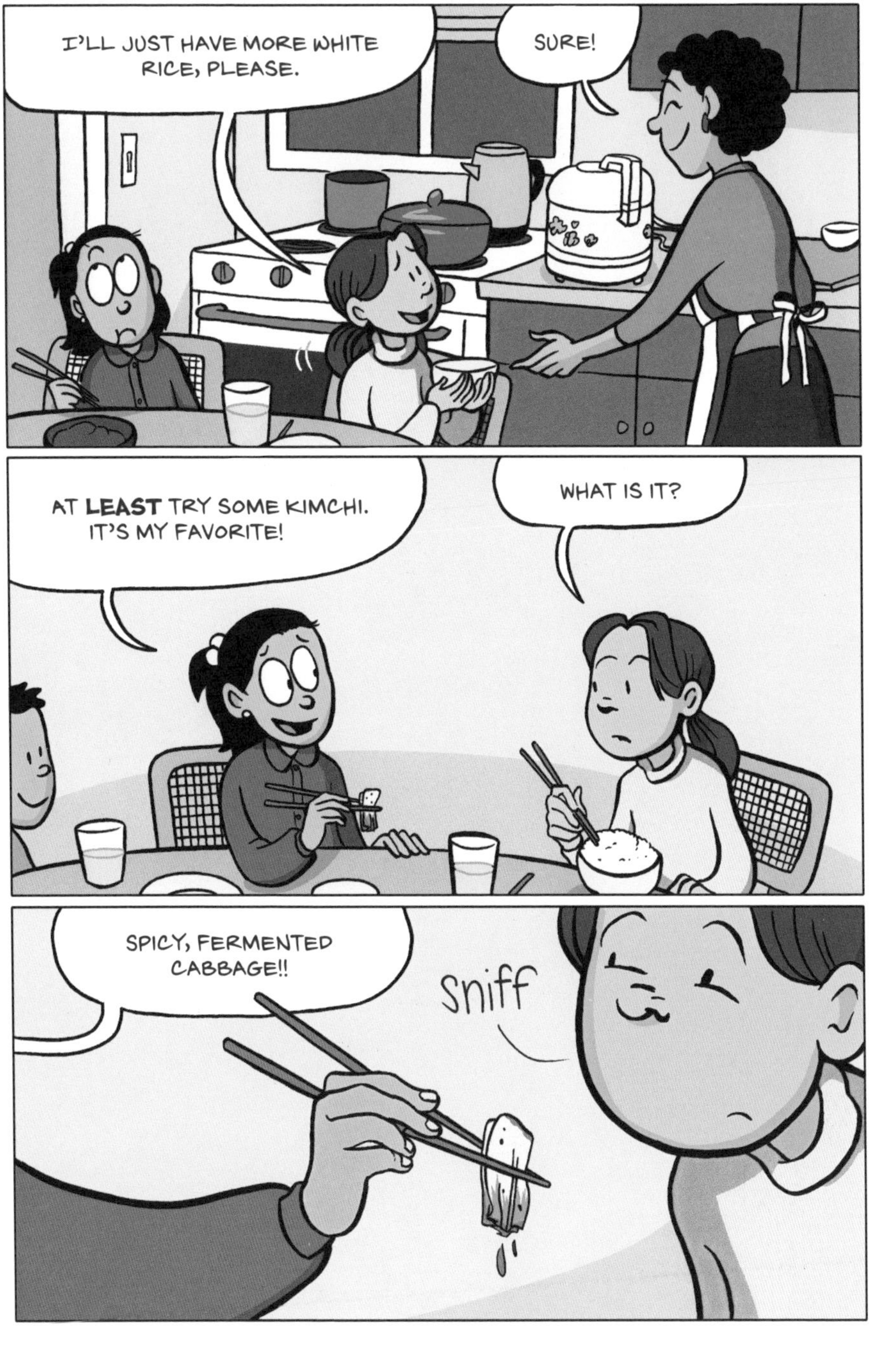
I'LL JUST HAVE MORE WHITE RICE, PLEASE.
SURE!
AT **LEAST** TRY SOME KIMCHI. IT'S MY FAVORITE!
WHAT IS IT?
SPICY, FERMENTED CABBAGE!!
sniff

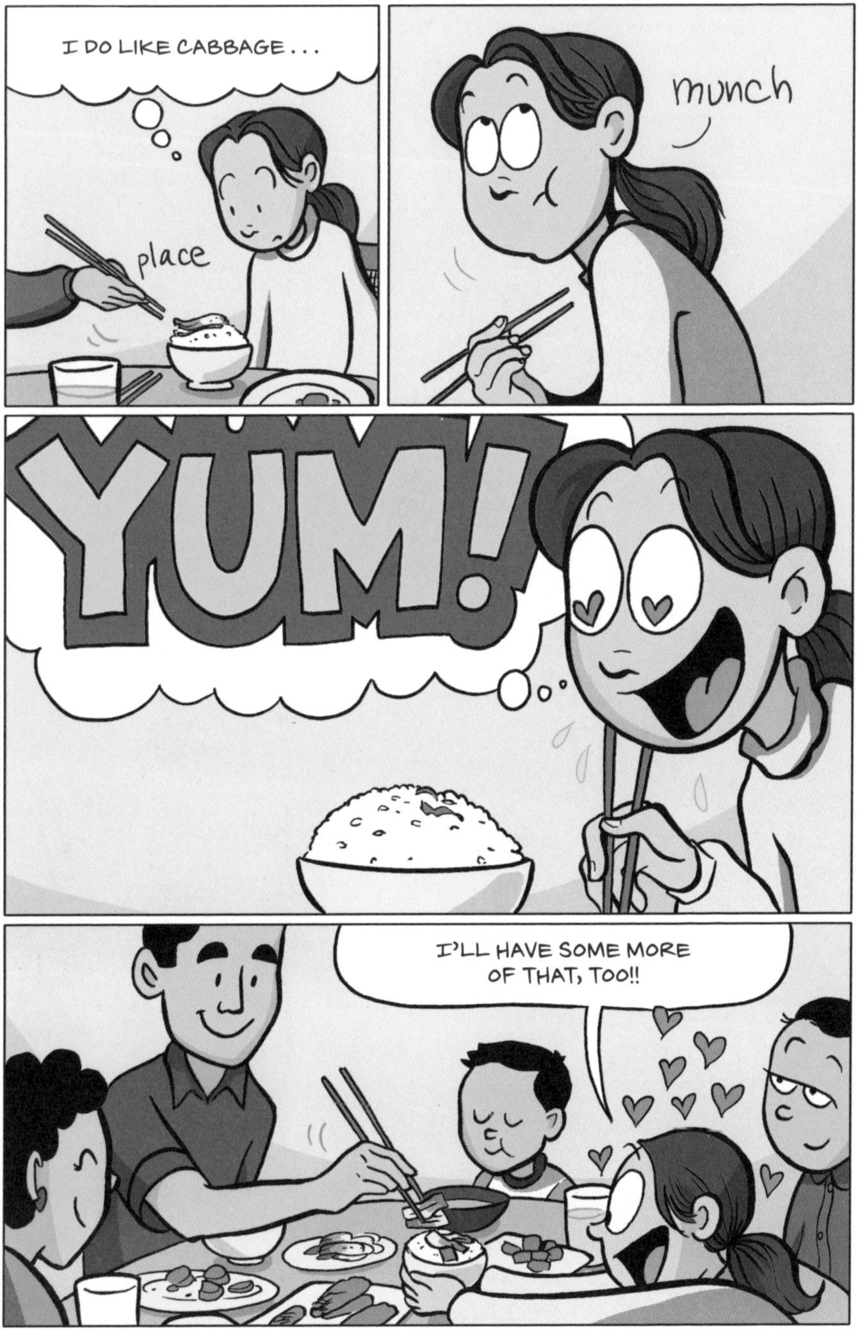
I DO LIKE CABBAGE . . .
place
munch
YUM!
I'LL HAVE SOME MORE OF THAT, TOO!!

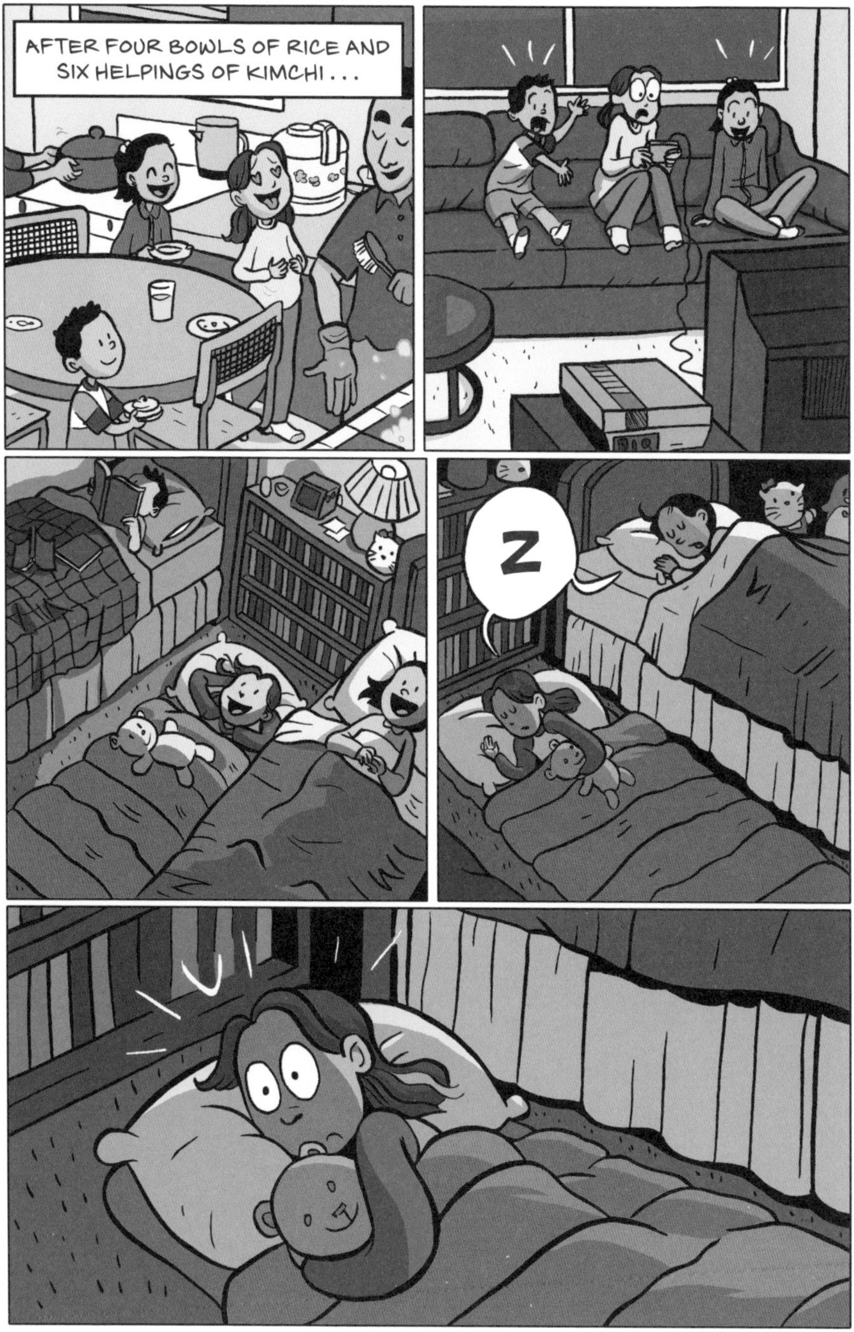
AFTER FOUR BOWLS OF RICE AND
SIX HELPINGS OF KIMCHI . . .
Z

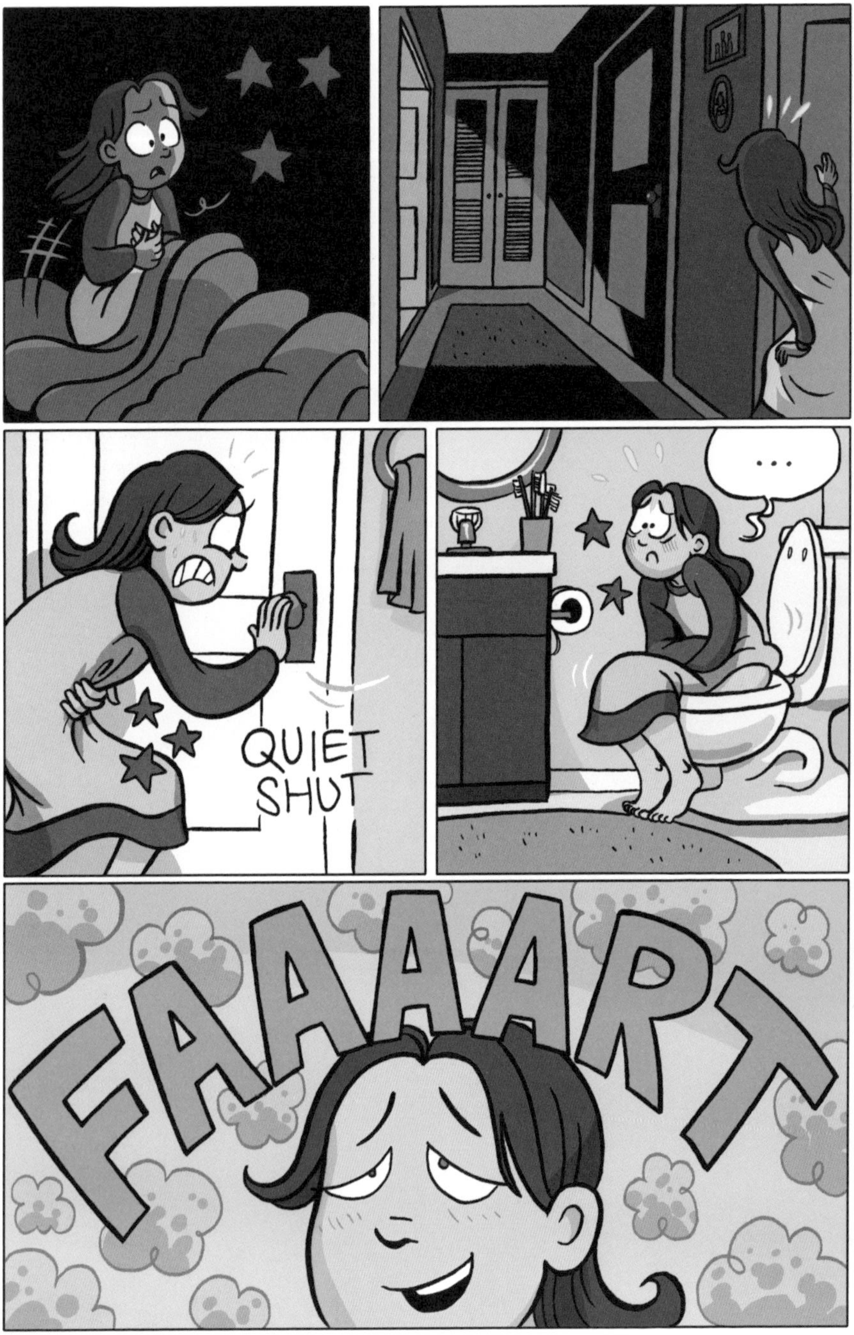
...
QUIET SHUT
FAAAART

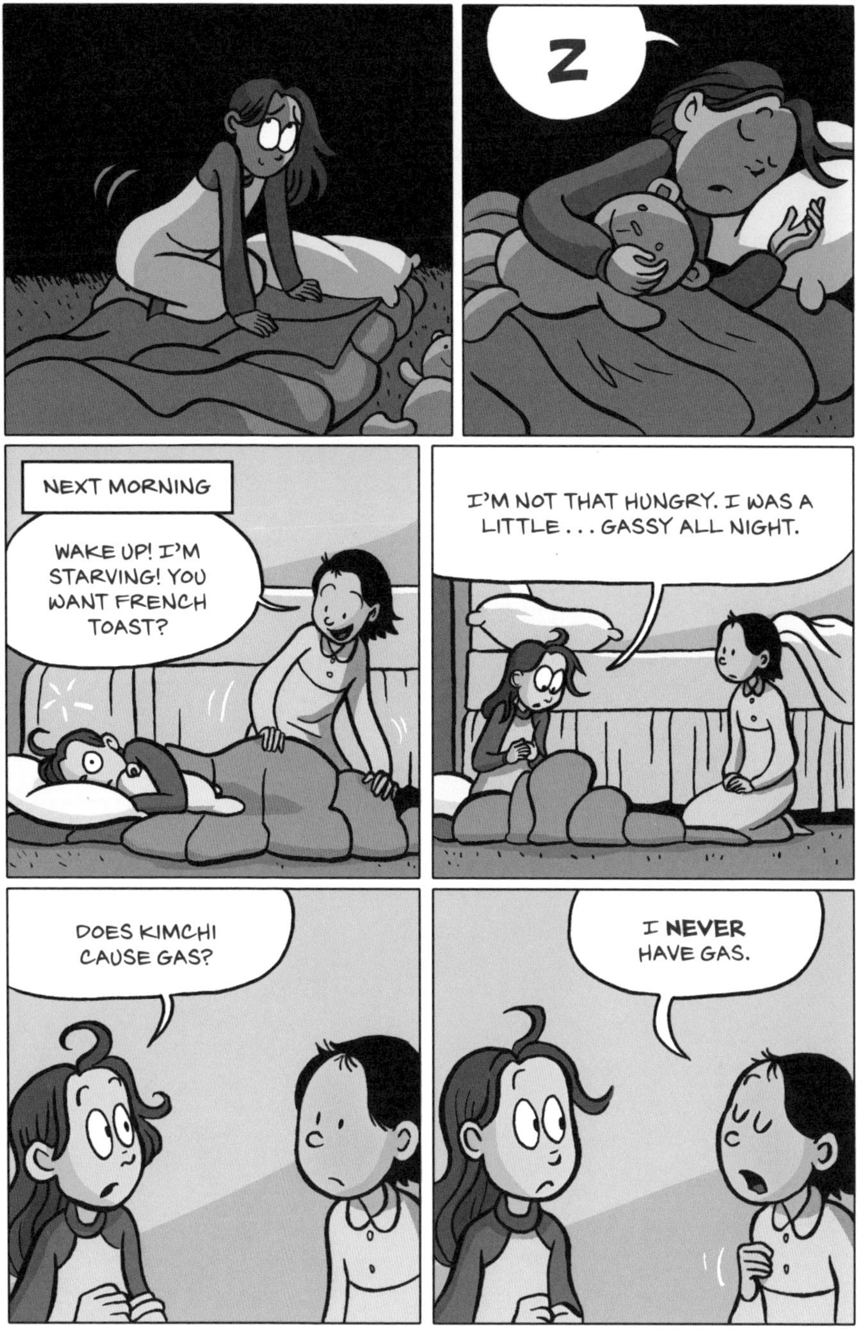
Z
NEXT MORNING
WAKE UP! I'M STARVING! YOU WANT FRENCH TOAST?
I'M NOT THAT HUNGRY. I WAS A LITTLE . . . GASSY ALL NIGHT.
DOES KIMCHI CAUSE GAS?
I **NEVER** HAVE GAS.

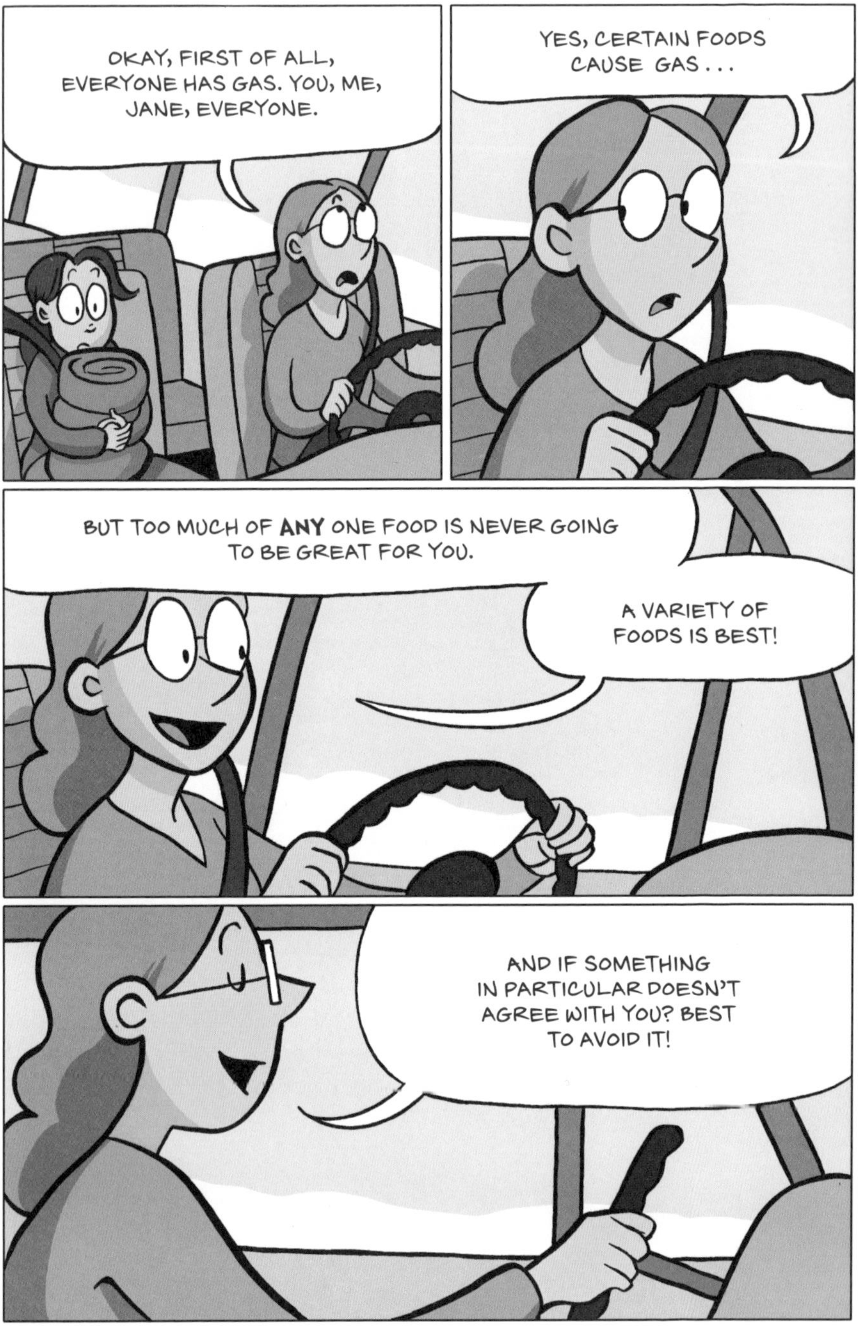
OKAY, FIRST OF ALL, EVERYONE HAS GAS. YOU, ME, JANE, EVERYONE.
YES, CERTAIN FOODS CAUSE GAS . . .
BUT TOO MUCH OF **ANY** ONE FOOD IS NEVER GOING TO BE GREAT FOR YOU.
A VARIETY OF FOODS IS BEST!
AND IF SOMETHING IN PARTICULAR DOESN'T AGREE WITH YOU? BEST TO AVOID IT!

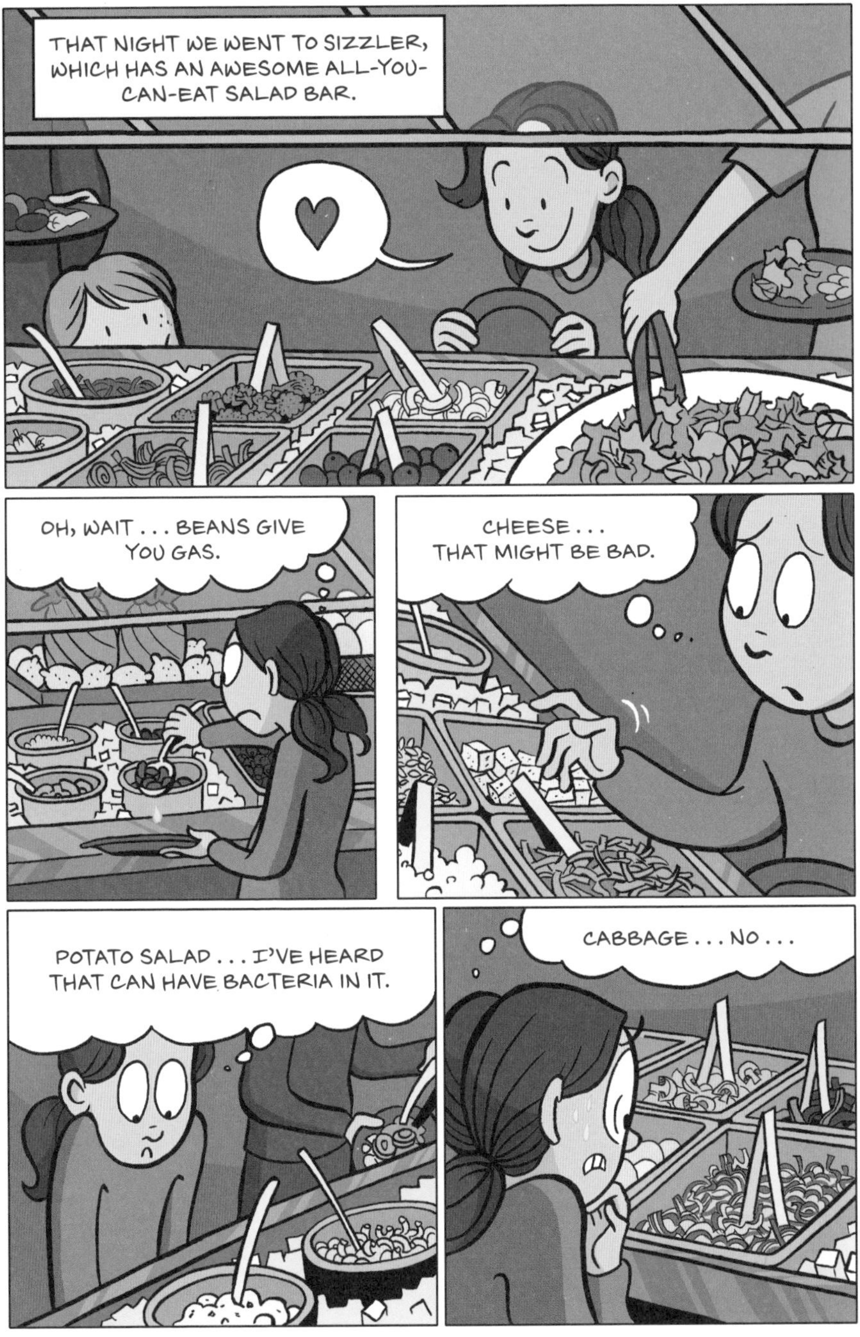
THAT NIGHT WE WENT TO SIZZLER, WHICH HAS AN AWESOME ALL-YOU-CAN-EAT SALAD BAR.
OH, WAIT . . . BEANS GIVE YOU GAS.
CHEESE . . . THAT MIGHT BE BAD.
POTATO SALAD . . . I'VE HEARD THAT CAN HAVE BACTERIA IN IT.
CABBAGE . . . NO . . .

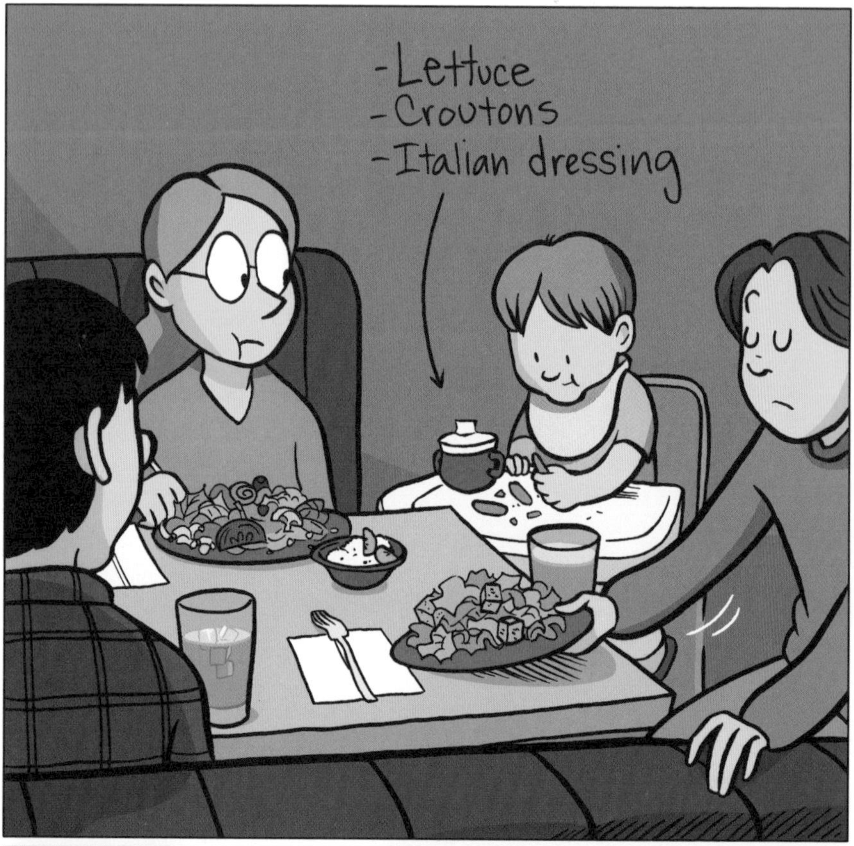
-Lettuce
-Croutons
-Italian dressing

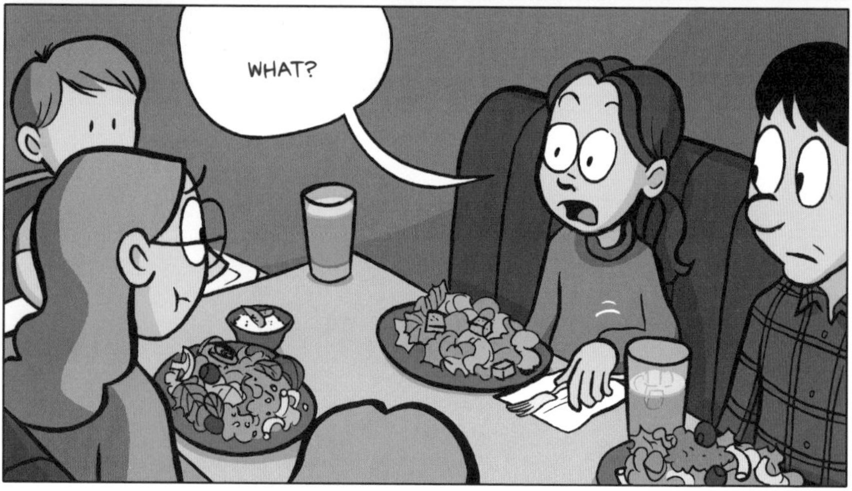
WHAT?

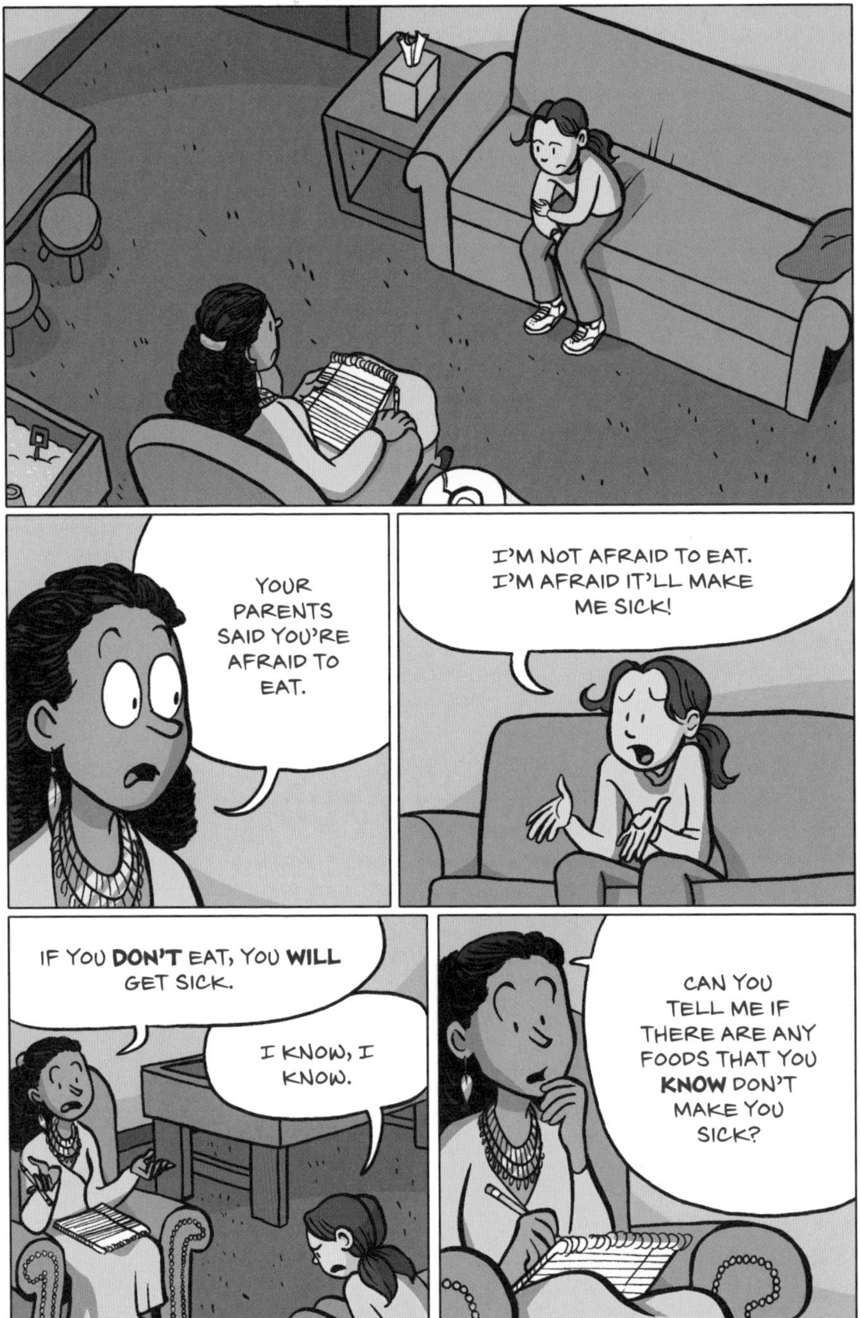
YOUR PARENTS SAID YOU'RE AFRAID TO EAT.
I'M NOT AFRAID TO EAT. I'M AFRAID IT'LL MAKE ME SICK!
IF YOU **DON'T** EAT, YOU **WILL** GET SICK.
I KNOW, I KNOW.
CAN YOU TELL ME IF THERE ARE ANY FOODS THAT YOU **KNOW** DON'T MAKE YOU SICK?

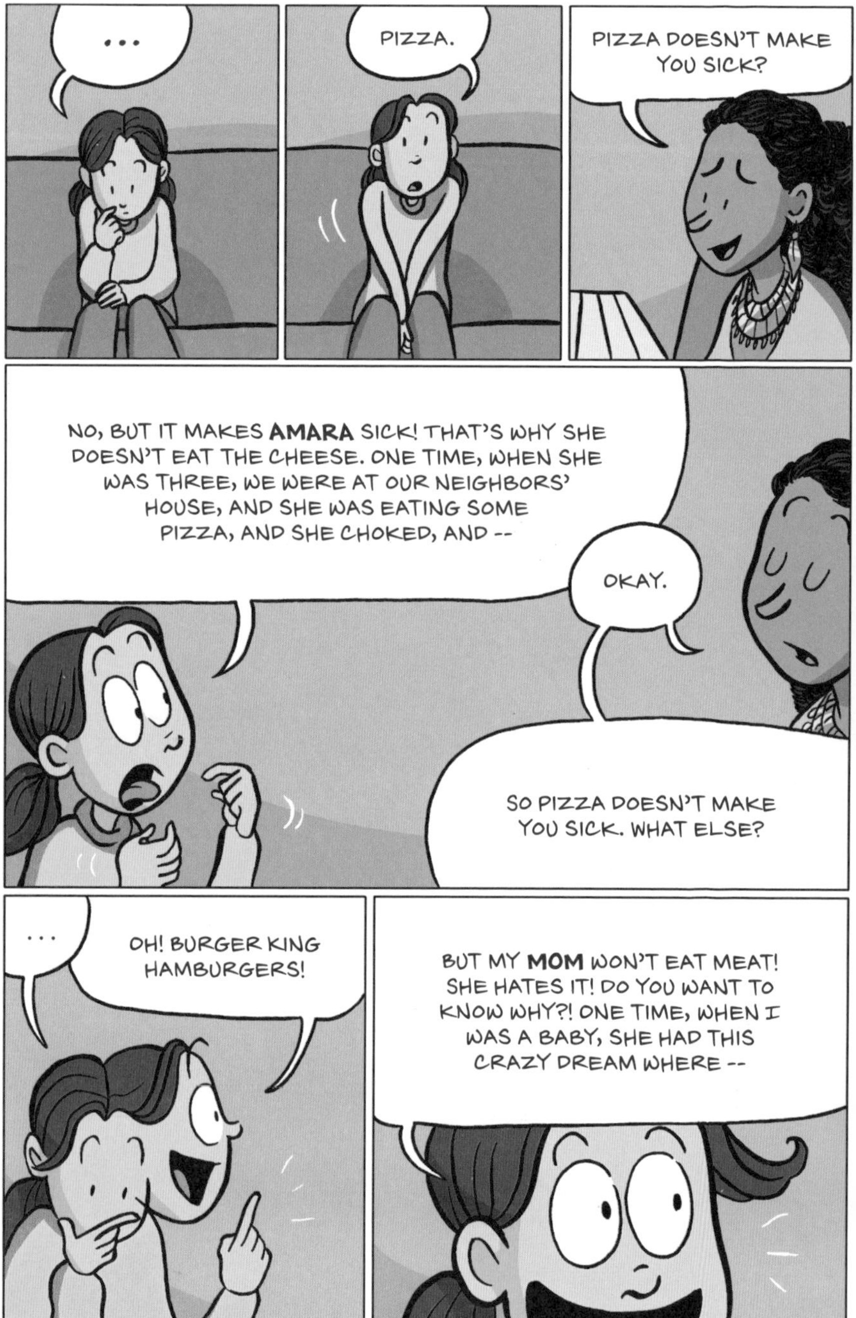
...
PIZZA.
PIZZA DOESN'T MAKE YOU SICK?
NO, BUT IT MAKES **AMARA** SICK! THAT'S WHY SHE DOESN'T EAT THE CHEESE. ONE TIME, WHEN SHE WAS THREE, WE WERE AT OUR NEIGHBORS' HOUSE, AND SHE WAS EATING SOME PIZZA, AND SHE CHOKED, AND --
OKAY.
SO PIZZA DOESN'T MAKE YOU SICK. WHAT ELSE?
...
OH! BURGER KING HAMBURGERS!
BUT MY **MOM** WON'T EAT MEAT! SHE HATES IT! DO YOU WANT TO KNOW WHY?! ONE TIME, WHEN I WAS A BABY, SHE HAD THIS CRAZY DREAM WHERE --

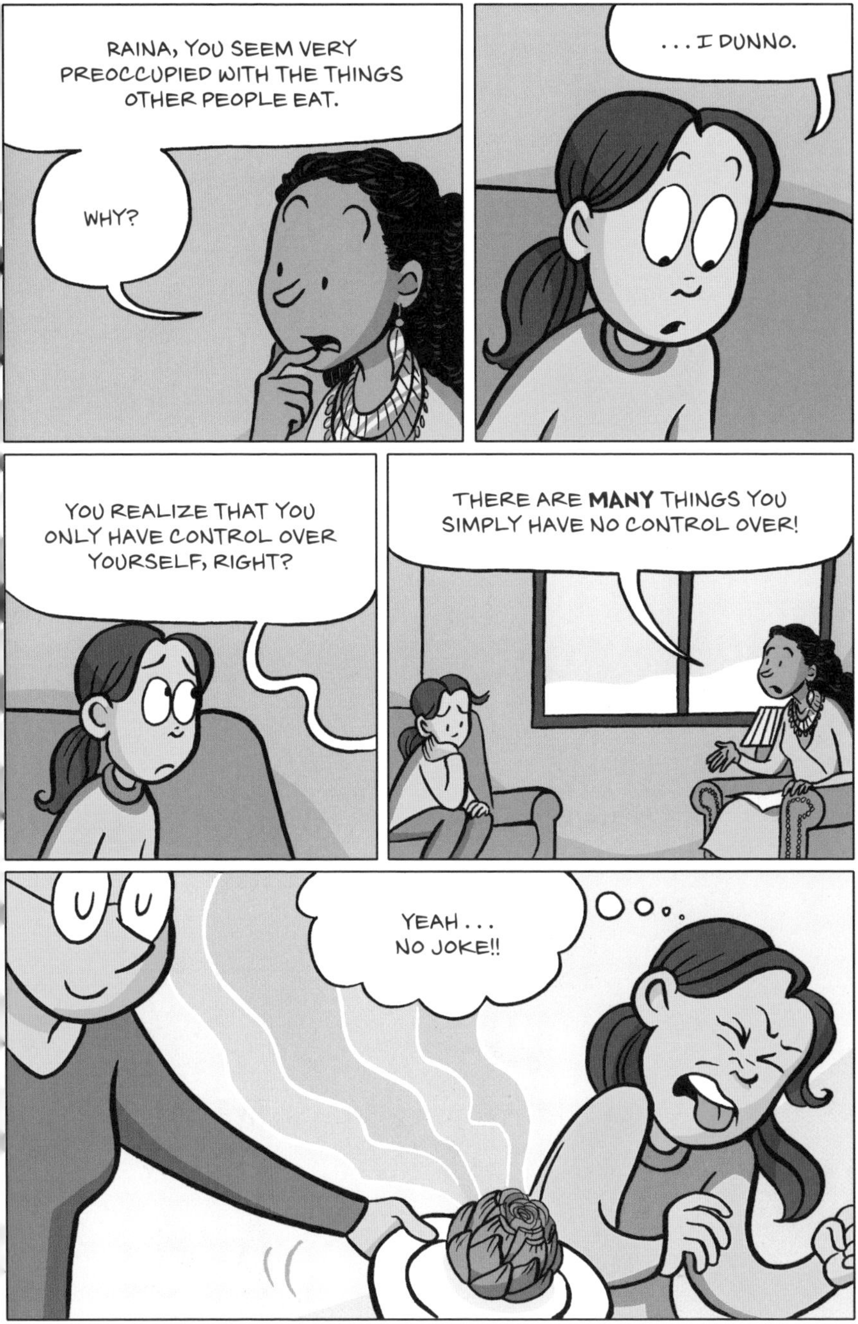
RAINA, YOU SEEM VERY PREOCCUPIED WITH THE THINGS OTHER PEOPLE EAT.
WHY?
. . . I DUNNO.
YOU REALIZE THAT YOU ONLY HAVE CONTROL OVER YOURSELF, RIGHT?
THERE ARE MANY THINGS YOU SIMPLY HAVE NO CONTROL OVER!
YEAH . . . NO JOKE!!

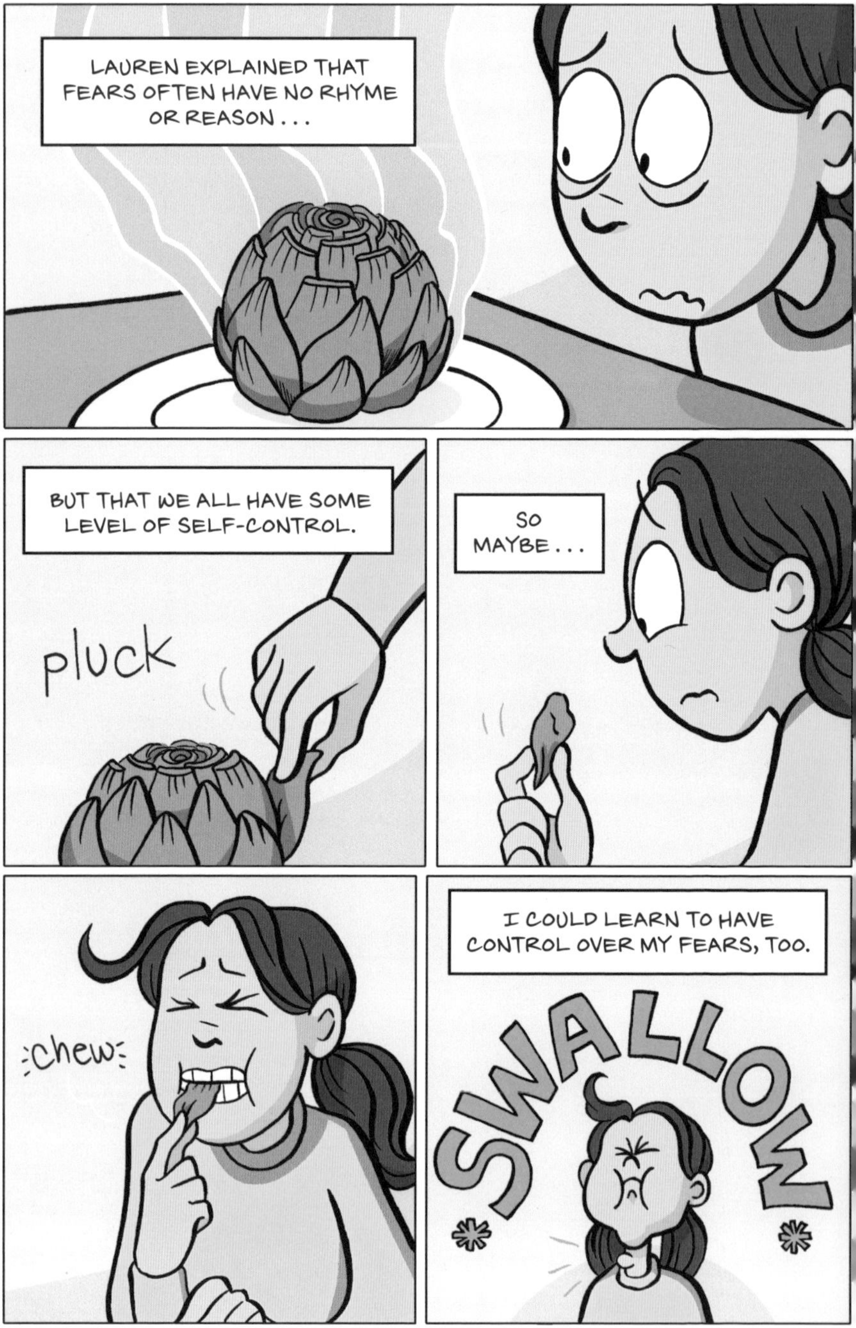
LAUREN EXPLAINED THAT FEARS OFTEN HAVE NO RHYME OR REASON . . .
BUT THAT WE ALL HAVE SOME LEVEL OF SELF-CONTROL.
pluck
SO MAYBE . . .
chew
I COULD LEARN TO HAVE CONTROL OVER MY FEARS, TOO.
SWALLOW

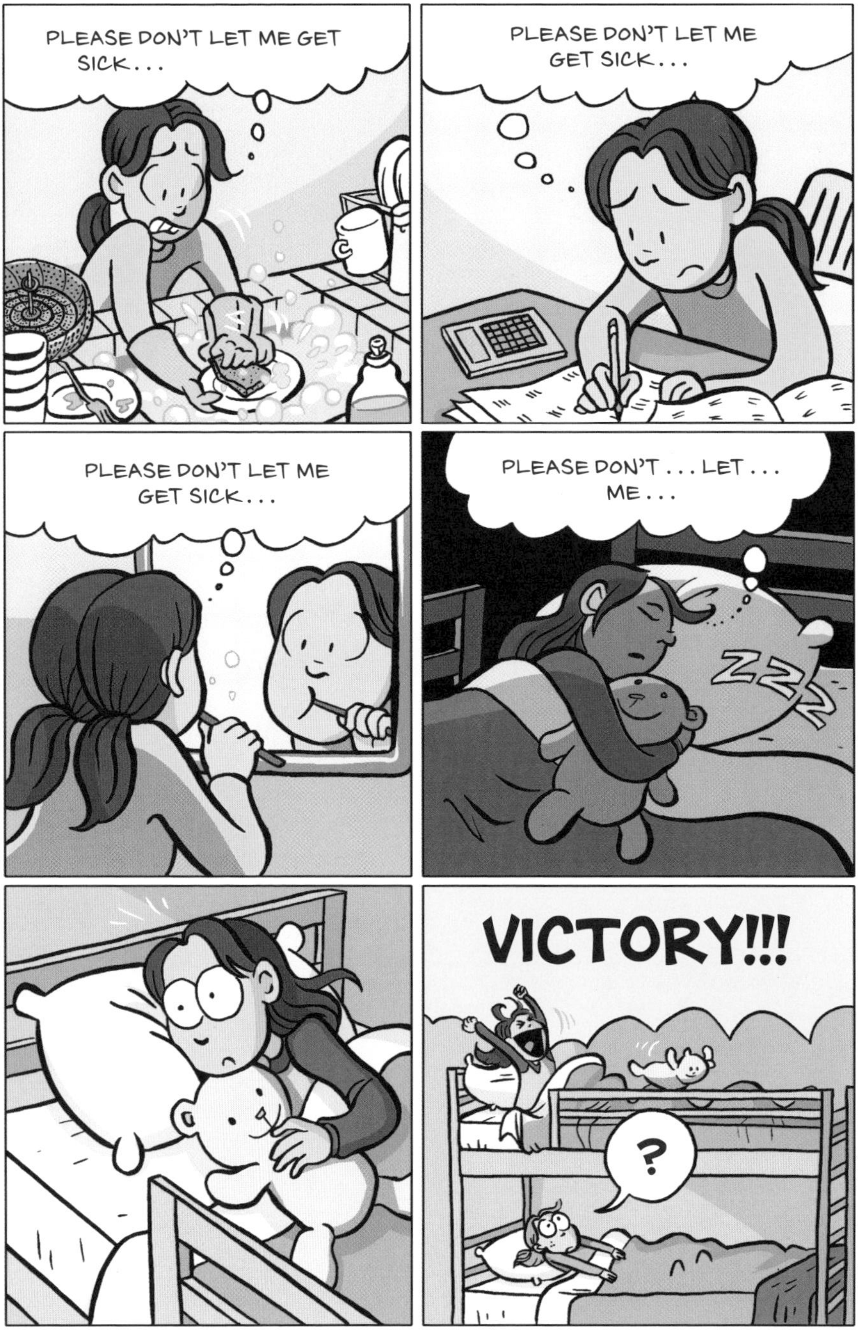
PLEASE DON'T LET ME GET SICK...
PLEASE DON'T LET ME GET SICK...
PLEASE DON'T LET ME GET SICK...
PLEASE DON'T ... LET ... ME ...
ZZZ
VICTORY!!!
?

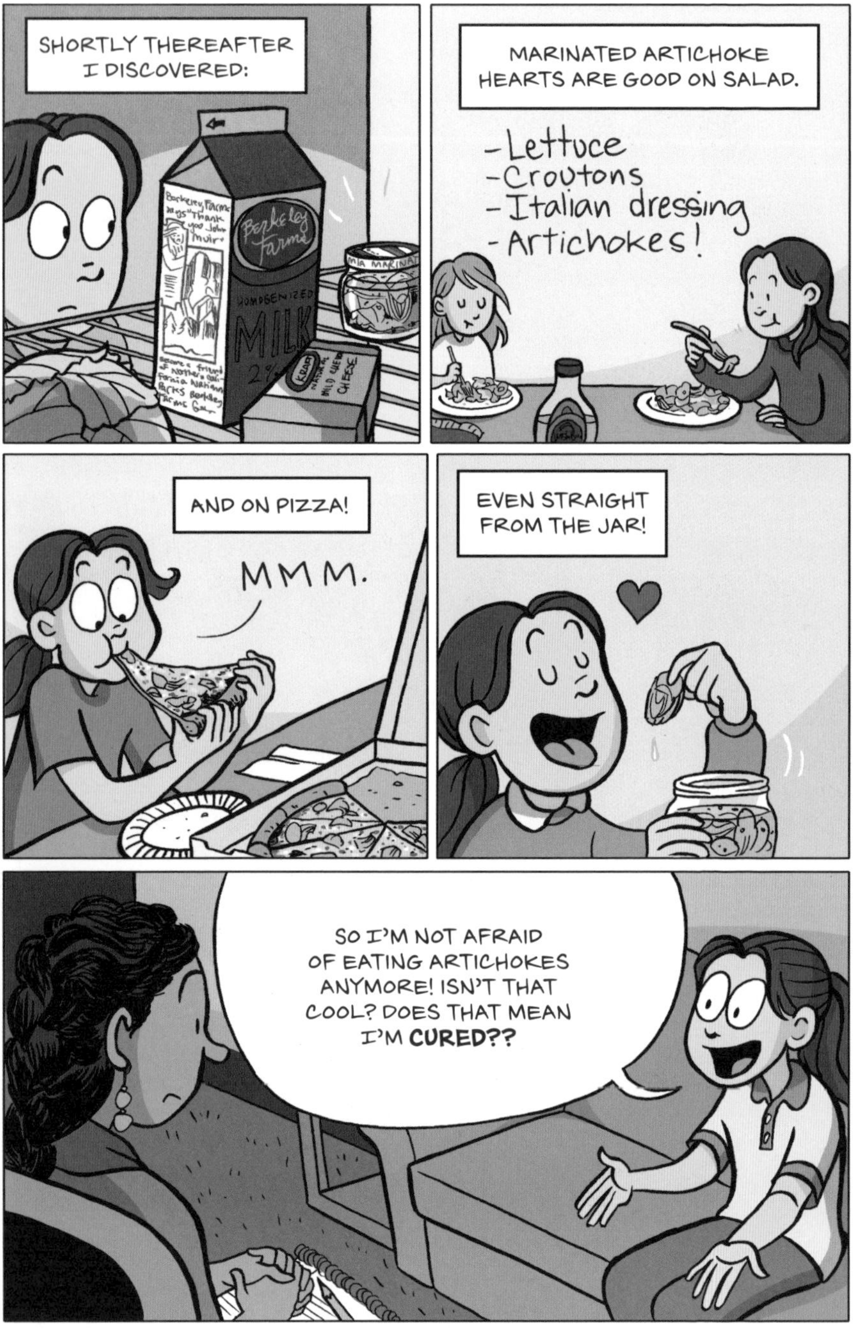

SHORTLY THEREAFTER I DISCOVERED:
MARINATED ARTICHOKE HEARTS ARE GOOD ON SALAD.
-Lettuce
-Croutons
-Italian dressing
-Artichokes!
AND ON PIZZA!
MMM.
EVEN STRAIGHT FROM THE JAR!
SO I'M NOT AFRAID OF EATING ARTICHOKES ANYMORE! ISN'T THAT COOL? DOES THAT MEAN I'M **CURED??**

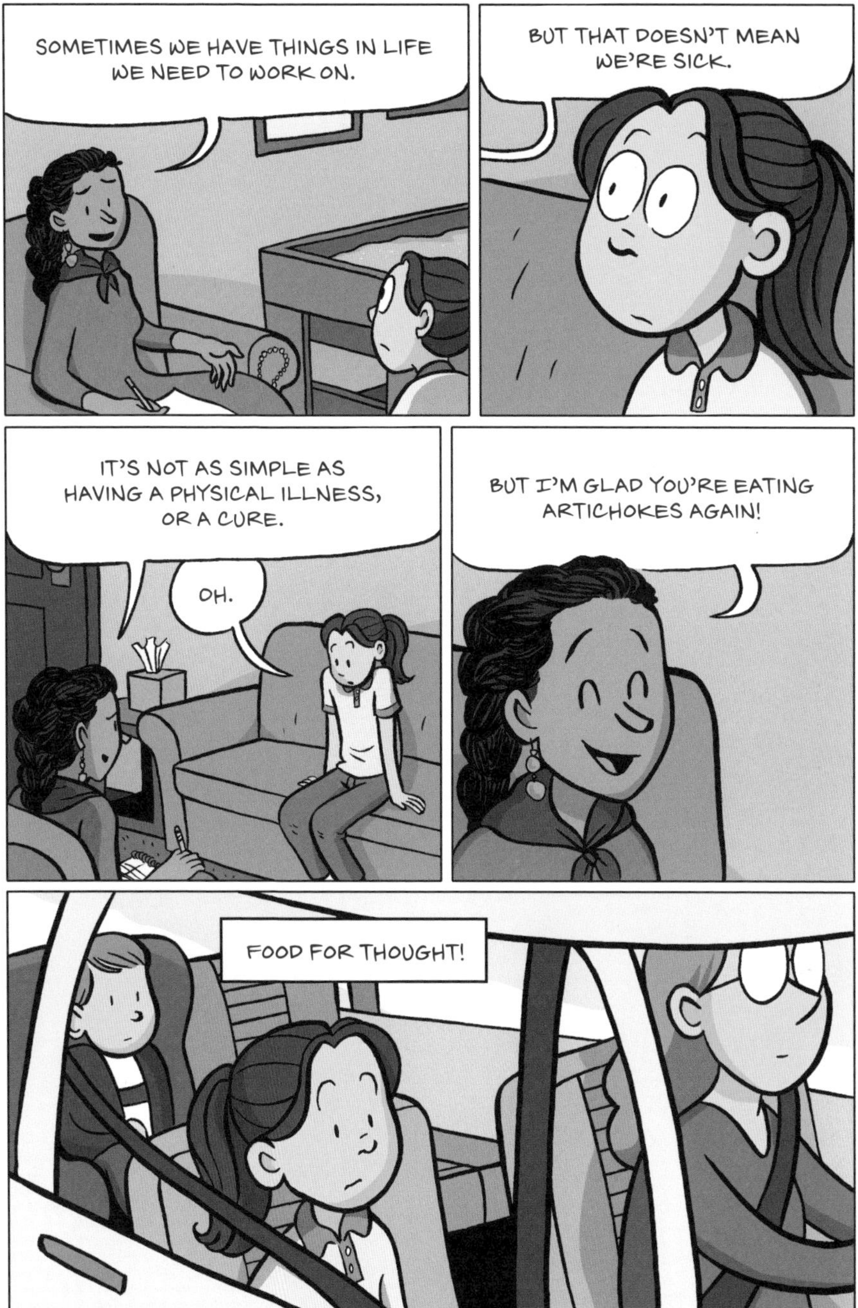
SOMETIMES WE HAVE THINGS IN LIFE WE NEED TO WORK ON.
BUT THAT DOESN'T MEAN WE'RE SICK.
IT'S NOT AS SIMPLE AS HAVING A PHYSICAL ILLNESS, OR A CURE.
OH.
BUT I'M GLAD YOU'RE EATING ARTICHOKES AGAIN!
FOOD FOR THOUGHT!

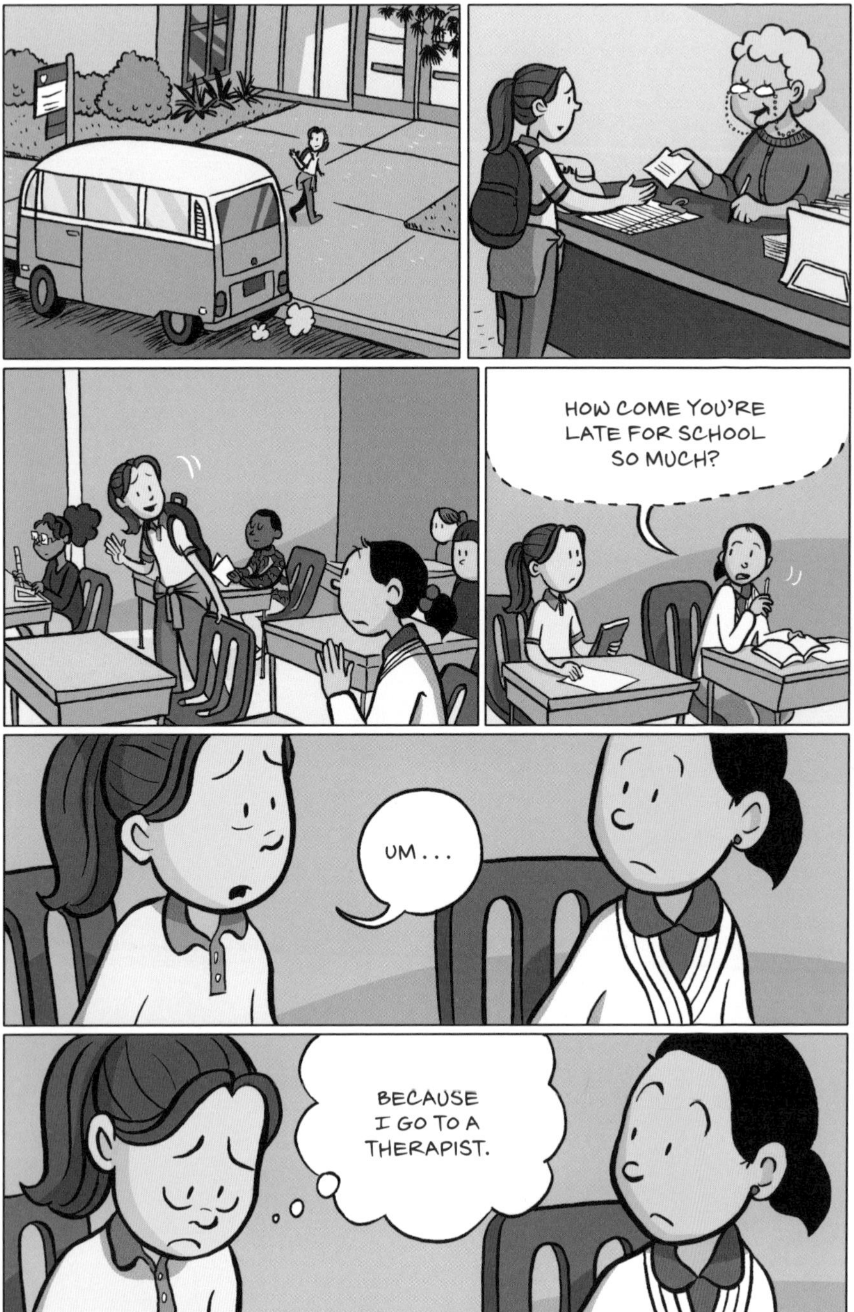
HOW COME YOU'RE LATE FOR SCHOOL SO MUCH?
UM . . .
BECAUSE I GO TO A THERAPIST.

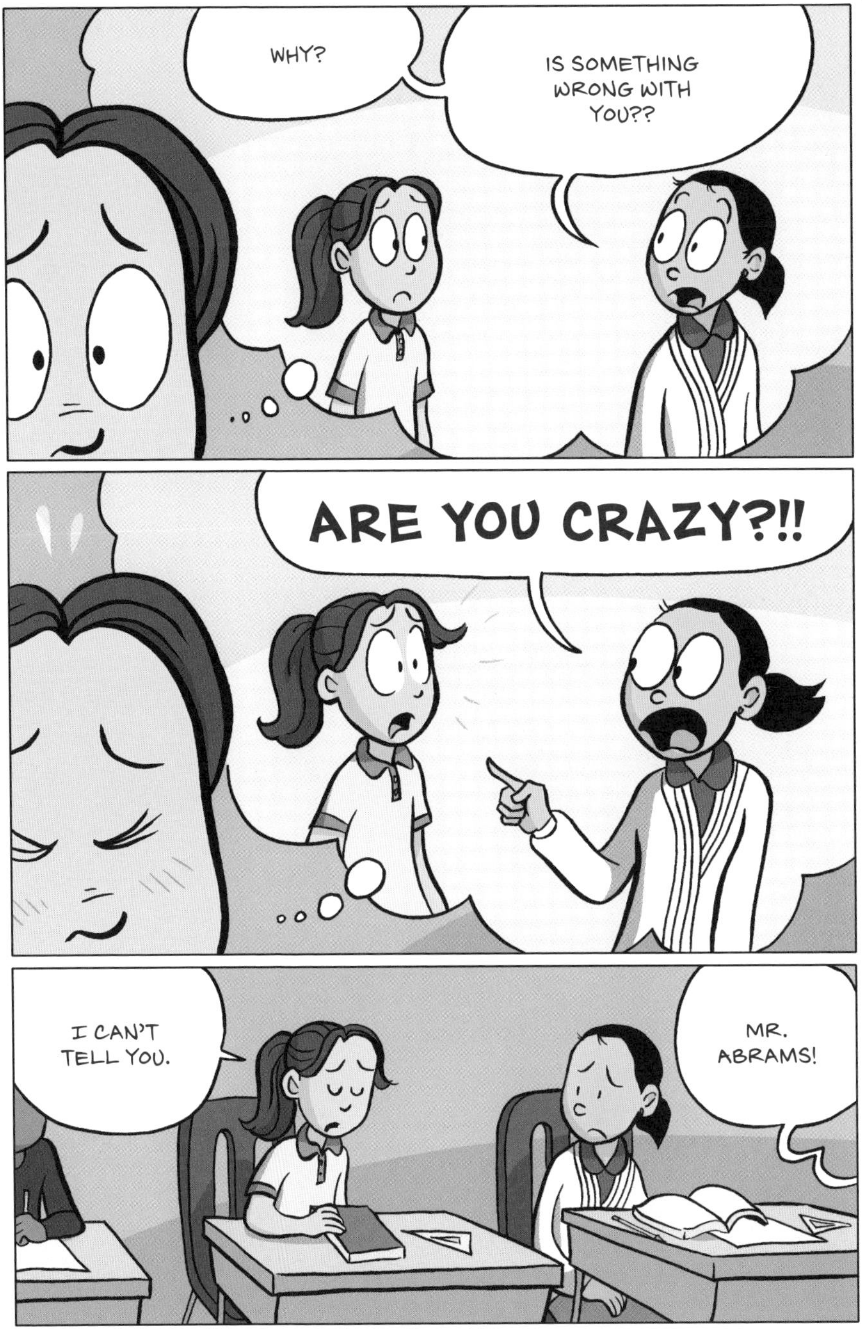
WHY?
IS SOMETHING WRONG WITH YOU??
ARE YOU CRAZY?!!
I CAN'T TELL YOU.
MR. ABRAMS!

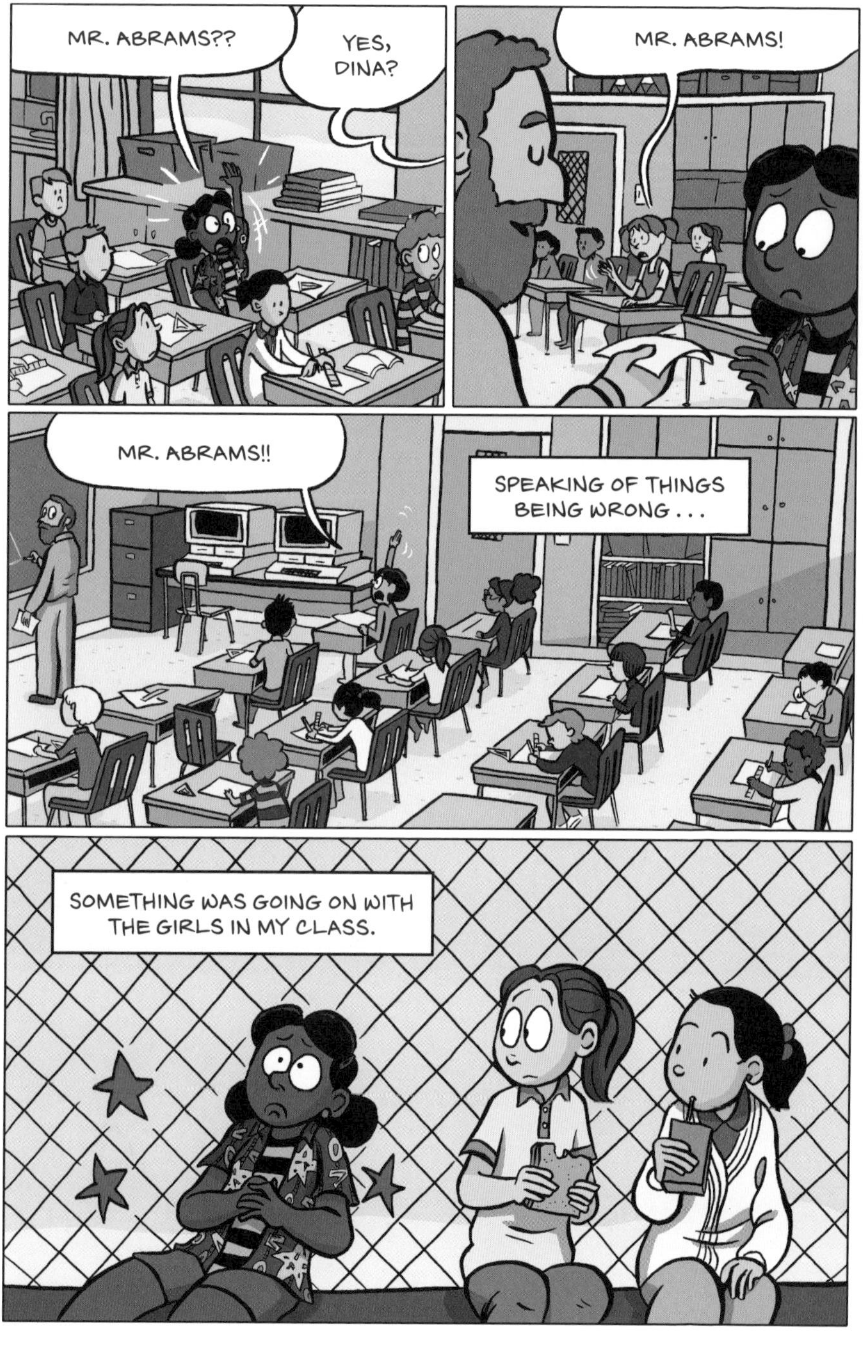
MR. ABRAMS??
YES, DINA?
MR. ABRAMS!
MR. ABRAMS!!
SPEAKING OF THINGS BEING WRONG . . .
SOMETHING WAS GOING ON WITH THE GIRLS IN MY CLASS.

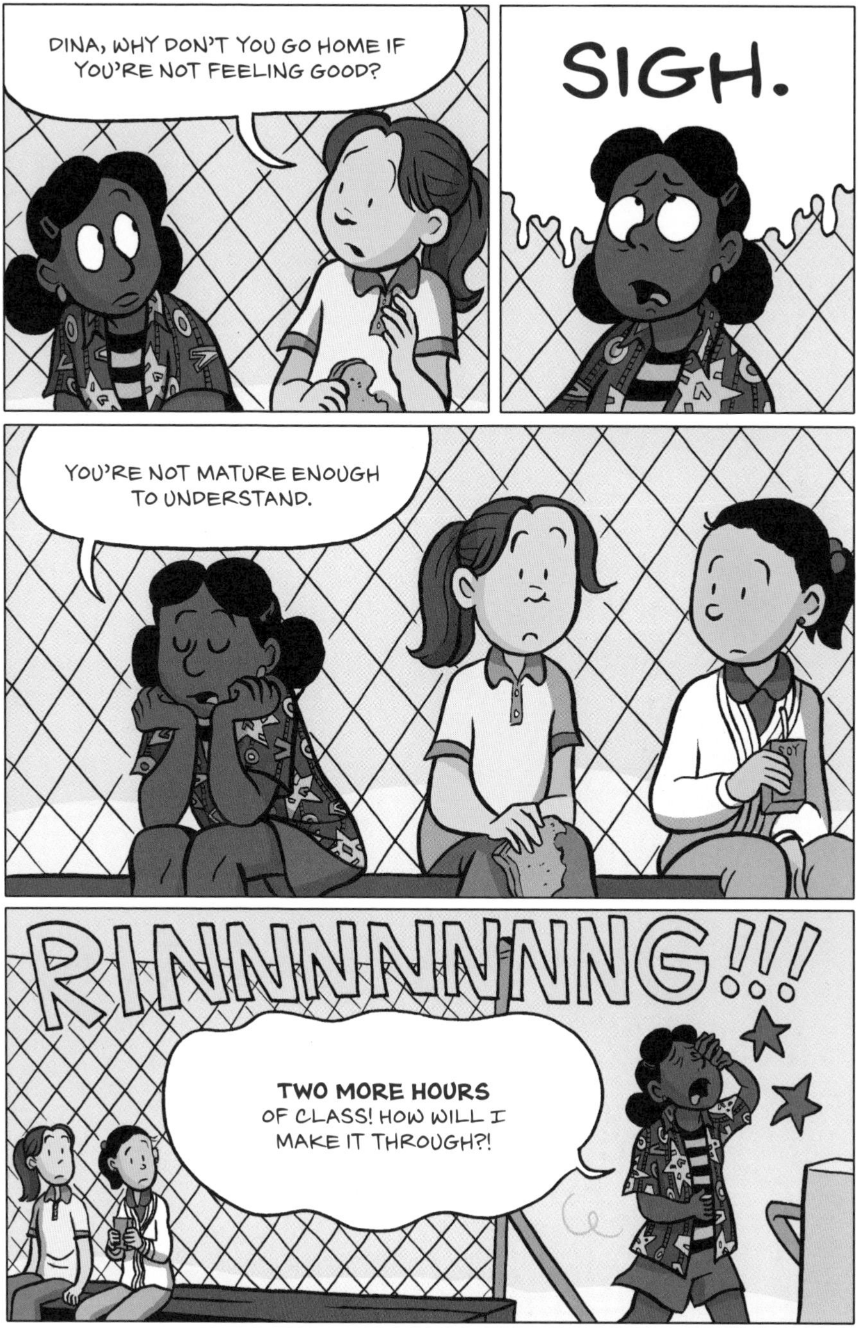
DINA, WHY DON'T YOU GO HOME IF YOU'RE NOT FEELING GOOD?
SIGH.
YOU'RE NOT MATURE ENOUGH TO UNDERSTAND.
RINNNNNNNG!!!
TWO MORE HOURS OF CLASS! HOW WILL I MAKE IT THROUGH?!

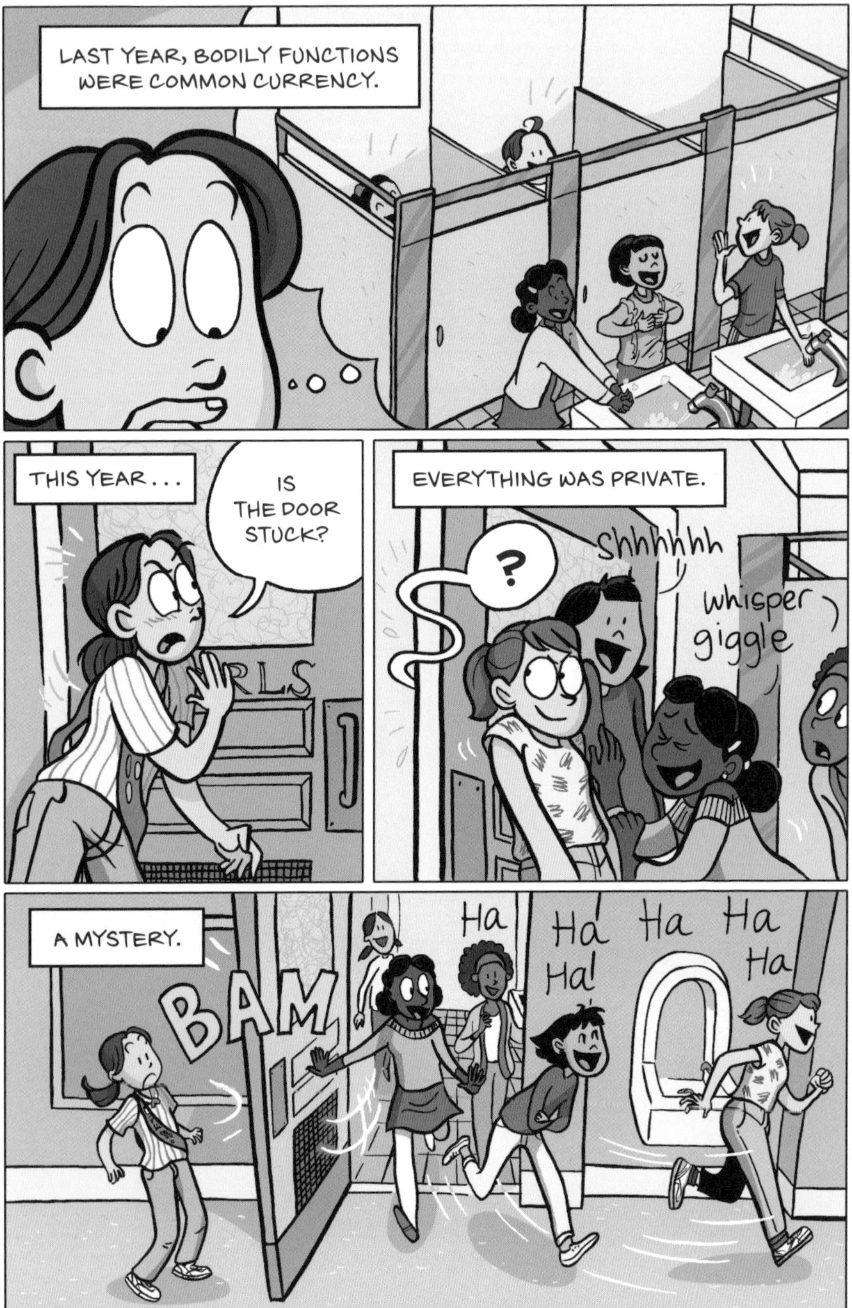
LAST YEAR, BODILY FUNCTIONS WERE COMMON CURRENCY.
THIS YEAR . . .
IS THE DOOR STUCK?
EVERYTHING WAS PRIVATE.
?
Shhhhhh
whisper
giggle
A MYSTERY.
BAM
Ha
Ha
Ha
Ha
Ha!
Ha

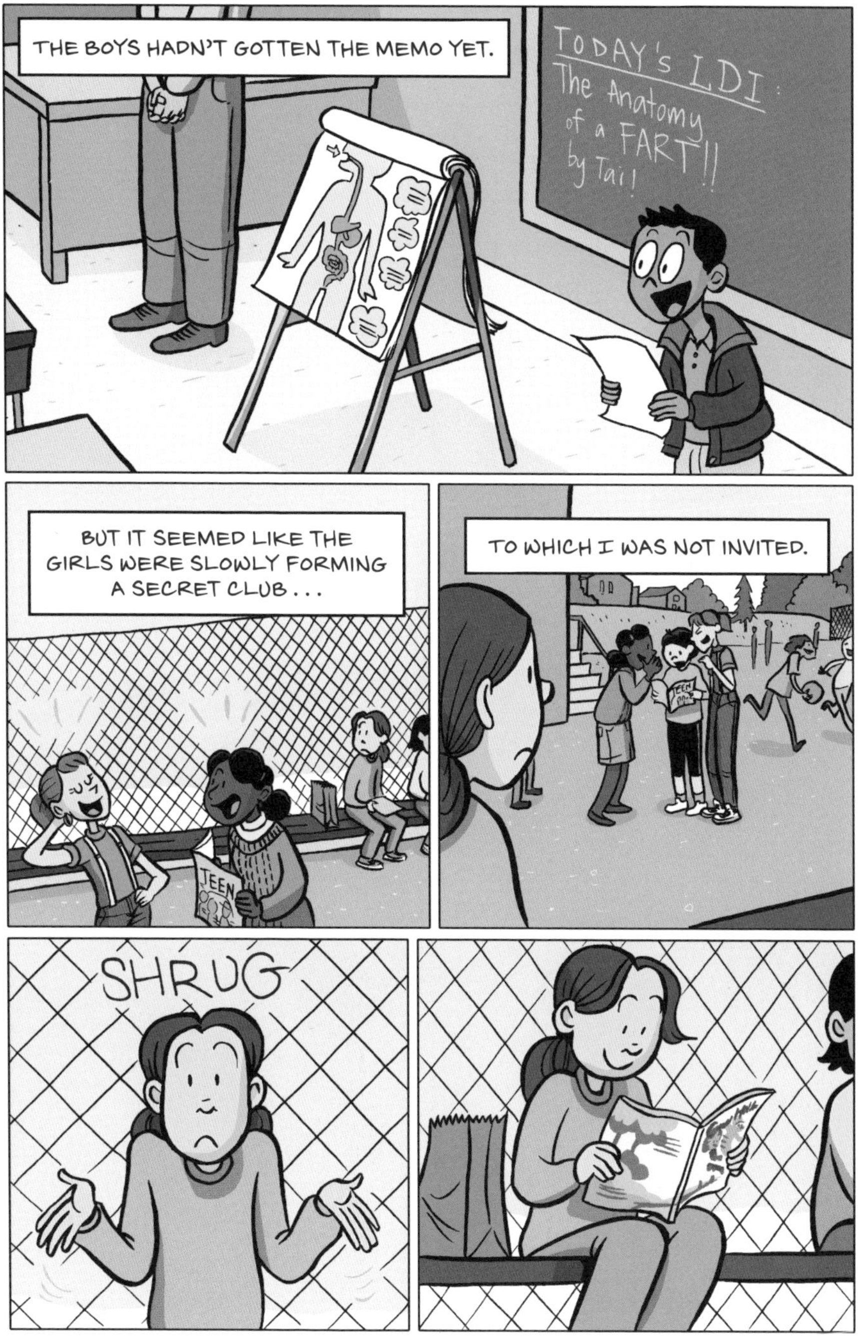
THE BOYS HADN'T GOTTEN THE MEMO YET.
TODAY's LDI: The Anatomy of a FART!! by Tai!
BUT IT SEEMED LIKE THE GIRLS WERE SLOWLY FORMING A SECRET CLUB . . .
TEEN
TO WHICH I WAS NOT INVITED.
SHRUG

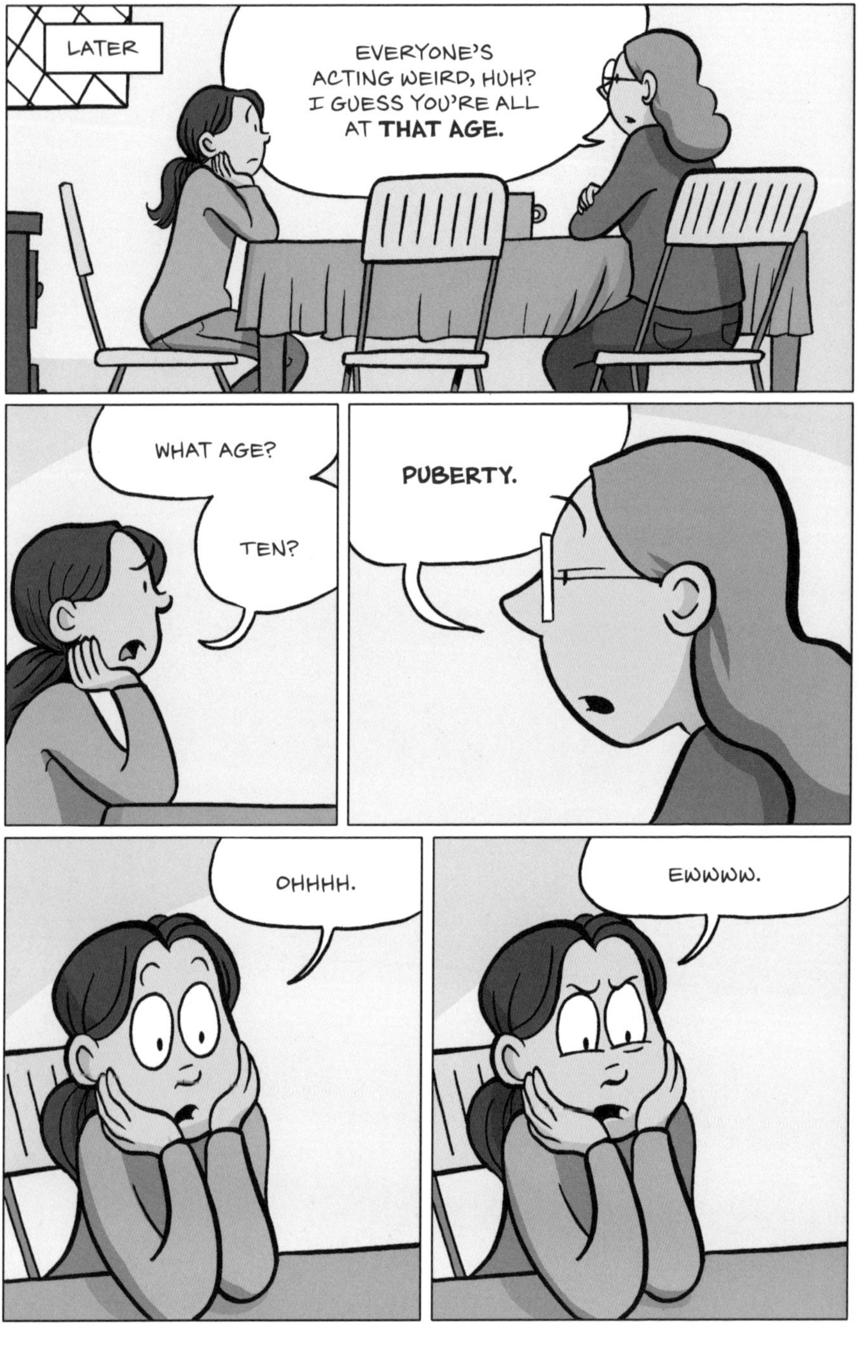
LATER
EVERYONE'S ACTING WEIRD, HUH? I GUESS YOU'RE ALL AT **THAT AGE.**
WHAT AGE?
TEN?
PUBERTY.
OHHHH.
EWWWW.

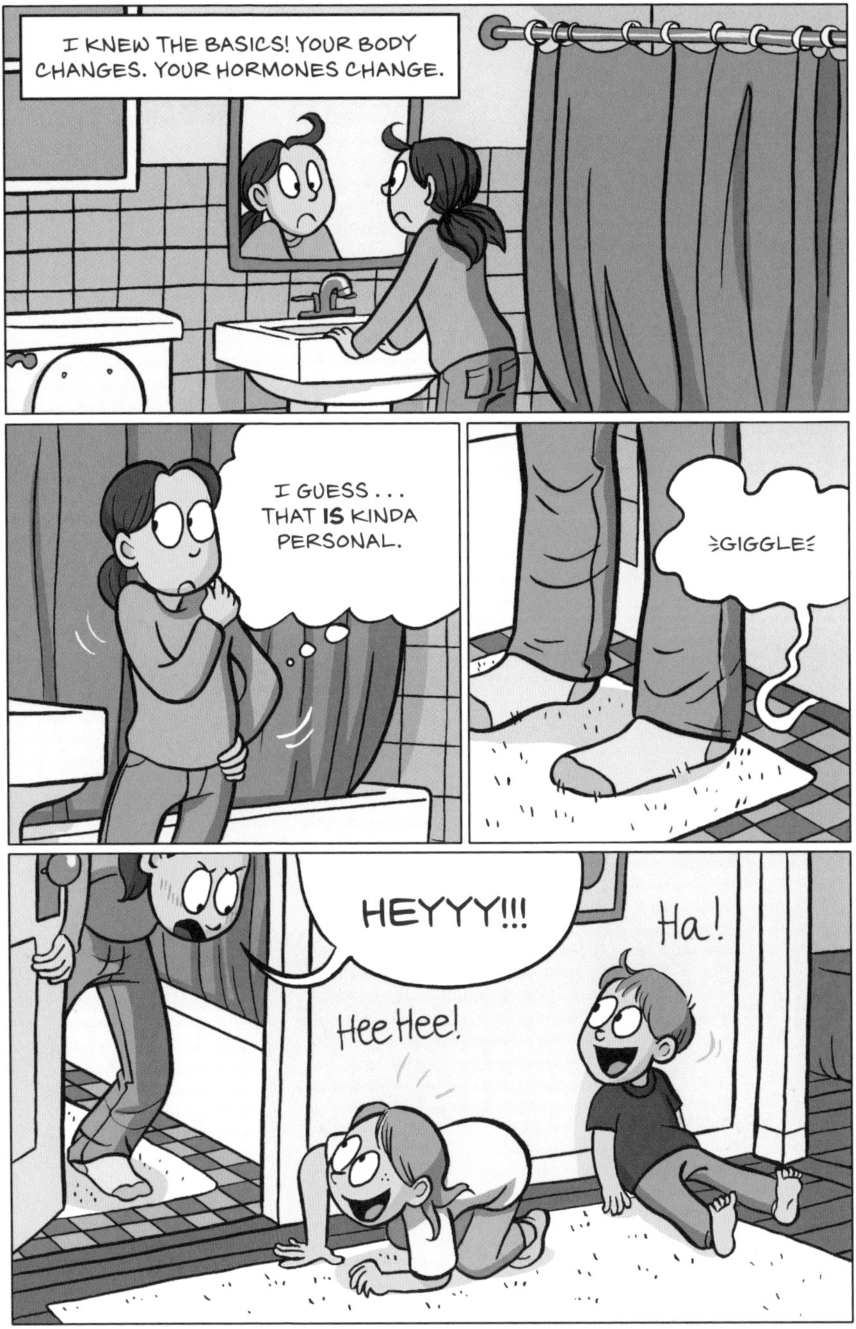
I KNEW THE BASICS! YOUR BODY CHANGES. YOUR HORMONES CHANGE.
I GUESS . . . THAT **IS** KINDA PERSONAL.
GIGGLE
HEYYY!!!
Ha!
Hee Hee!

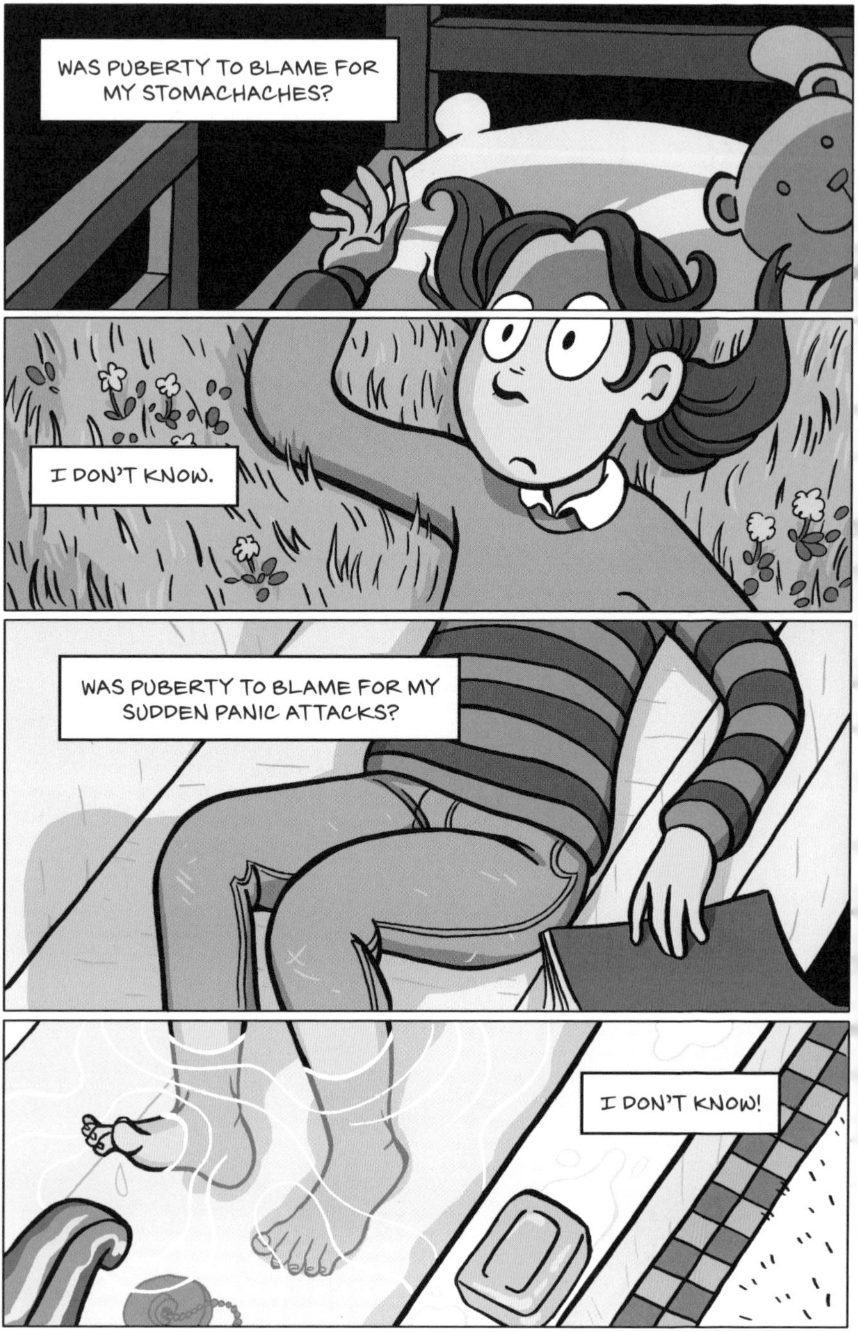
WAS PUBERTY TO BLAME FOR MY STOMACHACHES?
I DON'T KNOW.
WAS PUBERTY TO BLAME FOR MY SUDDEN PANIC ATTACKS?
I DON'T KNOW!

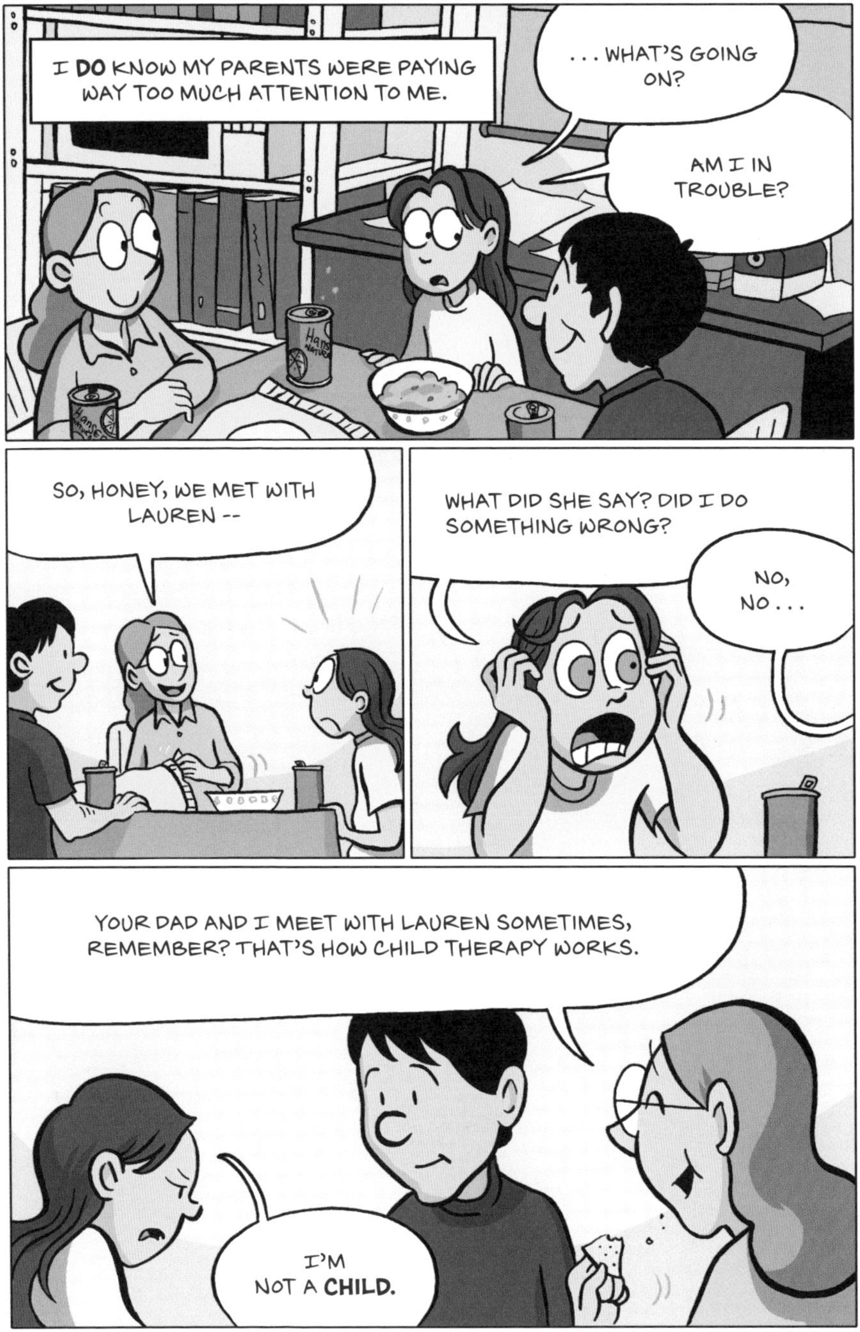
I DO KNOW MY PARENTS WERE PAYING WAY TOO MUCH ATTENTION TO ME.
. . . WHAT'S GOING ON?
AM I IN TROUBLE?
SO, HONEY, WE MET WITH LAUREN --
WHAT DID SHE SAY? DID I DO SOMETHING WRONG?
NO, NO . . .
YOUR DAD AND I MEET WITH LAUREN SOMETIMES, REMEMBER? THAT'S HOW CHILD THERAPY WORKS.
I'M NOT A CHILD.

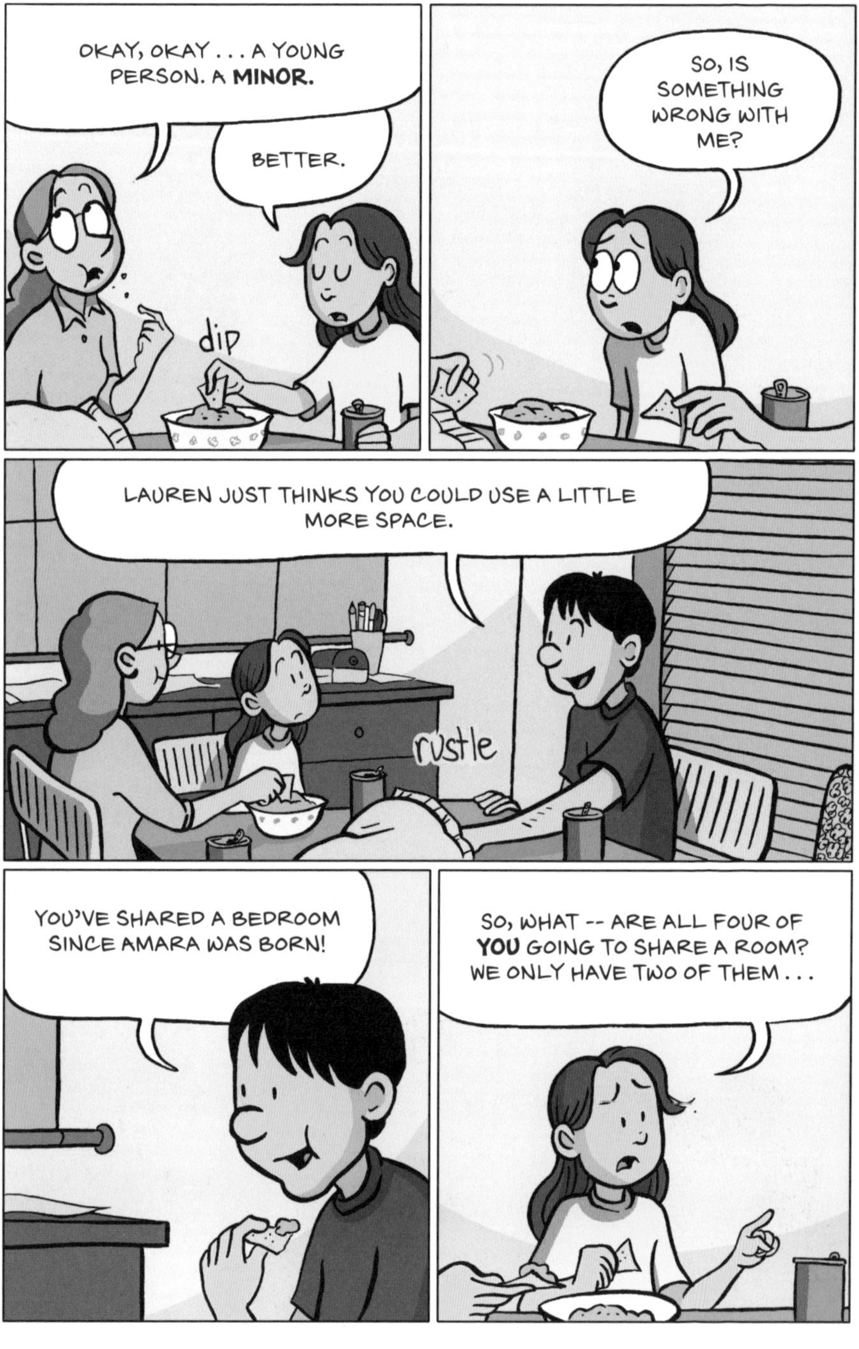
OKAY, OKAY . . . A YOUNG PERSON. A **MINOR.**
BETTER.
dip
SO, IS SOMETHING WRONG WITH ME?
LAUREN JUST THINKS YOU COULD USE A LITTLE MORE SPACE.
rustle
YOU'VE SHARED A BEDROOM SINCE AMARA WAS BORN!
SO, WHAT -- ARE ALL FOUR OF **YOU** GOING TO SHARE A ROOM? WE ONLY HAVE TWO OF THEM . . .

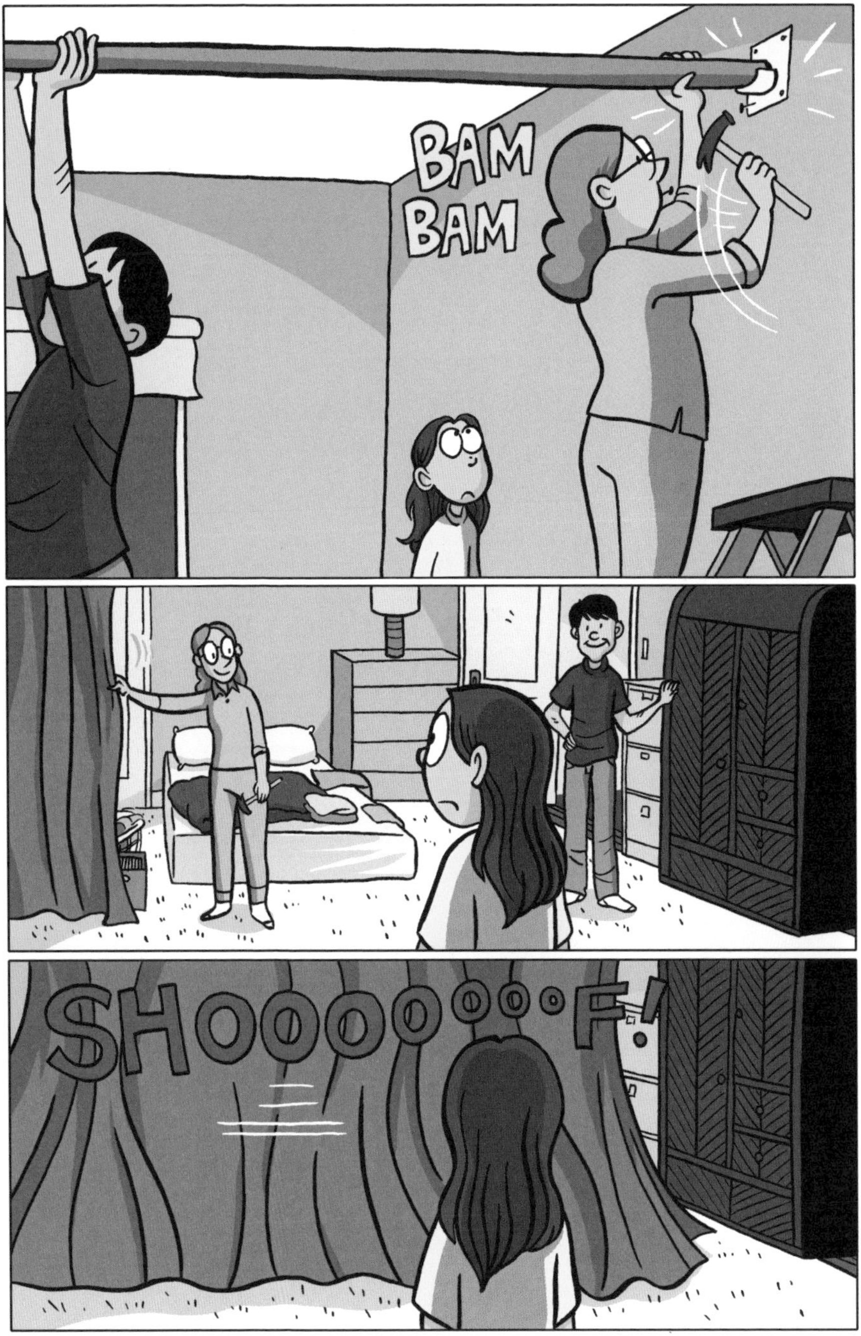
BAM
BAM
SHOOOOOOF!

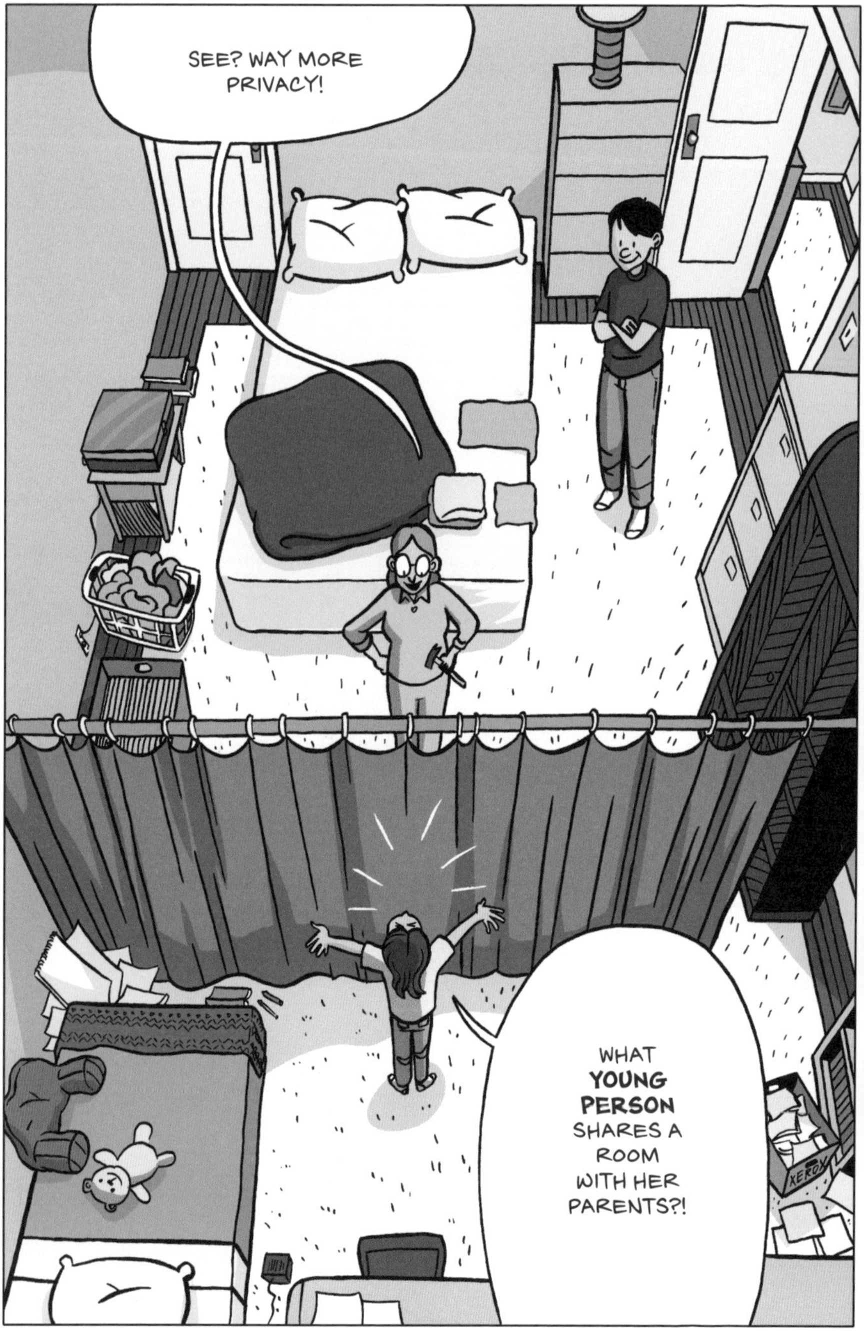
SEE? WAY MORE PRIVACY!
WHAT **YOUNG PERSON** SHARES A ROOM WITH HER PARENTS?!
XEROX

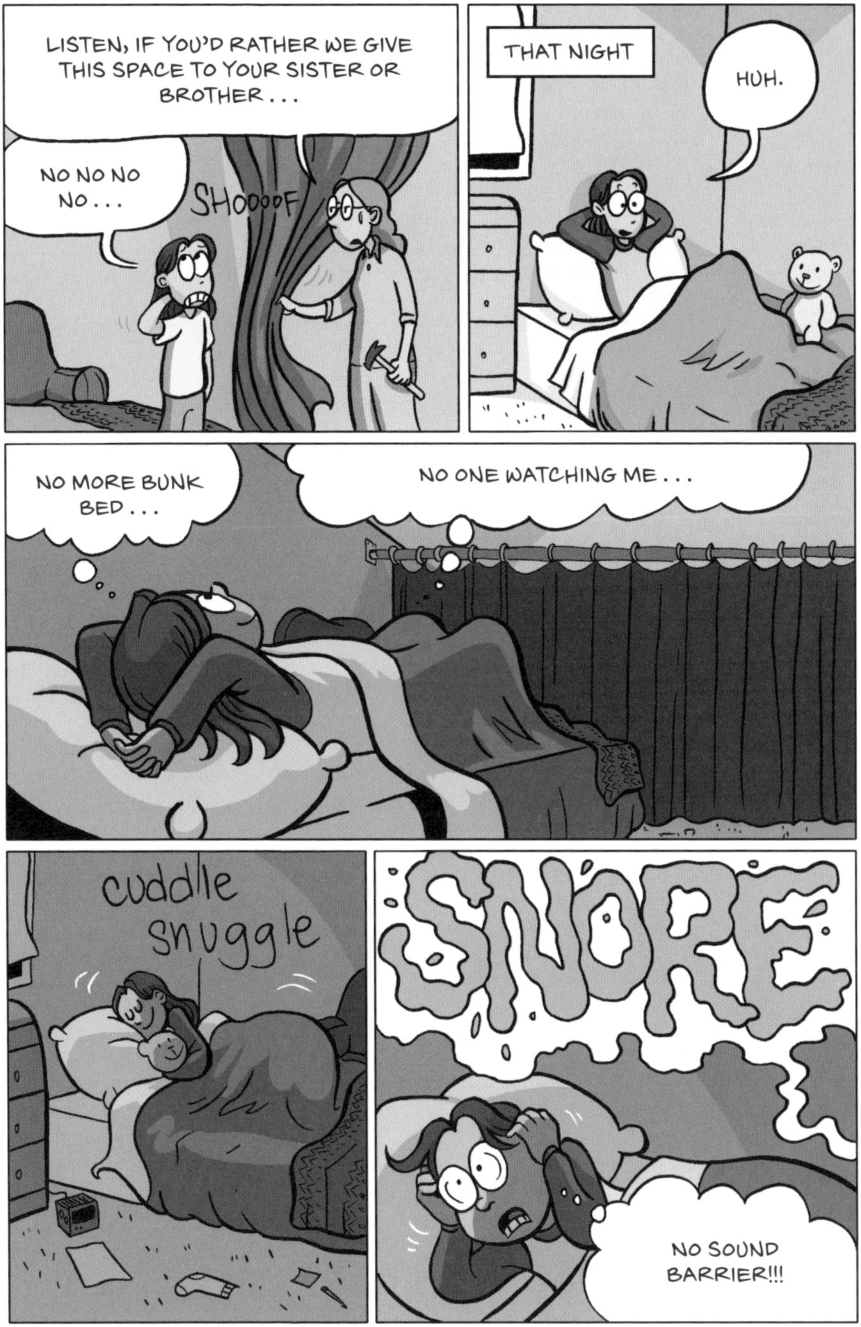
LISTEN, IF YOU'D RATHER WE GIVE THIS SPACE TO YOUR SISTER OR BROTHER . . .
NO NO NO NO . . .
SHOOOOF
THAT NIGHT
HUH.
NO MORE BUNK BED . . .
NO ONE WATCHING ME . . .
cuddle snuggle
SNORE
NO SOUND BARRIER!!!

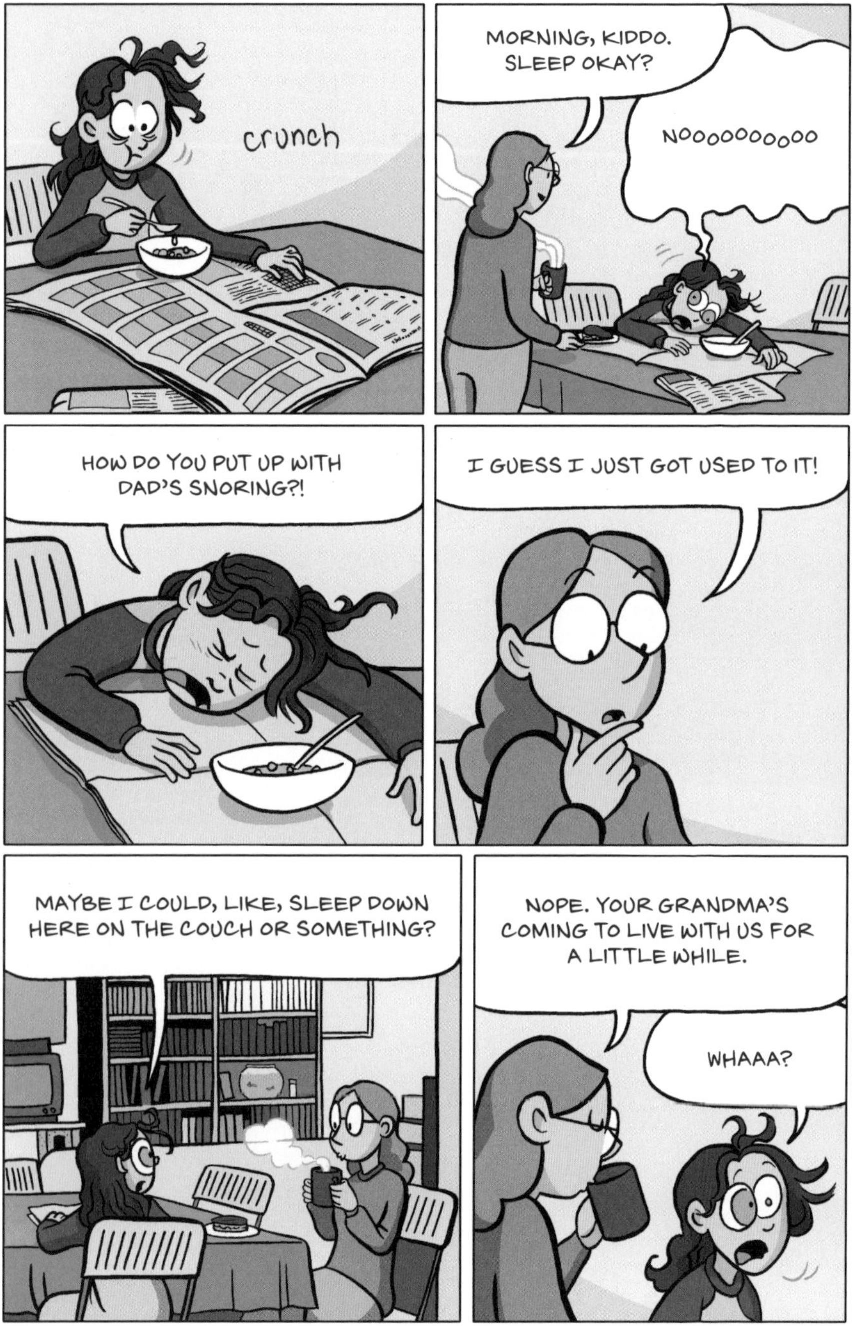
crunch
MORNING, KIDDO. SLEEP OKAY?
NOOOOOOOOOO
HOW DO YOU PUT UP WITH DAD'S SNORING?!
I GUESS I JUST GOT USED TO IT!
MAYBE I COULD, LIKE, SLEEP DOWN HERE ON THE COUCH OR SOMETHING?
NOPE. YOUR GRANDMA'S COMING TO LIVE WITH US FOR A LITTLE WHILE.
WHAAA?

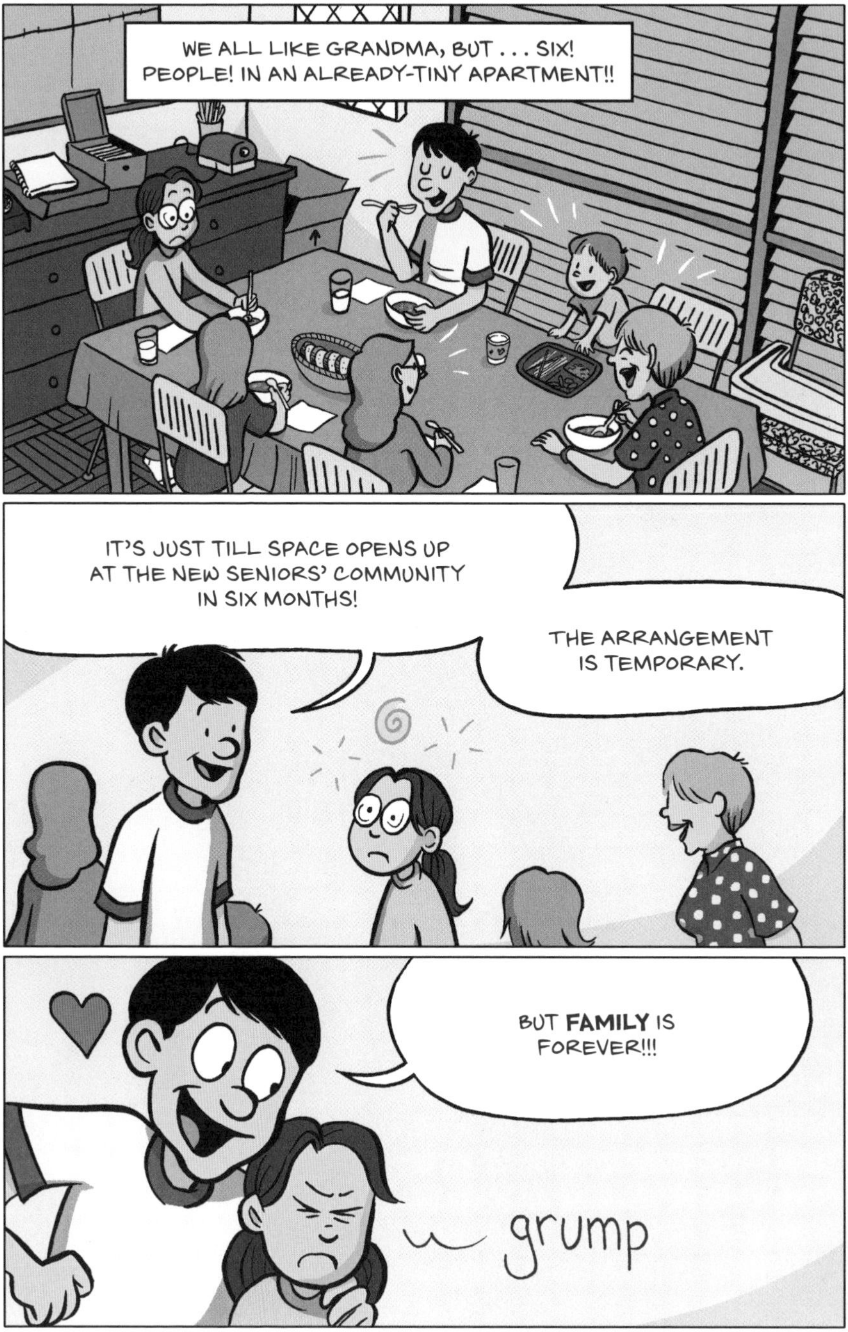
WE ALL LIKE GRANDMA, BUT . . . SIX! PEOPLE! IN AN ALREADY-TINY APARTMENT!!
IT'S JUST TILL SPACE OPENS UP AT THE NEW SENIORS' COMMUNITY IN SIX MONTHS!
THE ARRANGEMENT IS TEMPORARY.
BUT **FAMILY** IS FOREVER!!!
grump

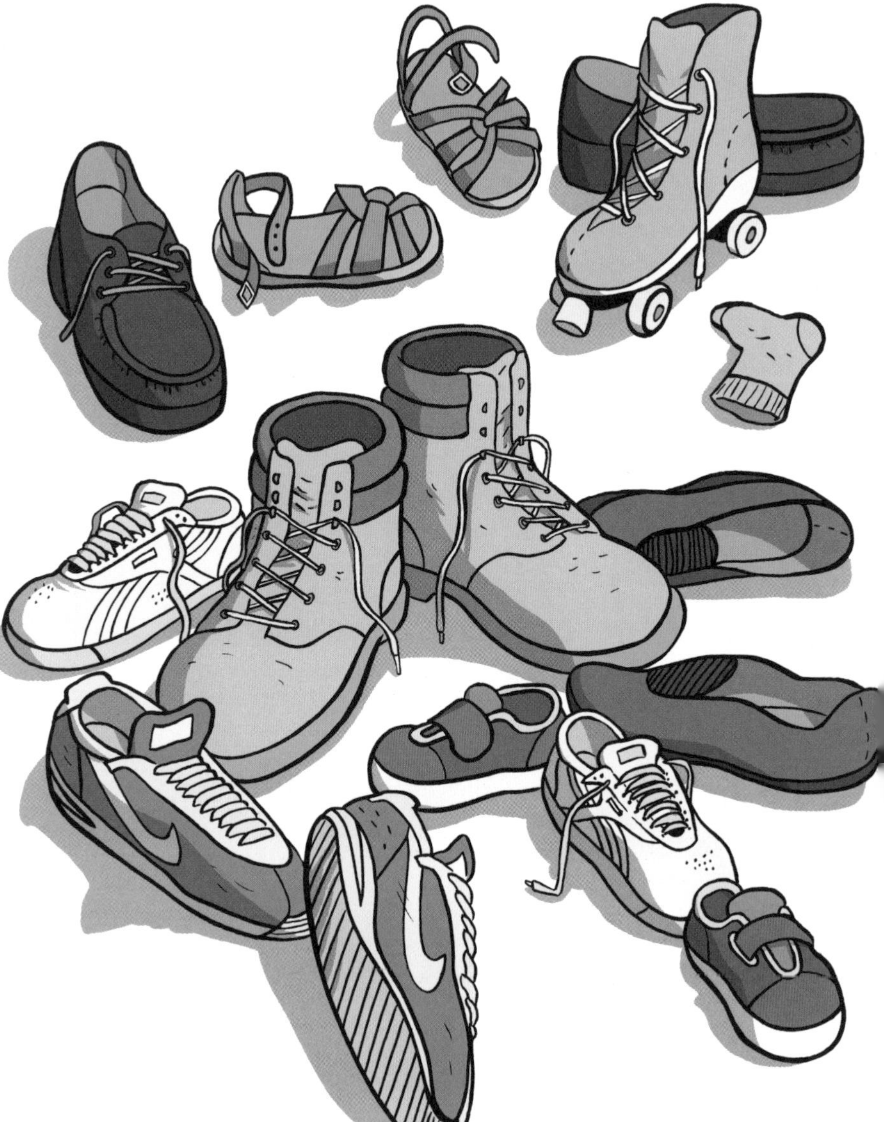

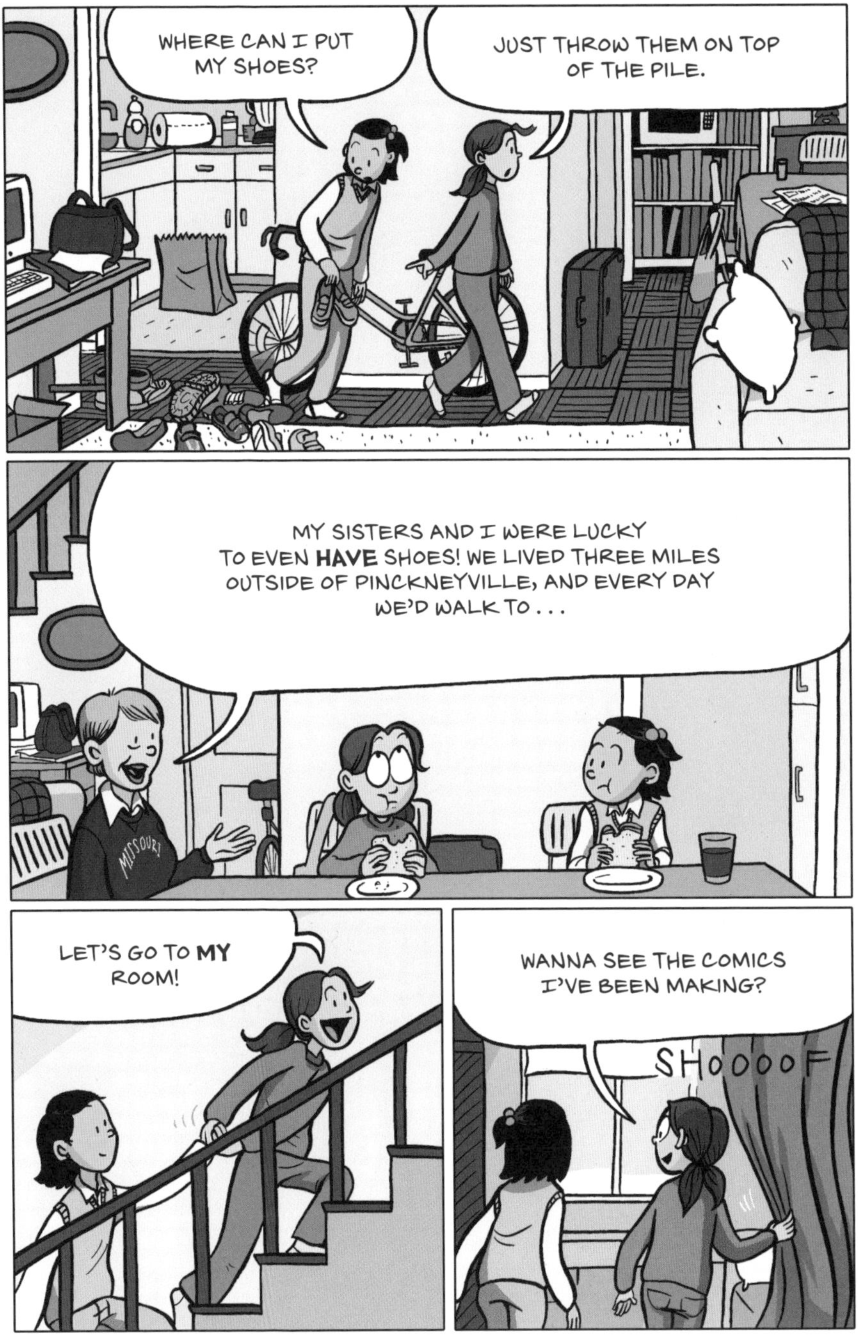
WHERE CAN I PUT MY SHOES?
JUST THROW THEM ON TOP OF THE PILE.
MY SISTERS AND I WERE LUCKY TO EVEN **HAVE** SHOES! WE LIVED THREE MILES OUTSIDE OF PINCKNEYVILLE, AND EVERY DAY WE'D WALK TO . . .
MISSOURI
LET'S GO TO **MY** ROOM!
WANNA SEE THE COMICS I'VE BEEN MAKING?
SHOOOOF

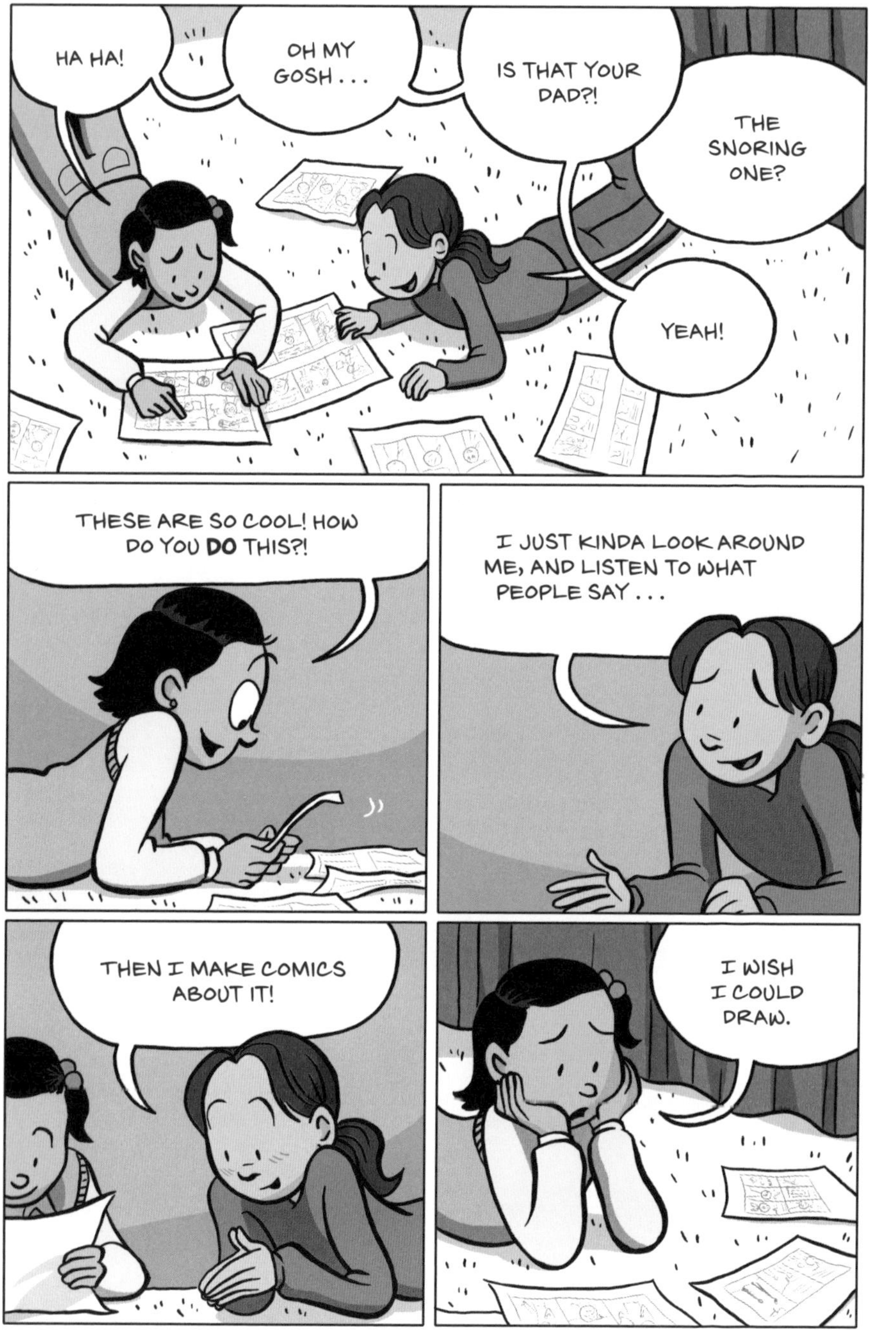
HA HA!
OH MY GOSH . . .
IS THAT YOUR DAD?!
THE SNORING ONE?
YEAH!
THESE ARE SO COOL! HOW DO YOU **DO** THIS?!
I JUST KINDA LOOK AROUND ME, AND LISTEN TO WHAT PEOPLE SAY . . .
THEN I MAKE COMICS ABOUT IT!
I WISH I COULD DRAW.

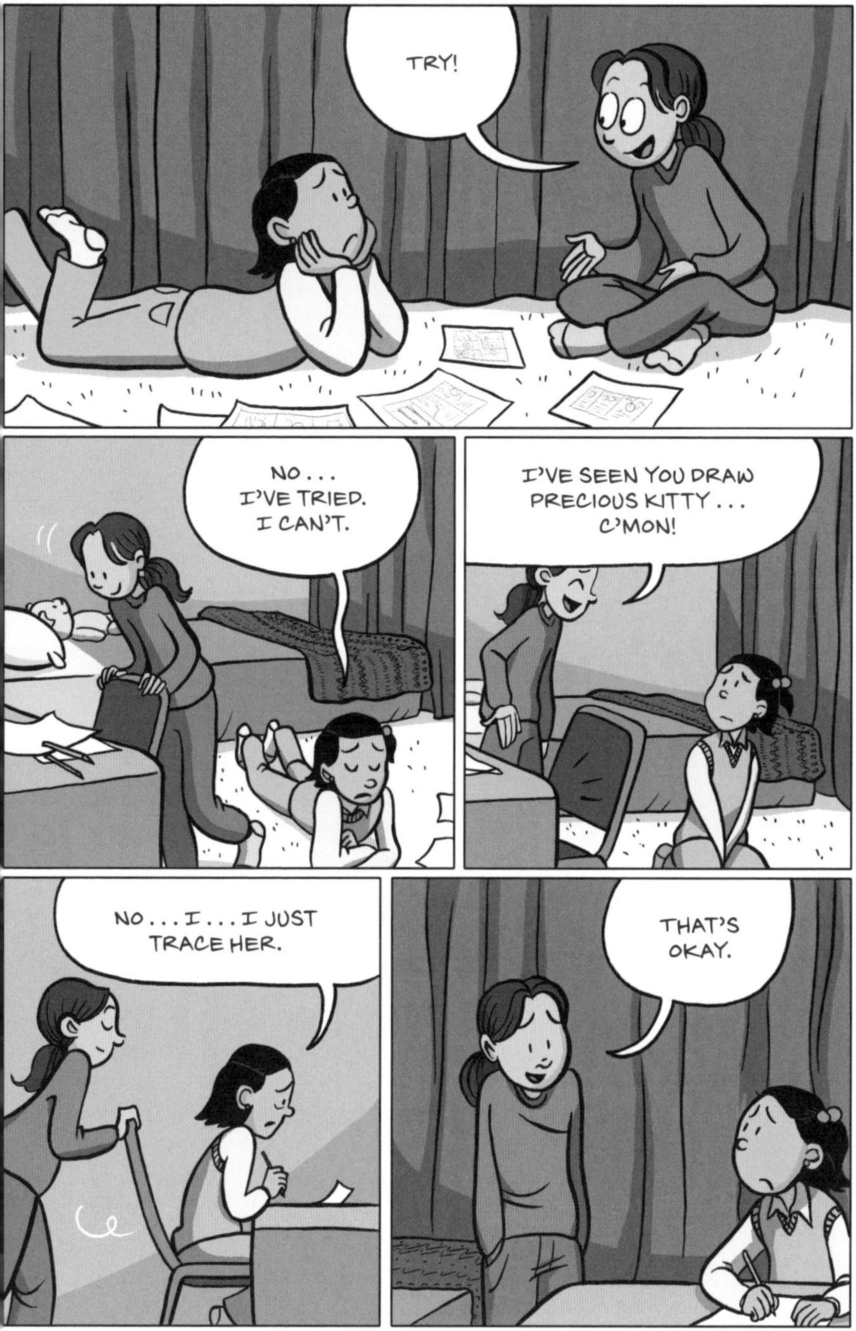
TRY!
NO . . . I'VE TRIED. I CAN'T.
I'VE SEEN YOU DRAW PRECIOUS KITTY . . . C'MON!
NO . . . I . . . I JUST TRACE HER.
THAT'S OKAY.

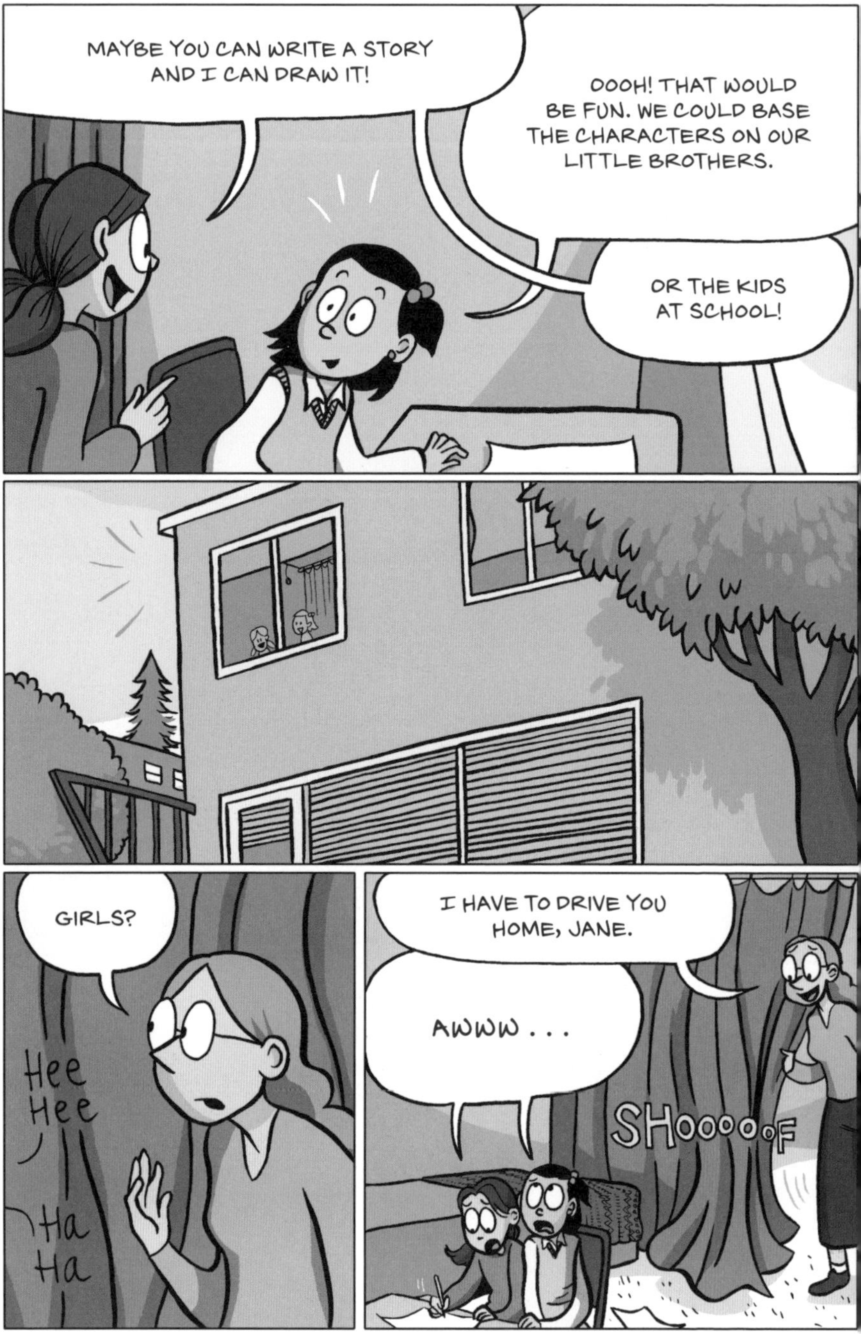
MAYBE YOU CAN WRITE A STORY AND I CAN DRAW IT!
OOOH! THAT WOULD BE FUN. WE COULD BASE THE CHARACTERS ON OUR LITTLE BROTHERS.
OR THE KIDS AT SCHOOL!
GIRLS?
Hee Hee
Ha Ha
I HAVE TO DRIVE YOU HOME, JANE.
AWWW . . .
SHooooOF

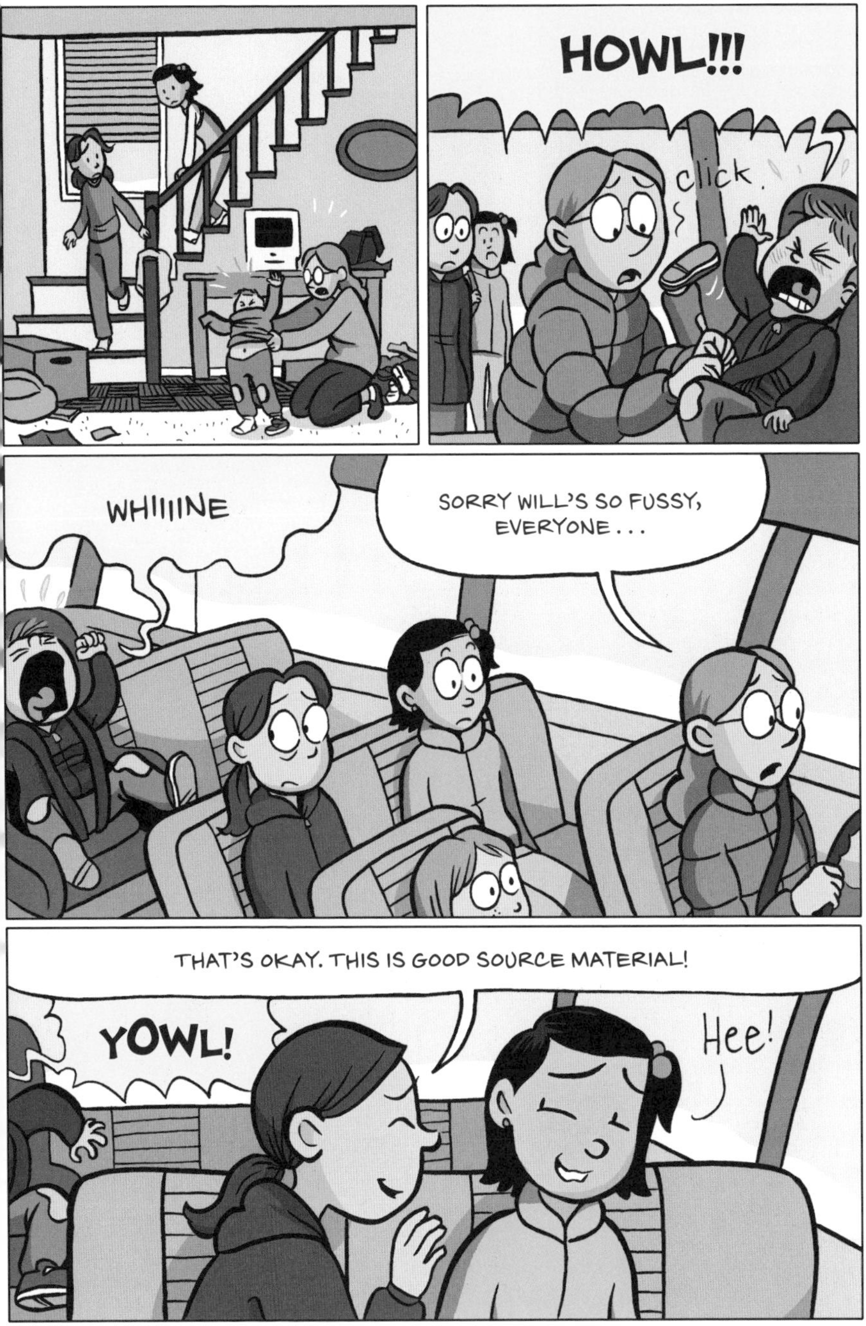
HOWL!!!
click
WHIIIINE
SORRY WILL'S SO FUSSY, EVERYONE . . .
THAT'S OKAY. THIS IS GOOD SOURCE MATERIAL!
YOWL!
Hee!

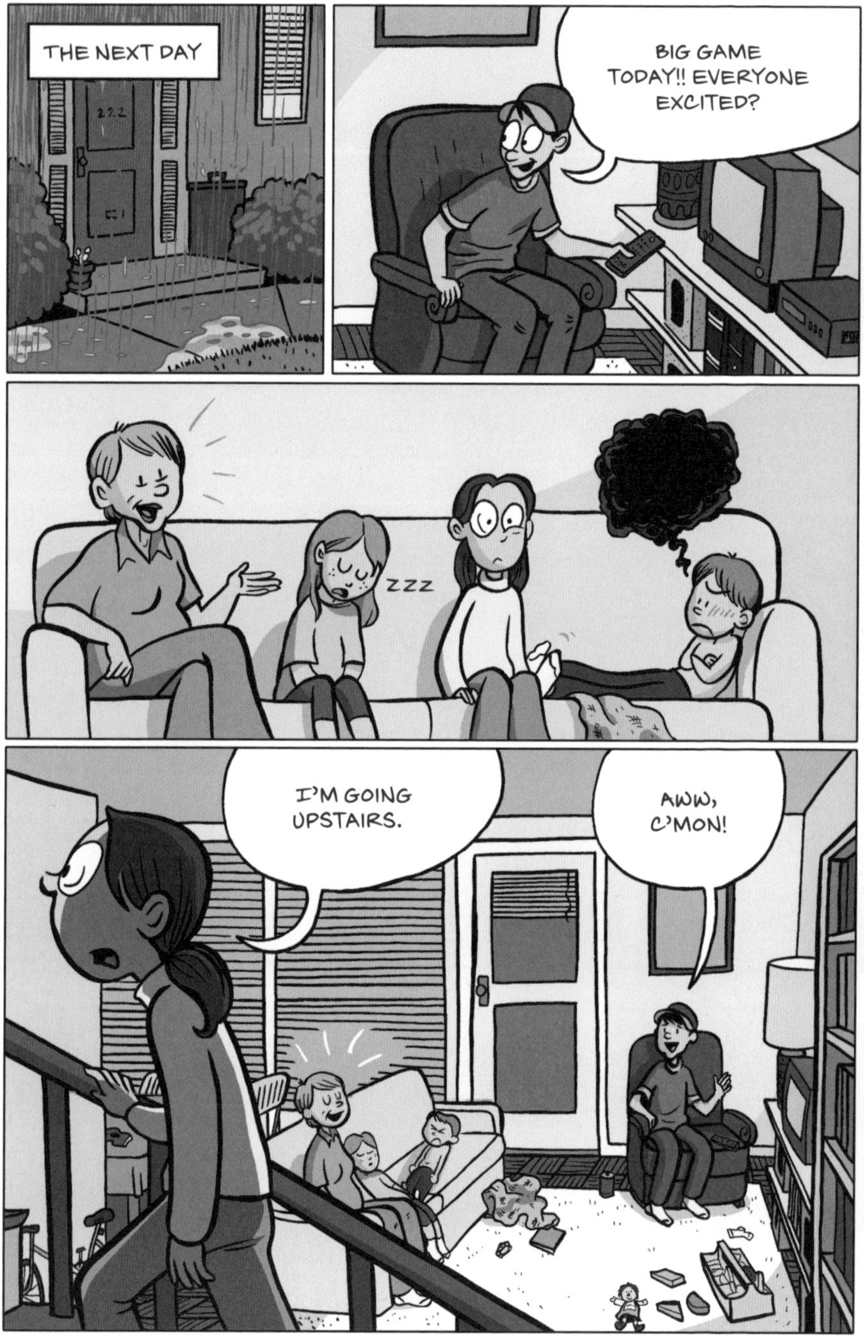
THE NEXT DAY
BIG GAME TODAY!! EVERYONE EXCITED?
ZZZ
I'M GOING UPSTAIRS.
AWW, C'MON!

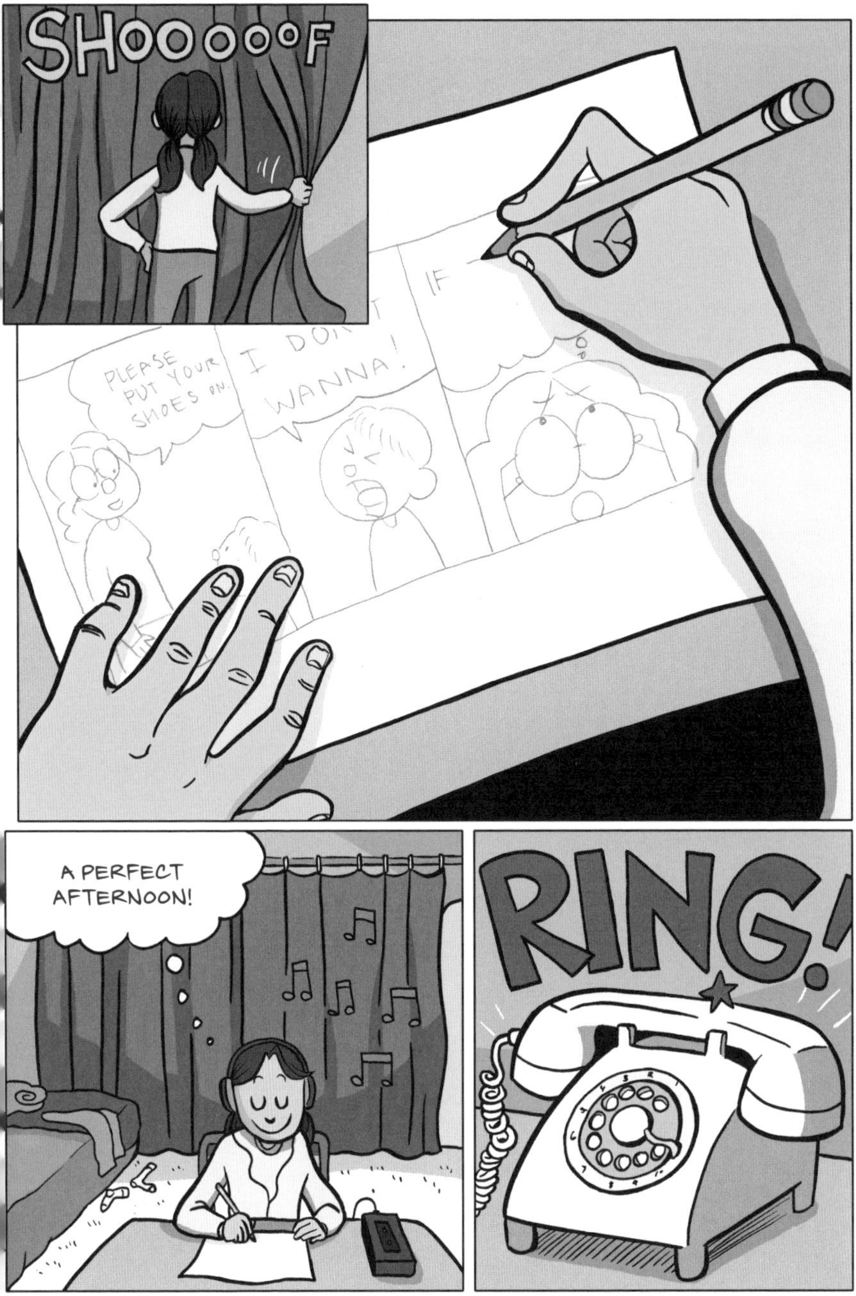
SHOOOOOF
PLEASE PUT YOUR SHOES ON.
I DON'T WANNA!
IF
A PERFECT AFTERNOON!
RING!

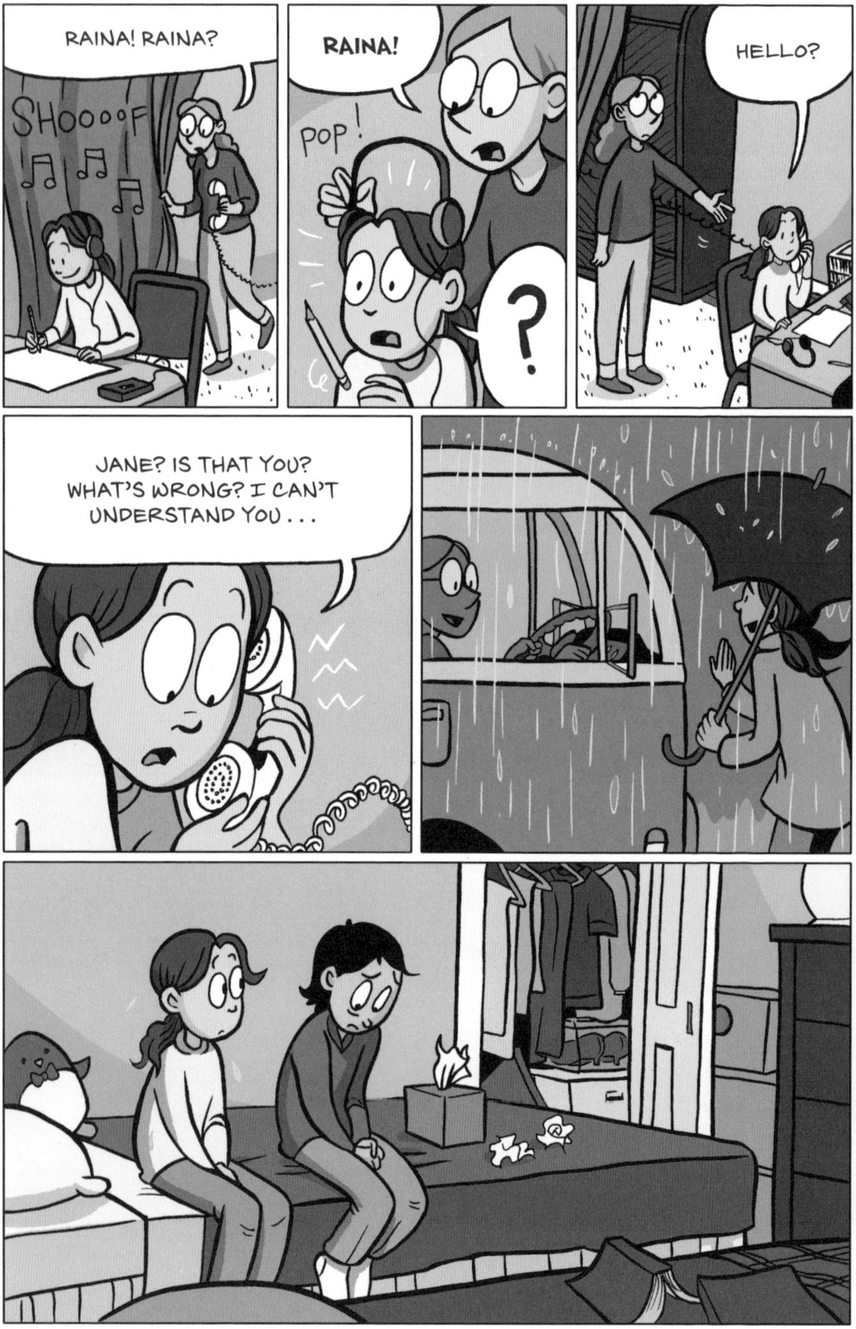
RAINA! RAINA?
SHOOooF
RAINA!
POP!
?
HELLO?
JANE? IS THAT YOU? WHAT'S WRONG? I CAN'T UNDERSTAND YOU . . .

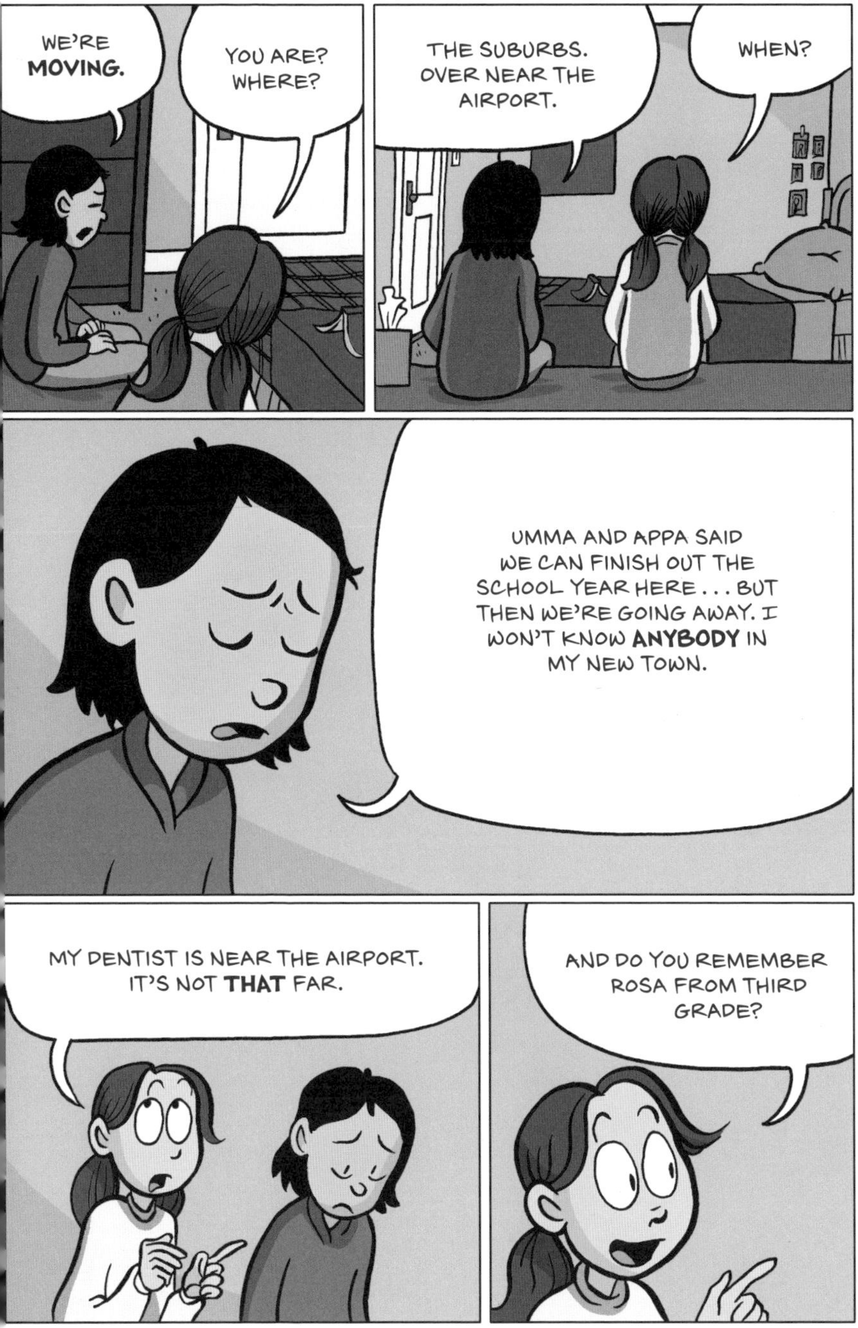
WE'RE **MOVING.**
YOU ARE? WHERE?
THE SUBURBS. OVER NEAR THE AIRPORT.
WHEN?
UMMA AND APPA SAID WE CAN FINISH OUT THE SCHOOL YEAR HERE . . . BUT THEN WE'RE GOING AWAY. I WON'T KNOW **ANYBODY** IN MY NEW TOWN.
MY DENTIST IS NEAR THE AIRPORT. IT'S NOT **THAT** FAR.
AND DO YOU REMEMBER ROSA FROM THIRD GRADE?

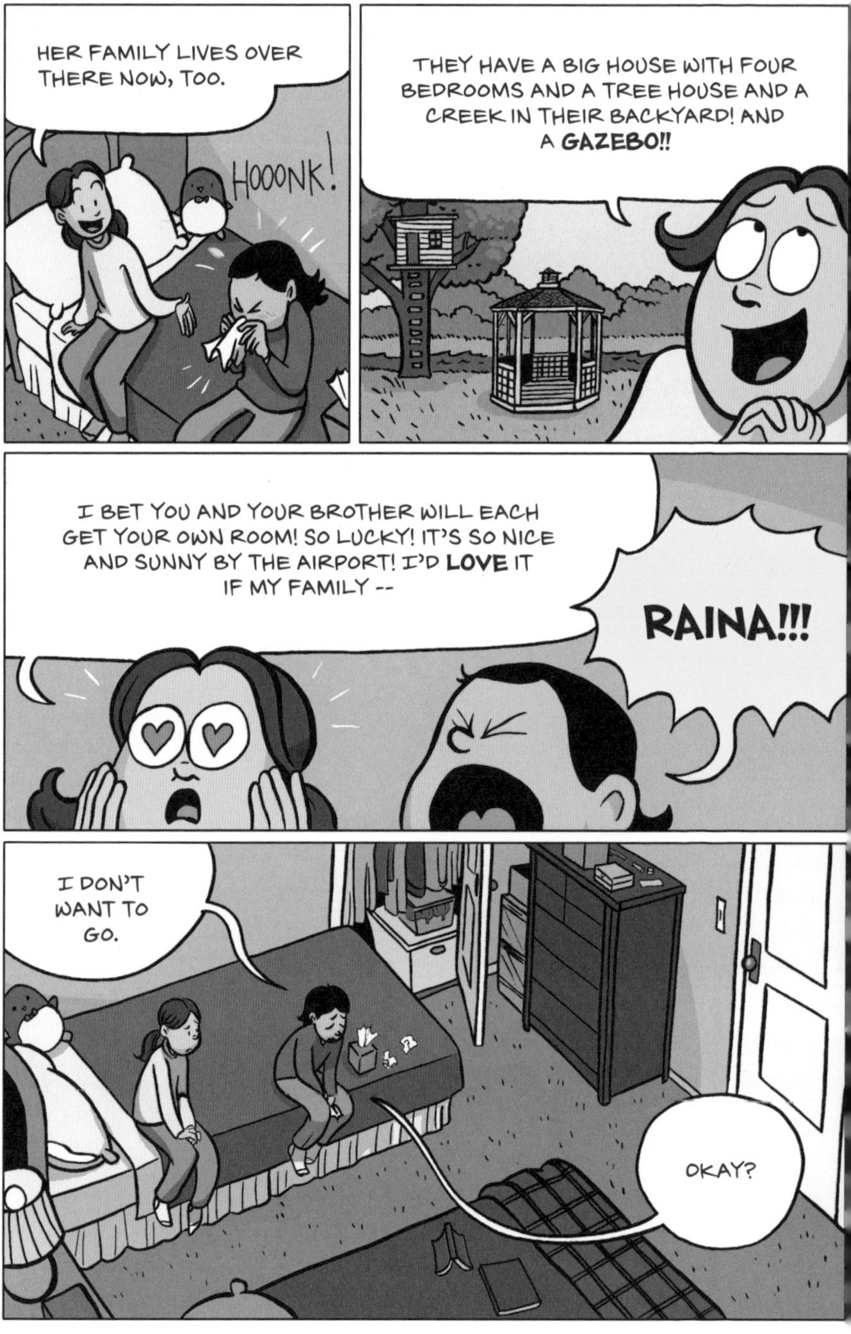
HER FAMILY LIVES OVER THERE NOW, TOO.
HOOONK!
THEY HAVE A BIG HOUSE WITH FOUR BEDROOMS AND A TREE HOUSE AND A CREEK IN THEIR BACKYARD! AND A **GAZEBO**!!
I BET YOU AND YOUR BROTHER WILL EACH GET YOUR OWN ROOM! SO LUCKY! IT'S SO NICE AND SUNNY BY THE AIRPORT! I'D **LOVE** IT IF MY FAMILY --
RAINA!!!
I DON'T WANT TO GO.
OKAY?

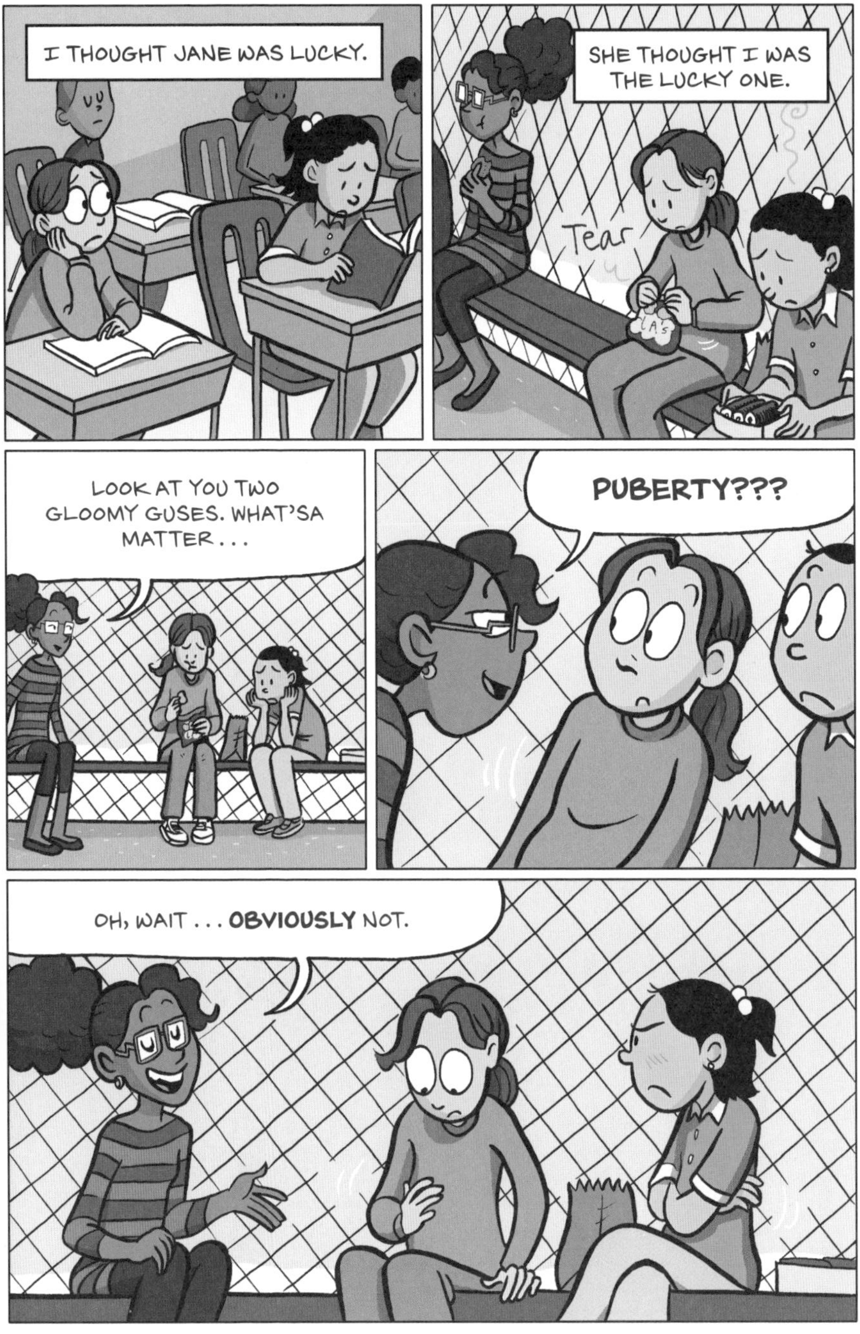
I THOUGHT JANE WAS LUCKY.
SHE THOUGHT I WAS THE LUCKY ONE.
Tear
LA's
LOOK AT YOU TWO GLOOMY GUSES. WHAT'SA MATTER . . .
PUBERTY???
OH, WAIT . . . OBVIOUSLY NOT.

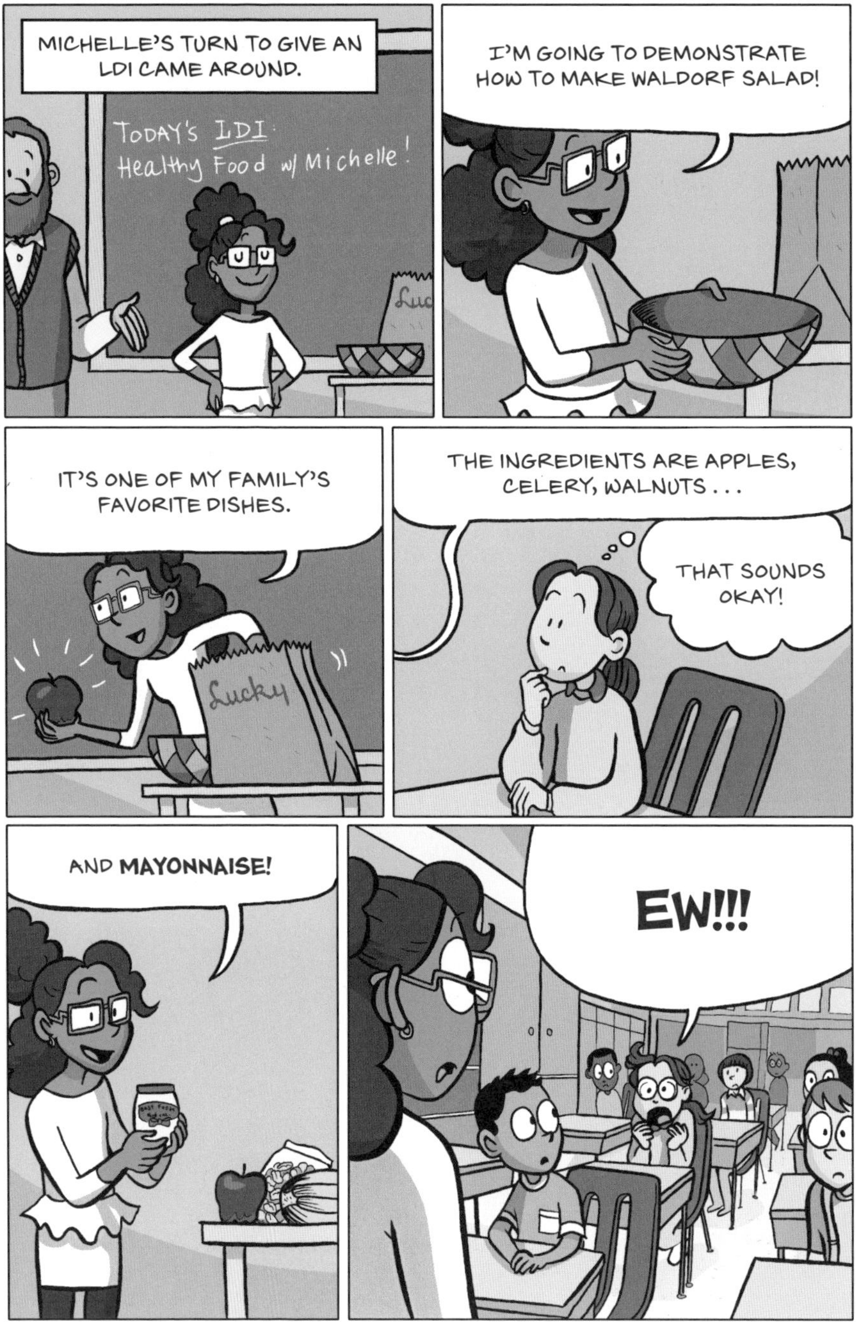
MICHELLE'S TURN TO GIVE AN LDI CAME AROUND.
TODAY'S LDI: Healthy Food w/ Michelle!
I'M GOING TO DEMONSTRATE HOW TO MAKE WALDORF SALAD!
IT'S ONE OF MY FAMILY'S FAVORITE DISHES.
Lucky
THE INGREDIENTS ARE APPLES, CELERY, WALNUTS . . .
THAT SOUNDS OKAY!
AND MAYONNAISE!
EW!!!

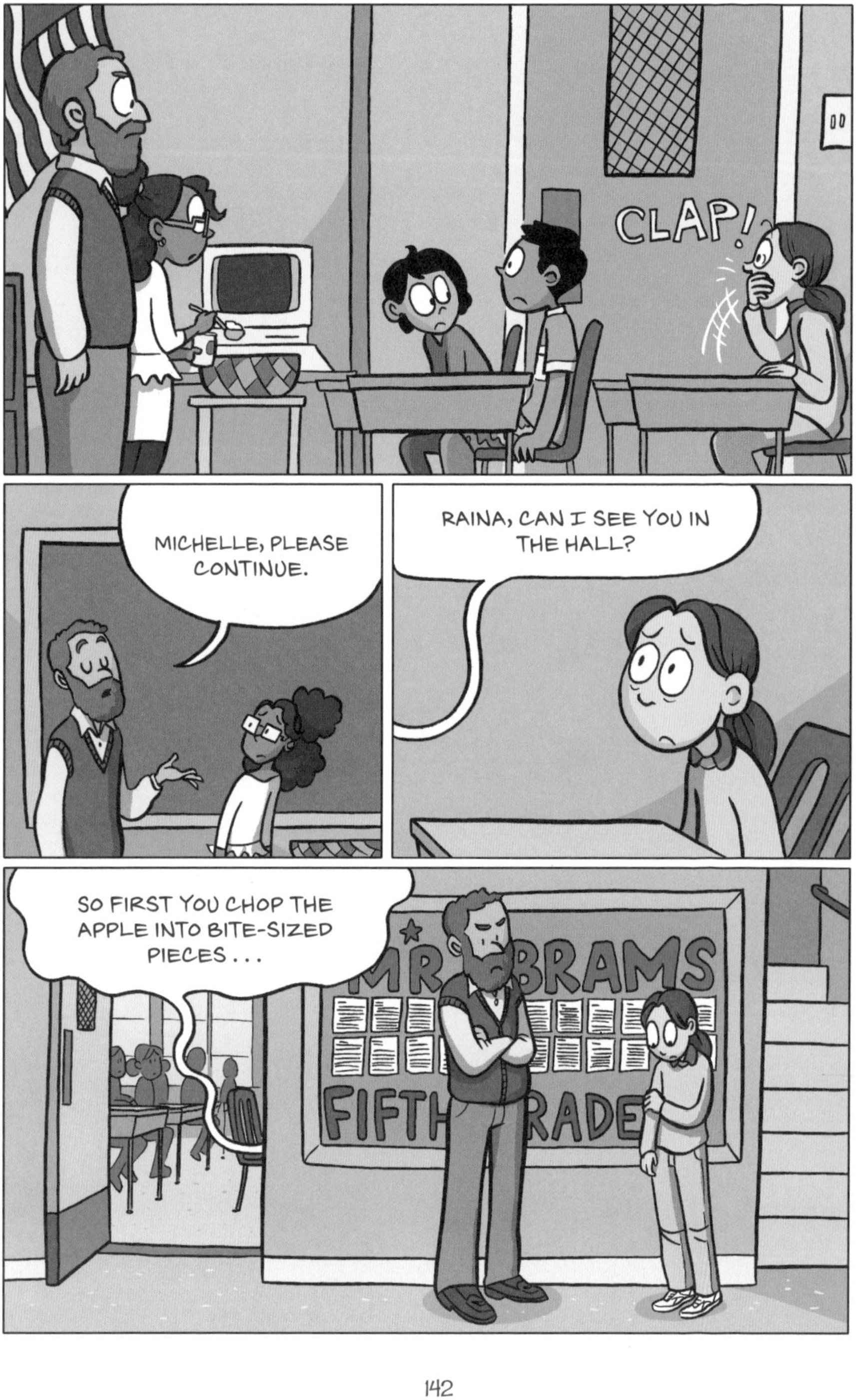
CLAP!
MICHELLE, PLEASE CONTINUE.
RAINA, CAN I SEE YOU IN THE HALL?
SO FIRST YOU CHOP THE APPLE INTO BITE-SIZED PIECES . . .
MR BRAMS
FIFTH RADE

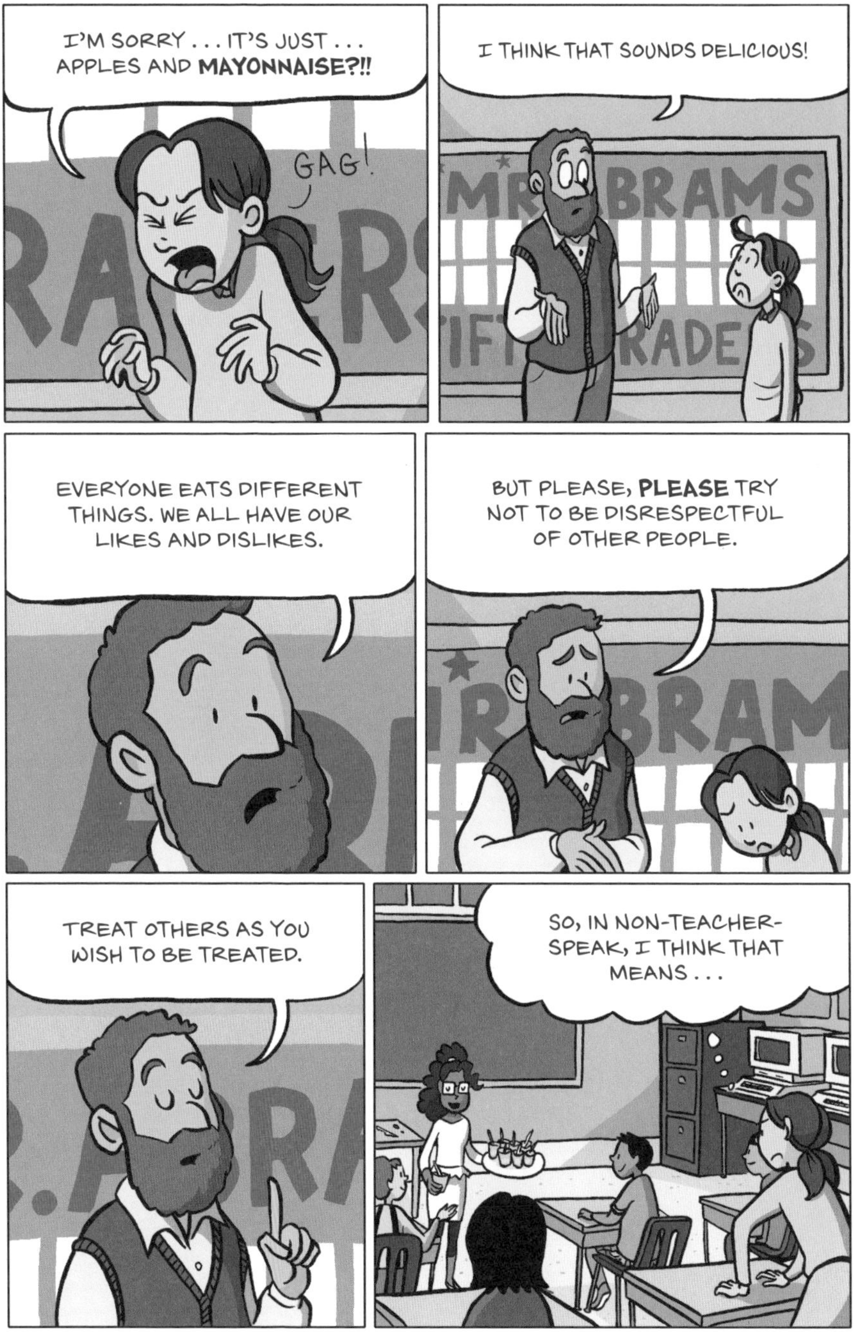
I'M SORRY . . . IT'S JUST . . . APPLES AND **MAYONNAISE?!!**
GAG!
I THINK THAT SOUNDS DELICIOUS!
MR. ABRAMS
EVERYONE EATS DIFFERENT THINGS. WE ALL HAVE OUR LIKES AND DISLIKES.
BUT PLEASE, **PLEASE** TRY NOT TO BE DISRESPECTFUL OF OTHER PEOPLE.
TREAT OTHERS AS YOU WISH TO BE TREATED.
SO, IN NON-TEACHER-SPEAK, I THINK THAT MEANS . . .

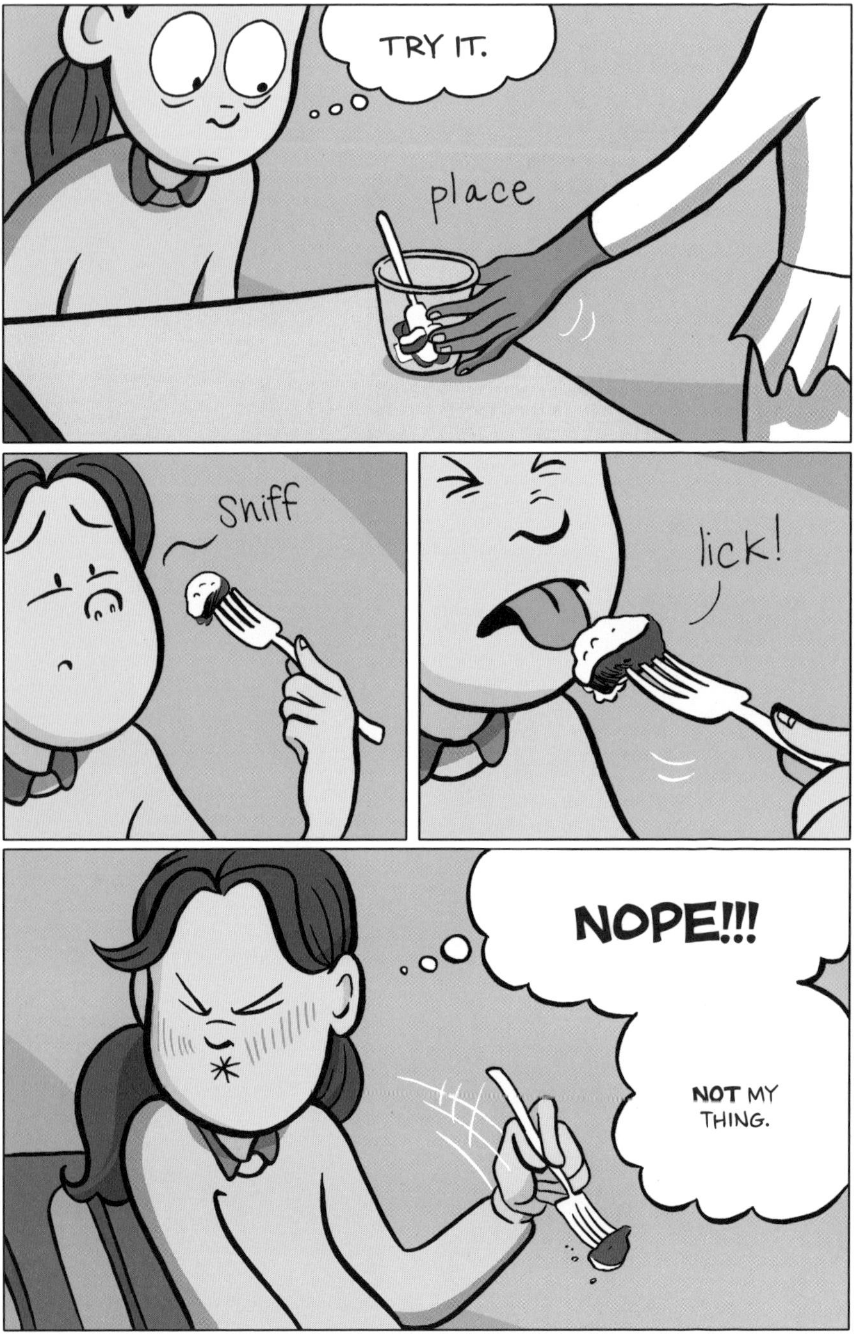
TRY IT.
place
sniff
lick!
NOPE!!!
NOT MY THING.

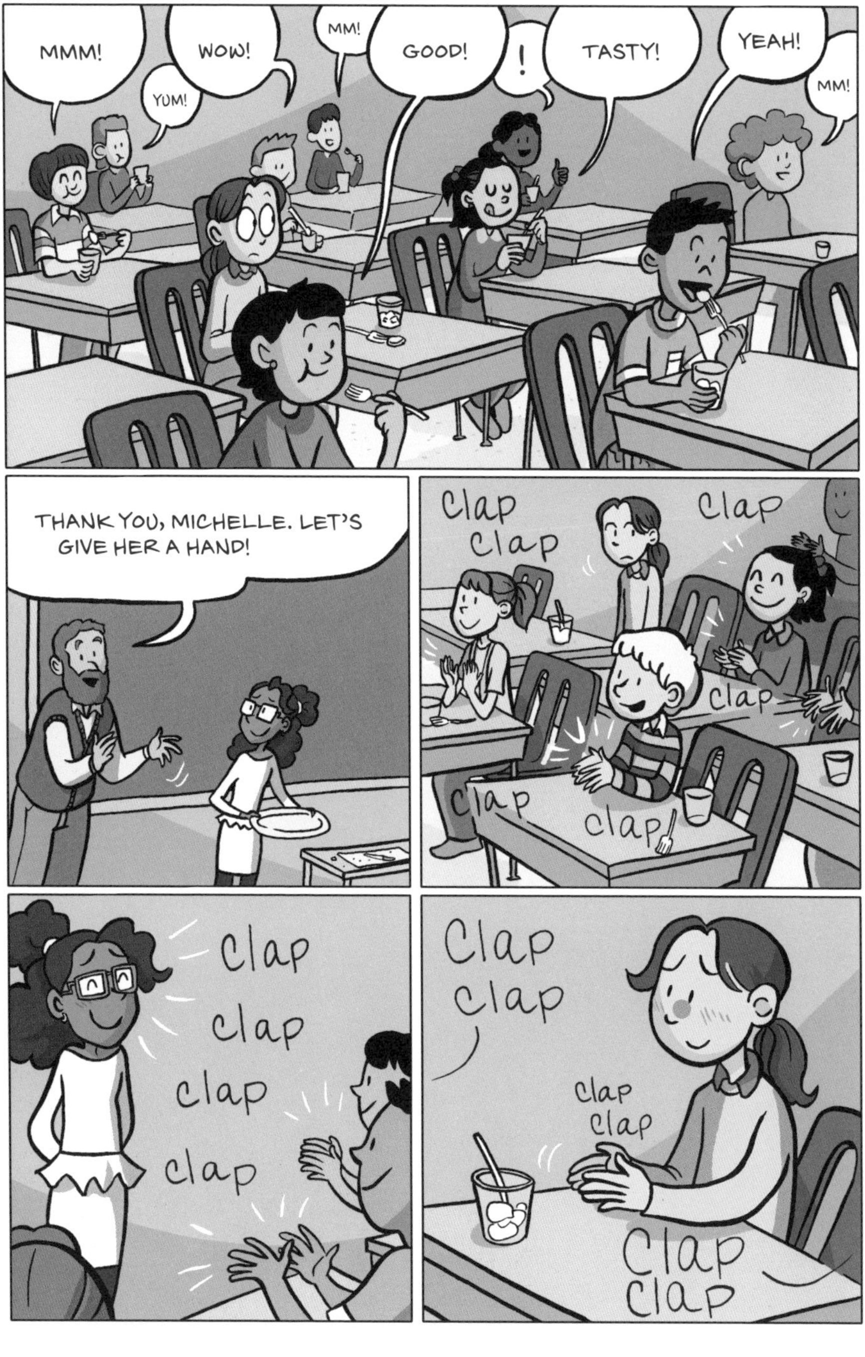
MMM!
YUM!
WOW!
MM!
GOOD!
!
TASTY!
YEAH!
MM!
THANK YOU, MICHELLE. LET'S GIVE HER A HAND!
Clap
Clap
Clap
clap
Clap
clap
Clap
clap
clap
clap
Clap
clap
Clap
Clap
Clap
Clap

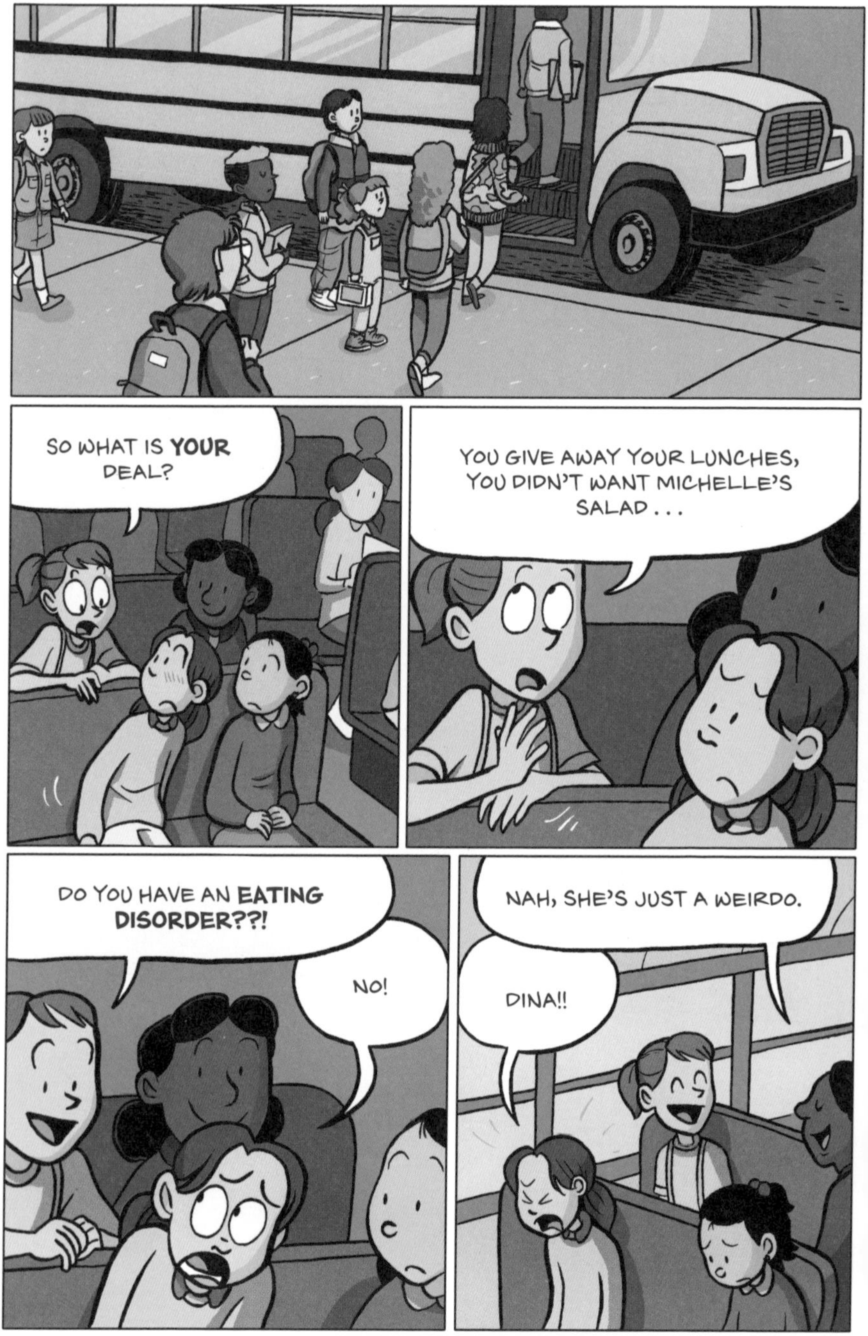

SO WHAT IS **YOUR** DEAL?
YOU GIVE AWAY YOUR LUNCHES, YOU DIDN'T WANT MICHELLE'S SALAD . . .
DO YOU HAVE AN **EATING DISORDER**??!
NO!
NAH, SHE'S JUST A WEIRDO.
DINA!!

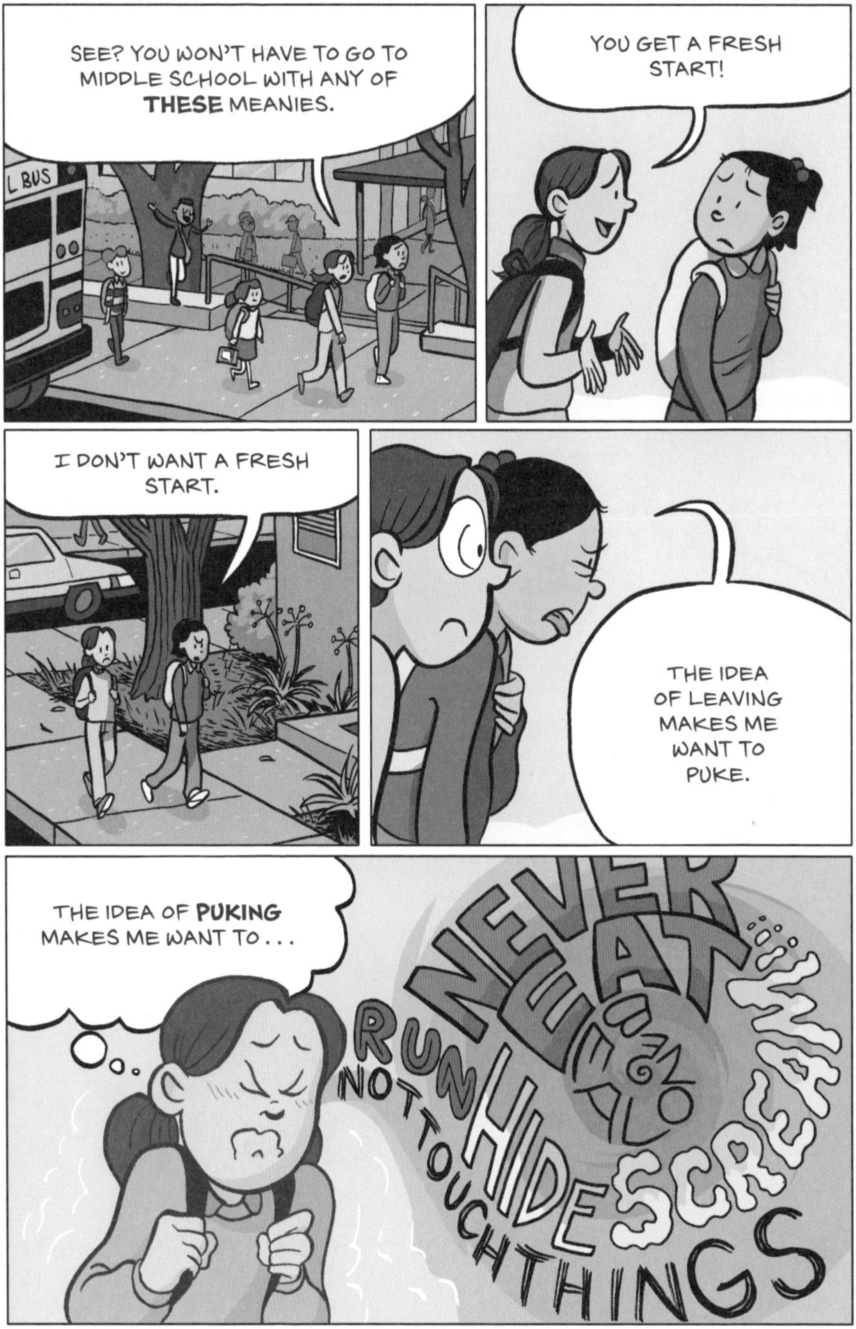
SEE? YOU WON'T HAVE TO GO TO MIDDLE SCHOOL WITH ANY OF **THESE** MEANIES.
L BUS
YOU GET A FRESH START!
I DON'T WANT A FRESH START.
THE IDEA OF LEAVING MAKES ME WANT TO PUKE.
THE IDEA OF **PUKING** MAKES ME WANT TO . . .
NEVER EAT
RUN
HIDE
SCREAM
NOT TOUCH THINGS

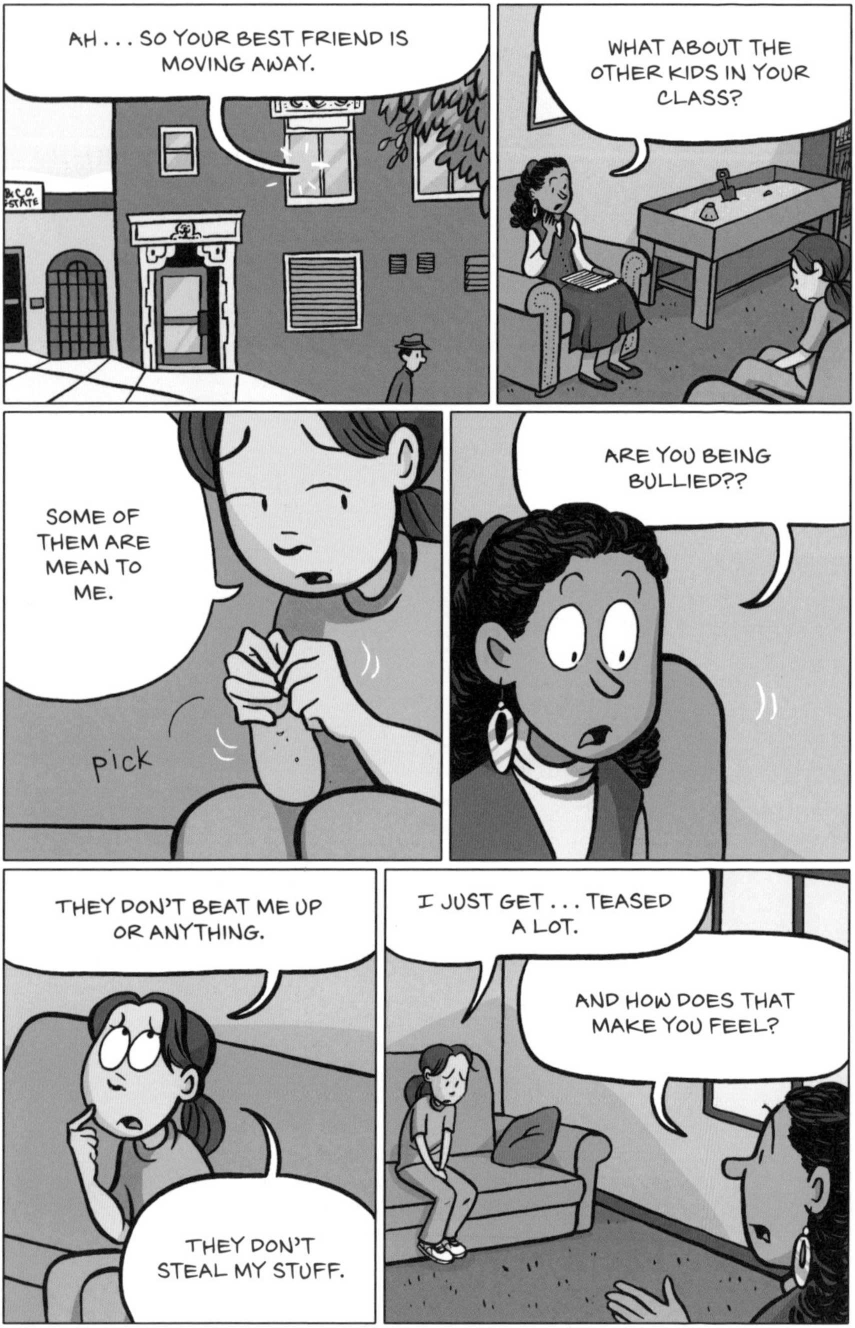

AH . . . SO YOUR BEST FRIEND IS MOVING AWAY.
B&C.O. ESTATE
WHAT ABOUT THE OTHER KIDS IN YOUR CLASS?
SOME OF THEM ARE MEAN TO ME.
pick
ARE YOU BEING BULLIED??
THEY DON'T BEAT ME UP OR ANYTHING.
THEY DON'T STEAL MY STUFF.
I JUST GET . . . TEASED A LOT.
AND HOW DOES THAT MAKE YOU FEEL?

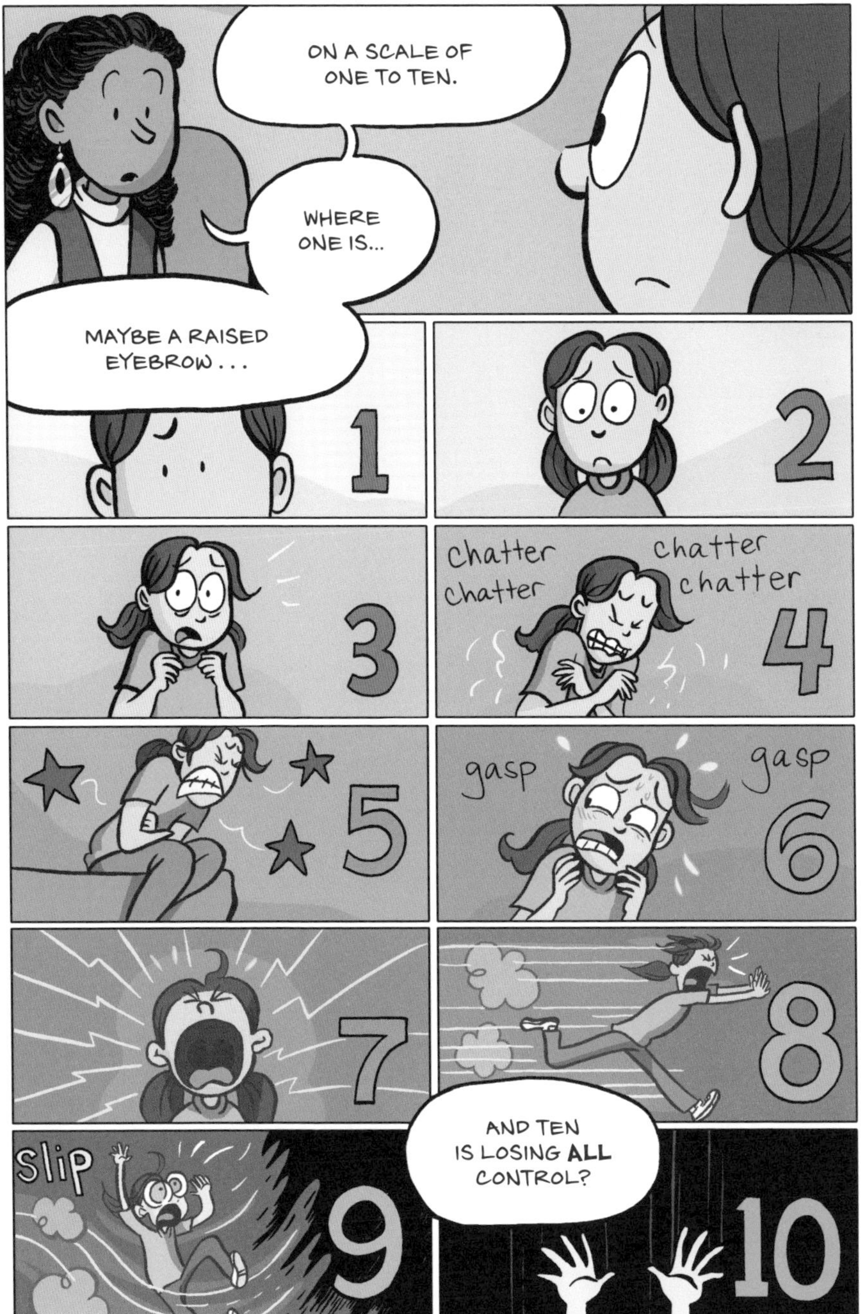

ON A SCALE OF ONE TO TEN.
WHERE ONE IS...
MAYBE A RAISED EYEBROW . . .
1
2
3
chatter chatter
chatter chatter
4
5
gasp
gasp
6
7
8
slip
9
AND TEN IS LOSING **ALL** CONTROL?
10

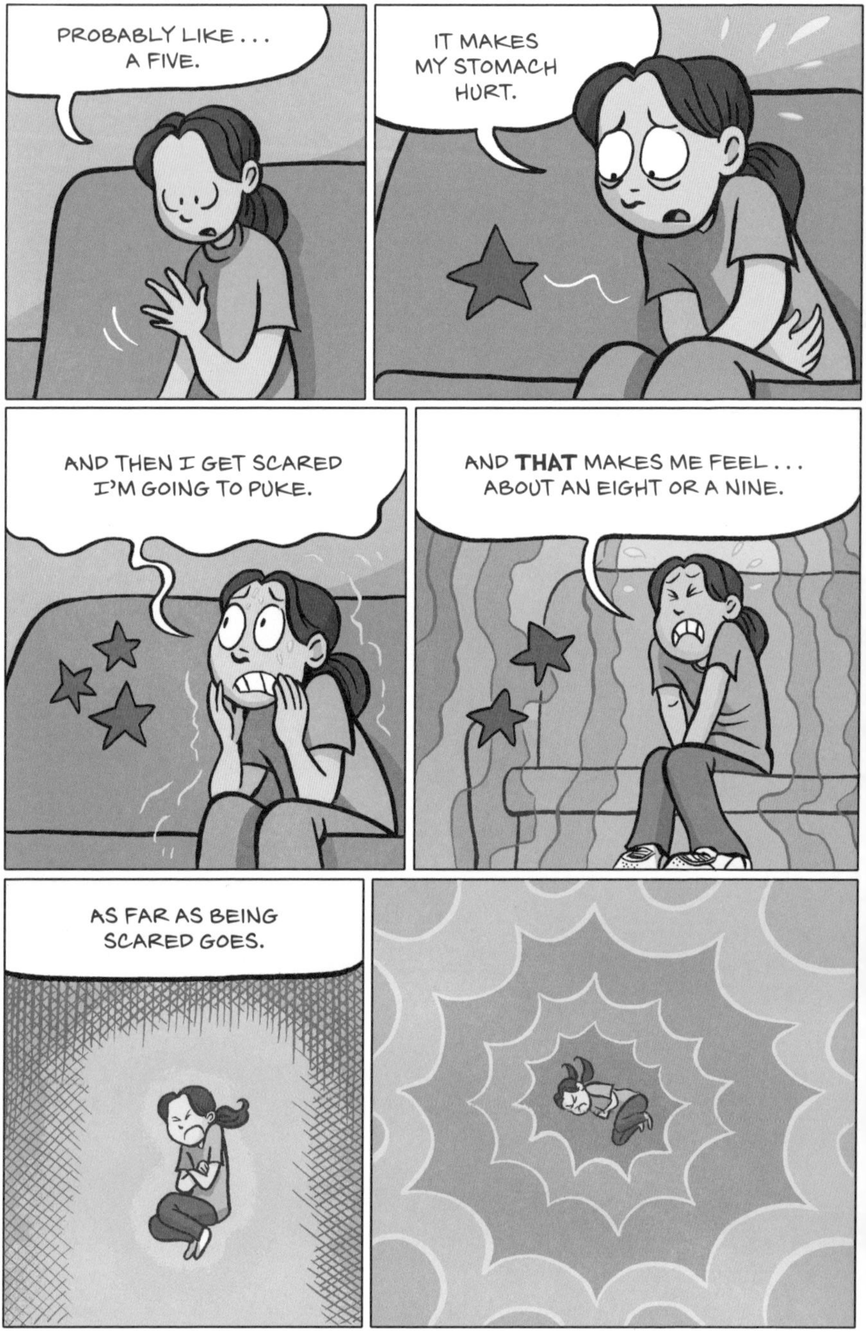
PROBABLY LIKE . . . A FIVE.
IT MAKES MY STOMACH HURT.
AND THEN I GET SCARED I'M GOING TO PUKE.
AND **THAT** MAKES ME FEEL . . . ABOUT AN EIGHT OR A NINE.
AS FAR AS BEING SCARED GOES.

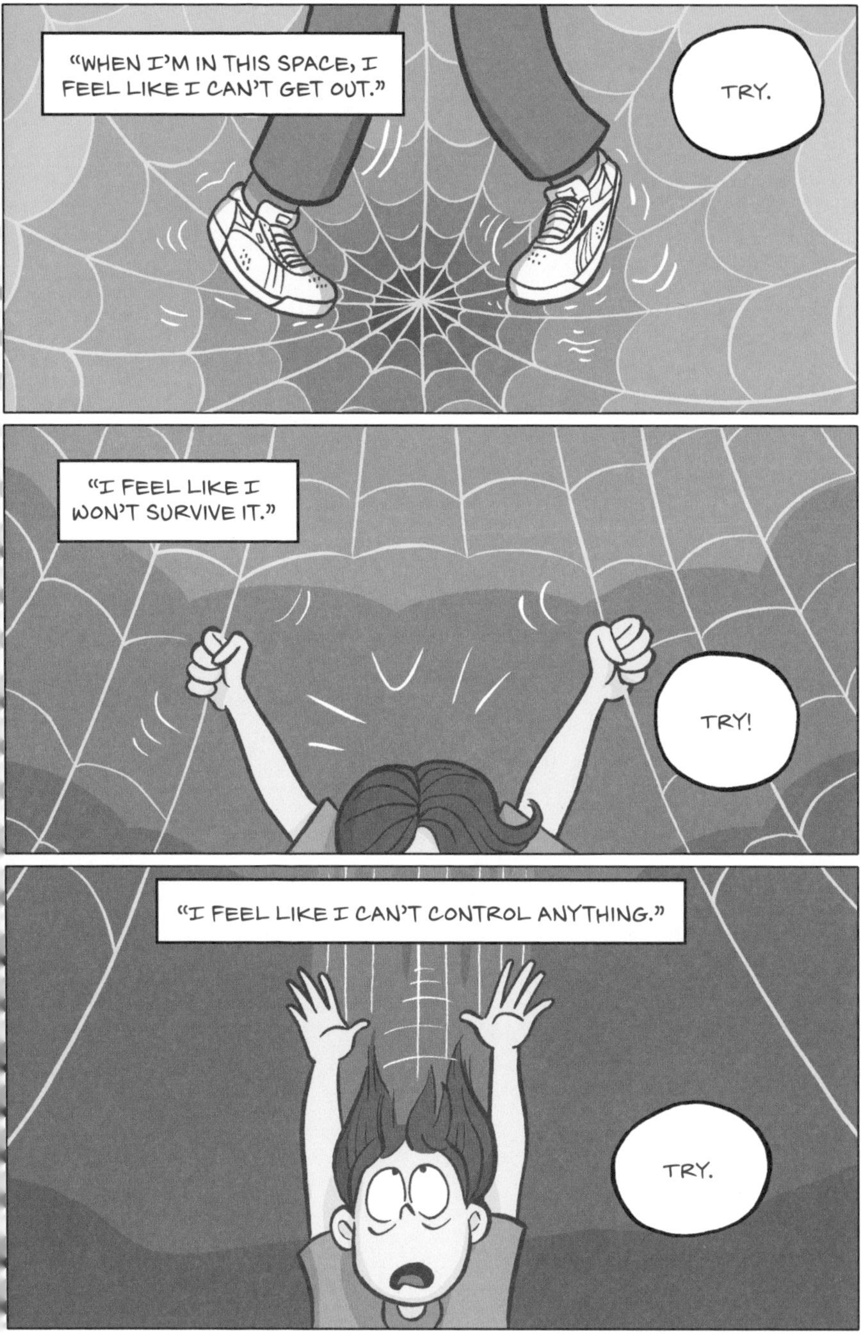
"WHEN I'M IN THIS SPACE, I FEEL LIKE I CAN'T GET OUT."
TRY.
"I FEEL LIKE I WON'T SURVIVE IT."
TRY!
"I FEEL LIKE I CAN'T CONTROL ANYTHING."
TRY.

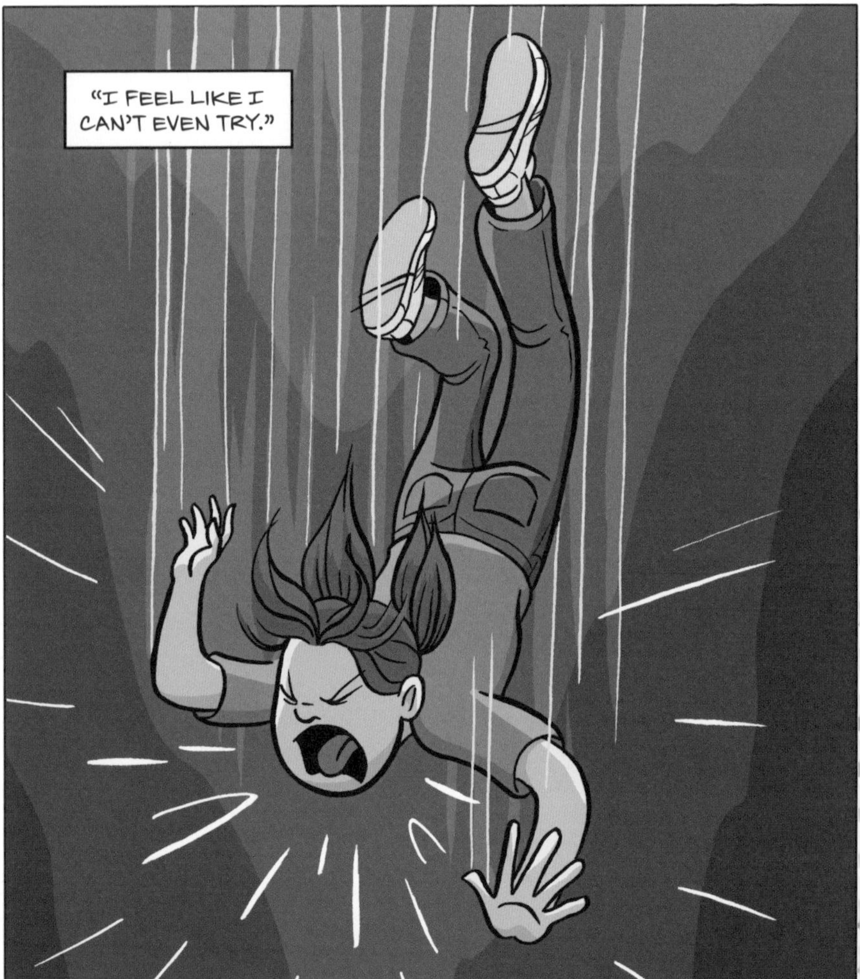
"I FEEL LIKE I CAN'T EVEN TRY."

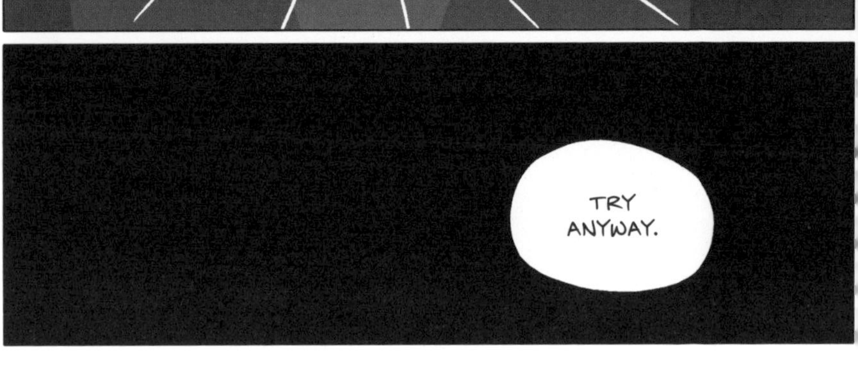
TRY ANYWAY.

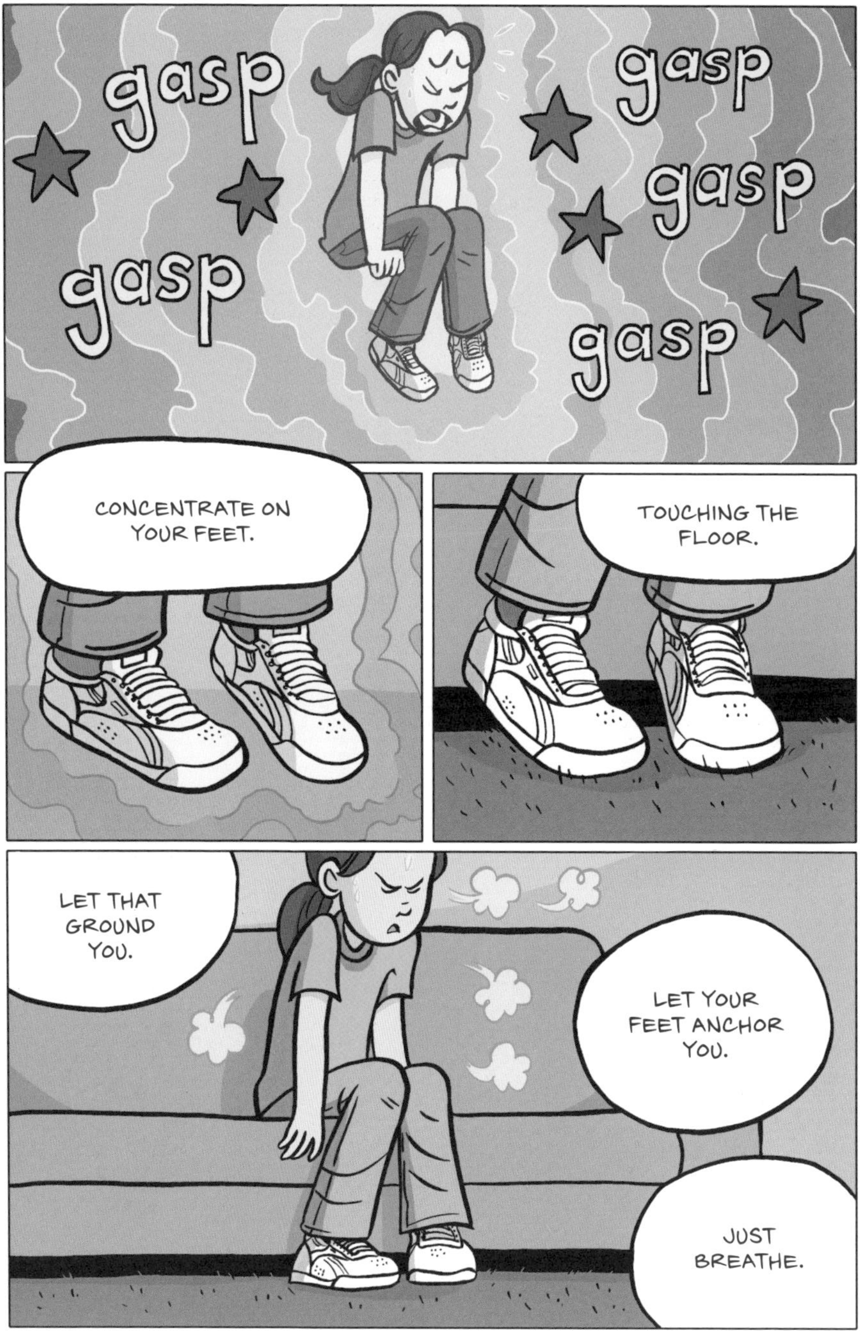
gasp
gasp
gasp
gasp
gasp
CONCENTRATE ON YOUR FEET.
TOUCHING THE FLOOR.
LET THAT GROUND YOU.
LET YOUR FEET ANCHOR YOU.
JUST BREATHE.

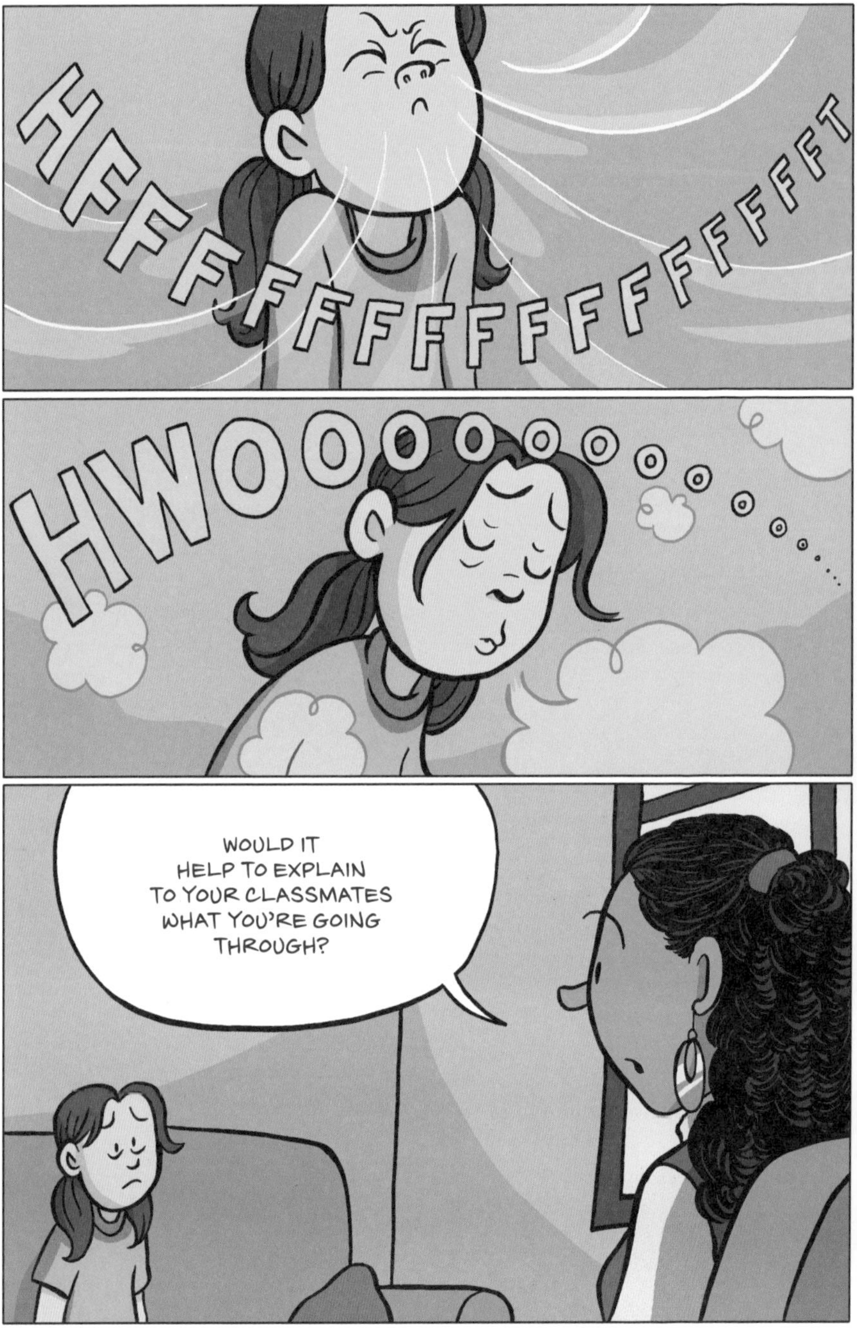
HFFFFFFFFFFFFFFFFT
HWOOOOOOOOOOO....
WOULD IT HELP TO EXPLAIN TO YOUR CLASSMATES WHAT YOU'RE GOING THROUGH?

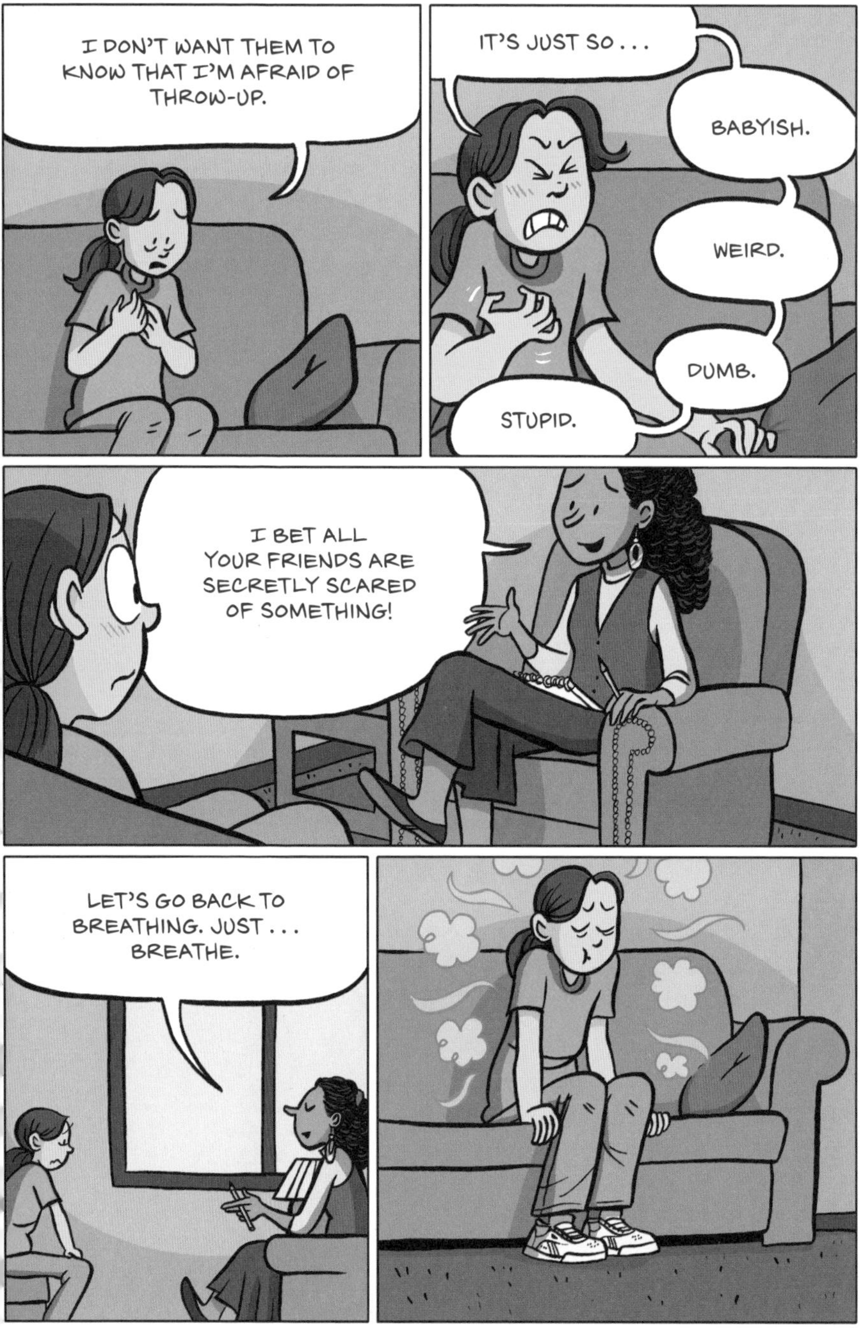
I DON'T WANT THEM TO KNOW THAT I'M AFRAID OF THROW-UP.
IT'S JUST SO . . .
BABYISH.
WEIRD.
DUMB.
STUPID.
I BET ALL YOUR FRIENDS ARE SECRETLY SCARED OF SOMETHING!
LET'S GO BACK TO BREATHING. JUST . . . BREATHE.

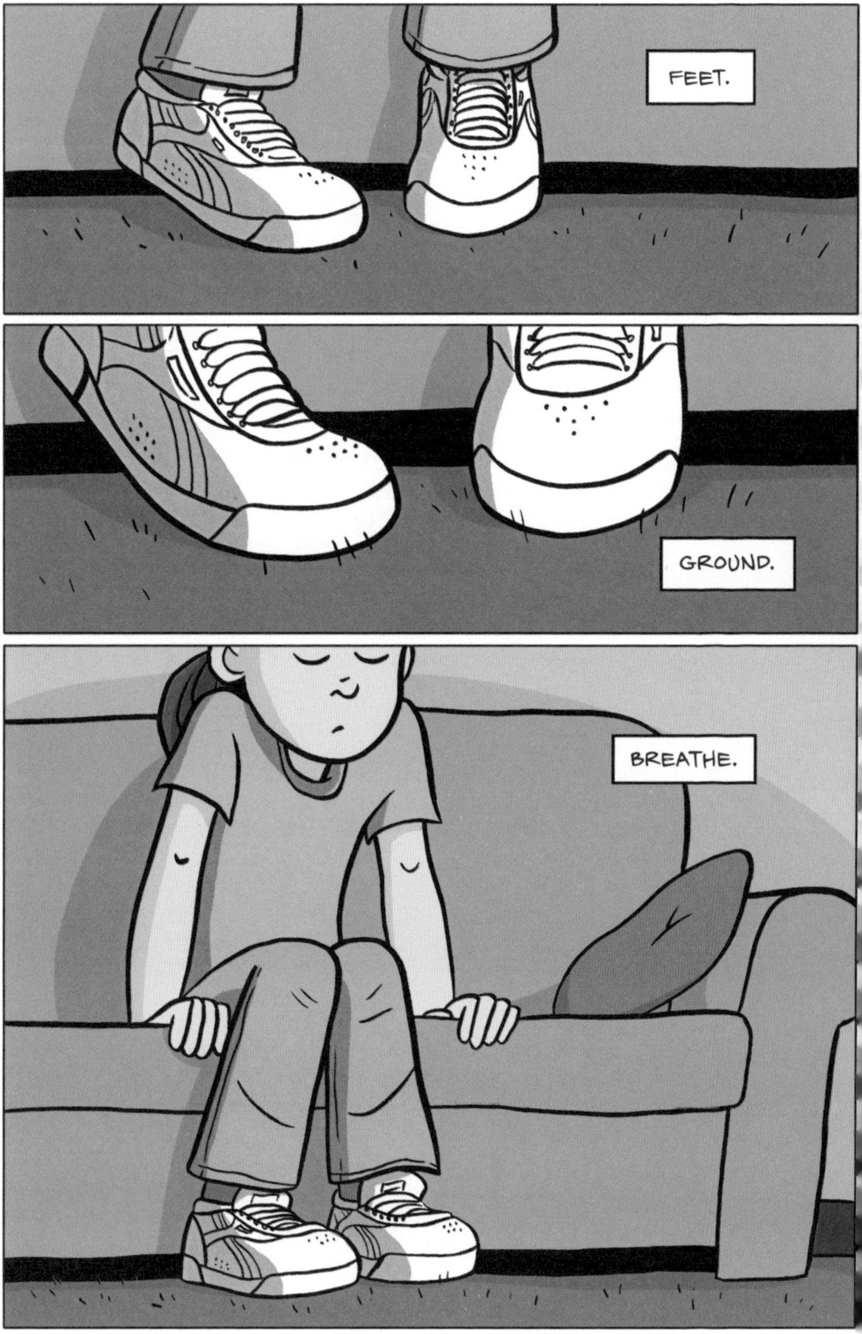
FEET.
GROUND.
BREATHE.

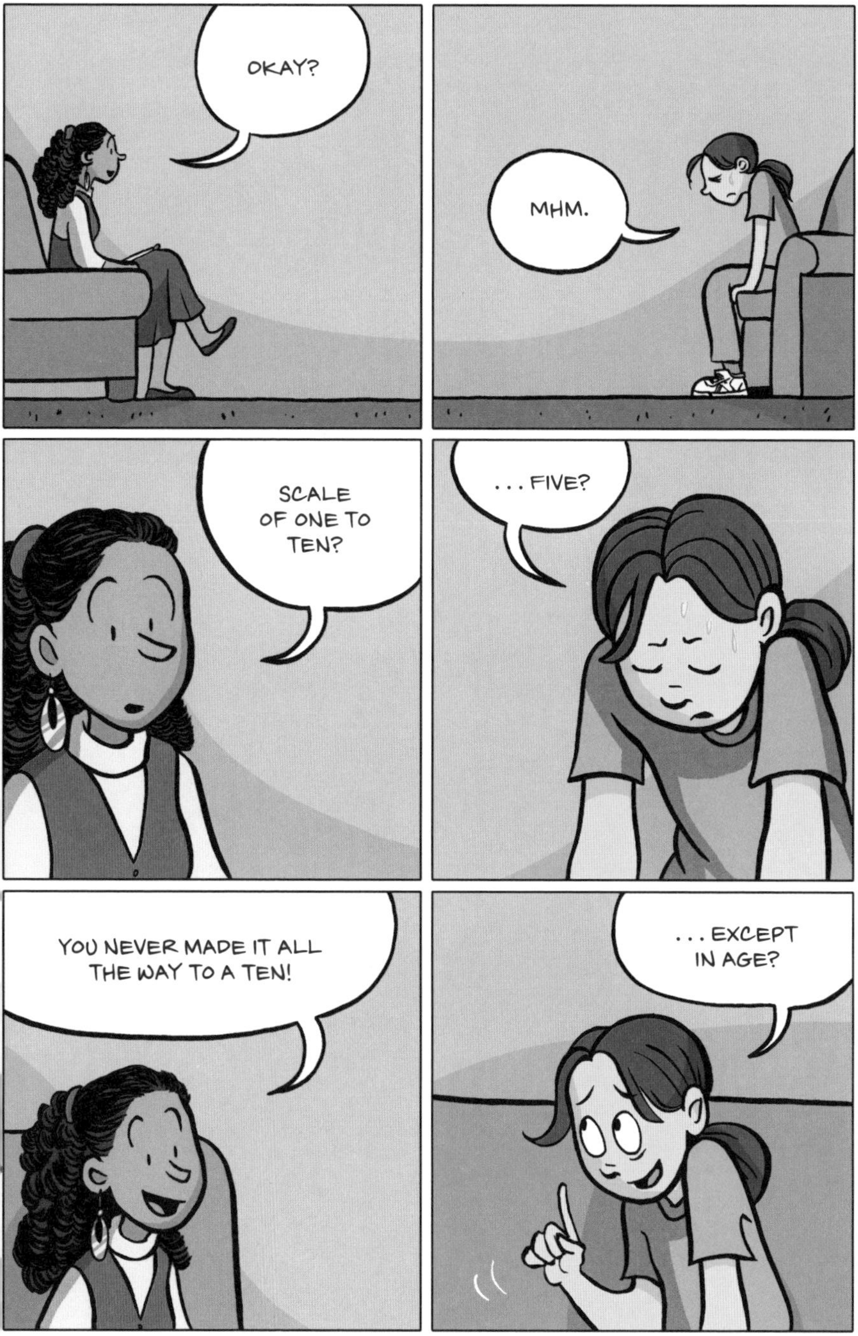
OKAY?
MHM.
SCALE OF ONE TO TEN?
. . . FIVE?
YOU NEVER MADE IT ALL THE WAY TO A TEN!
. . . EXCEPT IN AGE?

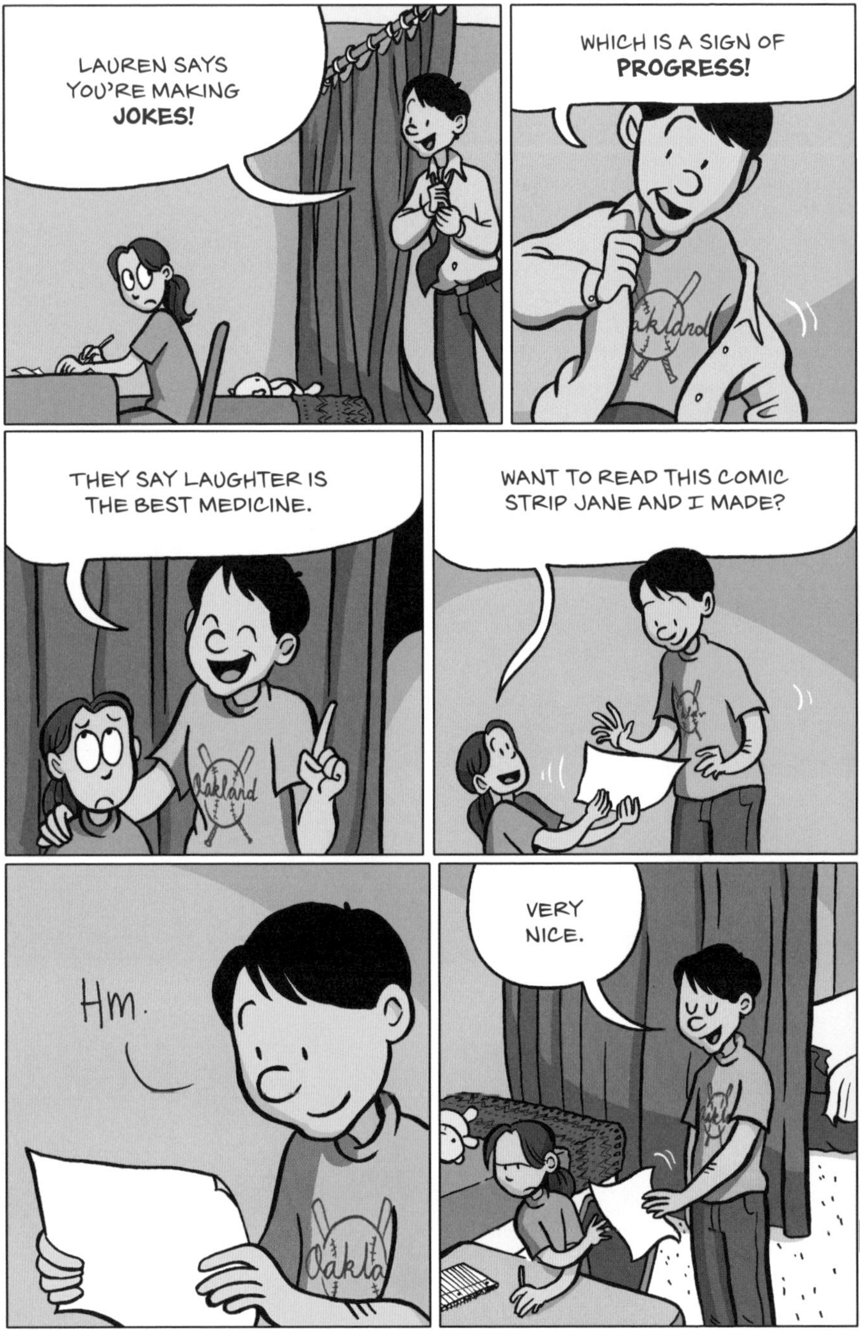
LAUREN SAYS YOU'RE MAKING **JOKES!**
WHICH IS A SIGN OF **PROGRESS!**
THEY SAY LAUGHTER IS THE BEST MEDICINE.
WANT TO READ THIS COMIC STRIP JANE AND I MADE?
Hm.
VERY NICE.

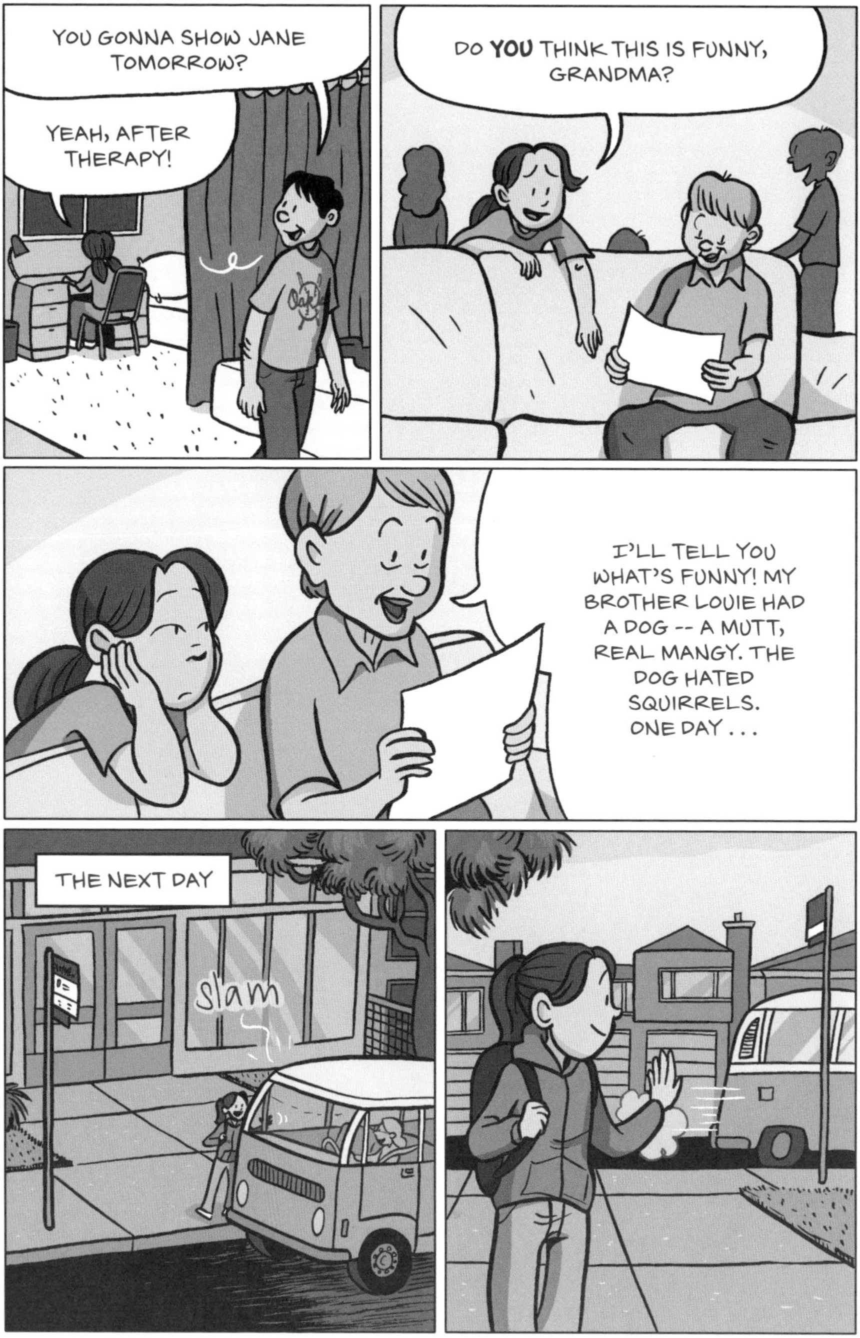

YOU GONNA SHOW JANE TOMORROW?
YEAH, AFTER THERAPY!
DO **YOU** THINK THIS IS FUNNY, GRANDMA?
I'LL TELL YOU WHAT'S FUNNY! MY BROTHER LOUIE HAD A DOG -- A MUTT, REAL MANGY. THE DOG HATED SQUIRRELS. ONE DAY . . .
THE NEXT DAY
slam

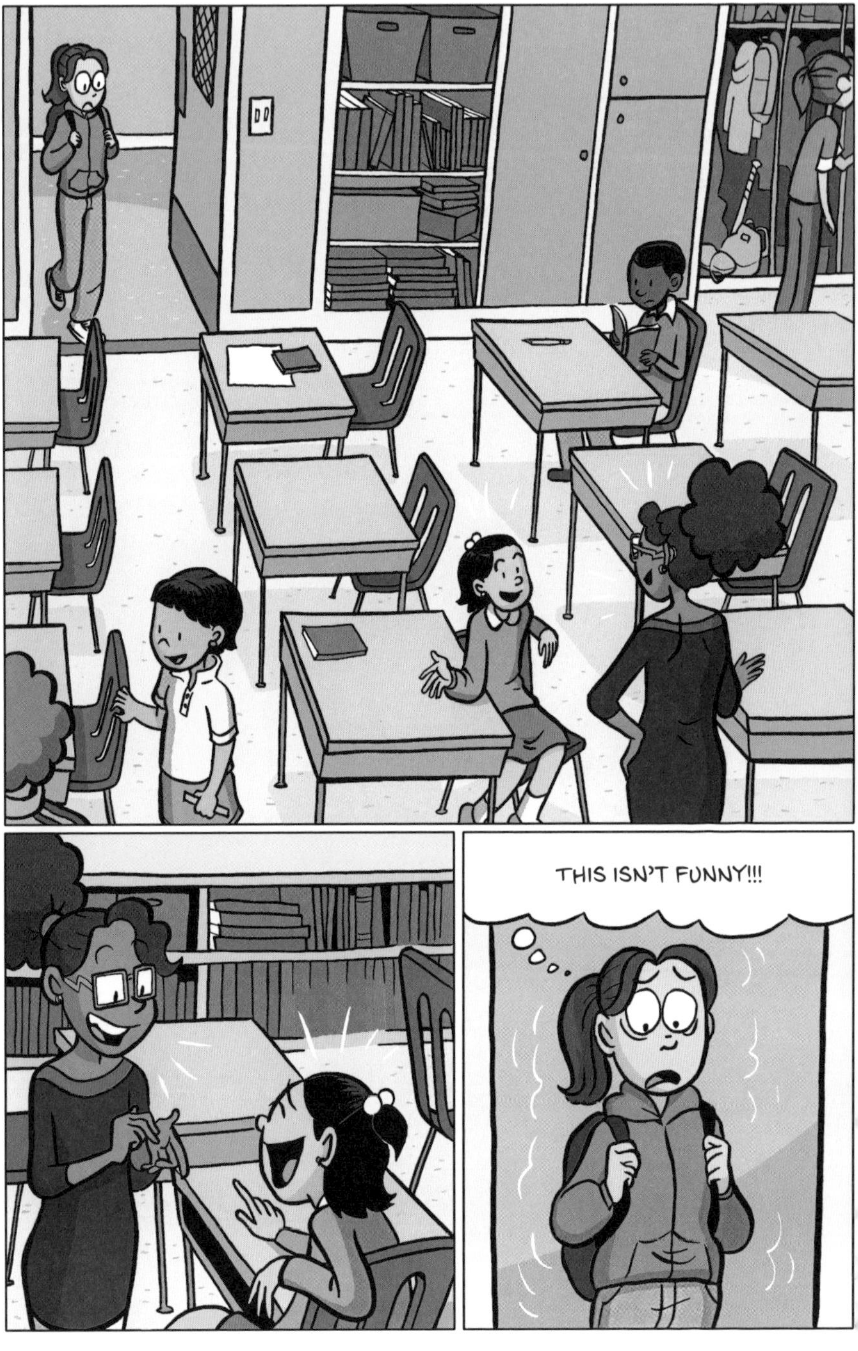
THIS ISN'T FUNNY!!!

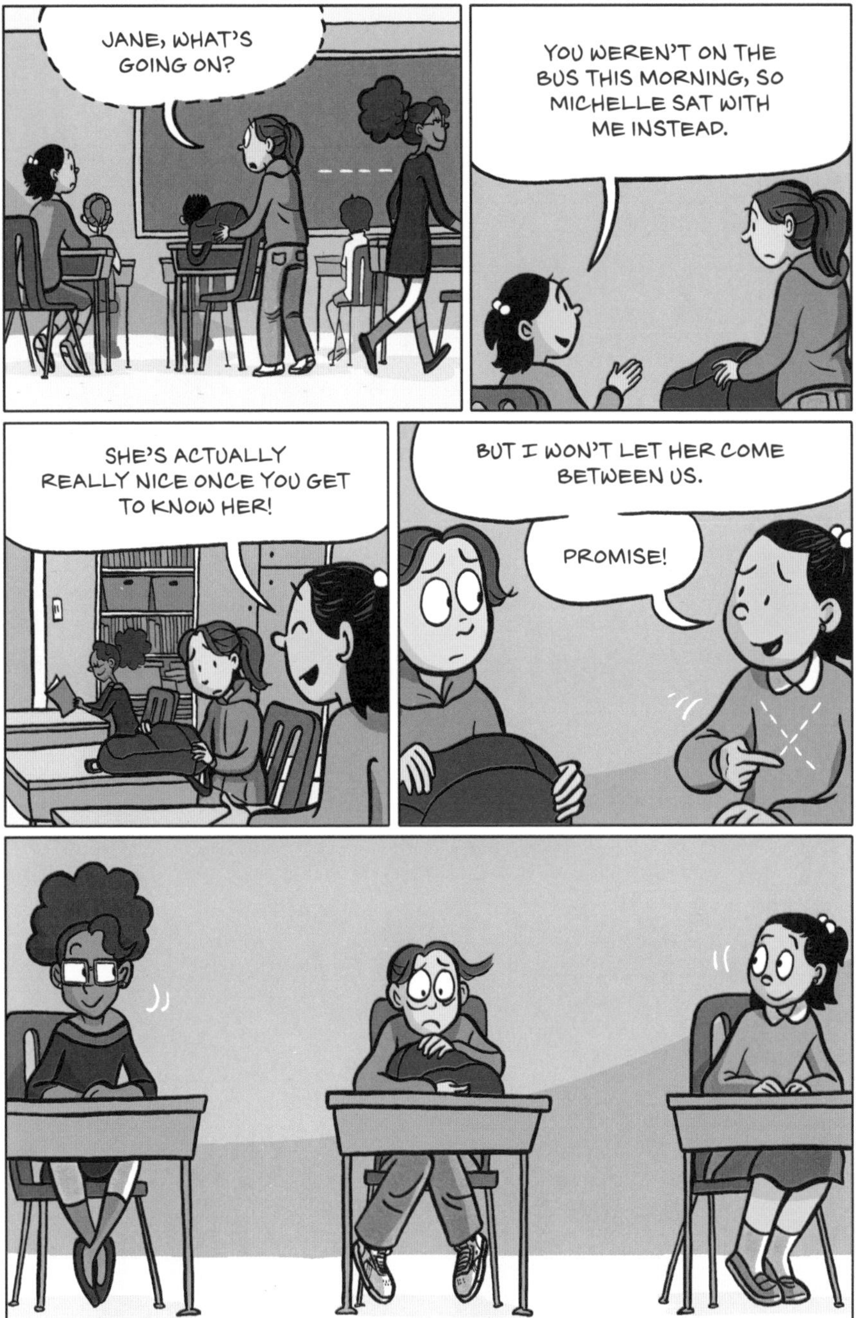

JANE, WHAT'S GOING ON?
YOU WEREN'T ON THE BUS THIS MORNING, SO MICHELLE SAT WITH ME INSTEAD.
SHE'S ACTUALLY REALLY NICE ONCE YOU GET TO KNOW HER!
BUT I WON'T LET HER COME BETWEEN US.
PROMISE!

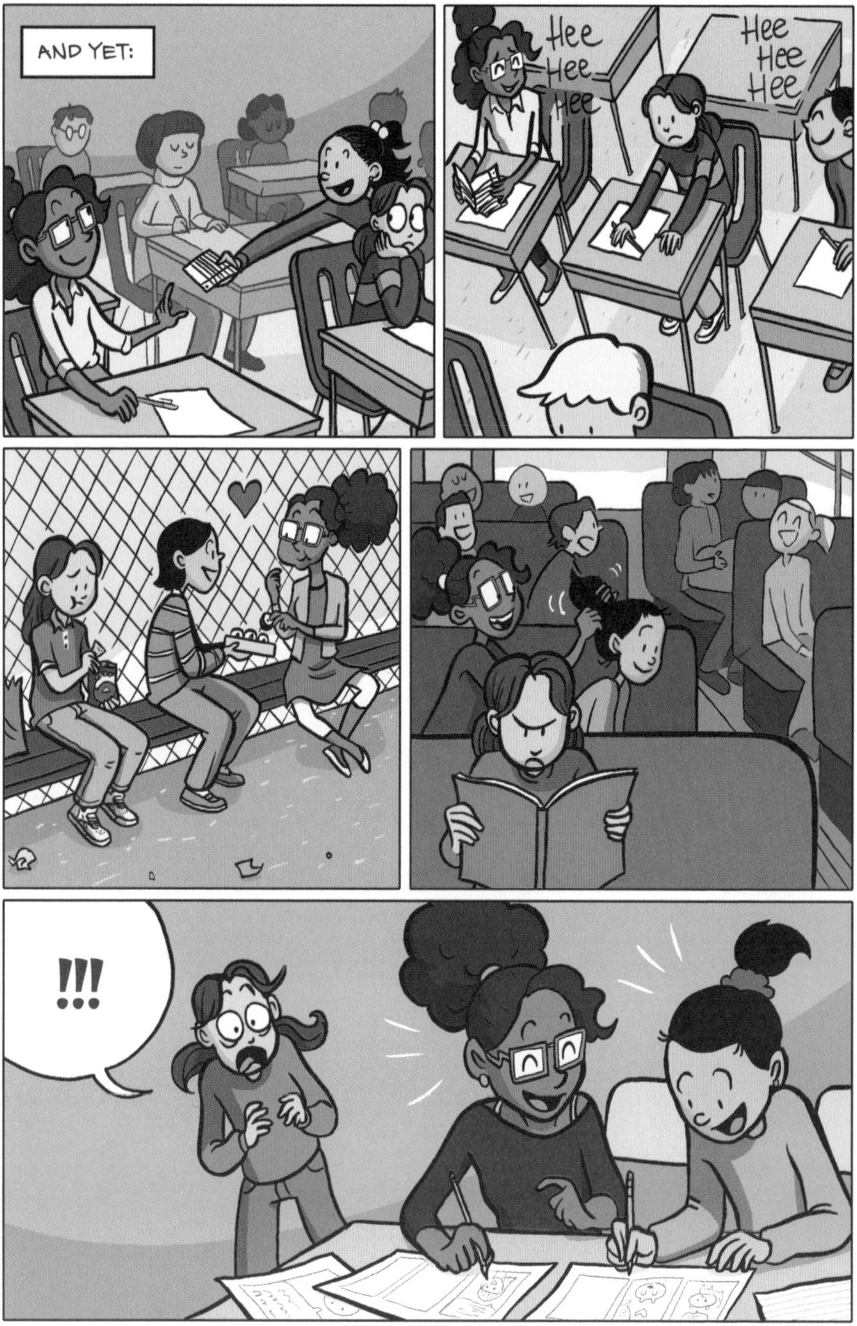
AND YET:
Hee
Hee
Hee
Hee
Hee
Hee
!!!

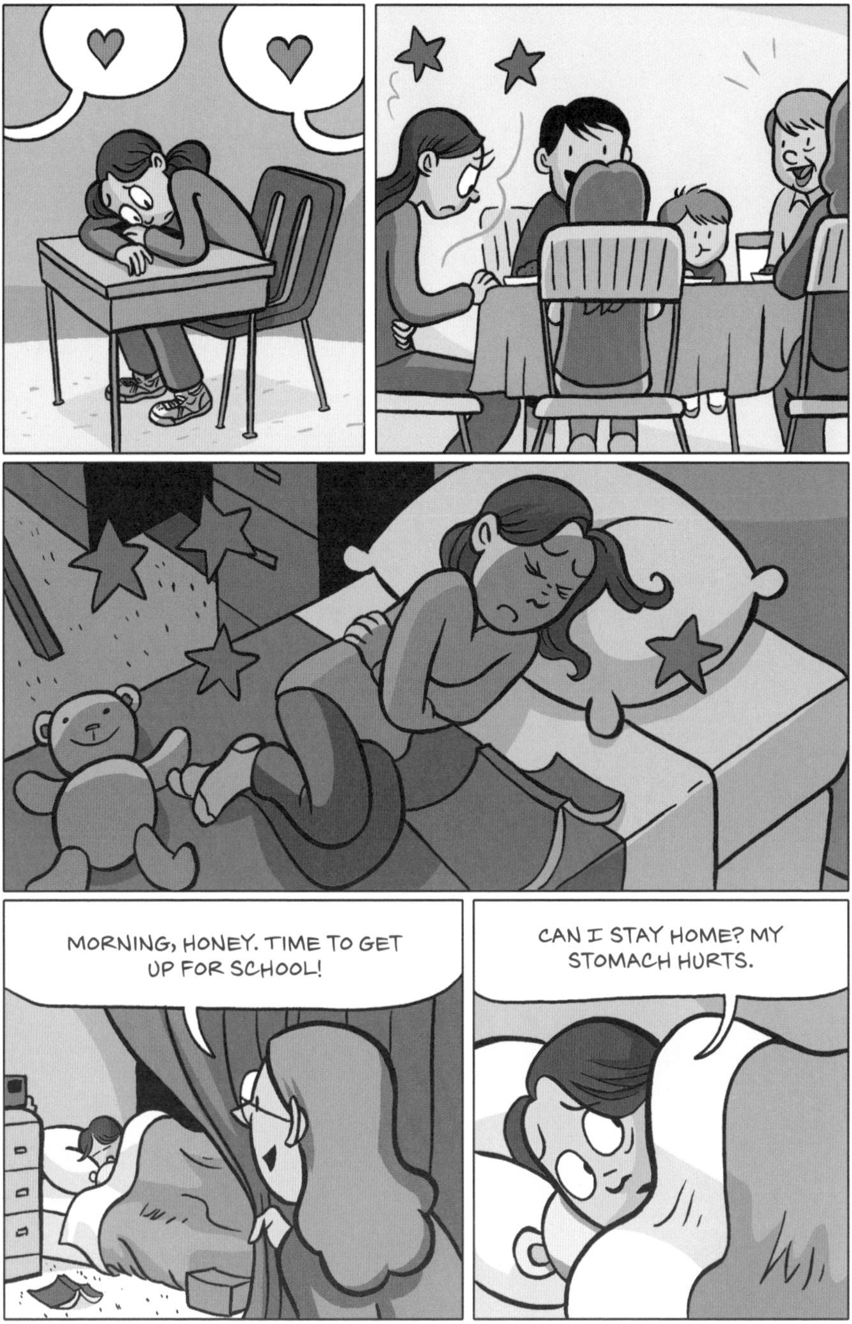
MORNING, HONEY. TIME TO GET UP FOR SCHOOL!
CAN I STAY HOME? MY STOMACH HURTS.

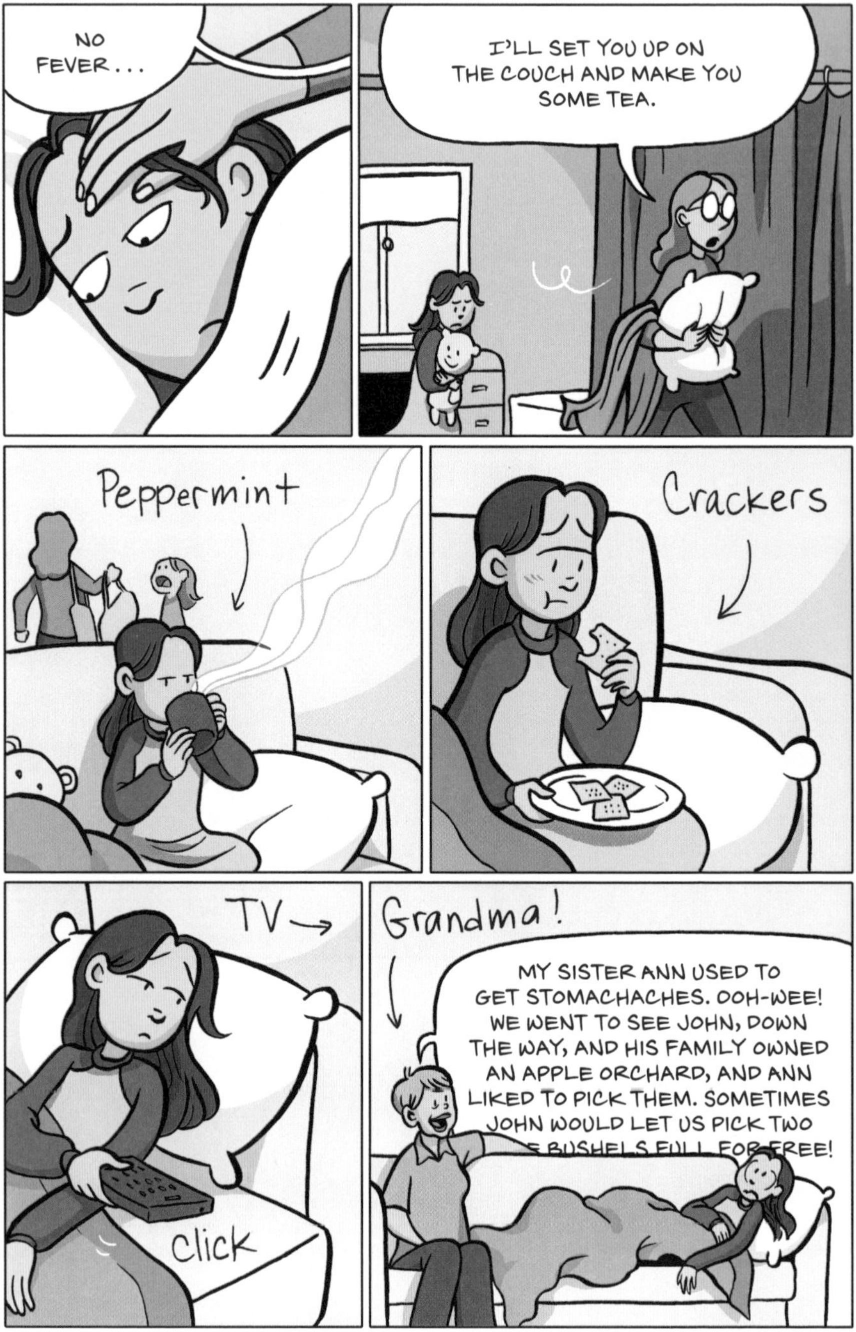
NO FEVER...
I'LL SET YOU UP ON THE COUCH AND MAKE YOU SOME TEA.
Peppermint
Crackers
TV
Click
Grandma!
MY SISTER ANN USED TO GET STOMACHACHES. OOH-WEE! WE WENT TO SEE JOHN, DOWN THE WAY, AND HIS FAMILY OWNED AN APPLE ORCHARD, AND ANN LIKED TO PICK THEM. SOMETIMES JOHN WOULD LET US PICK TWO

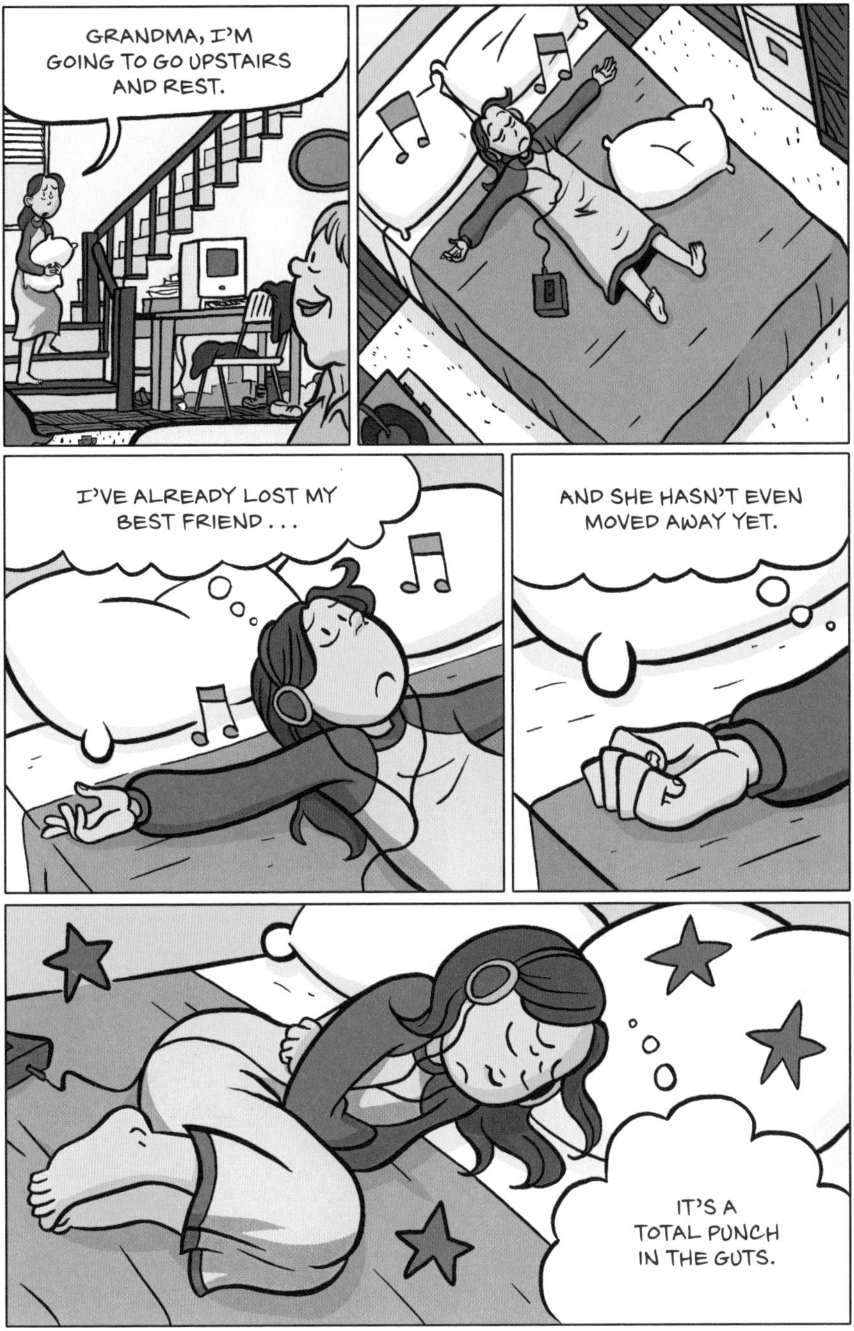
GRANDMA, I'M GOING TO GO UPSTAIRS AND REST.
I'VE ALREADY LOST MY BEST FRIEND . . .
AND SHE HASN'T EVEN MOVED AWAY YET.
IT'S A TOTAL PUNCH IN THE GUTS.

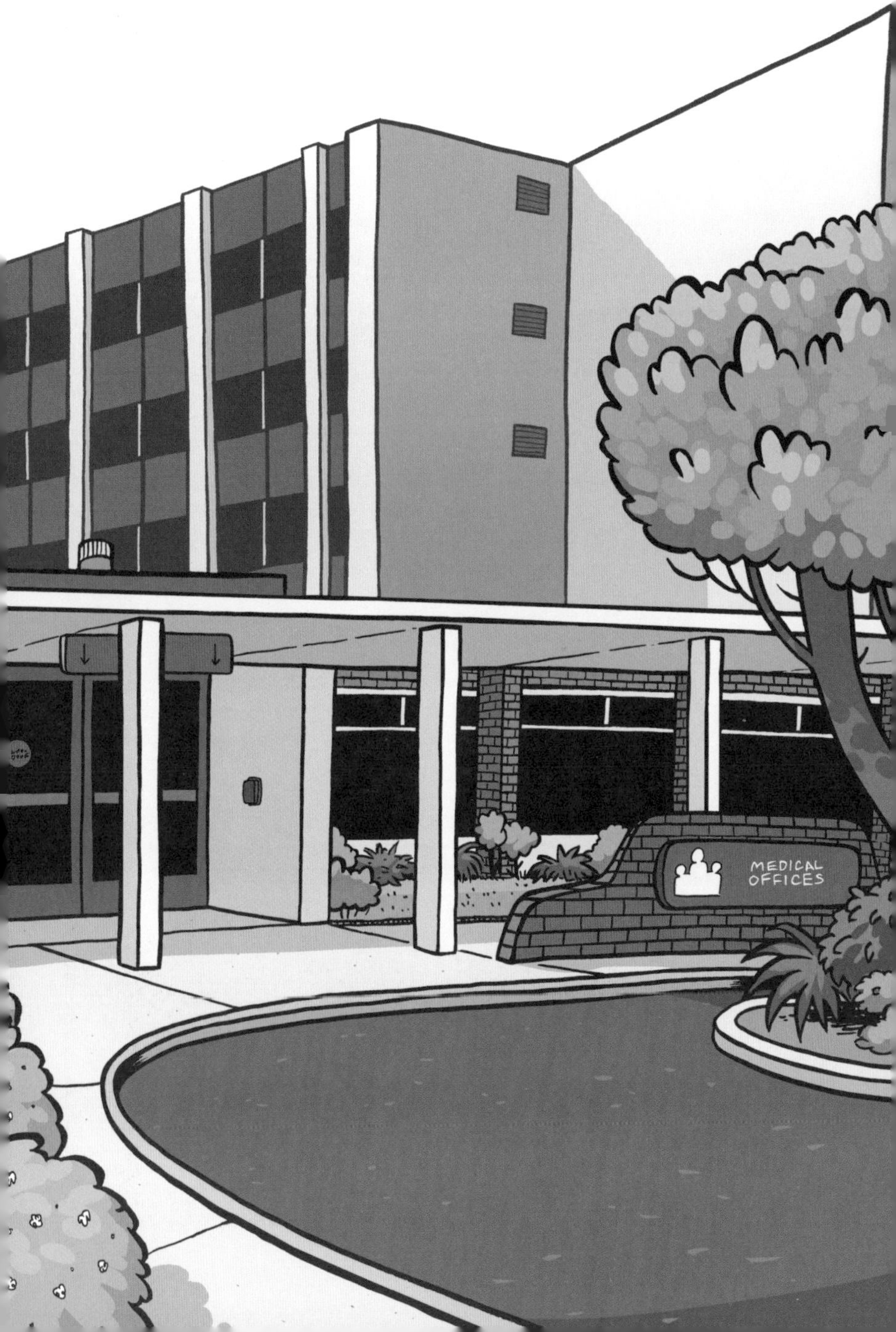
MEDICAL
OFFICES

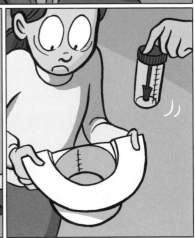

YEP . . . STILL HEALTHY AS A HORSE.

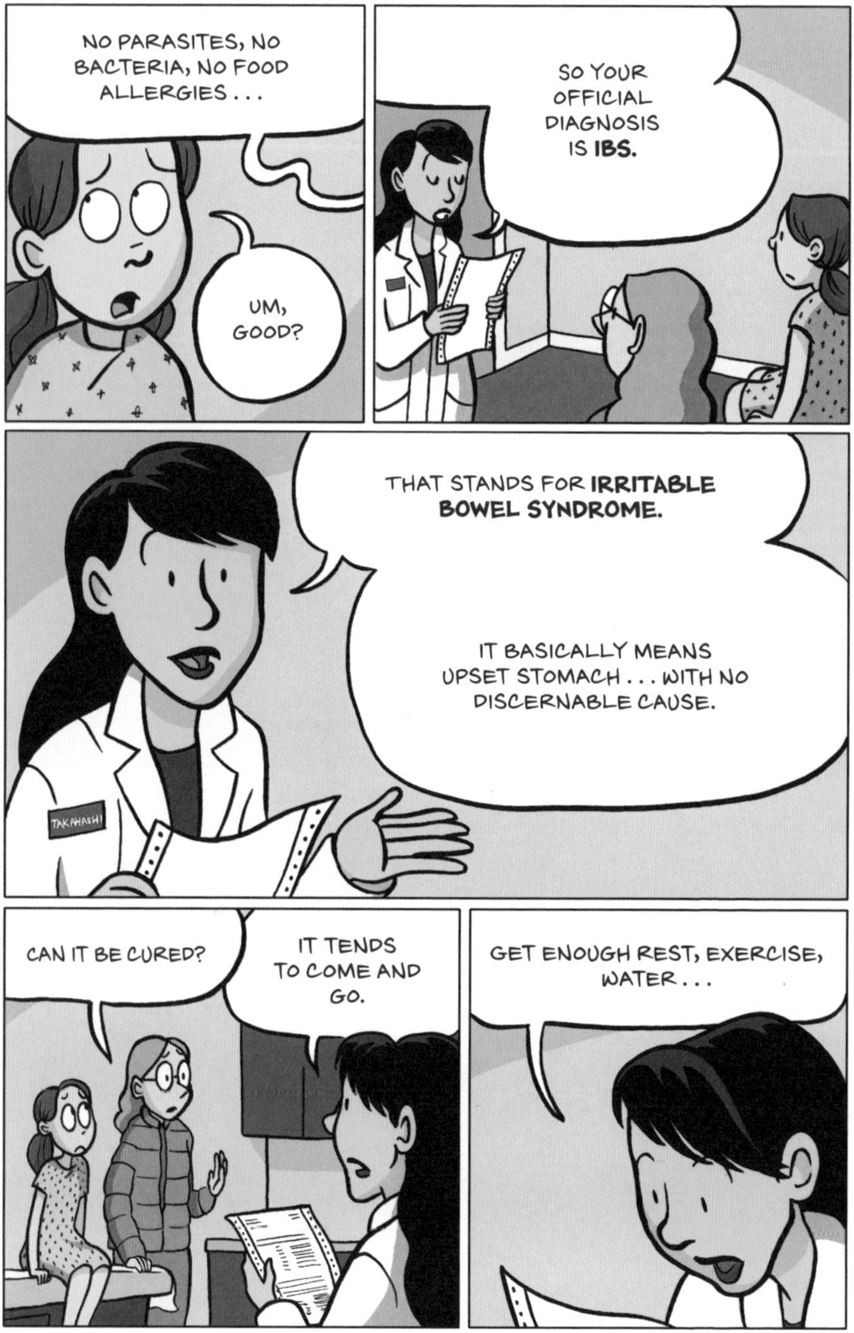
NO PARASITES, NO BACTERIA, NO FOOD ALLERGIES . . .
UM, GOOD?
SO YOUR OFFICIAL DIAGNOSIS IS **IBS.**
THAT STANDS FOR **IRRITABLE BOWEL SYNDROME.**
IT BASICALLY MEANS UPSET STOMACH . . . WITH NO DISCERNABLE CAUSE.
TAKAHASHI
CAN IT BE CURED?
IT TENDS TO COME AND GO.
GET ENOUGH REST, EXERCISE, WATER . . .

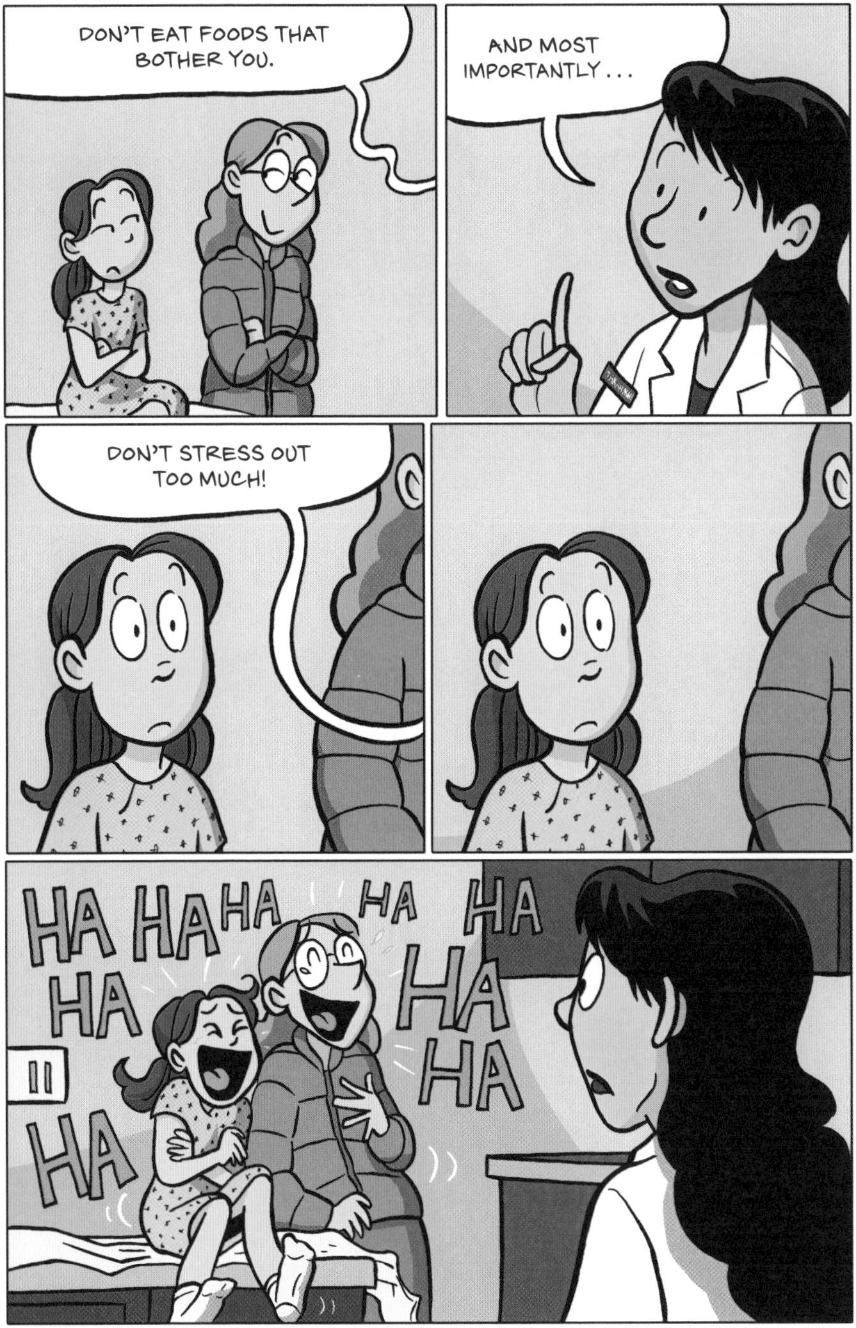
DON'T EAT FOODS THAT BOTHER YOU.
AND MOST IMPORTANTLY . . .
DON'T STRESS OUT TOO MUCH!
HA HA HA HA HA HA HA HA HA HA

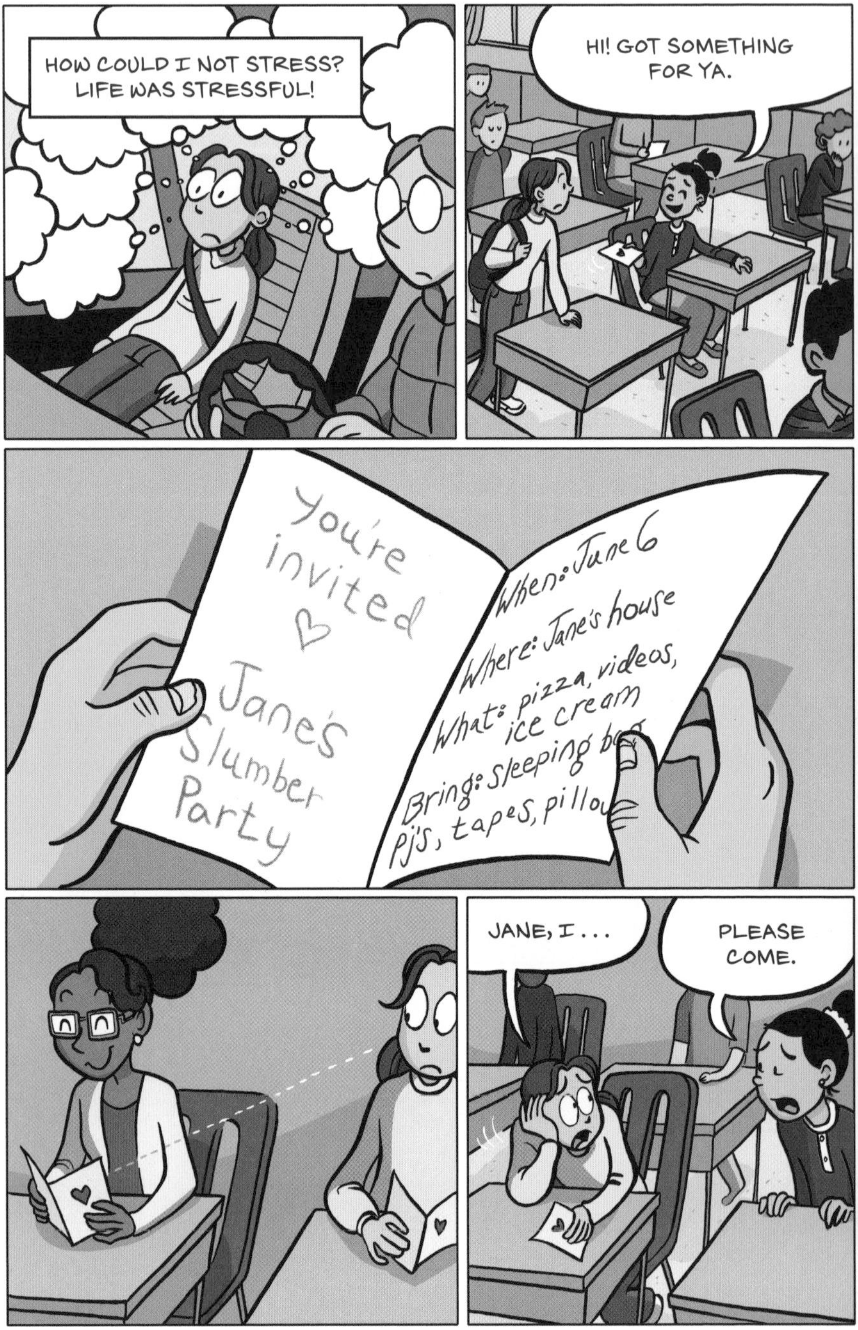
HOW COULD I NOT STRESS? LIFE WAS STRESSFUL!
HI! GOT SOMETHING FOR YA.
You're invited
Jane's Slumber Party
When: June 6
Where: Jane's house
What: pizza, videos, ice cream
Bring: sleeping ba
pj's, tapes, pillo
JANE, I . . .
PLEASE COME.

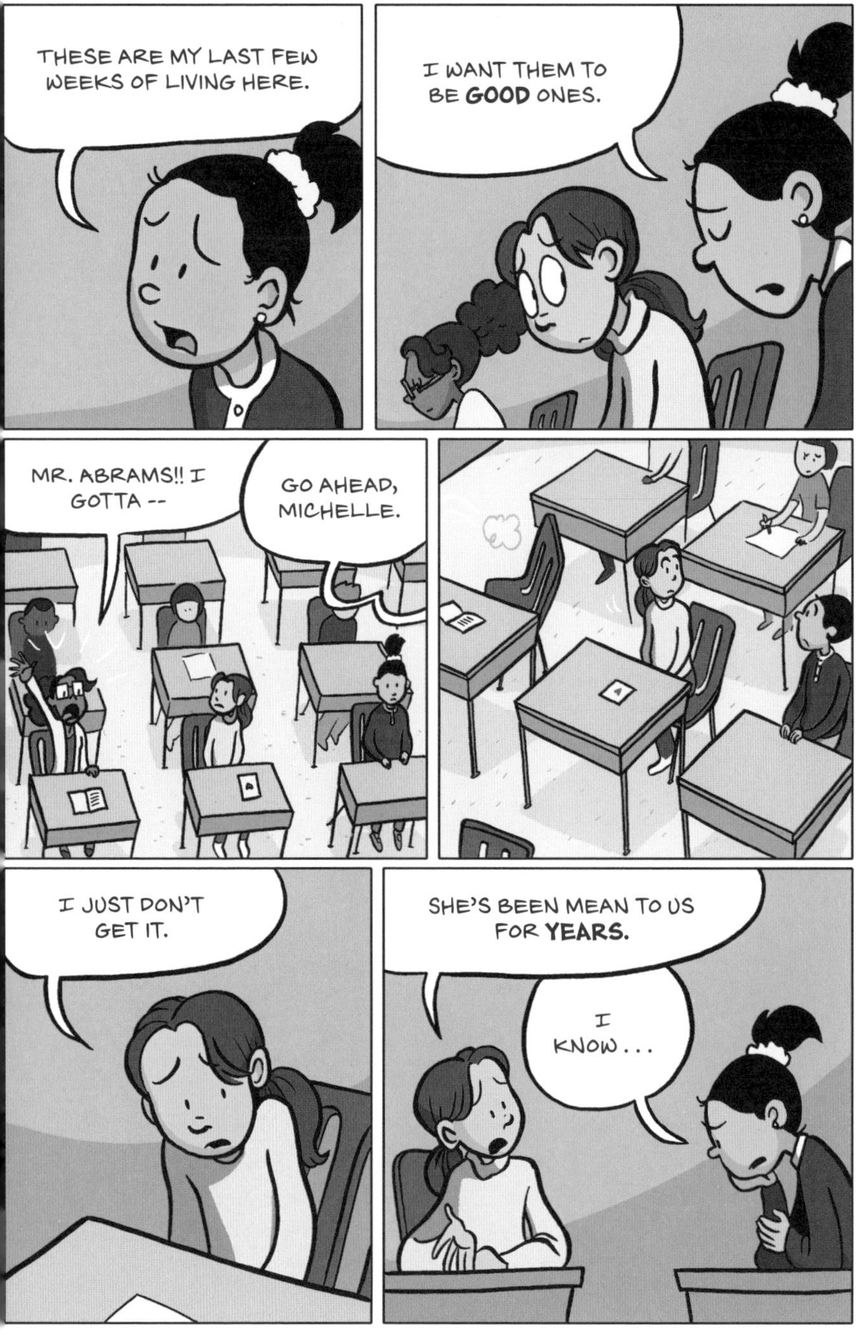
THESE ARE MY LAST FEW WEEKS OF LIVING HERE.
I WANT THEM TO BE **GOOD** ONES.
MR. ABRAMS!! I GOTTA --
GO AHEAD, MICHELLE.
I JUST DON'T GET IT.
SHE'S BEEN MEAN TO US FOR **YEARS.**
I KNOW . . .

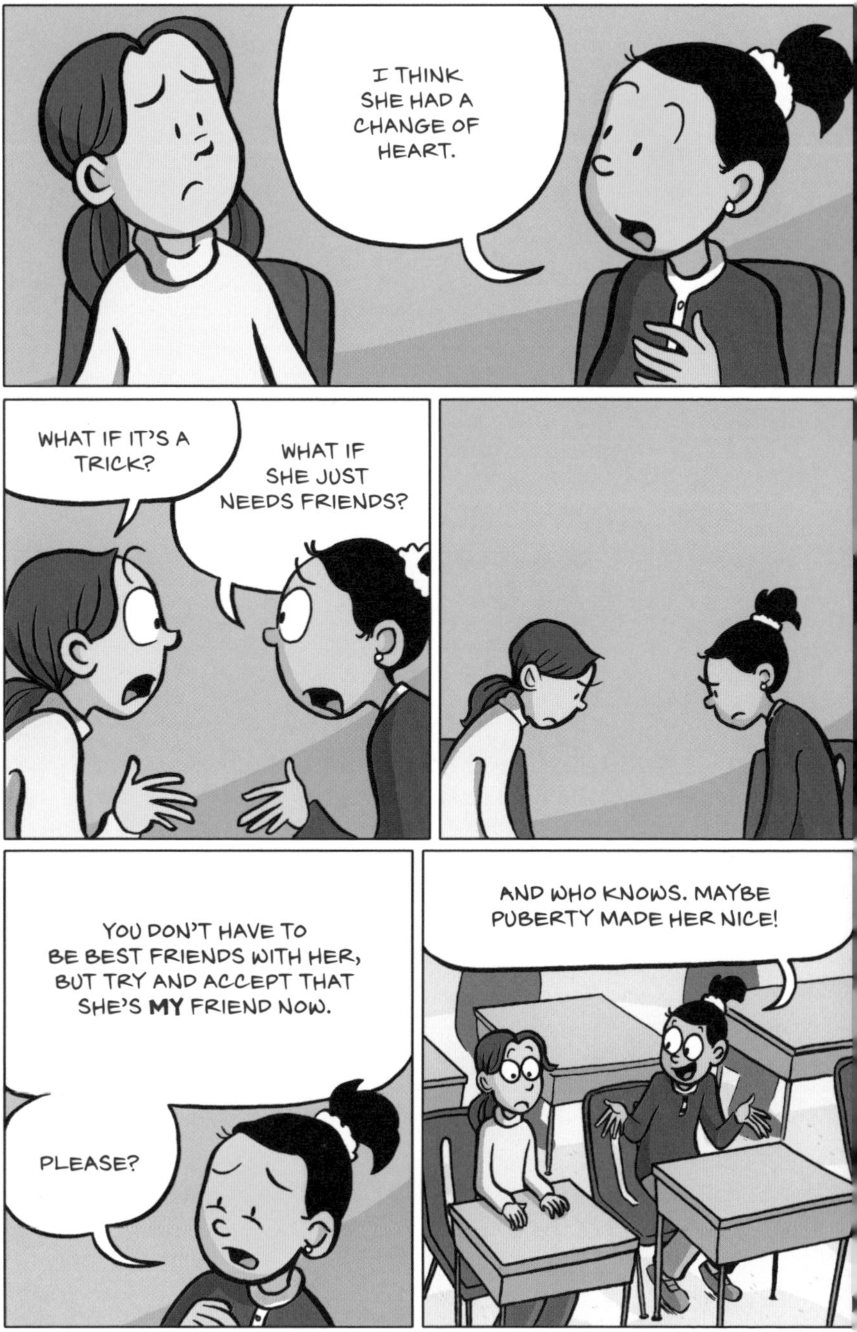
I THINK SHE HAD A CHANGE OF HEART.
WHAT IF IT'S A TRICK?
WHAT IF SHE JUST NEEDS FRIENDS?
YOU DON'T HAVE TO BE BEST FRIENDS WITH HER, BUT TRY AND ACCEPT THAT SHE'S **MY** FRIEND NOW.
PLEASE?
AND WHO KNOWS. MAYBE PUBERTY MADE HER NICE!

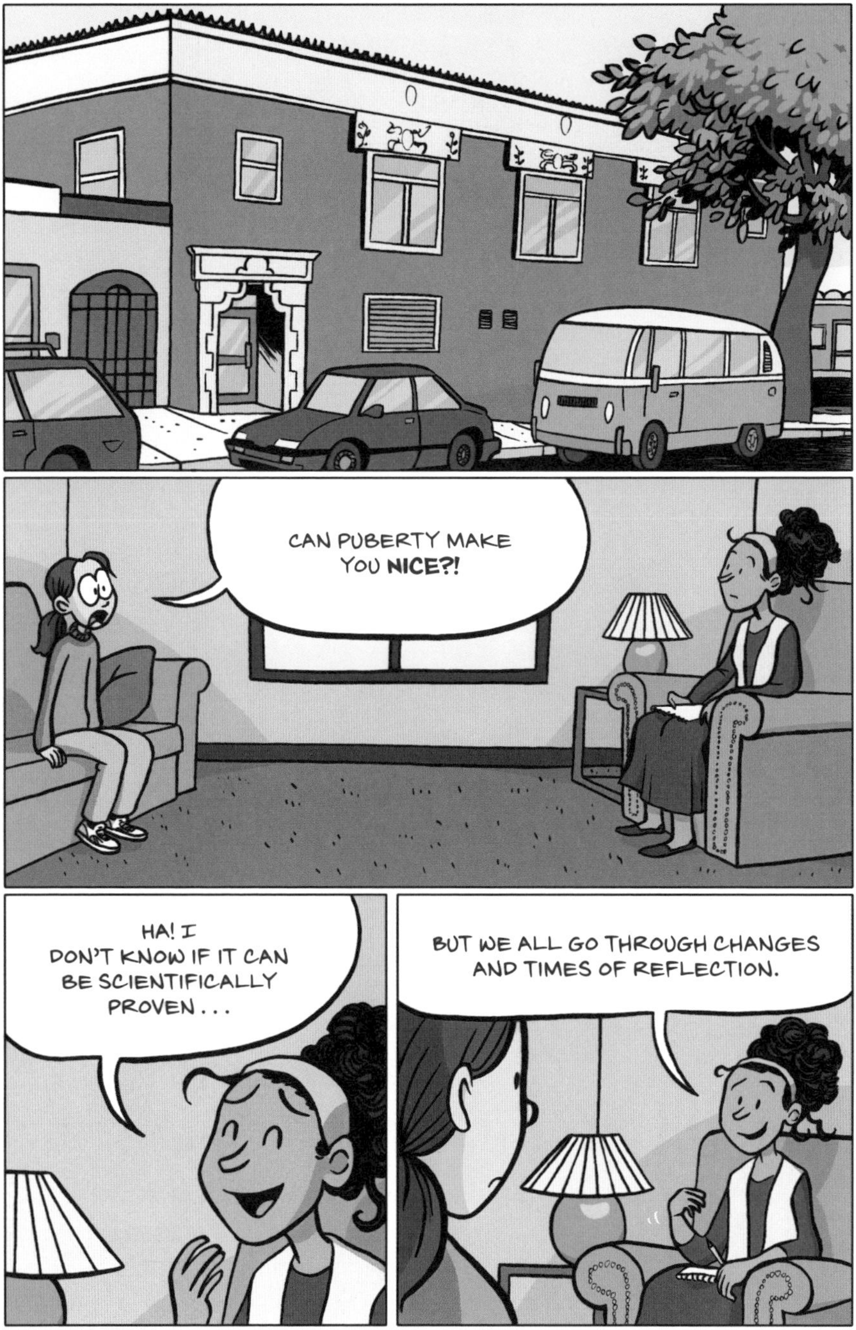
CAN PUBERTY MAKE YOU **NICE?!**
HA! I DON'T KNOW IF IT CAN BE SCIENTIFICALLY PROVEN . . .
BUT WE ALL GO THROUGH CHANGES AND TIMES OF REFLECTION.

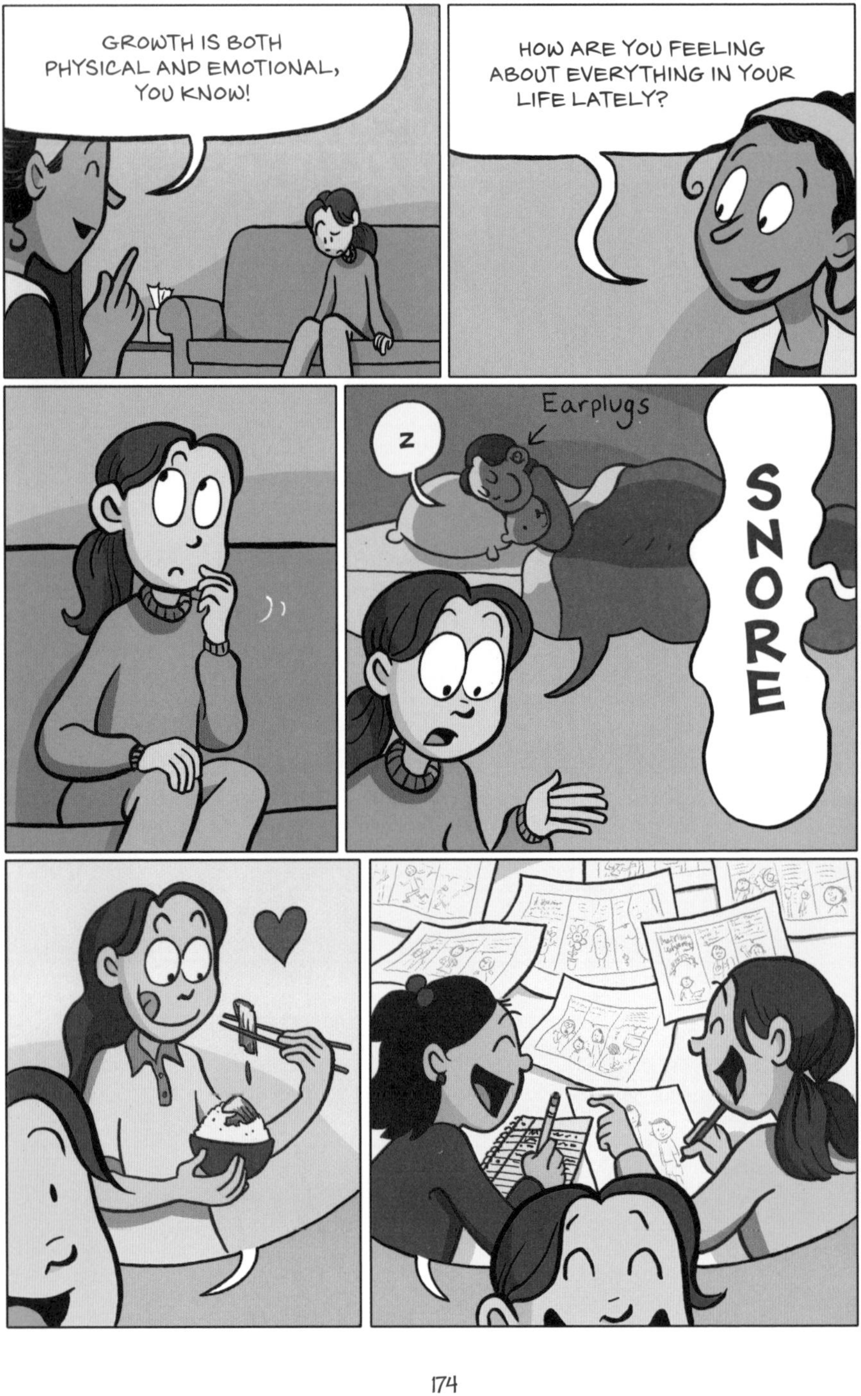
GROWTH IS BOTH PHYSICAL AND EMOTIONAL, YOU KNOW!
HOW ARE YOU FEELING ABOUT EVERYTHING IN YOUR LIFE LATELY?
Z
Earplugs
SNORE

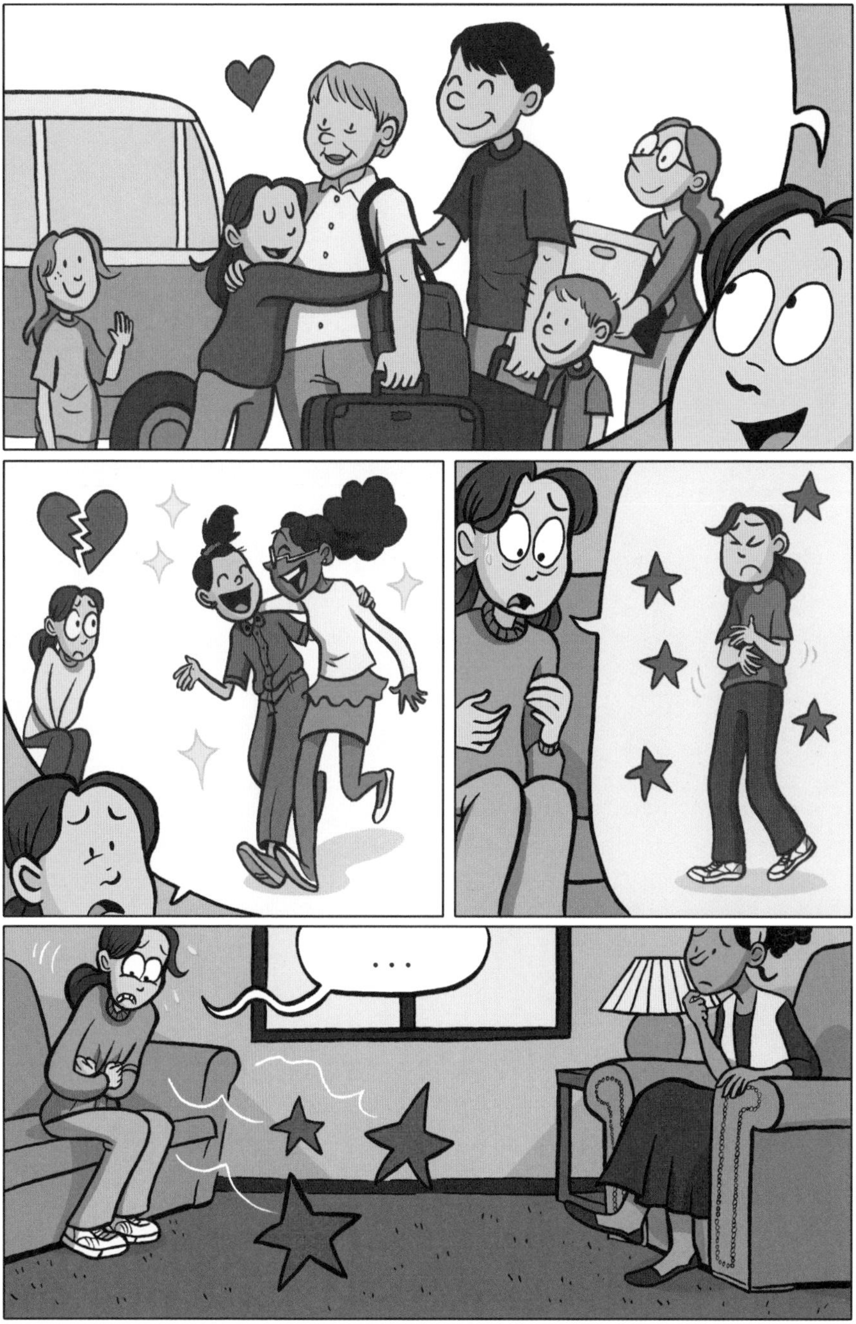
. . .

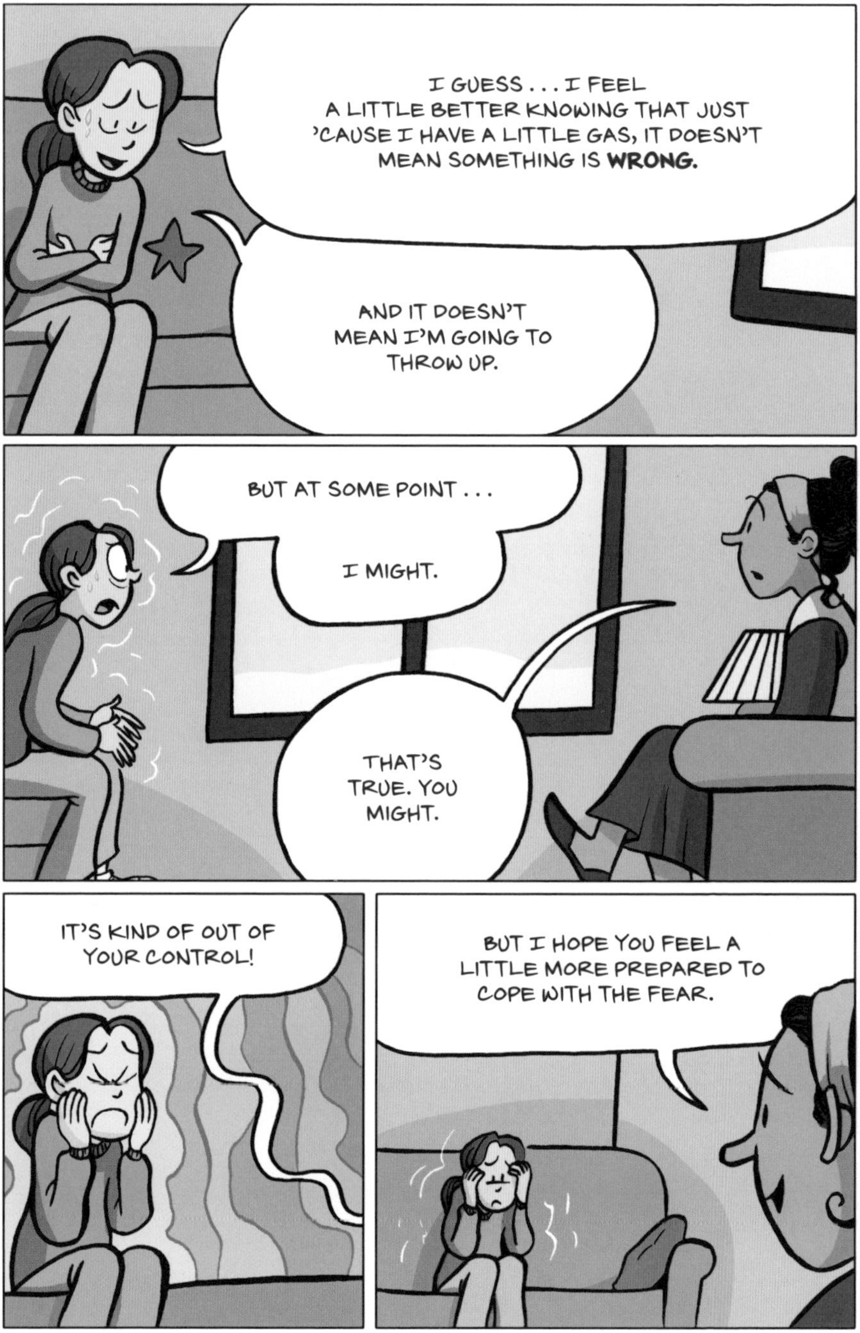

I GUESS . . . I FEEL A LITTLE BETTER KNOWING THAT JUST 'CAUSE I HAVE A LITTLE GAS, IT DOESN'T MEAN SOMETHING IS **WRONG.**
AND IT DOESN'T MEAN I'M GOING TO THROW UP.
BUT AT SOME POINT . . .
I MIGHT.
THAT'S TRUE. YOU MIGHT.
IT'S KIND OF OUT OF YOUR CONTROL!
BUT I HOPE YOU FEEL A LITTLE MORE PREPARED TO COPE WITH THE FEAR.

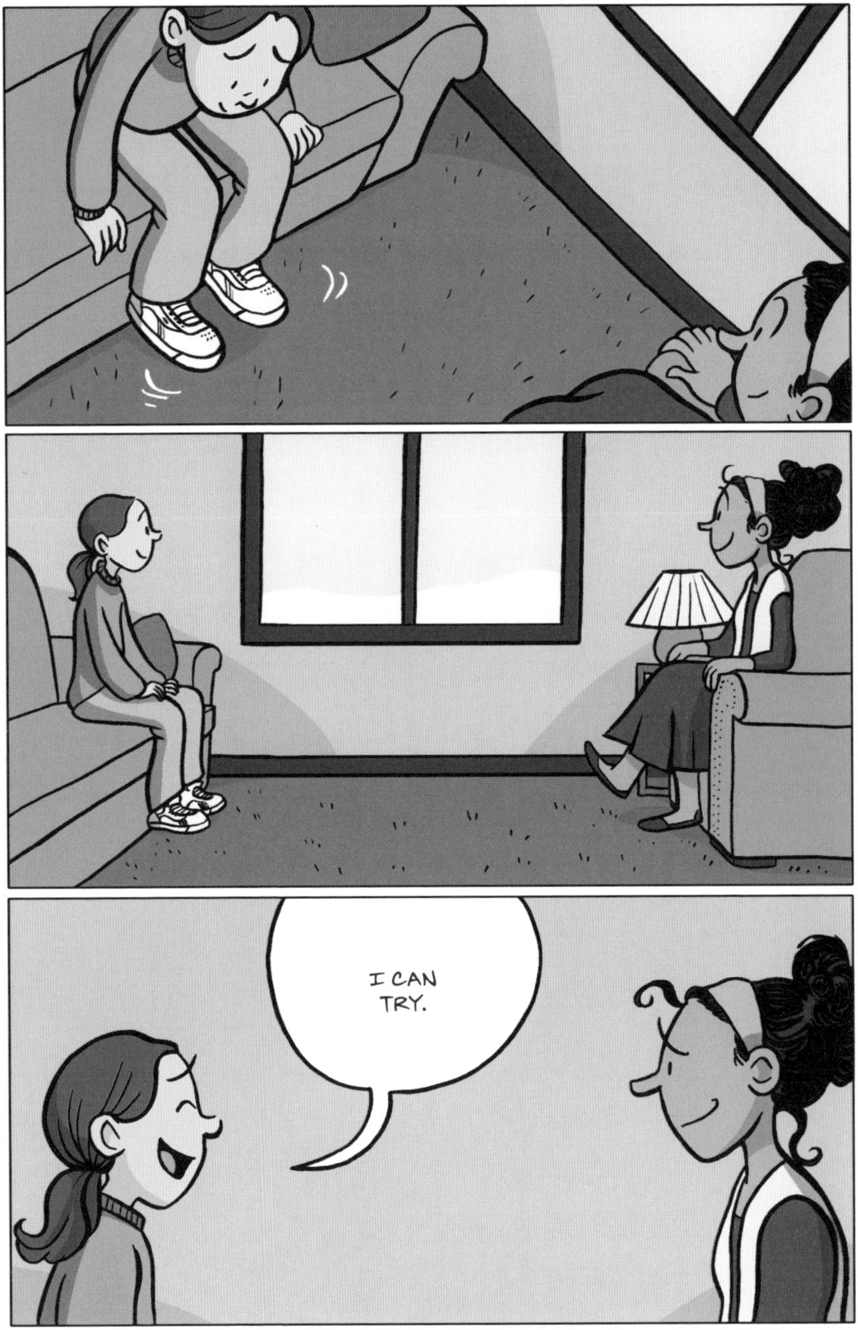
I CAN TRY.

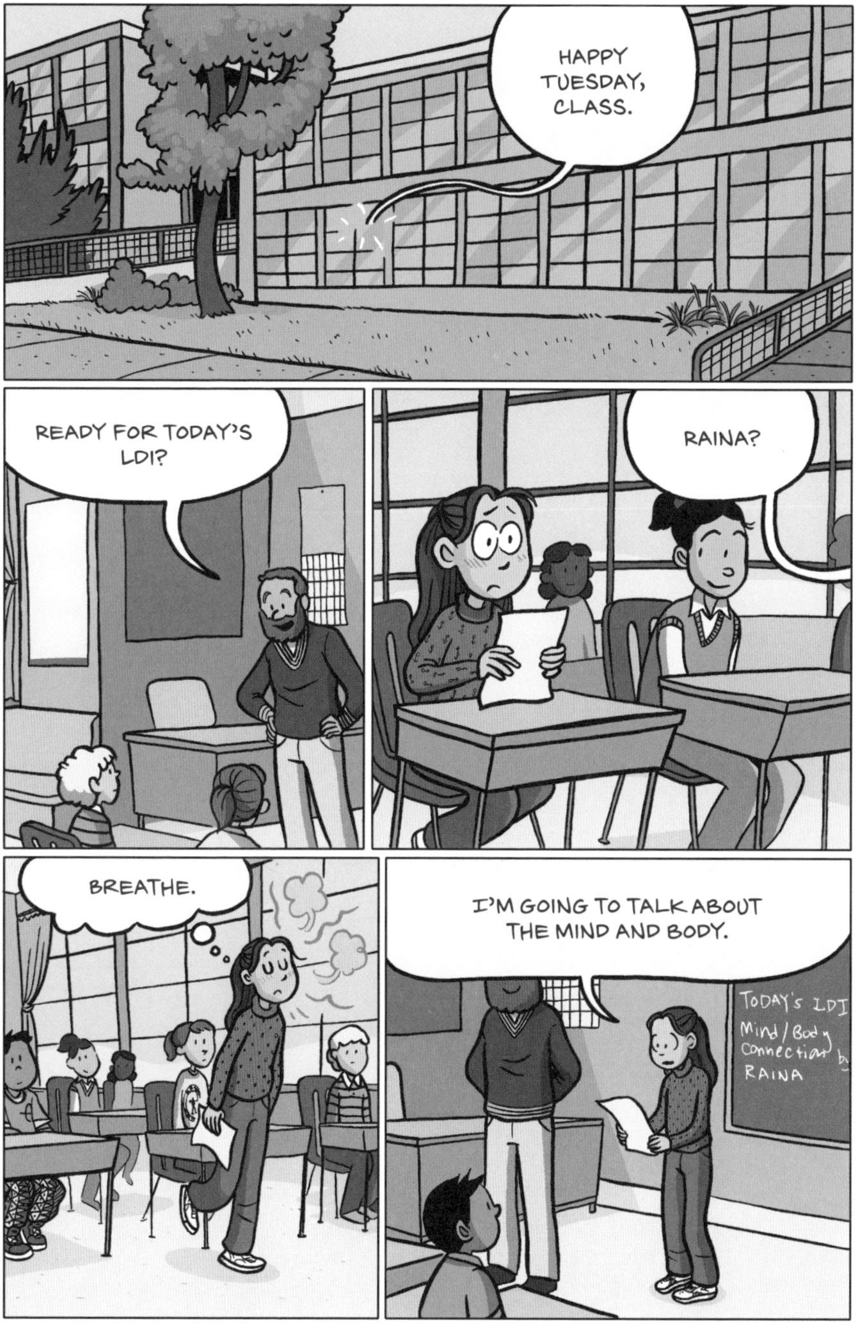
HAPPY TUESDAY, CLASS.
READY FOR TODAY'S LDI?
RAINA?
BREATHE.
I'M GOING TO TALK ABOUT THE MIND AND BODY.
TODAY'S LDI
Mind / Body Connection by RAINA

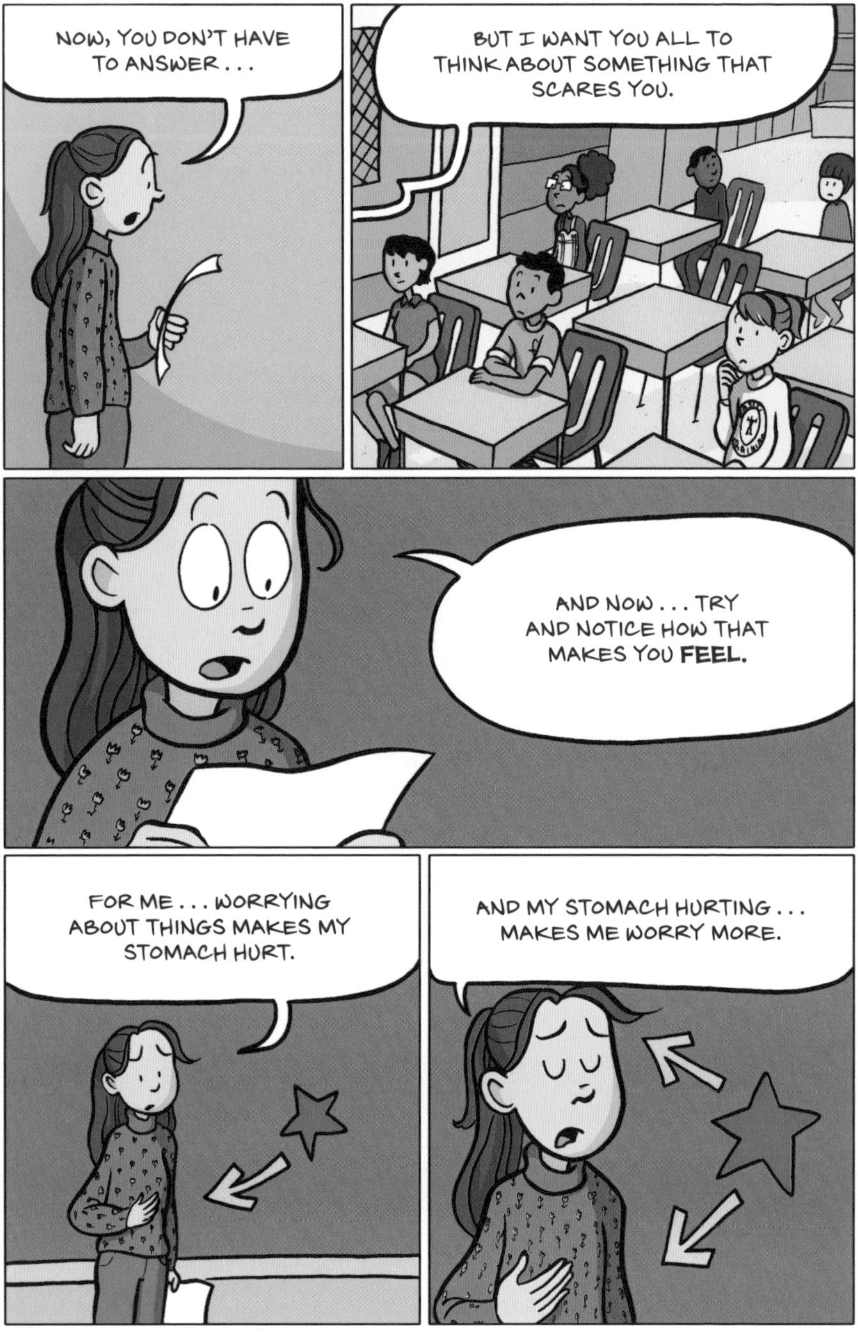
NOW, YOU DON'T HAVE TO ANSWER . . .
BUT I WANT YOU ALL TO THINK ABOUT SOMETHING THAT SCARES YOU.
AND NOW . . . TRY AND NOTICE HOW THAT MAKES YOU **FEEL.**
FOR ME . . . WORRYING ABOUT THINGS MAKES MY STOMACH HURT.
AND MY STOMACH HURTING . . . MAKES ME WORRY MORE.

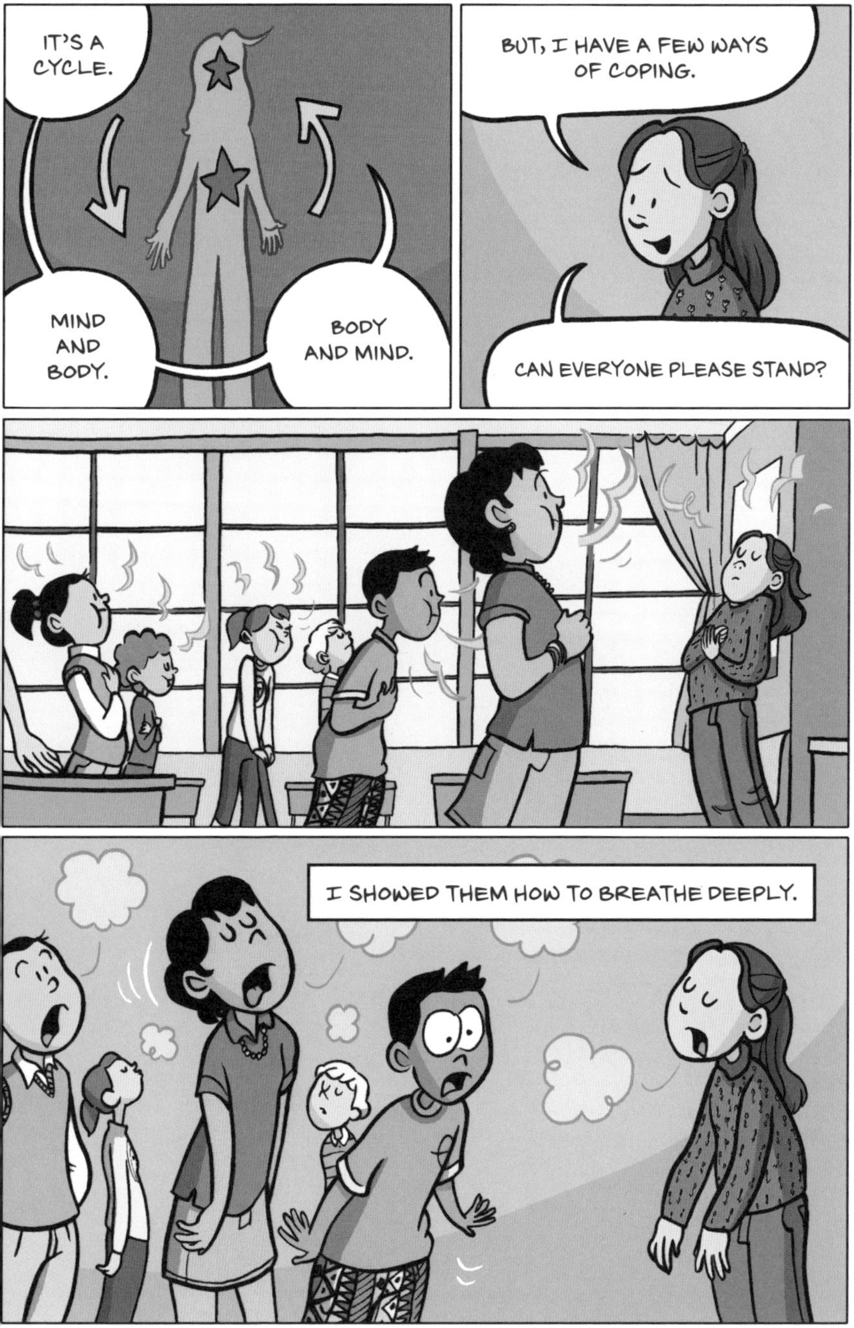
IT'S A CYCLE.
MIND AND BODY.
BODY AND MIND.
BUT, I HAVE A FEW WAYS OF COPING.
CAN EVERYONE PLEASE STAND?
I SHOWED THEM HOW TO BREATHE DEEPLY.

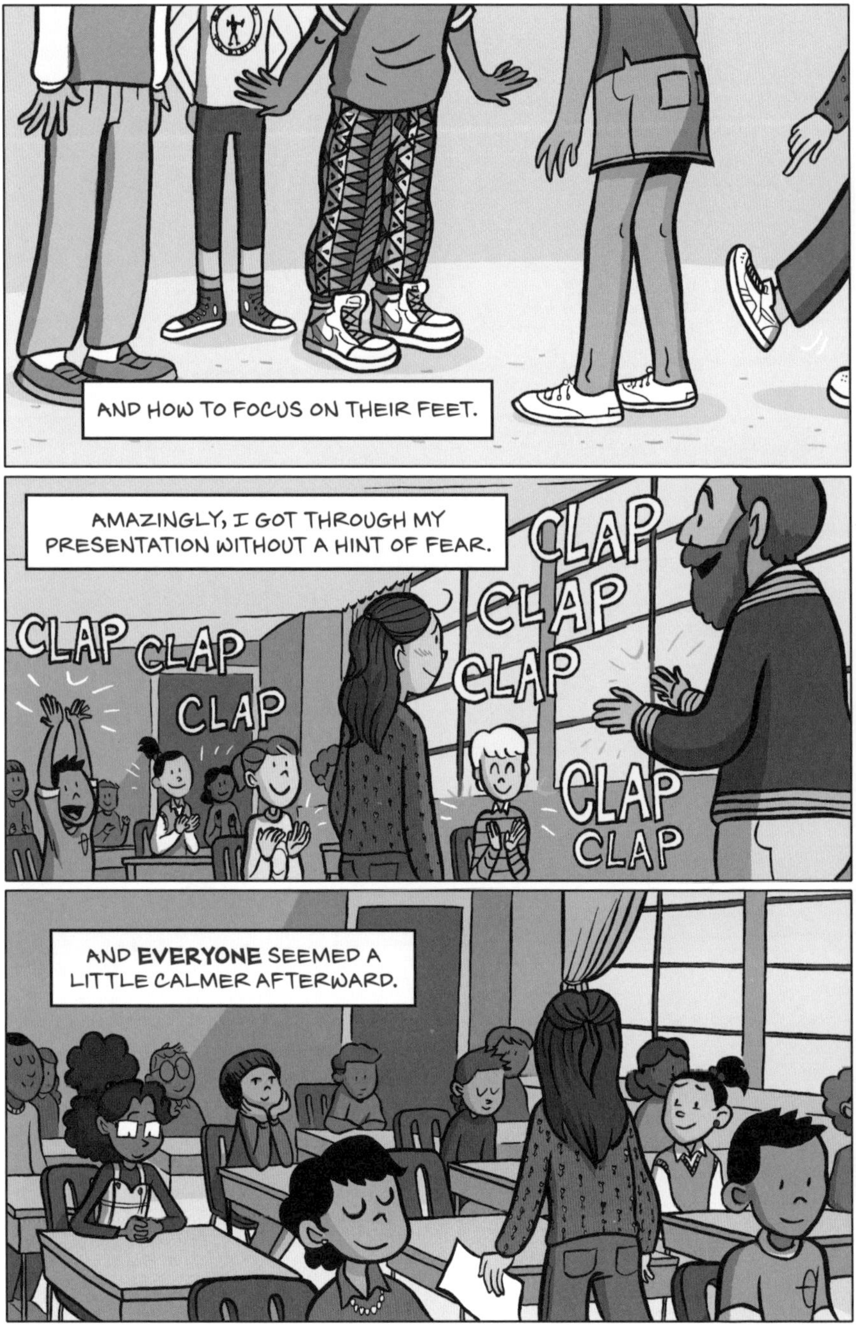
AND HOW TO FOCUS ON THEIR FEET.
AMAZINGLY, I GOT THROUGH MY PRESENTATION WITHOUT A HINT OF FEAR.
CLAP
CLAP
CLAP
CLAP CLAP
CLAP
CLAP
CLAP
AND **EVERYONE** SEEMED A LITTLE CALMER AFTERWARD.

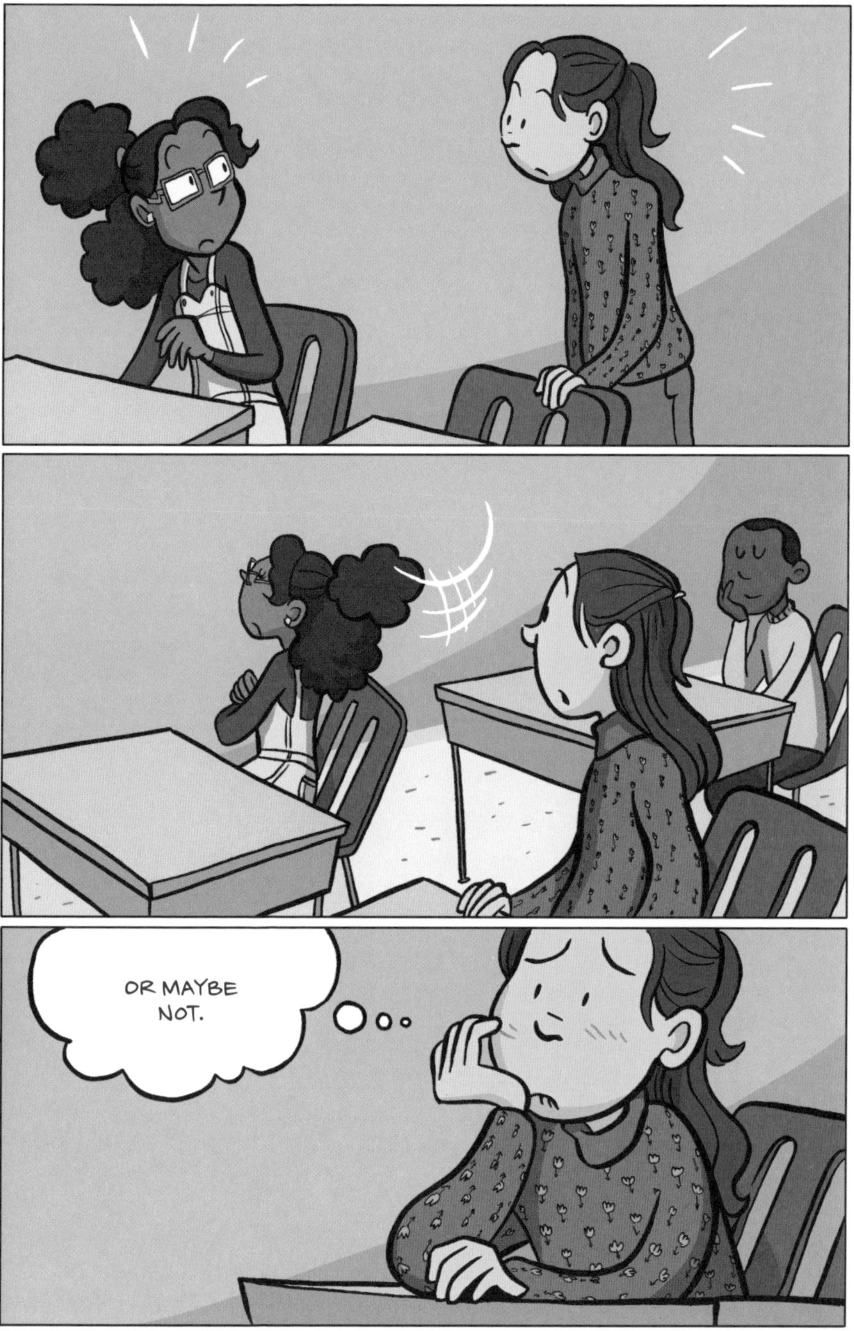
OR MAYBE NOT.

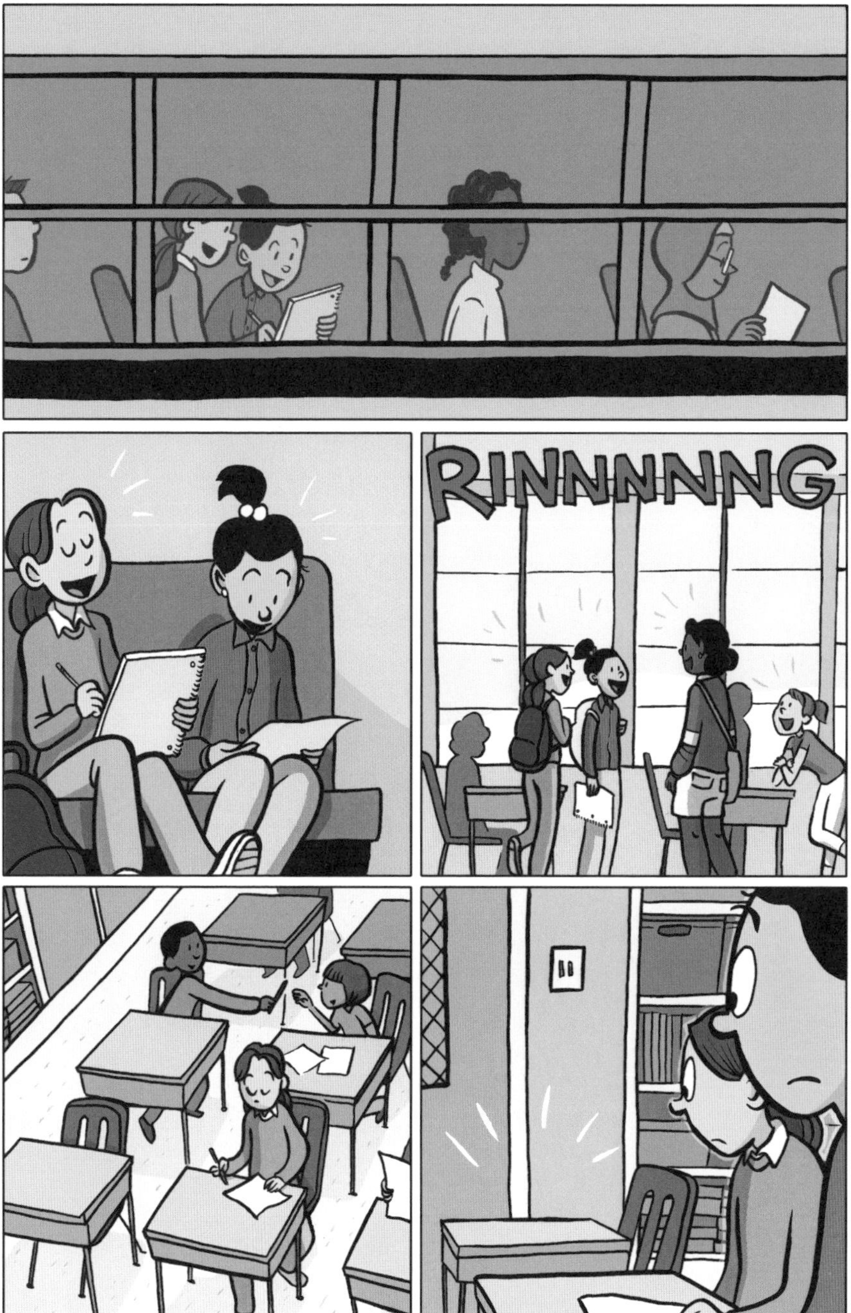
RINNNNNG

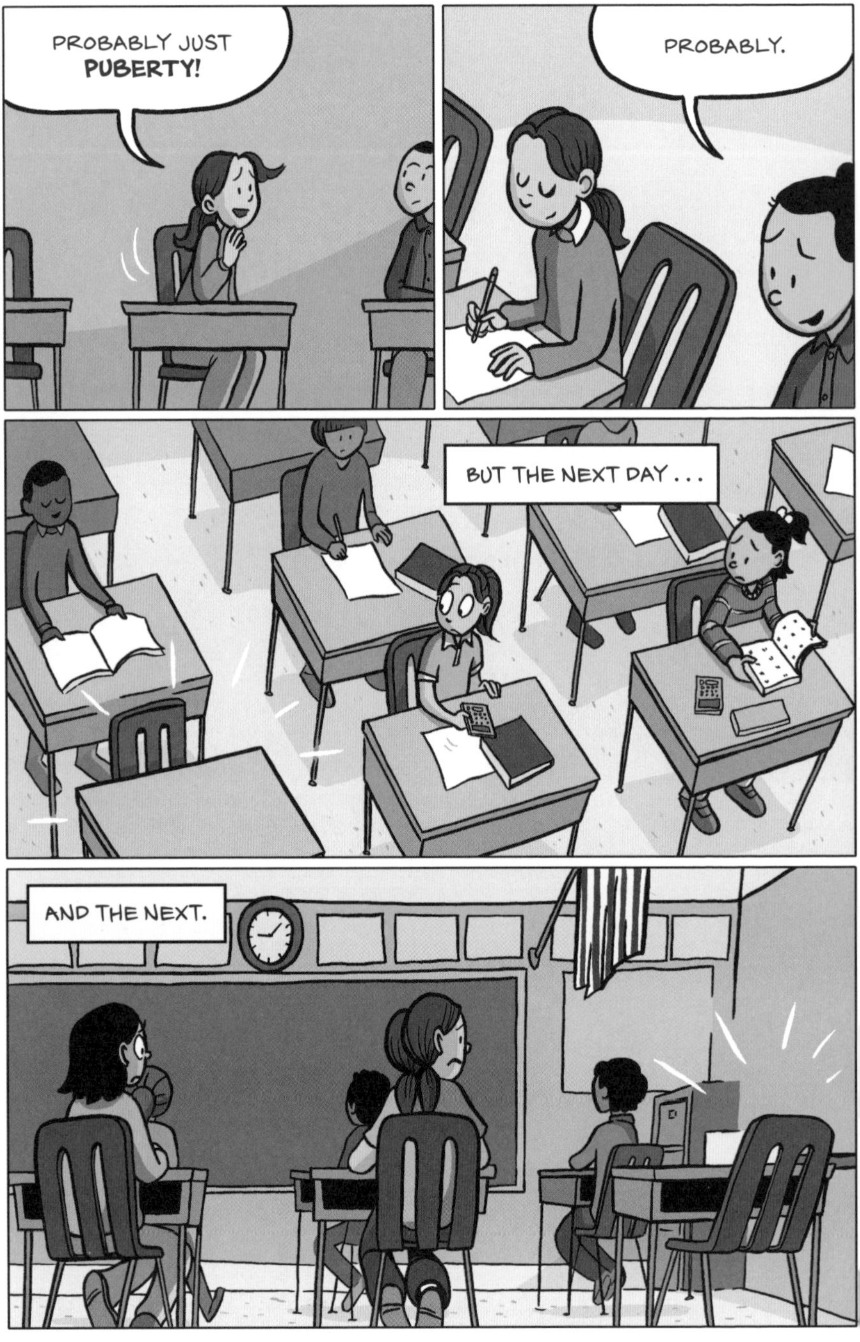
PROBABLY JUST PUBERTY!
PROBABLY.
BUT THE NEXT DAY . . .
AND THE NEXT.

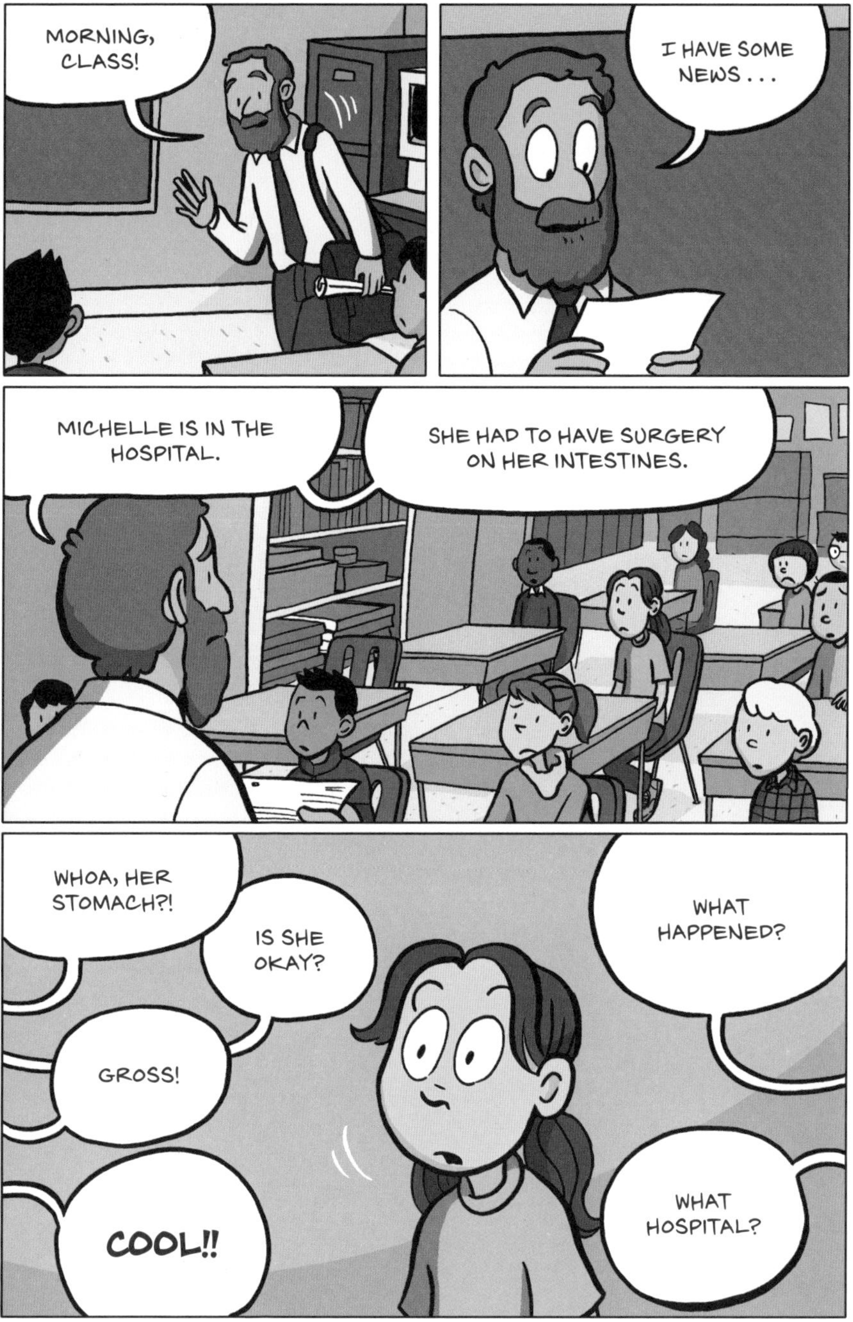
MORNING, CLASS!
I HAVE SOME NEWS . . .
MICHELLE IS IN THE HOSPITAL.
SHE HAD TO HAVE SURGERY ON HER INTESTINES.
WHOA, HER STOMACH?!
IS SHE OKAY?
WHAT HAPPENED?
GROSS!
COOL!!
WHAT HOSPITAL?

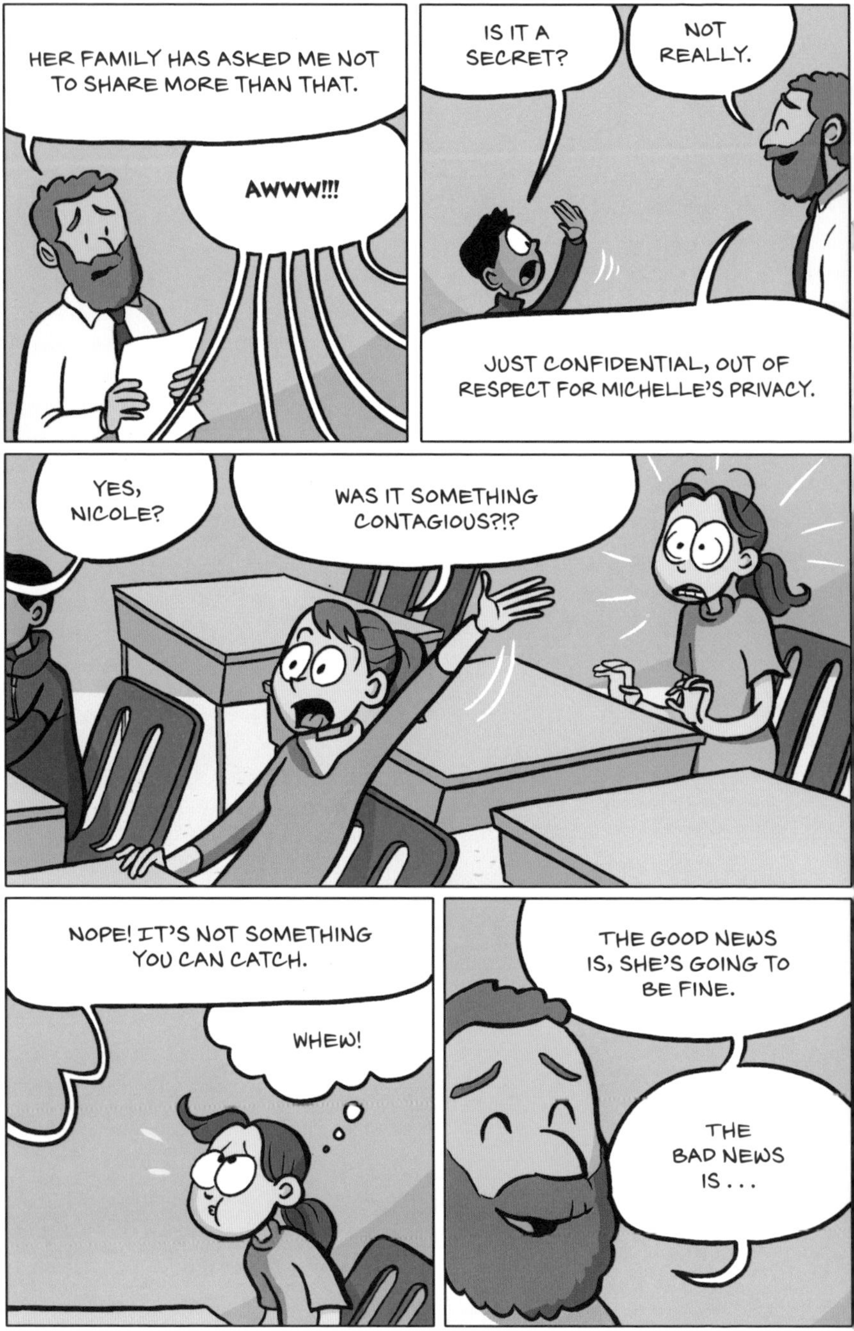
HER FAMILY HAS ASKED ME NOT TO SHARE MORE THAN THAT.
AWWW!!!
IS IT A SECRET?
NOT REALLY.
JUST CONFIDENTIAL, OUT OF RESPECT FOR MICHELLE'S PRIVACY.
YES, NICOLE?
WAS IT SOMETHING CONTAGIOUS?!?
NOPE! IT'S NOT SOMETHING YOU CAN CATCH.
WHEW!
THE GOOD NEWS IS, SHE'S GOING TO BE FINE.
THE BAD NEWS IS . . .

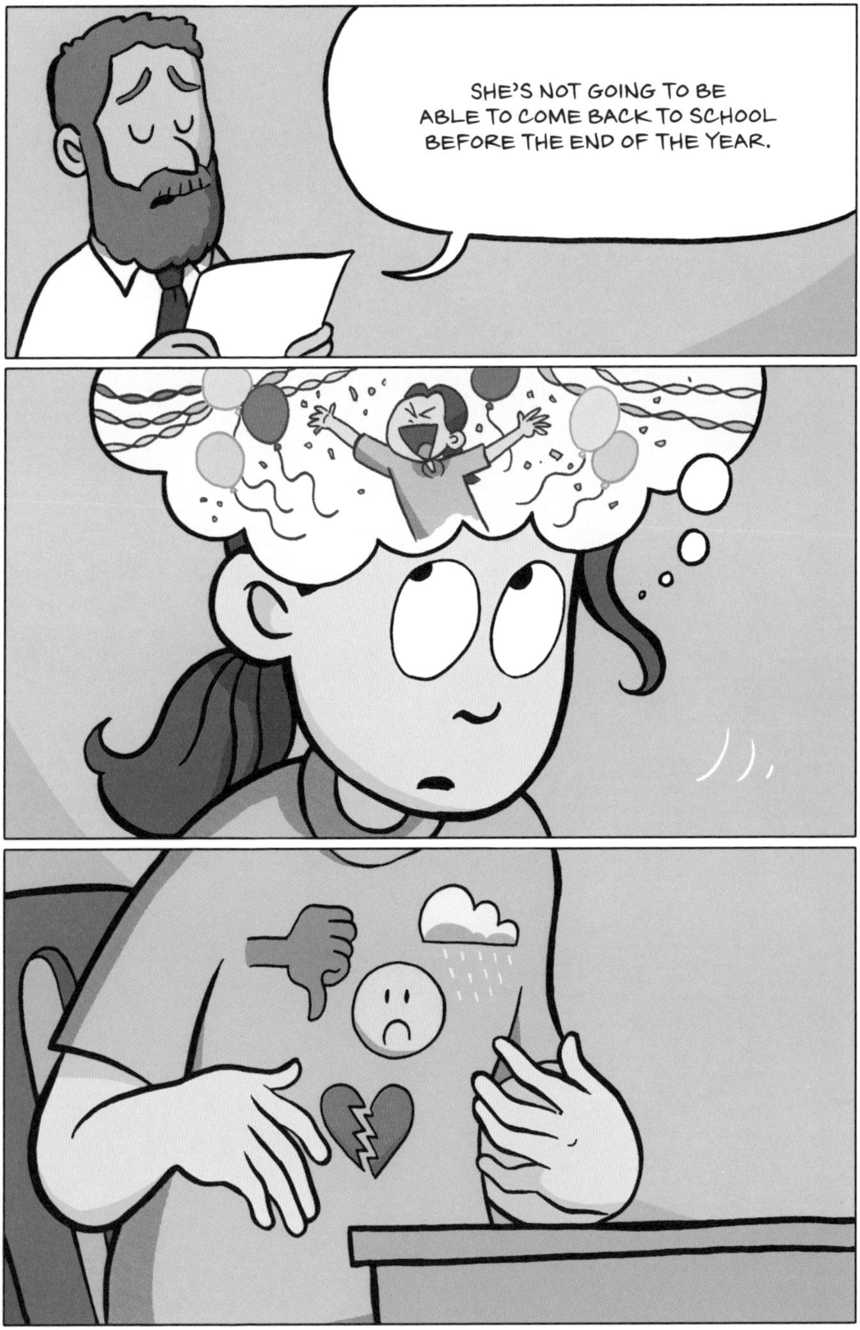
SHE'S NOT GOING TO BE ABLE TO COME BACK TO SCHOOL BEFORE THE END OF THE YEAR.

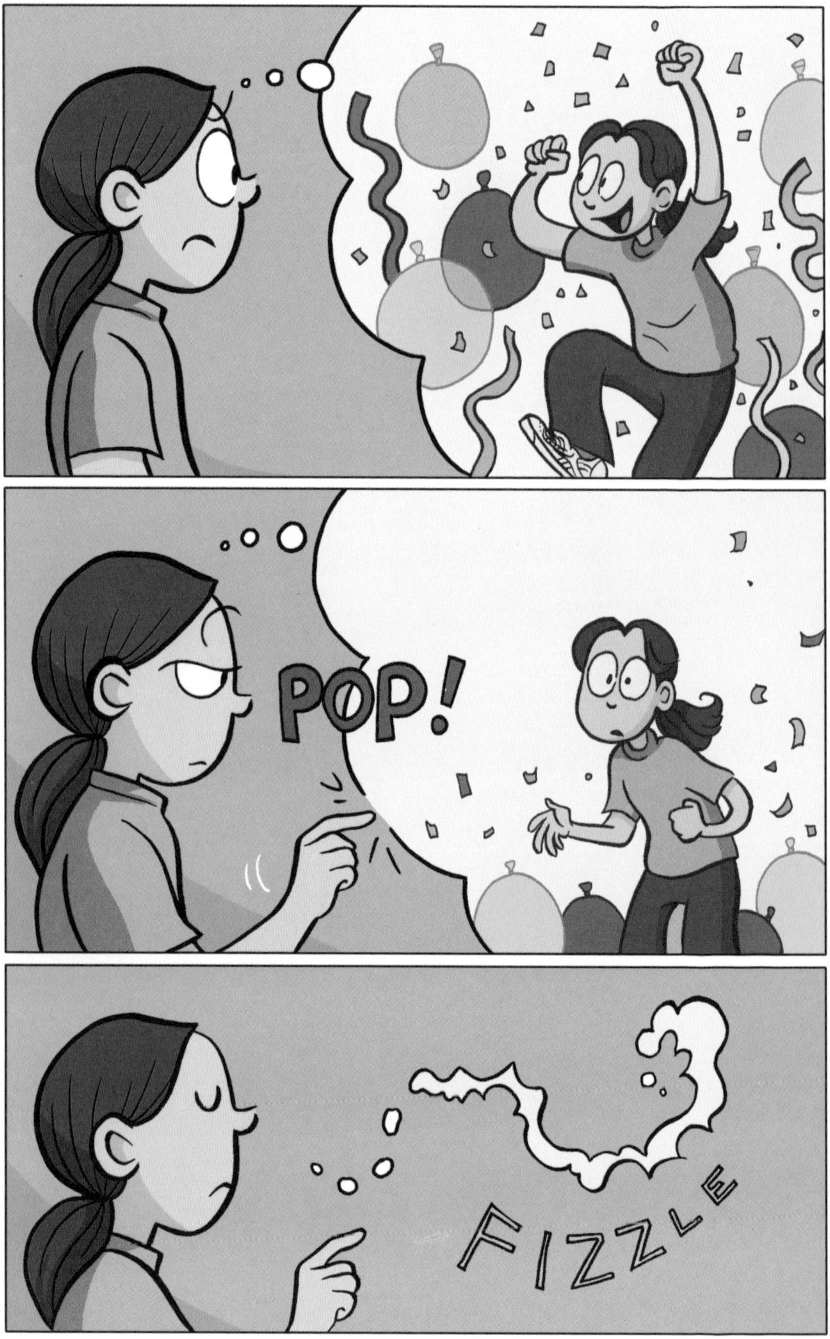
POP!
FIZZLE

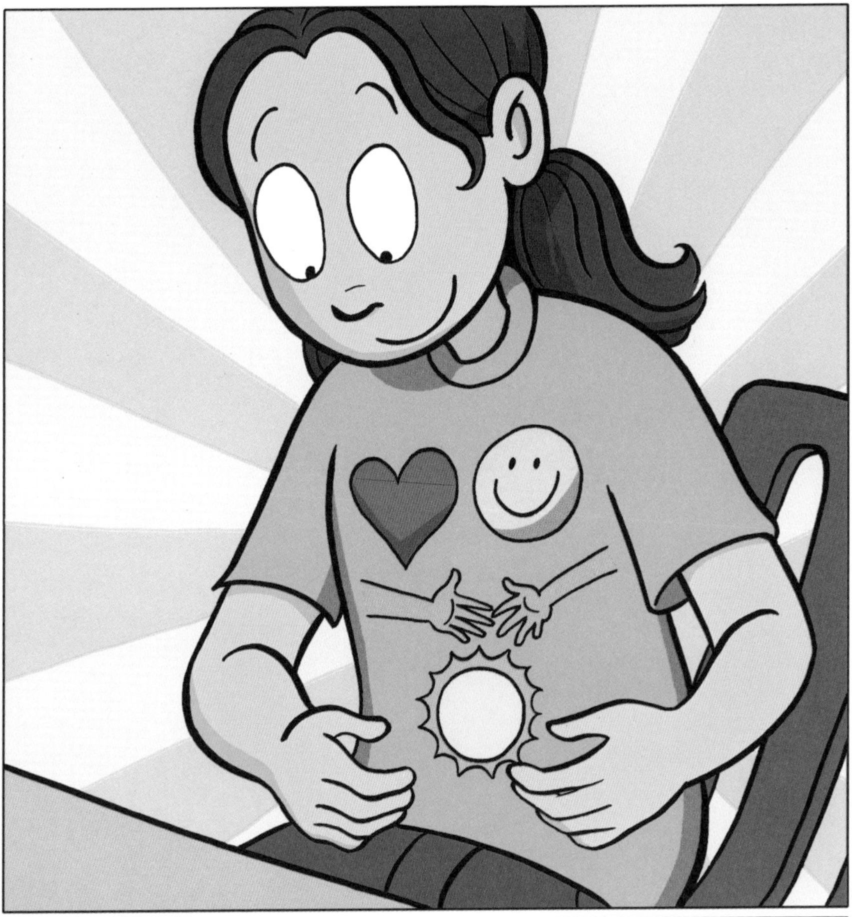

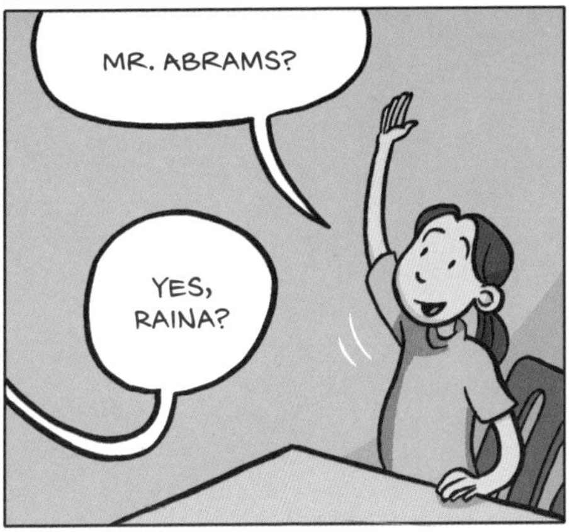
MR. ABRAMS?
YES, RAINA?

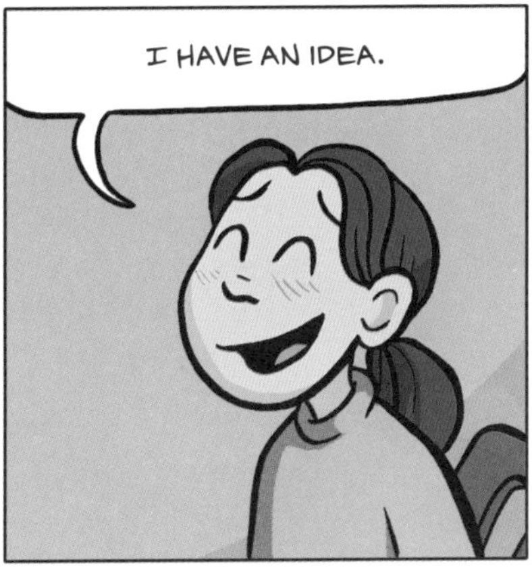
I HAVE AN IDEA.

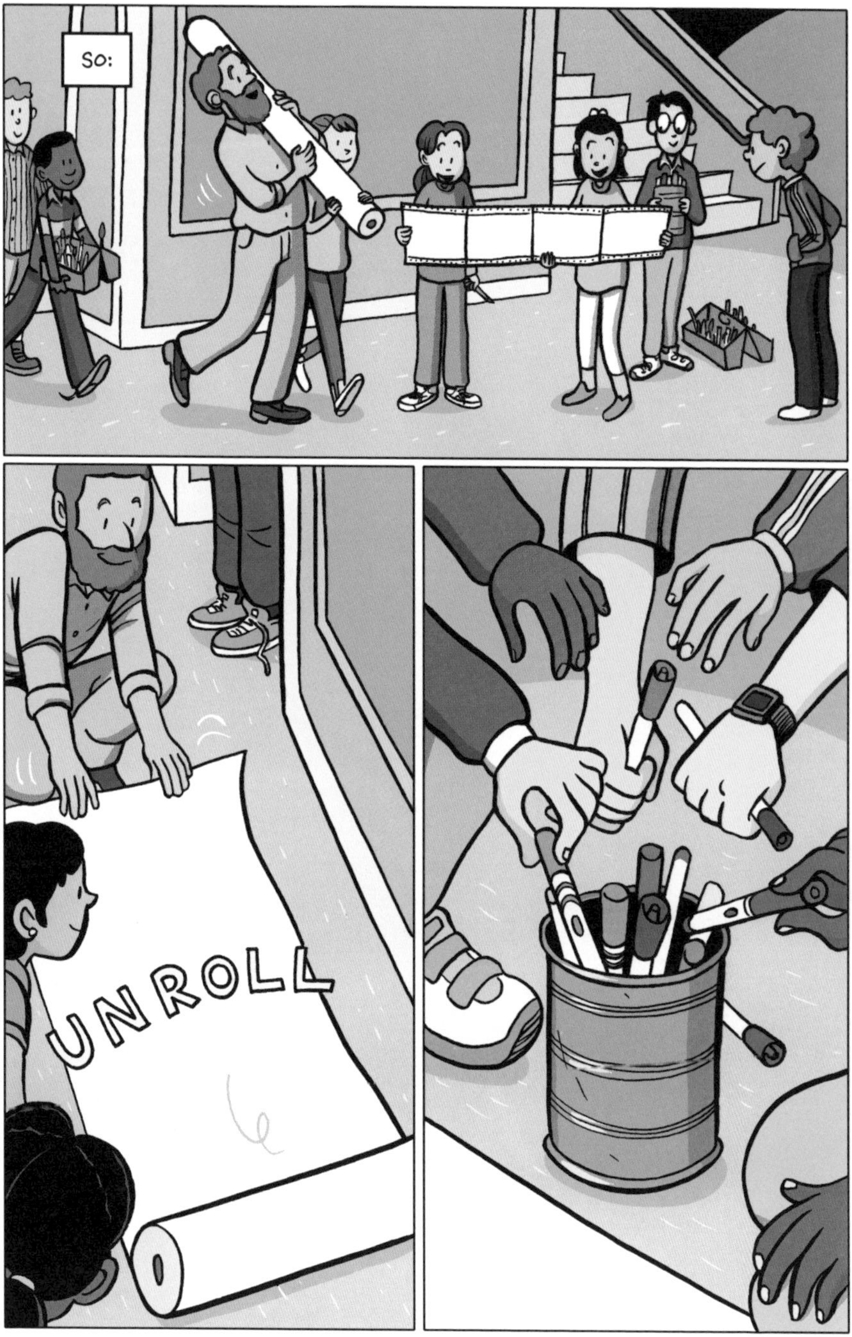
SO:
UNROLL

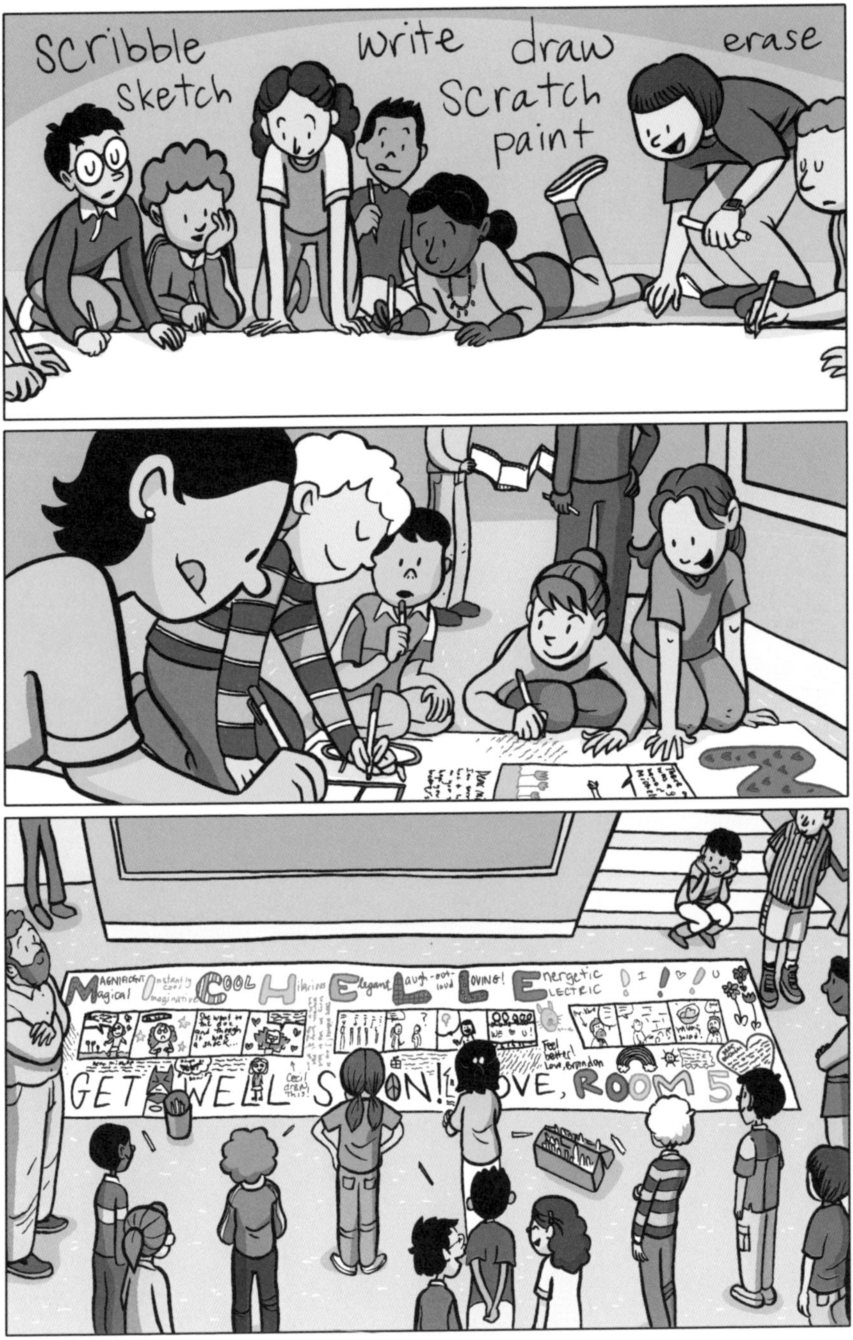
scribble
write
draw
erase
sketch
scratch
paint
MAGNIFICENT
Magical
Instantly cool
Imaginative
COOL
Hilarious
Elegant
Laugh-out-loud
LOVING!
Energetic
ELECTRIC
Feel better! Love, Brandon
Cecil drew this!
GET WELL S
ON!
OVE, ROOM 5

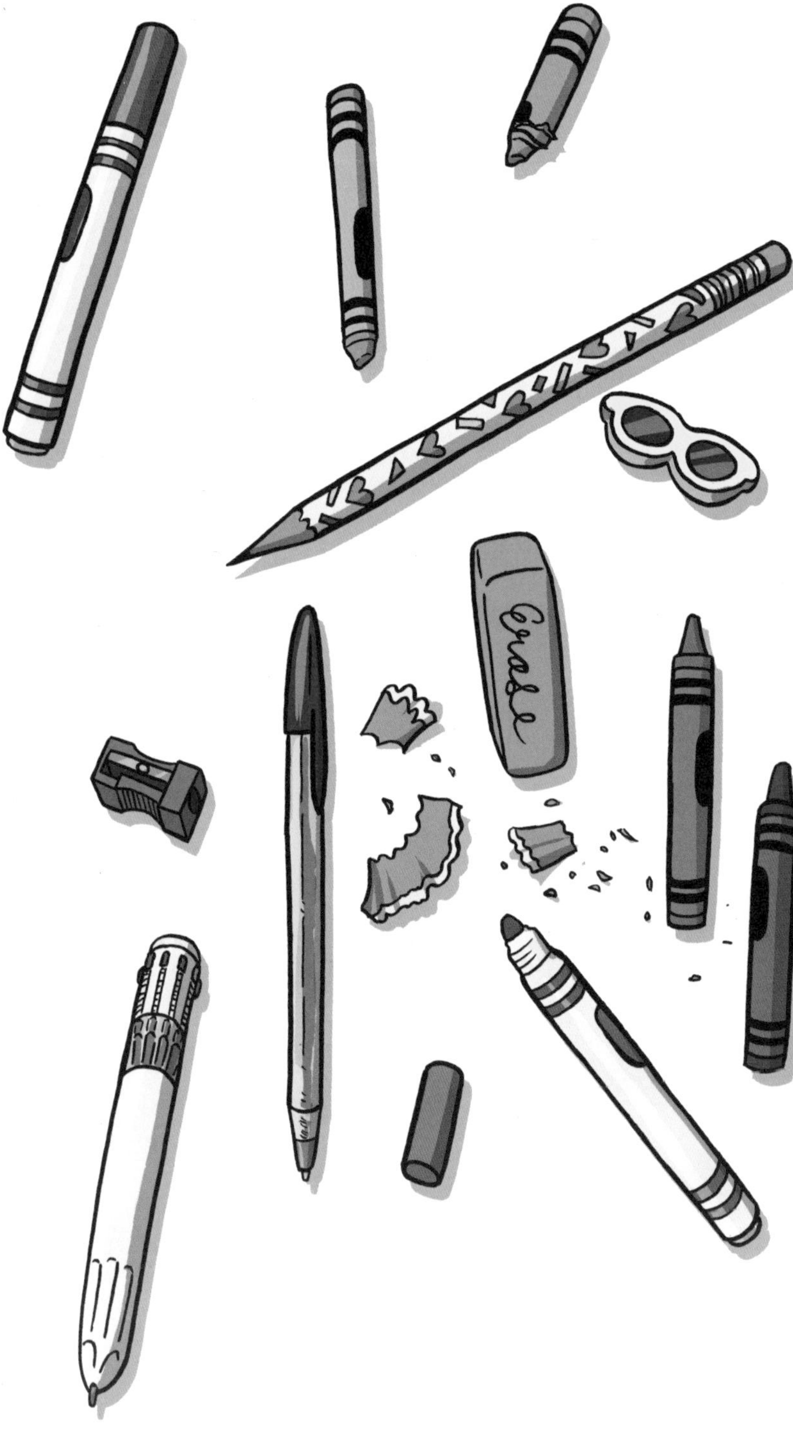
Erase

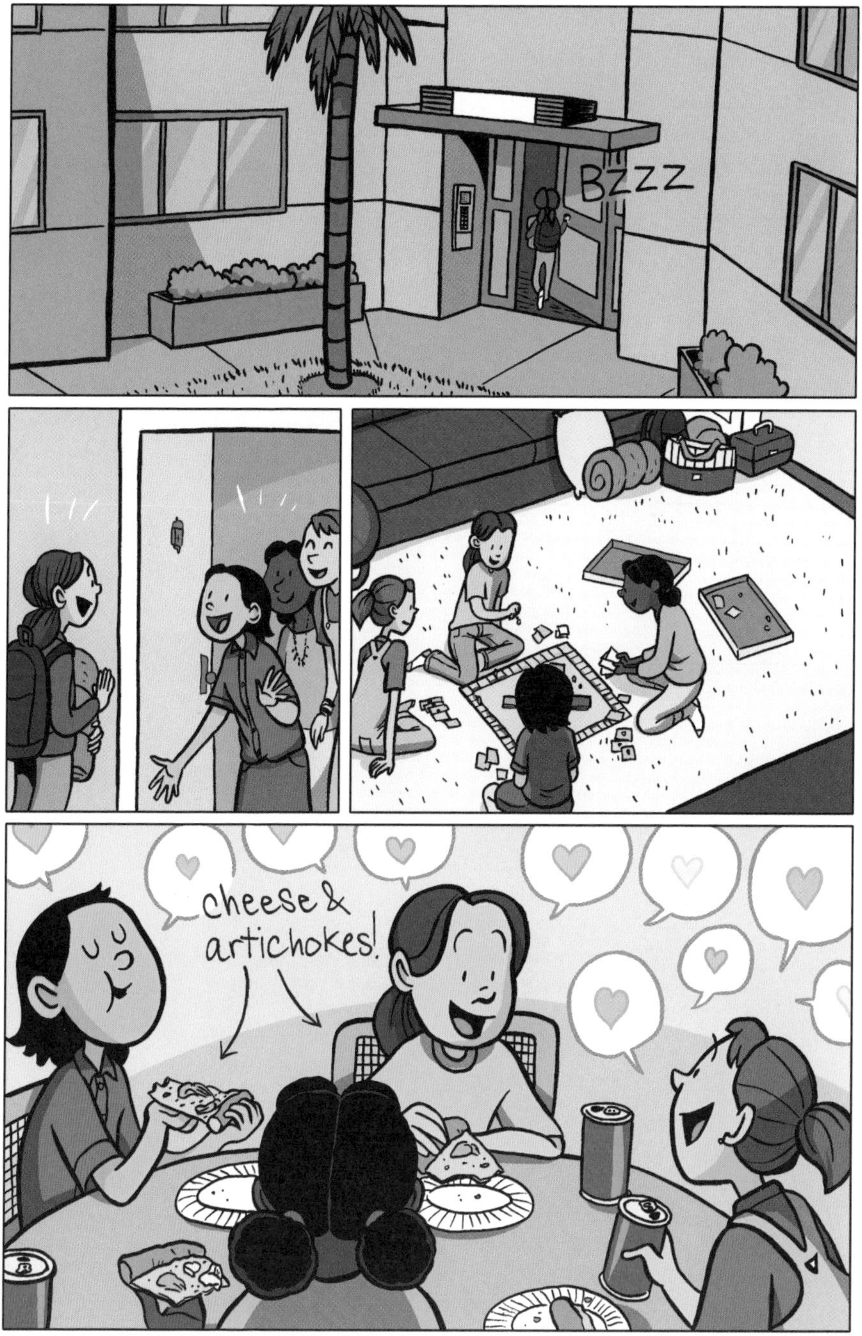
BZZZ
cheese & artichokes!

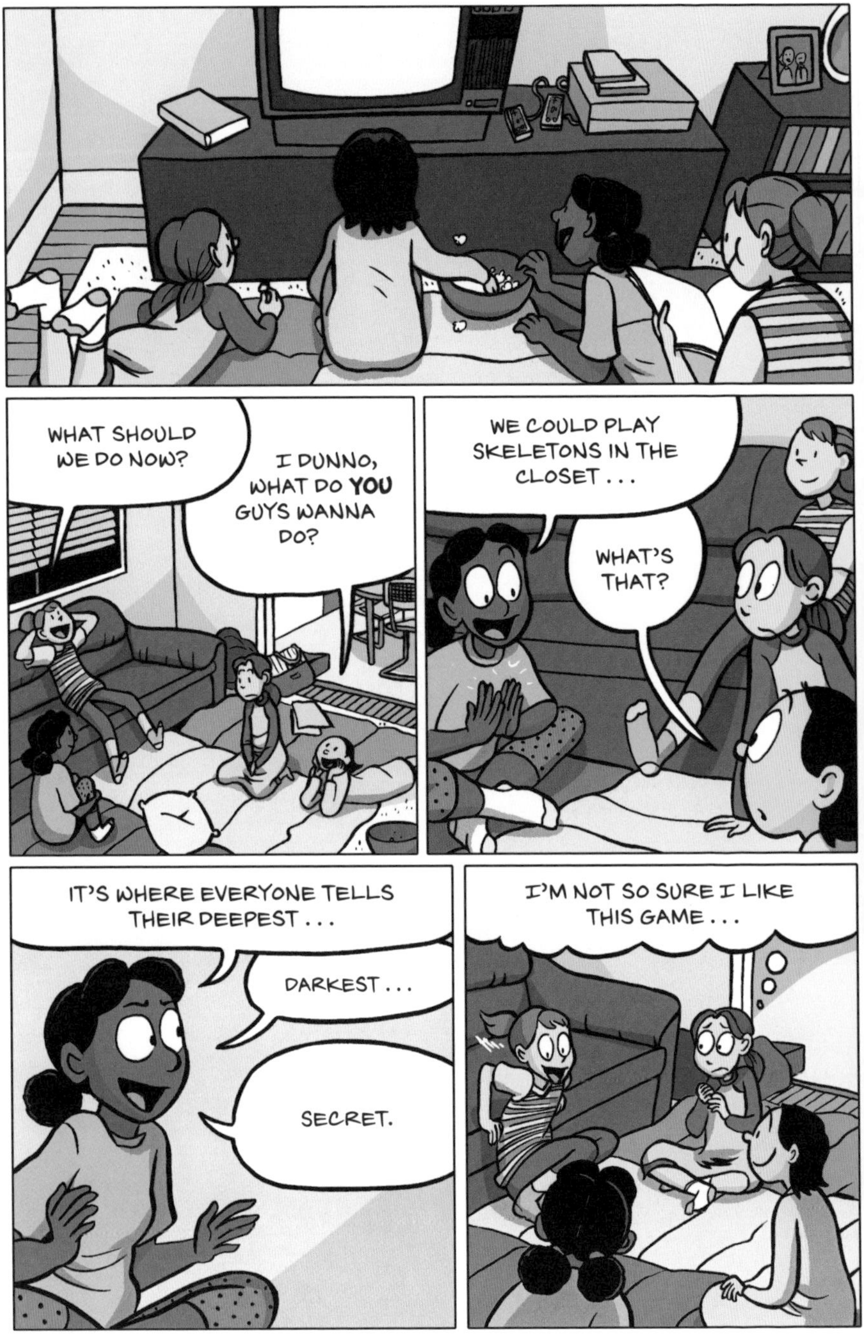
WHAT SHOULD WE DO NOW?
I DUNNO, WHAT DO **YOU** GUYS WANNA DO?
WE COULD PLAY SKELETONS IN THE CLOSET . . .
WHAT'S THAT?
IT'S WHERE EVERYONE TELLS THEIR DEEPEST . . .
DARKEST . . .
SECRET.
I'M NOT SO SURE I LIKE THIS GAME . . .

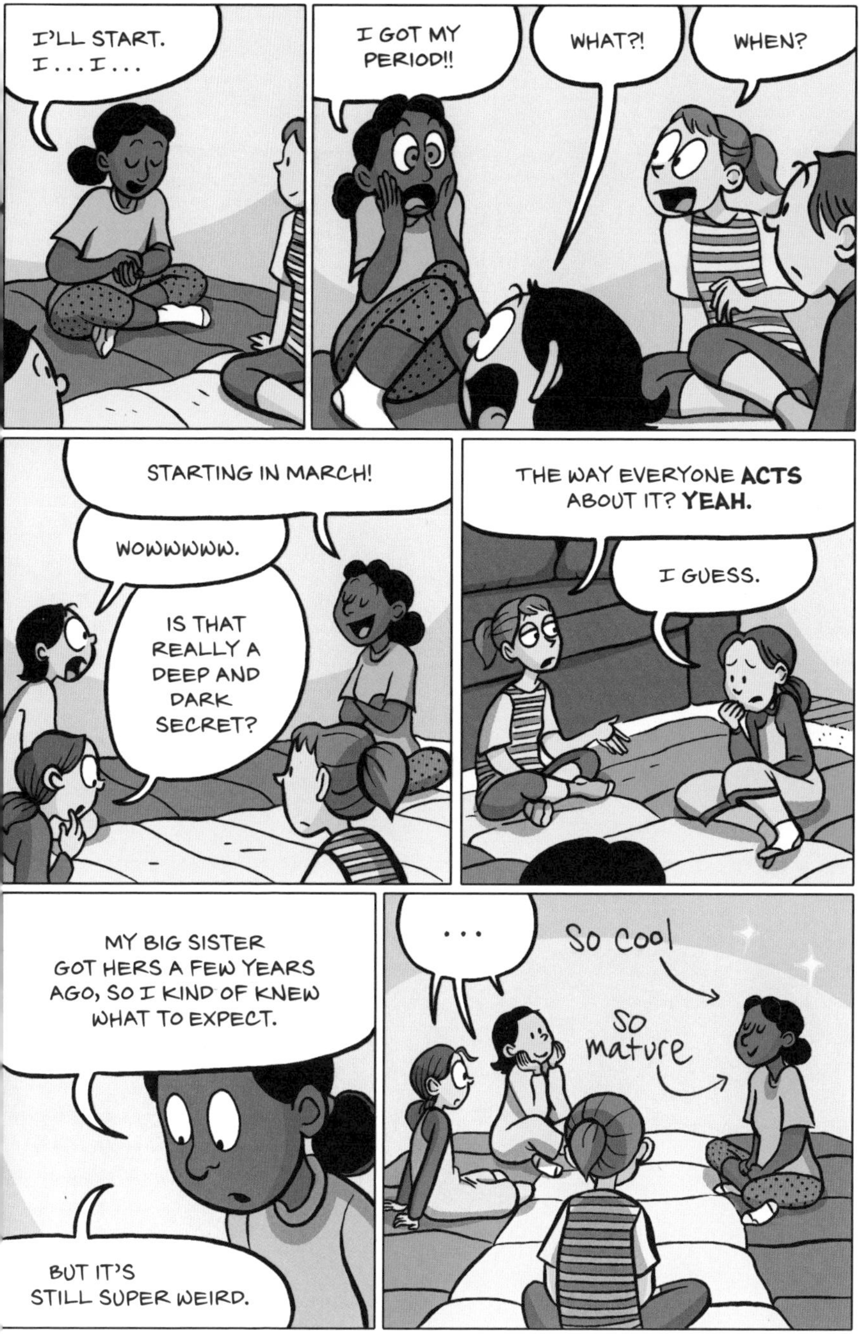
I'LL START. I . . . I . . .
I GOT MY PERIOD!!
WHAT?!
WHEN?
STARTING IN MARCH!
WOWWWWW.
IS THAT REALLY A DEEP AND DARK SECRET?
THE WAY EVERYONE ACTS ABOUT IT? YEAH.
I GUESS.
MY BIG SISTER GOT HERS A FEW YEARS AGO, SO I KIND OF KNEW WHAT TO EXPECT.
BUT IT'S STILL SUPER WEIRD.
. . .
So cool
so mature

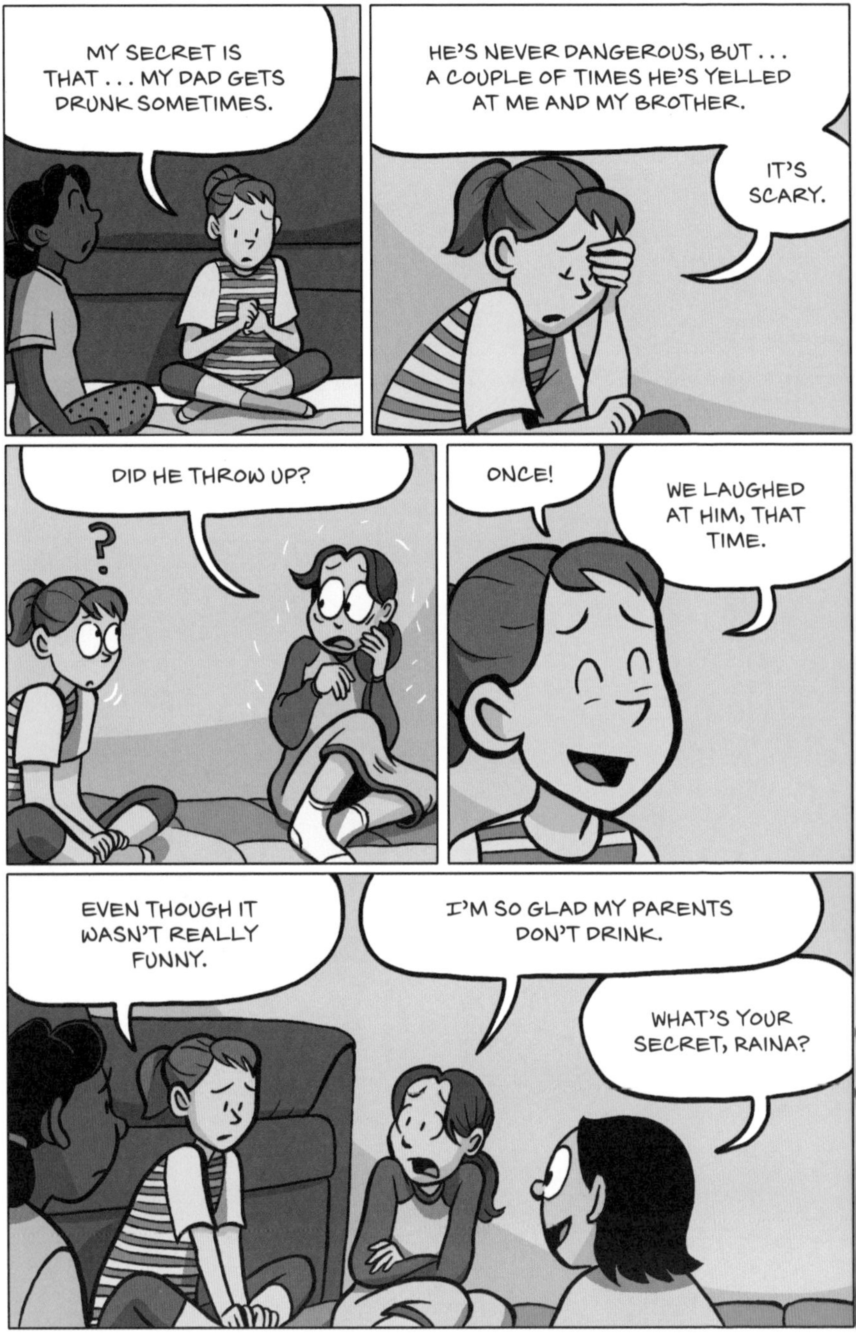
MY SECRET IS THAT . . . MY DAD GETS DRUNK SOMETIMES.
HE'S NEVER DANGEROUS, BUT . . . A COUPLE OF TIMES HE'S YELLED AT ME AND MY BROTHER.
IT'S SCARY.
DID HE THROW UP?
?
ONCE!
WE LAUGHED AT HIM, THAT TIME.
EVEN THOUGH IT WASN'T REALLY FUNNY.
I'M SO GLAD MY PARENTS DON'T DRINK.
WHAT'S YOUR SECRET, RAINA?

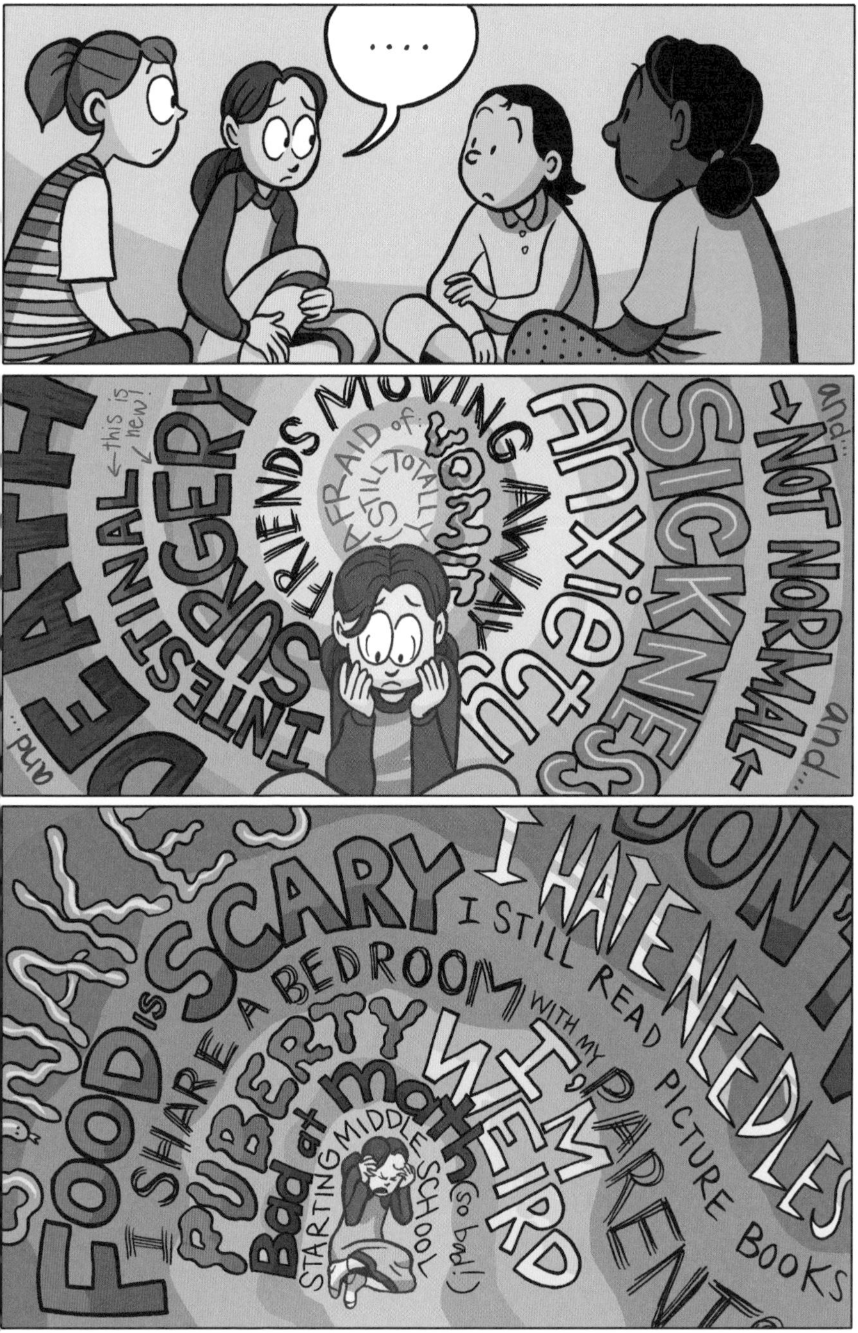
....
and...
DEATH
INTESTINAL
← this is new!
SURGERY
FRIENDS MOVING AWAY
AFRAID of:
STILL TOTALLY
VOMIT
anxiety
SICKNESS
and...
NOT NORMAL
and...
FOOD is SCARY
I HATE NEEDLES
I STILL READ PICTURE BOOKS
I SHARE A BEDROOM WITH MY PARENTS
PUBERTY
I'M WEIRD
Bad at math
STARTING MIDDLE SCHOOL
(so bad!)

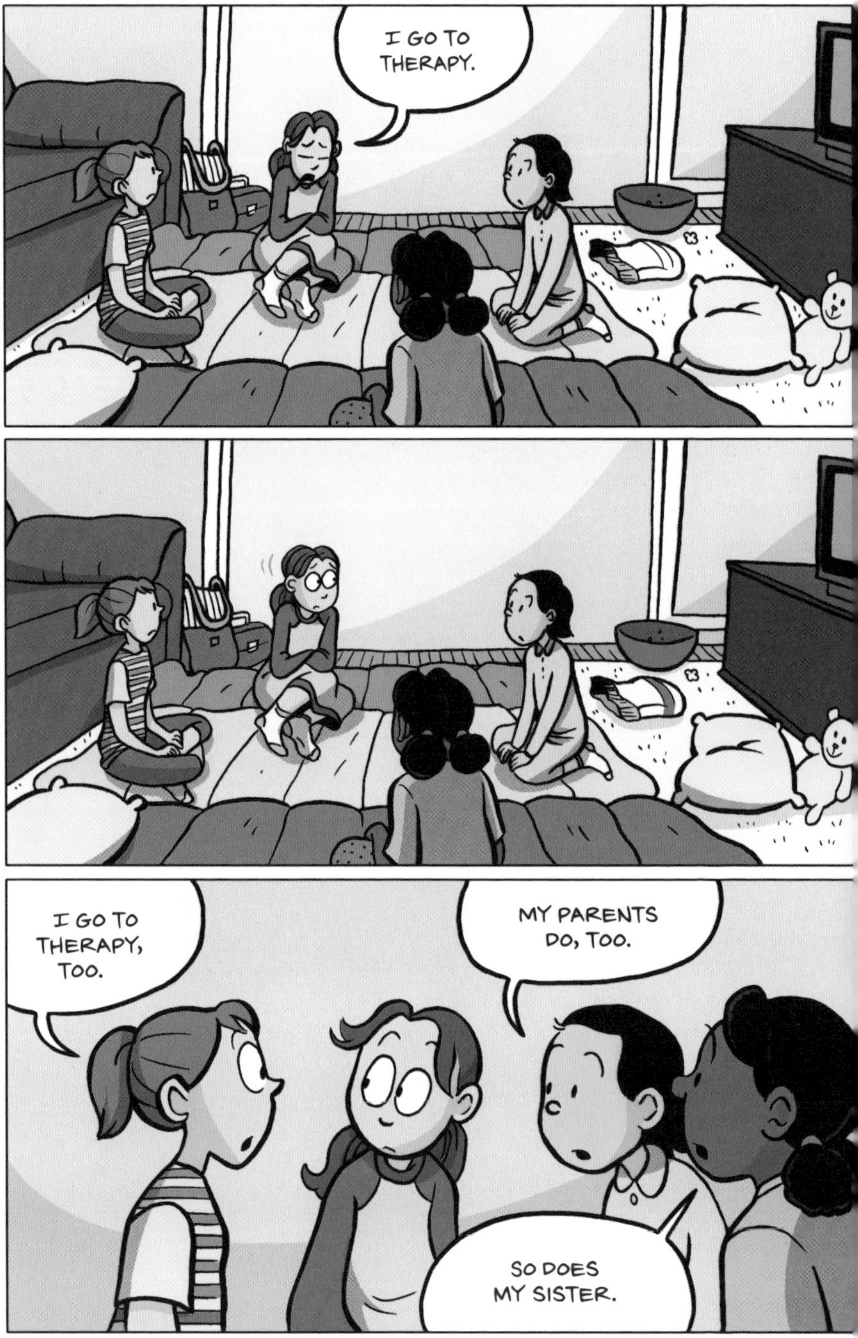
I GO TO THERAPY.
I GO TO THERAPY, TOO.
MY PARENTS DO, TOO.
SO DOES MY SISTER.

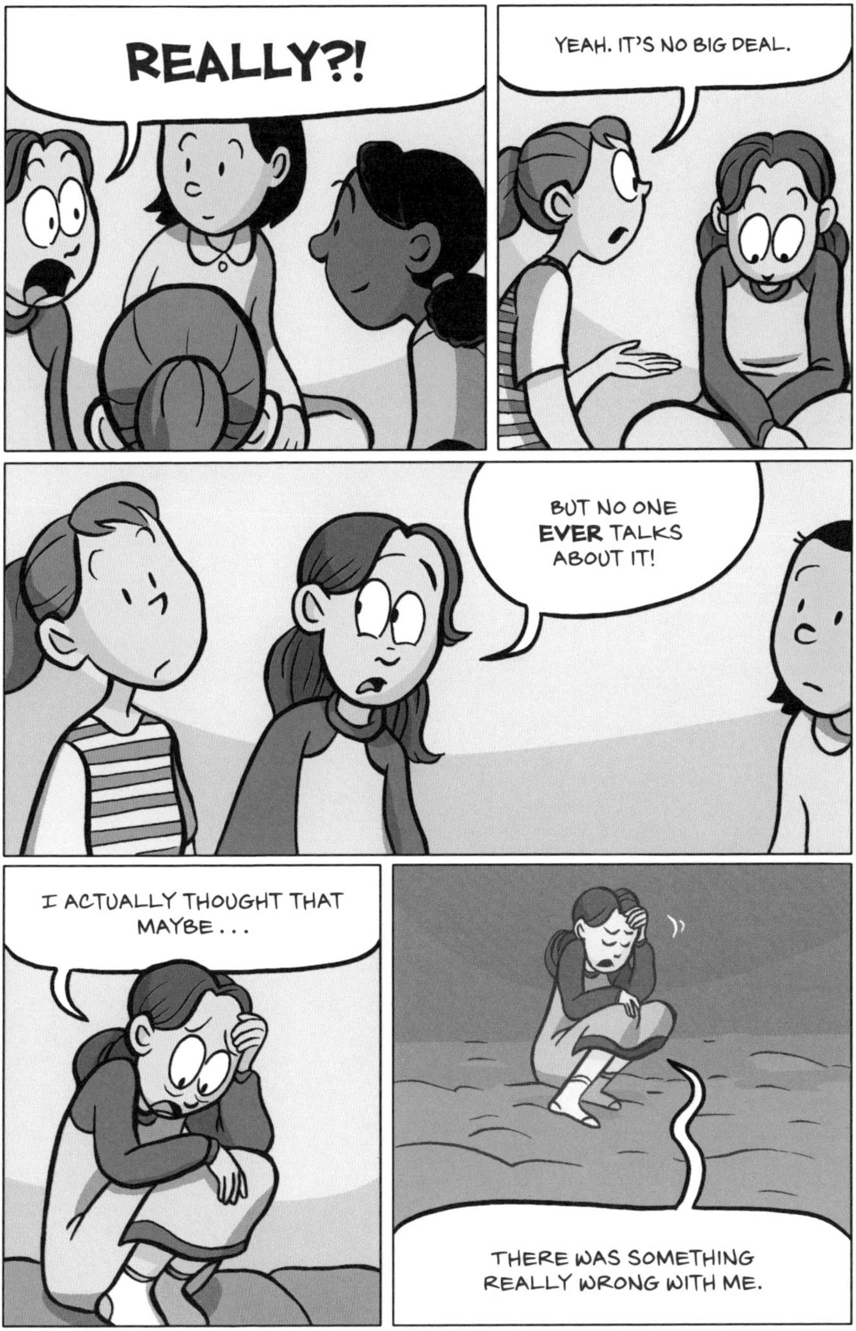

REALLY?!
YEAH. IT'S NO BIG DEAL.
BUT NO ONE EVER TALKS ABOUT IT!
I ACTUALLY THOUGHT THAT MAYBE . . .
THERE WAS SOMETHING REALLY WRONG WITH ME.

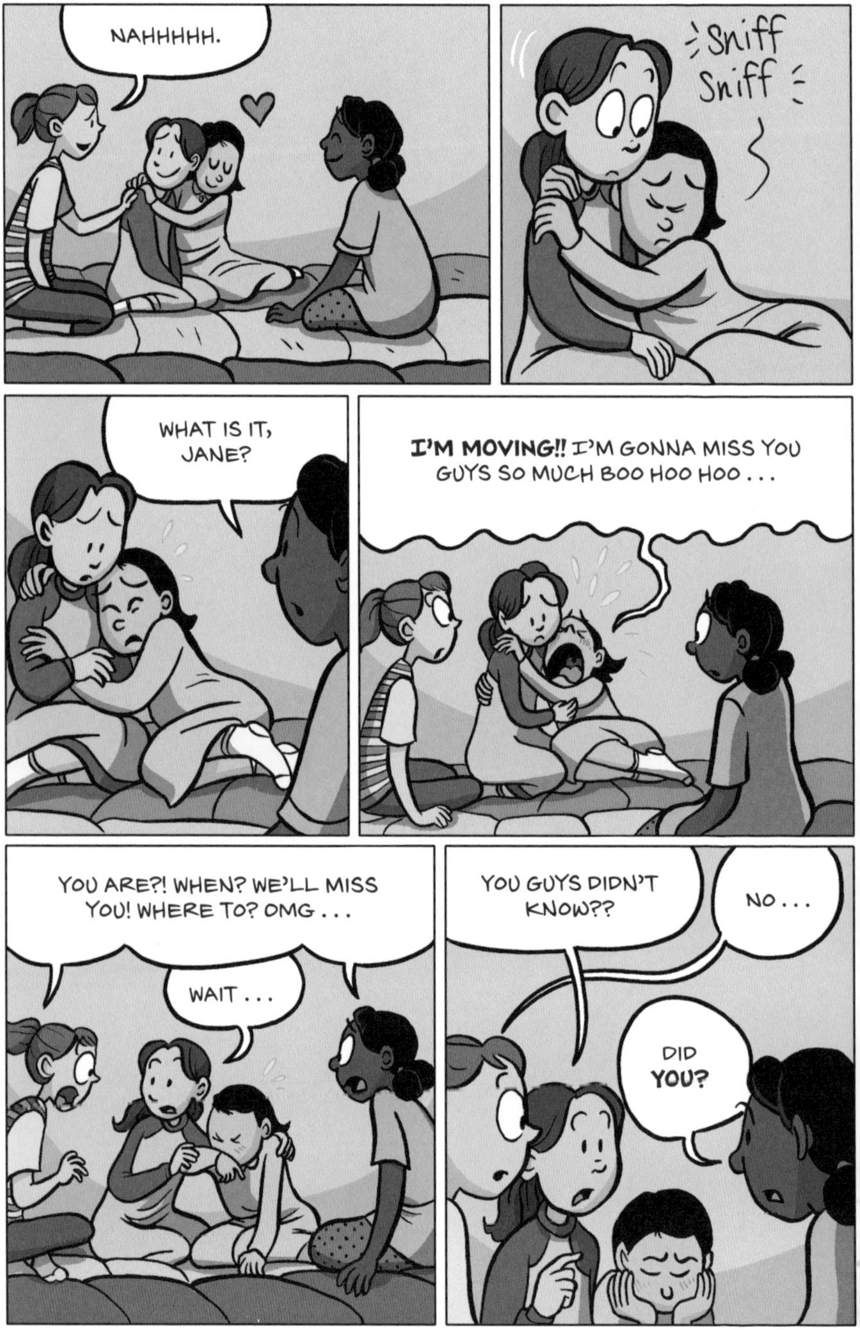
NAHHHHH.
Sniff
Sniff
WHAT IS IT, JANE?
I'M MOVING!! I'M GONNA MISS YOU GUYS SO MUCH BOO HOO HOO . . .
YOU ARE?! WHEN? WE'LL MISS YOU! WHERE TO? OMG . . .
WAIT . . .
YOU GUYS DIDN'T KNOW??
NO . . .
DID YOU?

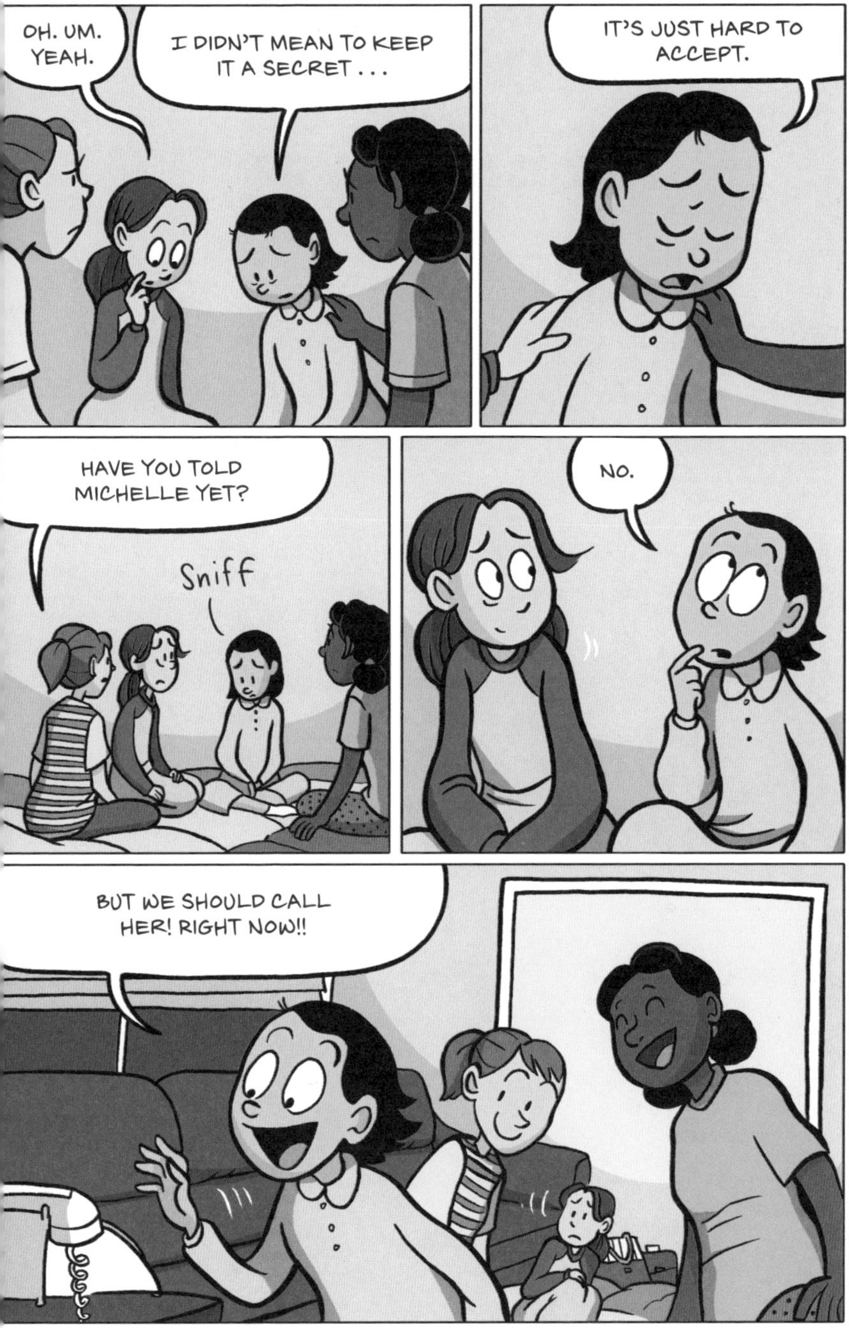
OH. UM. YEAH.
I DIDN'T MEAN TO KEEP IT A SECRET . . .
IT'S JUST HARD TO ACCEPT.
HAVE YOU TOLD MICHELLE YET?
Sniff
NO.
BUT WE SHOULD CALL HER! RIGHT NOW!!

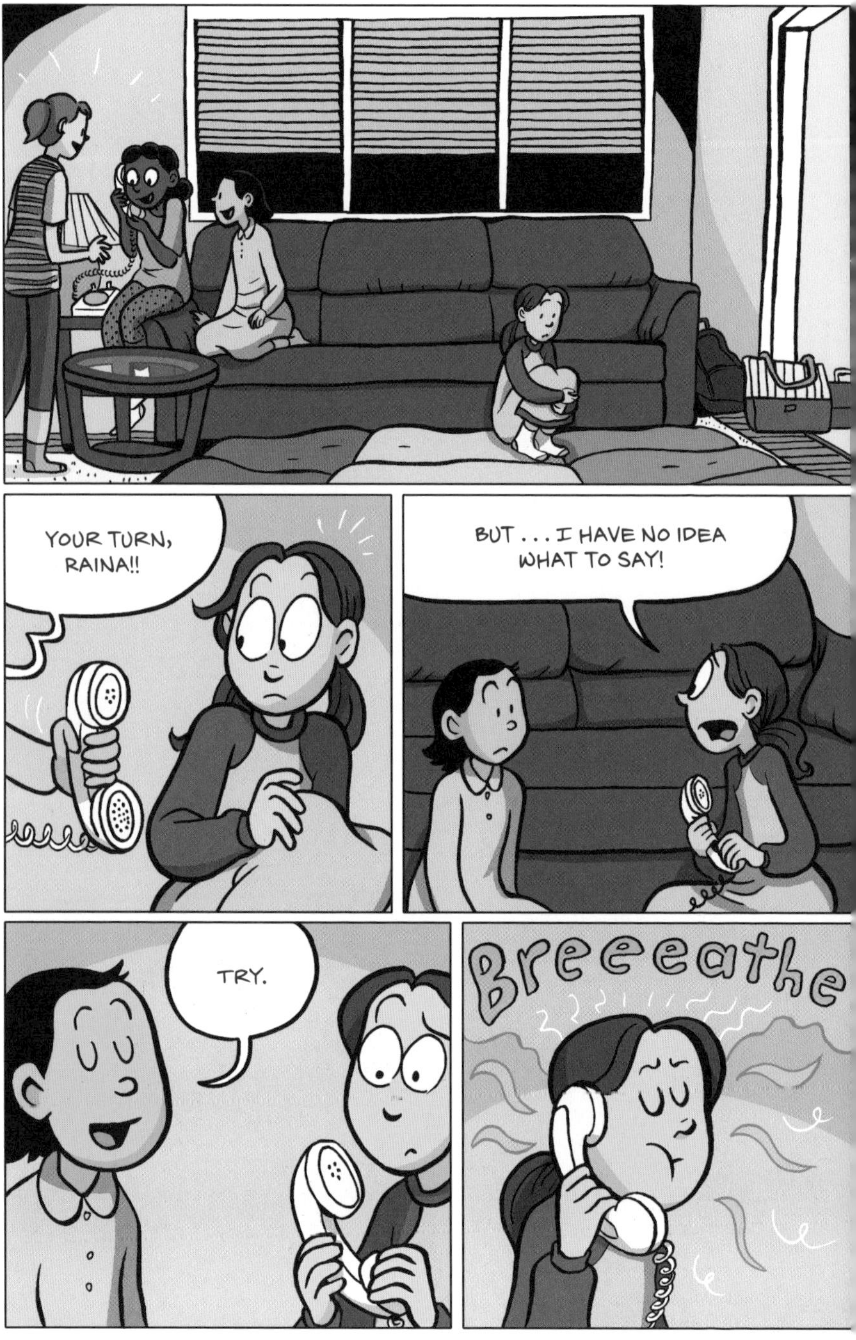
YOUR TURN, RAINA!!
BUT . . . I HAVE NO IDEA WHAT TO SAY!
TRY.
Breeeathe

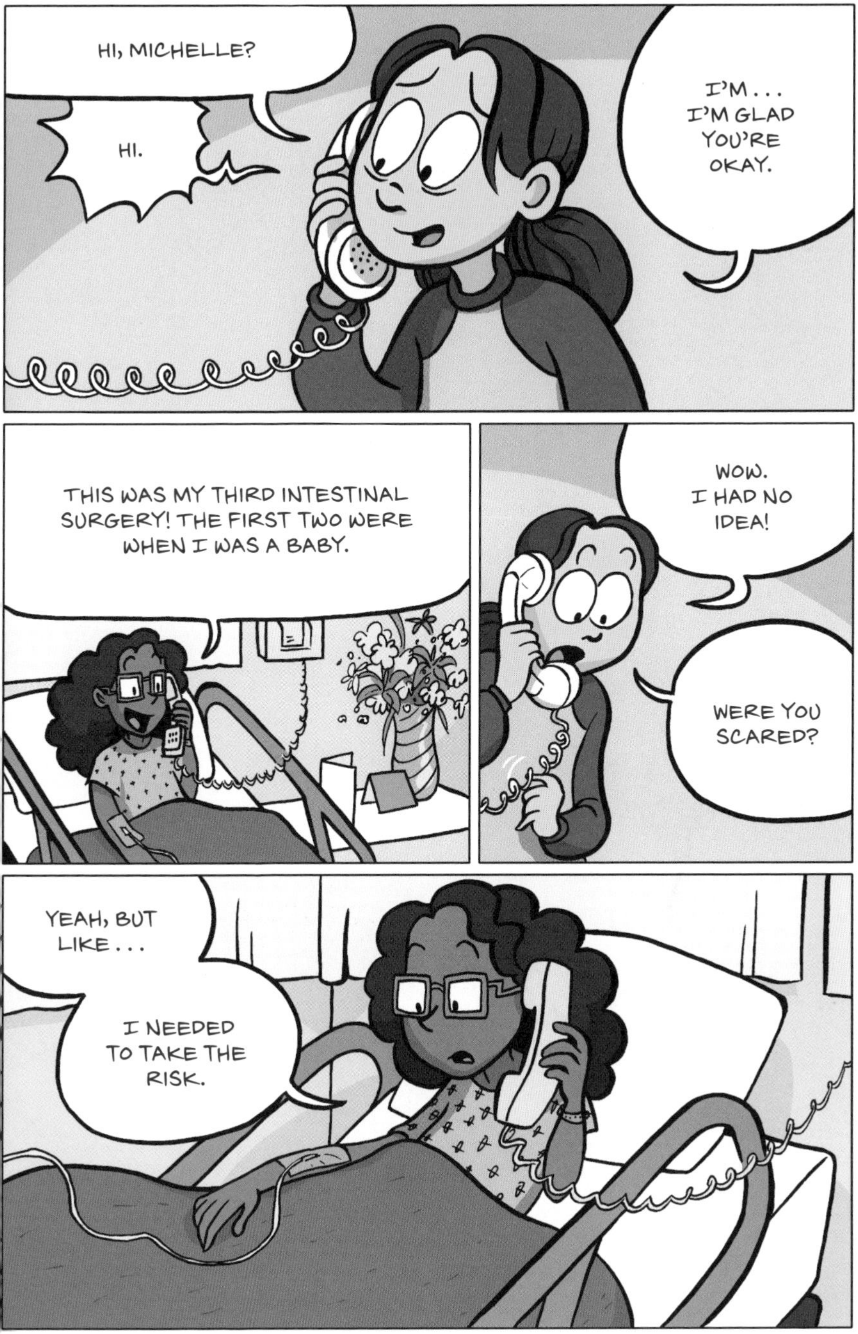
HI, MICHELLE?
HI.
I'M . . . I'M GLAD YOU'RE OKAY.
THIS WAS MY THIRD INTESTINAL SURGERY! THE FIRST TWO WERE WHEN I WAS A BABY.
WOW. I HAD NO IDEA!
WERE YOU SCARED?
YEAH, BUT LIKE . . .
I NEEDED TO TAKE THE RISK.

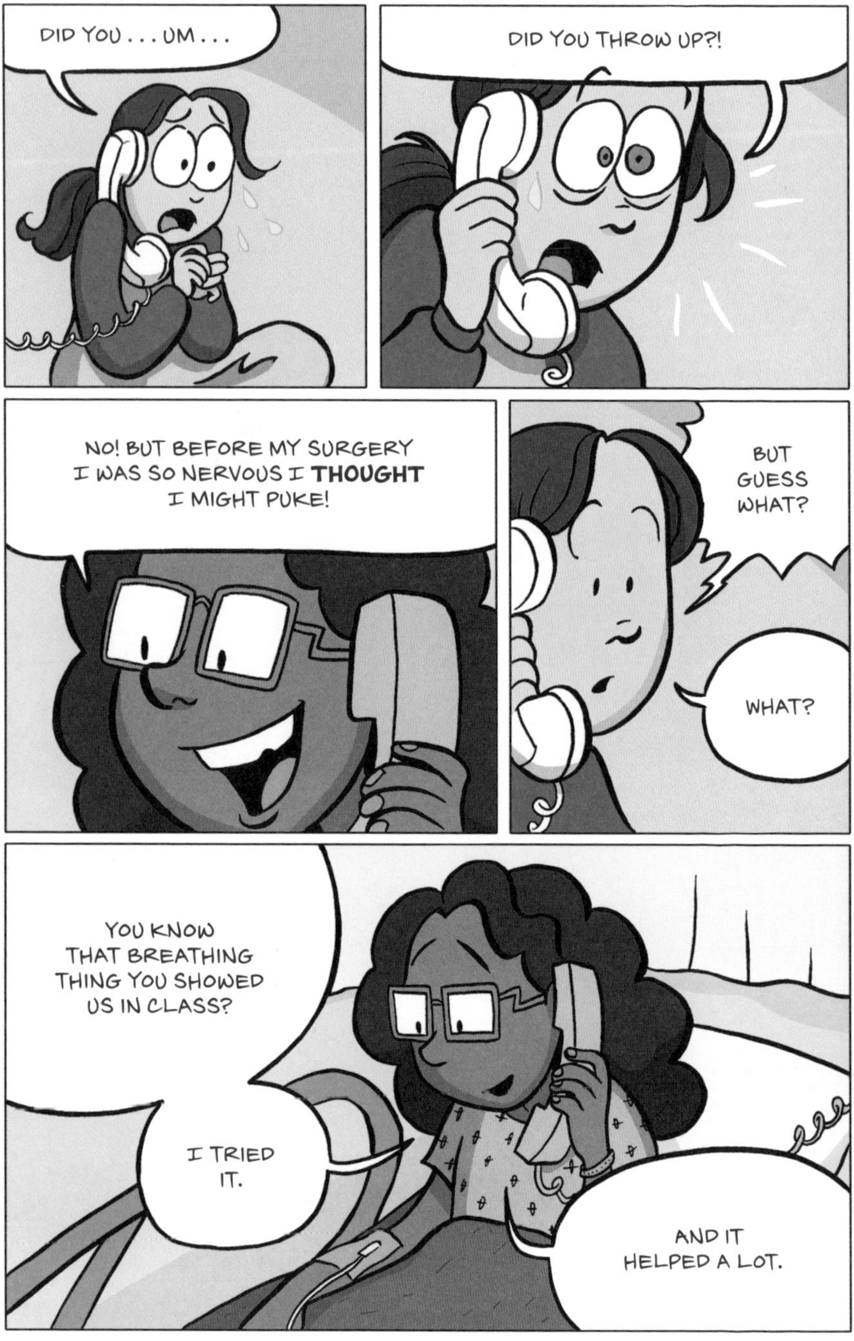
DID YOU . . . UM . . .
DID YOU THROW UP?!
NO! BUT BEFORE MY SURGERY I WAS SO NERVOUS I **THOUGHT** I MIGHT PUKE!
BUT GUESS WHAT?
WHAT?
YOU KNOW THAT BREATHING THING YOU SHOWED US IN CLASS?
I TRIED IT.
AND IT HELPED A LOT.

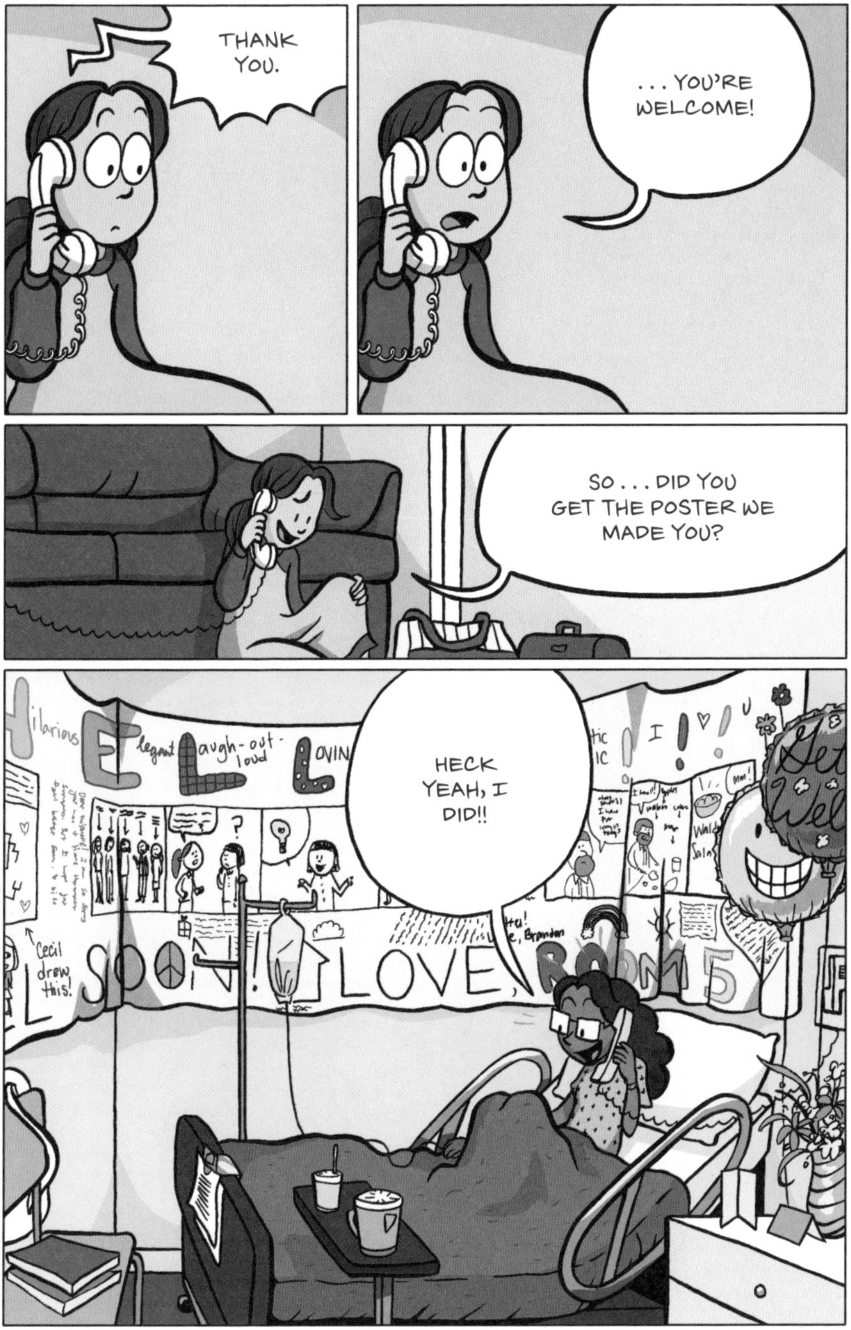
THANK YOU.
. . . YOU'RE WELCOME!
SO . . . DID YOU GET THE POSTER WE MADE YOU?
HECK YEAH, I DID!!
Cecil drew this!

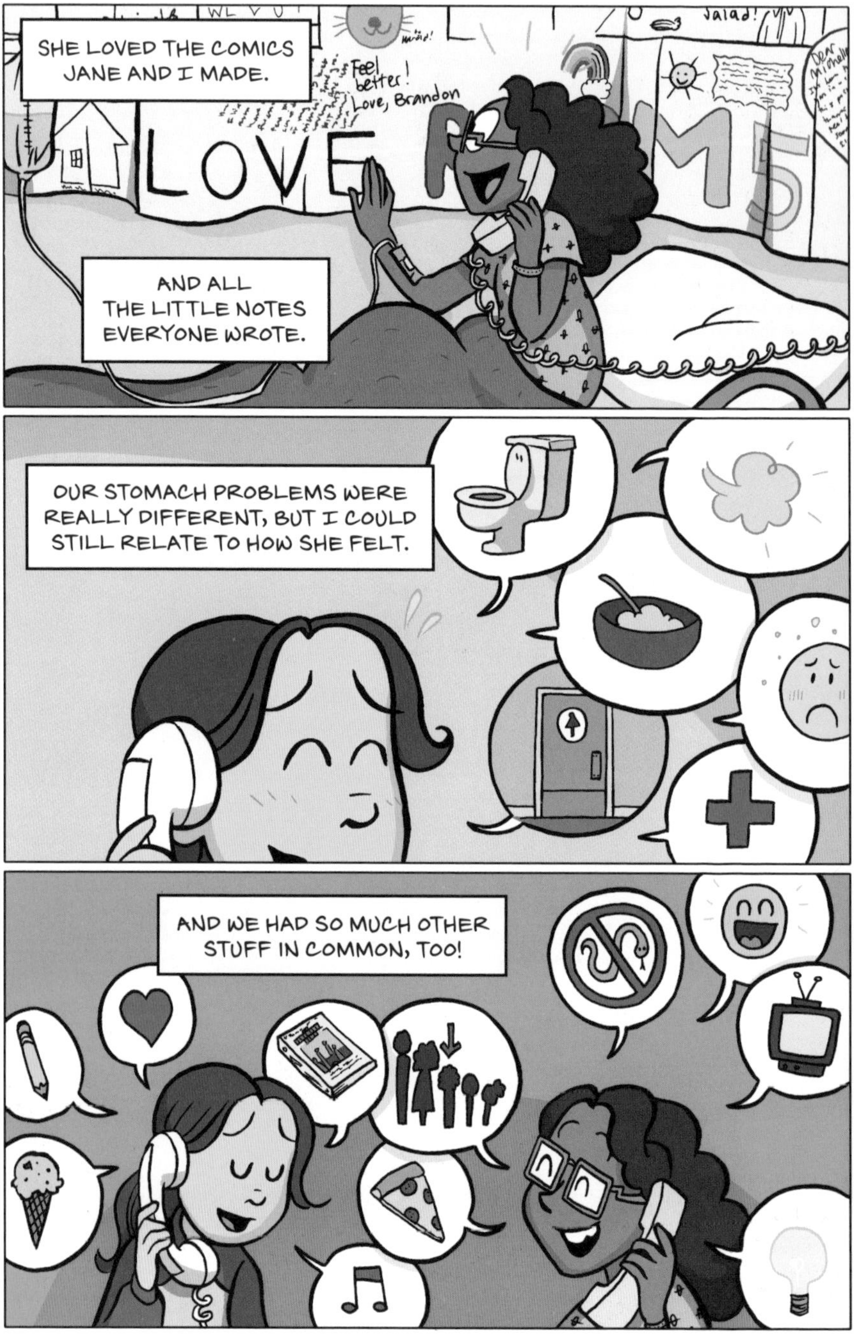
SHE LOVED THE COMICS JANE AND I MADE.
Feel better! Love, Brandon
LOVE
AND ALL THE LITTLE NOTES EVERYONE WROTE.
OUR STOMACH PROBLEMS WERE REALLY DIFFERENT, BUT I COULD STILL RELATE TO HOW SHE FELT.
AND WE HAD SO MUCH OTHER STUFF IN COMMON, TOO!

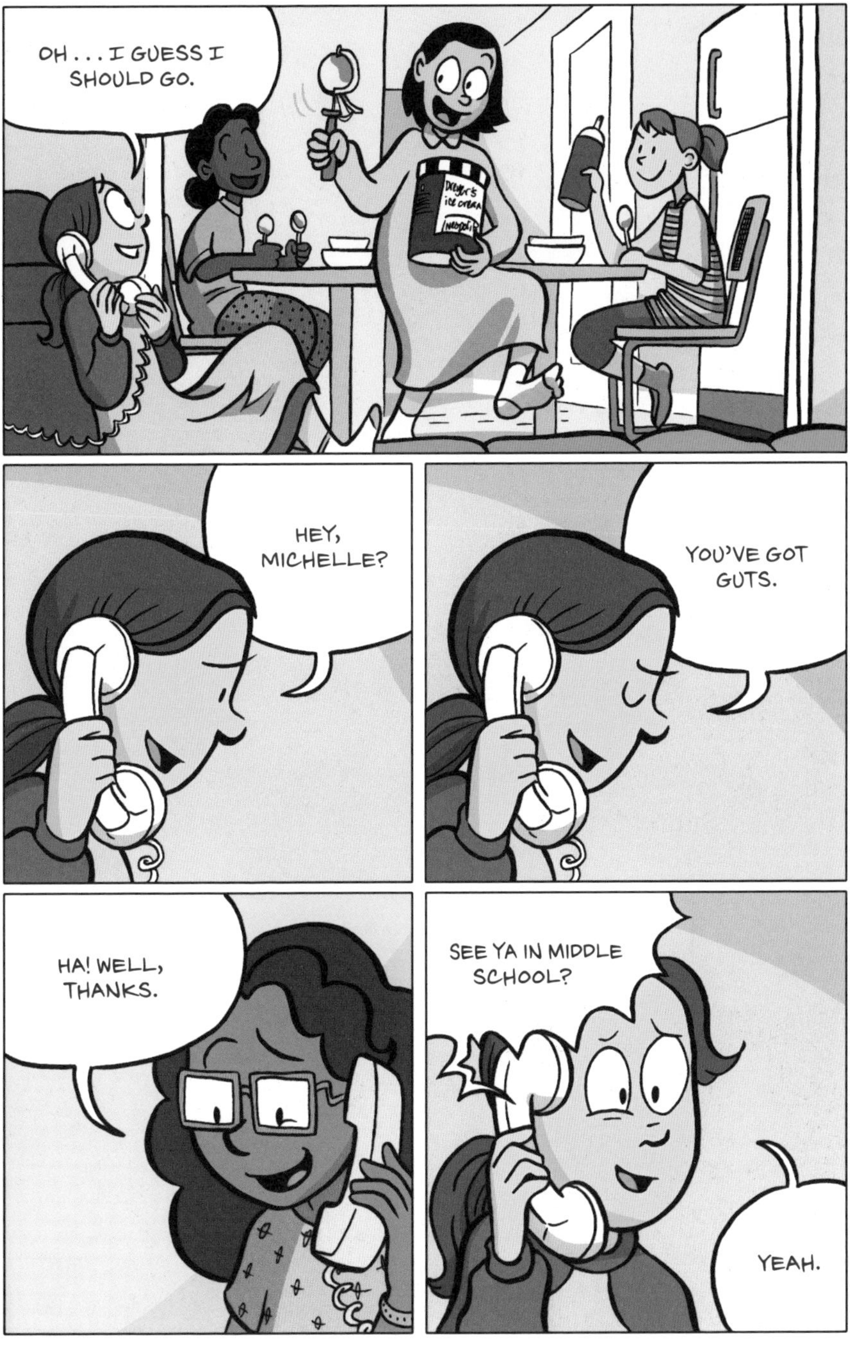
OH . . . I GUESS I SHOULD GO.
Dreyer's ice cream Neapolitan
HEY, MICHELLE?
YOU'VE GOT GUTS.
HA! WELL, THANKS.
SEE YA IN MIDDLE SCHOOL?
YEAH.

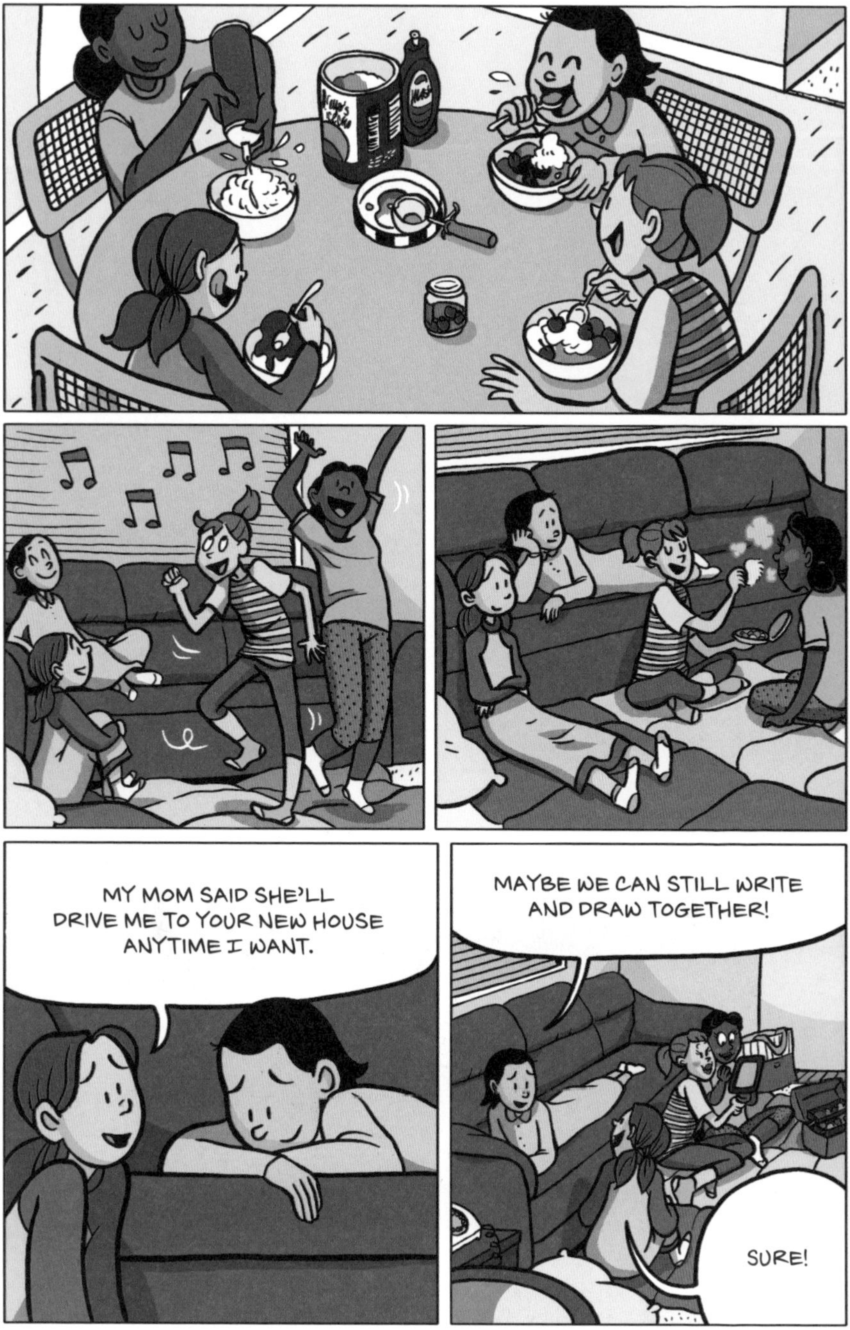

MY MOM SAID SHE'LL DRIVE ME TO YOUR NEW HOUSE ANYTIME I WANT.
MAYBE WE CAN STILL WRITE AND DRAW TOGETHER!
SURE!

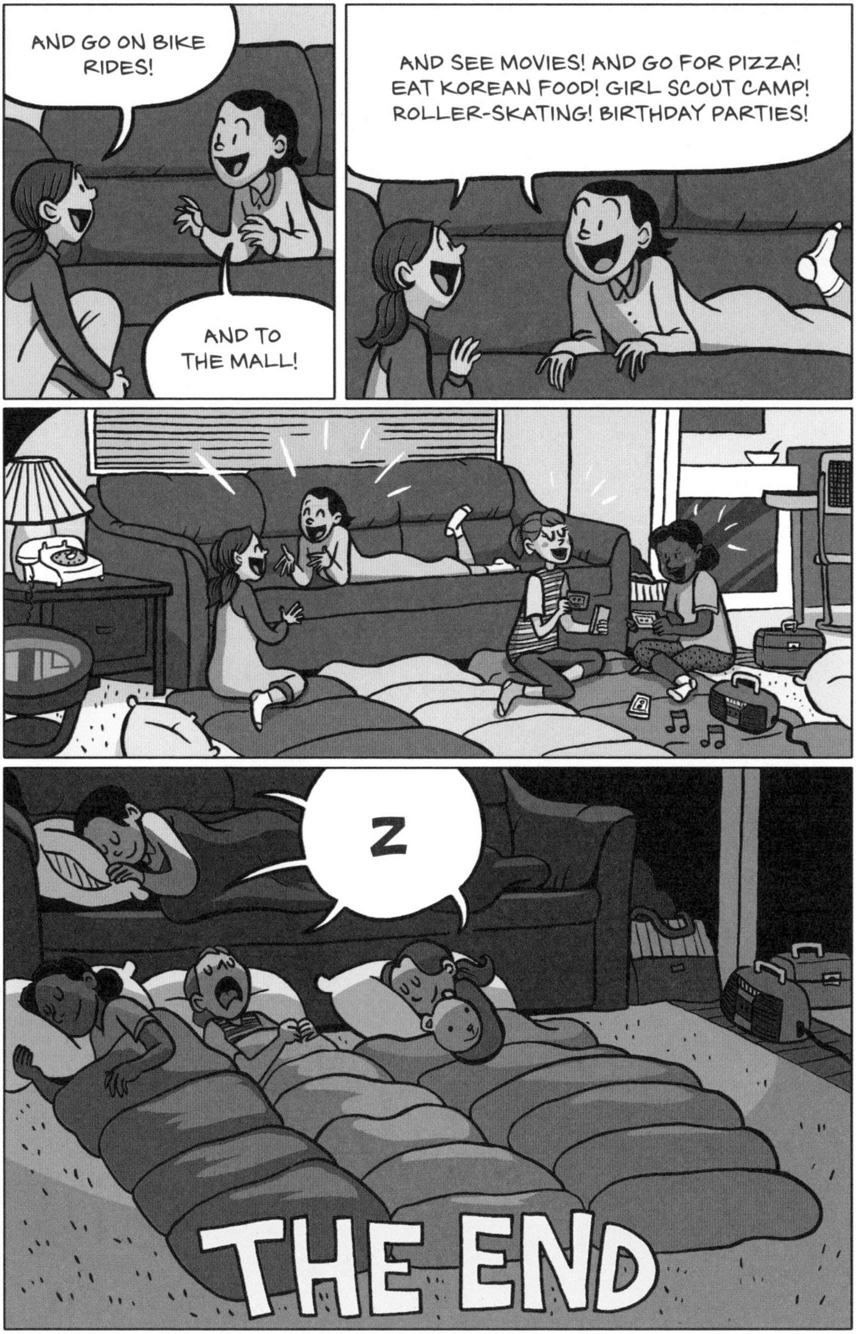
AND GO ON BIKE RIDES!
AND TO THE MALL!
AND SEE MOVIES! AND GO FOR PIZZA! EAT KOREAN FOOD! GIRL SCOUT CAMP! ROLLER-SKATING! BIRTHDAY PARTIES!
Z
THE END

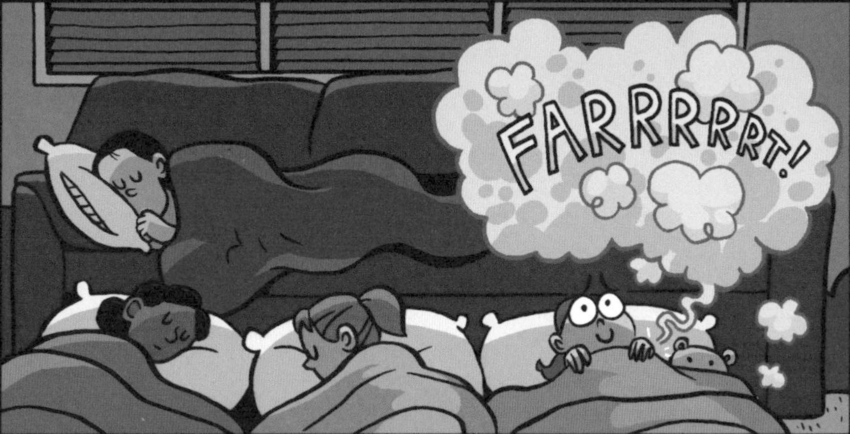
FARRRRRT!

Thanks to...

Early readers: Andy Runton, Vera Brosgol, Casey Gilly, Mike Jung, Shannon Hale, and Sue Telgemeier.

Consultants: Dr. Judy Pelham and Dr. Frank F. Escobar-Roger.

Production assistant: Meggie Ramm.

The team at Scholastic: Cassandra Pelham Fulton, David Saylor, Phil Falco, Lauren Donovan, Ellie Berger, Tracy van Straaten, Lizette Serrano, Julie Amitie, Carmen Alvarez, Susan Lee, Holland Baker, Celia Lee, Akshaya Iyer, and Shivana Sookdeo.

Colorists: Braden Lamb and Shelli Paroline.

My agent, Judy Hansen.

My family!

My therapists!!

My lovely and comforting group of friends, for whom no topic is off-limits.

My readers, who always ask the best questions.

—Raina

Author's Note

Guts was inspired by real people, real therapy, and real memories from my fourth- and fifth-grade years, though I adjusted some minor details to make the reading experience more streamlined.

I've dealt with stomachaches and anxiety for most of my life. It has never been easy, but it's gotten better as I've learned how to manage it over the years. My panic attacks came out of nowhere, starting at age nine. I missed a lot of school. I became obsessed with every little funny feeling in my stomach. I was terrified of eating the "wrong" foods, convinced they would make me ill. (The clinical term for fear of vomit is *emetophobia*, and it's actually pretty common!)

So, how am I doing now, more than three decades after this story takes place?

In the past five years I have done talk therapy, cognitive behavioral therapy, mindfulness training, EMDR, and exposure therapy. I tried anxiety medication. I use meditation apps. They've all helped, but I've realized that my phobias and worries are just part of who I am. I do my best to manage them!

I've been tested for everything from celiac disease to Crohn's disease to ulcerative colitis, and, after many negative results, I've learned to accept that there's nothing medically "wrong" with my stomach. I just have a sensitive system and must be careful about what I eat. My anxiety also affects how my body feels! So when I'm stressed out, I'm more likely to have digestion issues.

I want to make sure my readers know that this is my personal story. You may recognize some of my struggles, or yours might be totally different. You might not experience physical or emotional stress at all. If you do find yourself feeling stressed, or you're hurting in a way that you don't understand, please talk to an adult you know and trust. I was very lucky to have people in my life who supported me and helped me find ways to feel better.

Finally, I want to encourage you to talk about how you feel. You can write it down, draw pictures or comics, make music or plays, or simply share with your friends. It takes guts to admit how you feel on the inside, but chances are, others will be able to relate. You won't know unless you try!

Also by
Raina Telgemeier

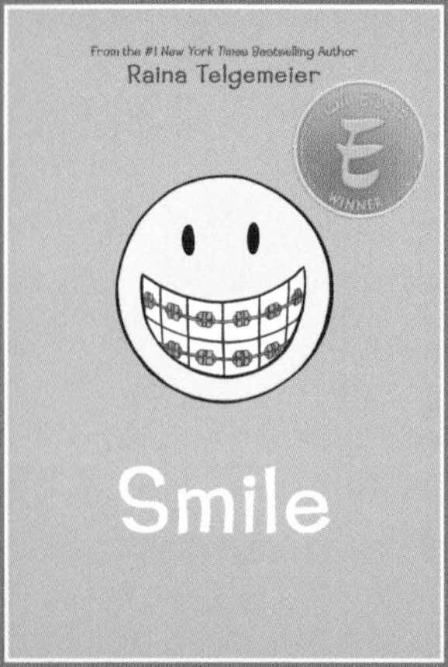
From the #1 New York Times Bestselling Author
Raina Telgemeier
Smile

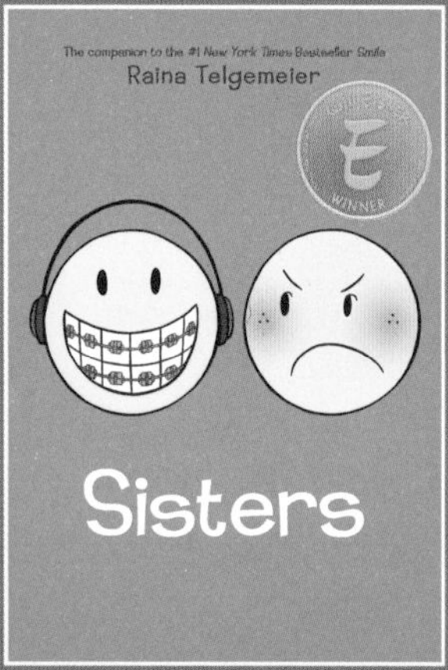
The companion to the #1 New York Times Bestseller Smile
Raina Telgemeier
Sisters

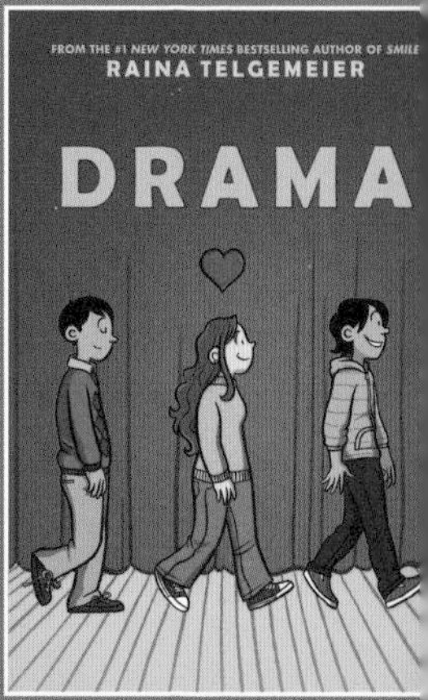
FROM THE #1 NEW YORK TIMES BESTSELLING AUTHOR OF SMILE
RAINA TELGEMEIER
DRAMA

By Ann M. Martin and Raina Telgemeier

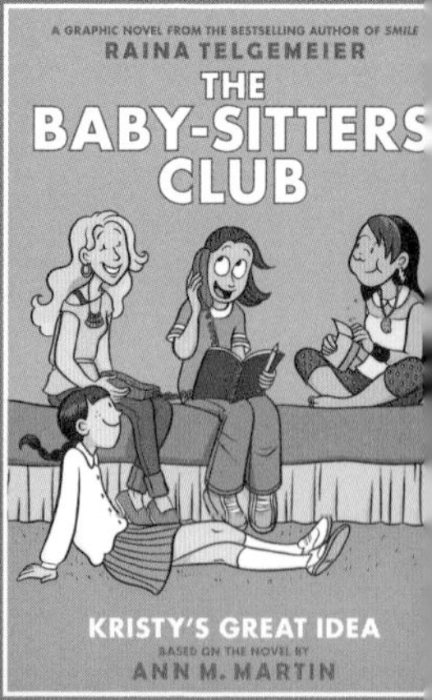
A GRAPHIC NOVEL FROM THE BESTSELLING AUTHOR OF SMILE
RAINA TELGEMEIER
THE BABY-SITTERS CLUB
KRISTY'S GREAT IDEA
BASED ON THE NOVEL BY
ANN M. MARTIN